ECU

THE CURRENCY
OF EUROPE

ECU
THE CURRENCY OF EUROPE

Edited by Christopher Johnson

Published by Euromoney Books
in association with

Banco Bilbao Vizcaya

Deutsche Bank Capital Markets Limited

The Industrial Bank of Japan Group

Istituto Mobiliare Italiano

MATIF

Nomura

Paribas Capital Markets Group

Published by
Euromoney Publications PLC
Nestor House, Playhouse Yard
London EC4V 5EX

ISBN 1 85564 009 0

Euromoney is grateful to Banco Bilbao Vizcaya, Deutsche Bank Capital Markets Limited, The Industrial Bank of Japan Group, Istituto Mobiliare Italiano, MATIF, Nomura and Paribas Capital Markets Group for their support and assistance in the preparation of this book.

Typeset by PW Graphics, London

Printed in Great Britain by Jolly & Barber Ltd, Rugby

Contents

The Authors

BECKER, Dr Werner, Economics Department, Deutsche Bank AG.
BISHOP, Graham, EC Specialist, Salomon Brothers International.
BROWN, J. T., Clifford Chance, Paris, and SHEA, A. M., Clifford Chance, London.
BRUCE, Philip, Head of Fixed Income and Money Market Instruments, LIFFE.
CAHEN, Didier, President, Association Eurocitoyen.
CHOWN, John, Director, J F Chown & Co Ltd.
DE MAIGRET, Bertrand, Director General, and COLLIGNON, Dr Stefan, Director for Research and Communication, Association for the Monetary Union of Europe.
DE THOMAZ, Bernard, Banque Bruxelles Lambert SA.
DURRANT, Jim, Head of Fixed Income Research Department, Paribas Capital Markets.
GROS, Dr Daniel, Head of Financial Markets Unit, Centre for European Policy Studies.
GROSVENOR, Jonathan P., Global Sales Manager, Banco Bilbao Vizcaya.
JAILLET, Pierre, Principal Administrator, and VISSOL, Thierry, Head of Ecu Section, Commission of the European Communities.
JONES, Steven Warren, Manager of Product Strategy, FINEX.
JOZZO, Dr Alfonso, General Manager, International Division, Istituto Bancario San Paolo di Torino.
LEDWARD, William, Senior European Economist, SALOJARVI, Liisa, International Board and Currency Strategy, and YASUOKA, Akira, Director, Economic Research Department, Nomura Research Institute Europe Ltd.
KOIZUMI, Toshinaga, Joint General Manager, Capital Markets, The Industrial Bank of Japan, Limited.
LEVITT, Malcolm, former visiting fellow, National Institute of Economic and Social Research, now EC Adviser, Barclays Bank.
LOMAX, Roger, Finance Manager, B.A.T Industries.
MASERA, Dr Rainer S., Director General, Istituto Mobiliare Italiano.
MENTRE, Paul, Président Directeur Général, Banque CSIA.
MOORE, Sue, freelance writer.
PLENDERLEITH, Ian, Associate Director, Bank of England.
PORTE, Thierry, Managing Director, Morgan Stanley International, and O'BRIEN, James, Principal, Morgan Stanley & Co., Inc.
PRIOR, Robert, Assistant Vice-President, Timber Hill Inc.
RAMBURE, Dominique, Chairman, Banking Association, and Head of International Relations Department, Istituto Bancario San Paolo di Torino.
RICHARDS, O. P., Director, Samuel Montagu and Co. Limited.
ROGERS, Neil, Ecu Analyst, UBS Phillips & Drew.
SCHOFIELD, Jennifer M. M., Bond Research Department, Deutsche Bank Group.
STEINHERR, Professor Alfred, Head of Financial Research Department, and PEREE, Eric, Economist, Financial Research Department, European Investment Bank.
WERREN, Jacques, Senior Vice-President, Research and Marketing, MATIF.

Editor's Foreword

There is already a considerable amount of literature about the Ecu in both the banking and the academic worlds. The pace of change is such that constant updating is required to keep up with the latest developments. The publication of the Delors Report, and the holding of the Intergovernmental Conference on economic and monetary union, have given the Ecu a new and even more important role as not only the common currency but the future single currency of Europe. The authors of this book, introduced by President Delors himself, are leading authorities on different aspects of the Ecu in both its private and official roles. If the markets are to be the test of whether there is a demand for the Ecu, then some of them have already given a positive response. The currency of the new economic and monetary union is too important, however, to be left entirely to the markets. Governments are now playing a crucial role in setting up the indispensable framework within which the Ecu can flourish as a credible currency not only for the EC, but for the rest of Europe, notably the Eastern countries, and for the world as a whole.

Christopher Johnson
Former Chief Economic Adviser, Lloyds Bank
UK Adviser, Association for the Monetary Union of Europe
London, July 1991

Jacques Delors
President, Commission of the European Communities

Introduction

The European Council at its meeting in Rome in October 1990 in the declaration on Economic and Monetary Union said that "the Community will have a single currency – a strong and stable Ecu – which will be an expression of its identity and unity". Since then the Ecu markets have been particularly active and new Ecu products have been developed. Also the negotiations on Economic and Monetary Union (EMU) have been progressing in the Intergovernmental Conference.

Growing confidence in the Community's commitment to the Ecu will greatly enhance its attractiveness and give a strong boost to its use as a transaction currency, as the main obstacle is the remaining doubts about its future. It is therefore essential that the new Treaty designates the Ecu as the single currency of the Community.

There has been a continuous expansion of financial Ecu markets over recent years. They have been developing in breadth and depth. Private operators now offer all the financial instruments – short-term, long-term, futures, swaps – that are available in any major currency. On the international bond markets the Ecu has taken its place with the leading world currencies. Investors may now choose among liquid issues at various maturities from borrowers of the highest standing and use efficient markets for derivatives.

The Ecu is Europe's currency, but by no means a currency used exclusively by Europeans. It has long ago lost the image of being the "Belgian dentist's" investment currency. Investors and borrowers from all parts of the world have come to appreciate the qualities of the Ecu, and European suppliers of financial services on the Ecu markets are facing lively competition from outside Europe. Seen from a global view, the Ecu represents "Europe", covering both the currency risk and the political and economic perspectives.

While developments on the financial Ecu markets are encouraging, its commercial use is still quite limited. Some noticeable initiatives have been taken and there seems to have been more activity recently, but the use of the Ecu as a currency for quoting prices and for invoicing and settlement has not really taken off. This ground must be prepared in view of the Ecu's destiny as the future single currency of EMU.

There is a certain parallel between currencies and telephones. A telephone is a useless instrument if it is only possessed by one person; but when ownership is widespread, it becomes extremely useful. There is a point of critical mass. The same is true for the Ecu. Hence it is difficult to predict the point of take-off. As long as actions in the commercial field are isolated, the beneficiary of an Ecu payment tends to sell the Ecus against other currencies because he has no incentive to hold them for transaction purposes. Once a critical mass of transactions is reached, the incentive to accept payments in Ecus, to hold them and to use them for making payments to the next link in the chain, may spread quickly.

It will be easier and much quicker to reach this point if obstacles which stand in the way of a more general use are removed. This is a task for stage one of EMU.

Removing the obstacles implies as a first step identifying them precisely. There are first of all legal and administrative obstacles. The Ecu is not the currency of any one country in particular. It lacks national currency status. Legislation in the member states varies – in some it is pragmatic, in others dogmatic. Currency law matters in many areas of economic life, and paving the way for a new currency calls for a review of numerous national regulations. Areas which need to be examined include: accounting rules, the constitution of company capital, the provisions governing the issue and quotation of shares, the status of the Ecu in insurance business, pricing in Ecu, and its treatment as a currency in which taxes may be calculated and possibly paid.

The Ecu also faces hurdles which are quite natural for a newcomer among the currencies, and which are the result of operators' habits, market inertia and pockets of ignorance. Another form of obstacle which sometimes faces the Ecu is excessive transaction costs, especially for small operators.

The Commission will act to ensure that as far as possible the legal and administrative obstacles to Ecu use are eliminated. It will also continue to contribute to the removal of the barriers of inertia and lack of knowledge, and to the reduction of the obstacle of cost.

The reasons why the Ecu has been adopted by the financial markets have varied over time. Before the full liberalisation of capital movements which took place in much of the Community at the same time as the start of stage one of EMU, July 1990, the Ecu owed some of its development to restrictions on capital movements in some Community countries. At an earlier stage in the development of the European Monetary System (EMS) the Ecu was of interest to private users partly at times when inflation and interest rates were diverging. Being a basket of the currencies of the member states, it provided diversification and hence less risk. These reasons for the Ecu's use have now been largely eliminated, and yet its use has increased dramatically. This confirms what was evident from the beginning: the overriding factor behind the market's interest in the Ecu is that it is designed to become the single currency of Europe. Its future development, as in the past, will therefore require official involvement.

The Ecu is now benefiting from improved convergence, and it is acquiring the status of a strong currency. For more than four years it has been stable *vis-à-vis* the Deutschmark. In this period the differential between long-term interest rates of the two currencies has narrowed from about 4 per cent to 1 per cent. In the run-up to the final stage this trend will continue, as increased convergence is achieved in the process of EMU.

Hence, the Ecu will quite naturally – through greater stability of its components – strengthen further in the period ahead. This must be the main channel through which a strong and stable Ecu is achieved. To the extent that all its component currencies are stable, the basket offers the same degree of hardness as the best of them.

Some suggested that additional guarantees of hardness could, however, be offered to the markets by changes to its definition. A distinction should be made between those which would abandon any basket definition and those which would modify the basket. Abandoning the basket definition implies creating an abstract currency whose value depends upon the goods and services which it can purchase. Hence its value depends ultimately on the institution which is empowered to issue it. This approach therefore raises all the institutional questions which have to be settled for stage three of EMU. It is also open to the criticisms that have been levelled against the parallel-currency approach – that it risks being inflationary and that even if precautions are taken to avoid this, it is likely to create instability because it leads to confused signals being given about monetary policy.

Other suggestions involve modifying the basket in some way so as to increase the hardness of the Ecu. The question which has to be asked for these is whether the suggested modification gives a significant increase in the attractiveness of the Ecu. Quite simply, do the expected benefits of the extra stability outweigh the costs of complexity?

As the existing Ecu is now well known, the simplest solution would be to freeze the composition of the Ecu. This would remove an uncertainty which is specific to the Ecu, ie the five-yearly review of the basket, and it would simplify matters instead of complicating them. It may be noted in passing that 98 per cent of the weight of the Ecu is at present constituted by currencies which participate in the Exchange Rate Mechanism and 70 per cent by currencies which have been in the narrow band since 1979 and have not experienced realignments since January 1987.

As usual, the Community is proceeding in its own way. Creating a new currency from a basket of 12 national currencies is unique in monetary history. Citizens of all member states can find their identity reflected in the basket Ecu, just as all governments bear responsibility for its quality, since their national currency is a component of it.

1

Daniel Gros
Centre for European Policy Studies

The development of the Ecu

Origin and definition of the Ecu

The Ecu is older than most people realise. It it was born as the European Unit of Account (EUA), which was created in 1974 as an accounting unit for the European Development Fund. This unit was then renamed the Ecu when the European Monetary System (EMS) was established in 1979. It is not accidental that the origins of the Ecu are forgotten. The fact that the Ecu's development started only after the creation of the EMS shows that its fate was, and is, linked to progress on European monetary integration.

The EUA was supposed to represent a European average. This is why the Ecu contained all Community currencies, and the weights were to reflect the relative economic size of each country. Exhibit 1.1a shows the composition of the Ecu (then called the EUA) in 1974. The official economic criteria were, and still are, each country's share of: Community

Exhibit 1.1 **The Ecu weights in September 1974 and March 1979**

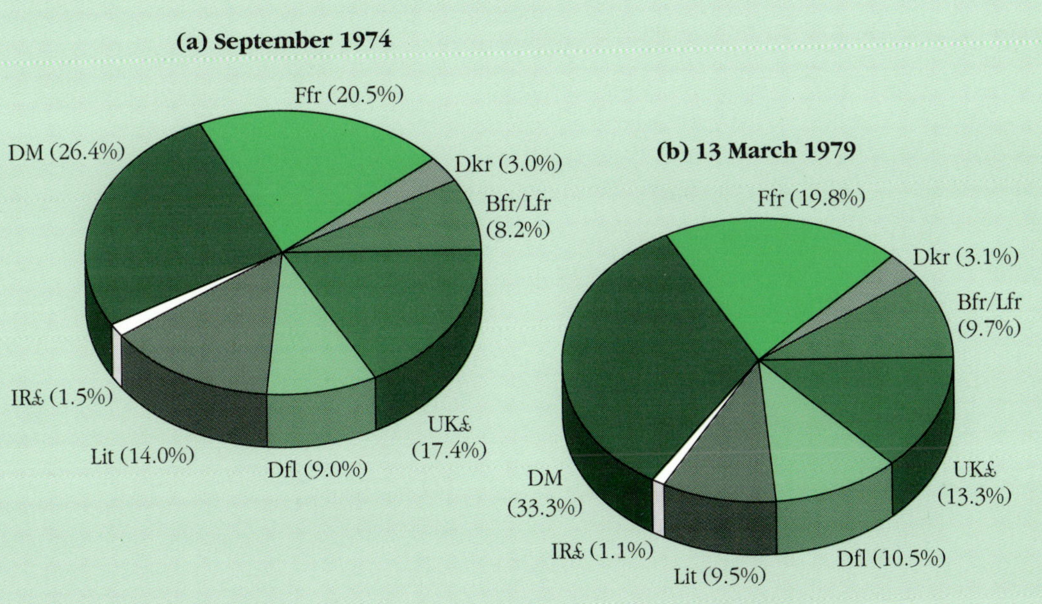

Source: Eurostat, Money and Finance, 1990/3.

GDP, intra-Community trade and the EMS financial support system. These objective criteria were used in 1974 to determine the initial composition of the Ecu basket. Thus Exhibit 1.1a also gives the relative economic weights.[1]

This concern to have a representative basket is also evident in the provision that the composition of the basket is re-examined and, if necessary, revised by the ECOFIN council (which represents the EC's economics and finance ministers) every five years, or on request if a change in weight exceeds 25 per cent. The creation of the EMS and the change of name in 1979 must have introduced additional considerations since this provision was not used even though, at that time, some imbalances had emerged. (For example, in 1979 the Italian lira's share in the Ecu basket had been reduced to less than one-third of the Deutschmark's). However, in 1984, when the Greek drachma was added to the basket, and in 1989, when the Portuguese escudo and the Spanish peseta were included, some judgmental adjustments were made which offset the increased weight of the stronger currencies. This implies that since 1979 the economic criteria have served only as broad indicators. This can also be seen in Exhibit 1.1b, which displays the weights in 1979, ie when the Ecu was officially born.

In 1979 the actual shares of the two strong currencies, the Deutschmark and the Dutch guilder, exceeded their economic weight (and correspondingly the shares of the weaker currencies were lower than their economic weights). According to economic criteria the share of the Deutschmark should have been 25 per cent in 1979, but its actual share was 33 per cent; conversely, the lira's share should have been 13 per cent, but its actual share in 1979 was only 9.5 per cent. The recompositions in 1984 and 1989 followed a similar pattern: the shares of the strong currencies (the Deutschmark and Dutch guilder) always remained well above their weights according to official economic criteria. In this sense the Ecu is already

1. The economic weights are calculated using 1979 to 1984 data; they are therefore not identical to the weights actually used in 1974 (which were based on a five-year average preceding that date). However, the 1979 to 1984 data are still a good approximation because the economic weights move only very slowly over time.

Exhibit 1.2 **The Ecu weights in September 1984**

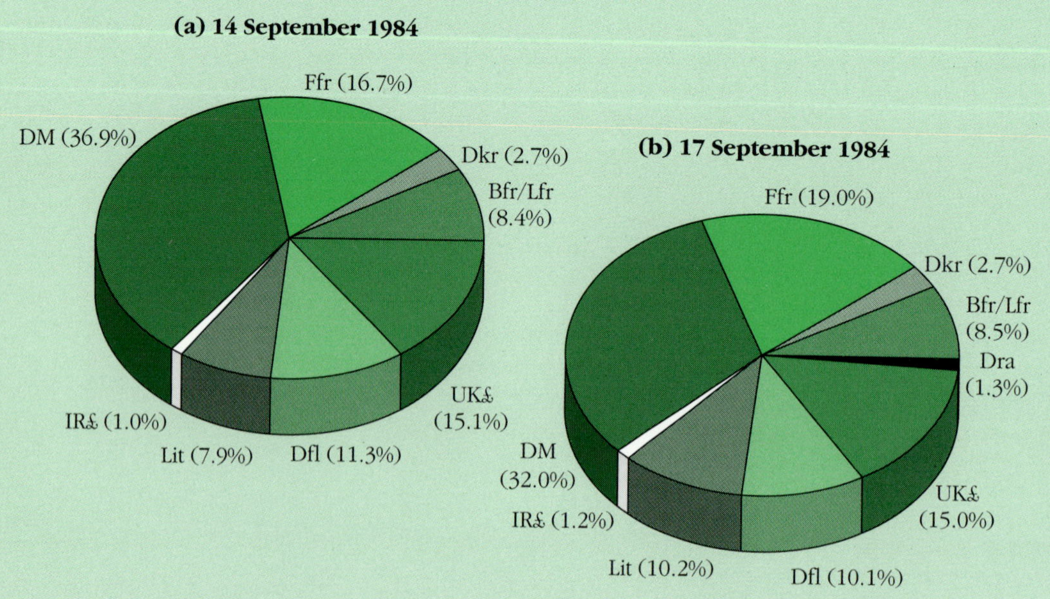

Source: IMF, Occasional Paper 48, Dec. 86.

Exhibit 1.3 **The Ecu weights in September 1989**

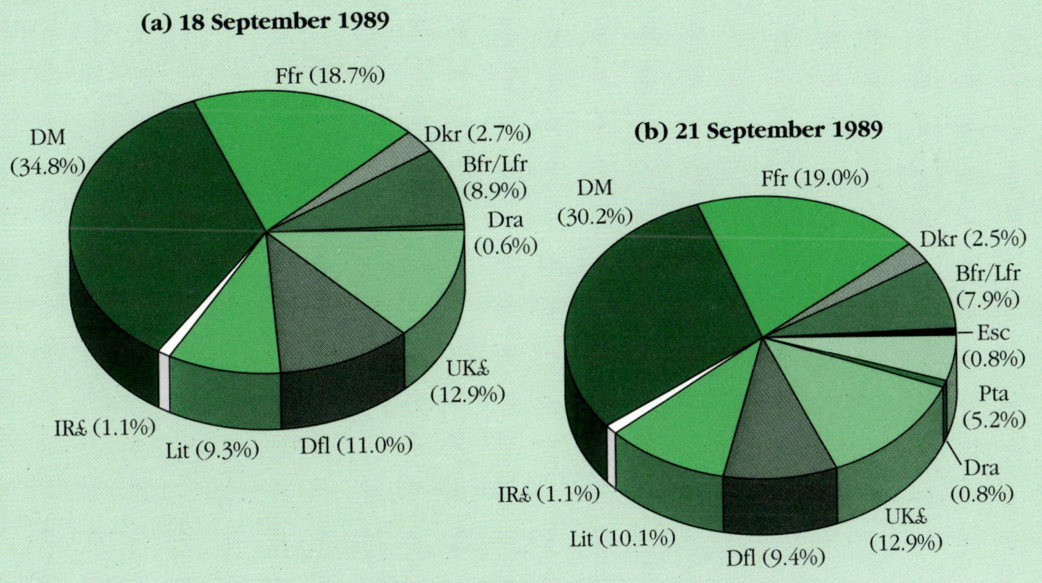

Source: Eurostat, Money and Finance, 1990/3.

stronger than the average value of the Community currencies. Exhibits 1.2 and 1.3 give a picture of the 1984 and 1989 recompositions.

Comparing Exhibit 1.1a to 1.2a shows how lira depreciation reduced its initial weight from 14 per cent to below 8 per cent in 1984. Conversely, the weight of the two strong currencies (the Deutschmark and Dutch guilder) increased from 35.4 per cent to almost 50 per cent in 1984. These changes in the relative weights were partially corrected during the 1984 recomposition, which, aside from adding the drachma, with a weight of 1.3 per cent, reduced the combined Dutch guilder and Deutschmark share by over 6 per cent but increased both the French franc and Italian lira shares by about 2 per cent.

Although the shares are the decisive considerations during the recompositions, the Ecu in fact consists of a basket of fixed amounts of 12 Community currencies. These amounts are fixed between recompositions and the weights can change only because of exchange-rate movements. Exhibit 1.4 shows the present composition of the Ecu. This will be valid at least until 1994 but probably until 1999, because it is unlikely that by 1994 additional members will have joined the Community. At the current, more stable exchange rates, the weights should not change so much that a recomposition is required by 1994. This is shown in the last column of Exhibit 1.4, which contains a projection of the composition of the Ecu in September 1994 based on present long-term interest rate differentials.

The fixed-amount basket definition thus has the drawback that, at times of large currency fluctuations, it creates a need for periodic revisions if the basket is to continue to reflect some representative average performance. It would have been possible to avoid this problem by adopting another basket definition, for example the fixed-weight basket. There are several different ways a fixed-weight basket can be achieved in practice. One solution would be to automatically increase the amounts of

Exhibit 1.4

The current composition of the Ecu

	Amounts in national currency	Percentage shares Market exchange rates (28/03/91)	Projection for 09/94
B/Lfr	3.43	8.1	8.32
Dkr	0.198	2.5	2.48
Ffr	1.332	19.1	18.72
DM	0.624	30.4	32.49
IR£	0.0085	1.1	1.04
Lit	151.8	9.9	8.61
Dfl	0.2198	9.5	10.09
UK£	0.0878	12.6	12.42
Gdr	1.44	0.6	0.5
Pta	6.885	5.4	4.71
Esc	1.393	0.8	0.62

Source: Own computations.

the depreciating currencies and to automatically reduce amounts of the appreciating currencies. Under this option, the average exchange rate of the fixed-weight basket could be close to that of the actual Ecu basket in the short term.

A further option, equivalent to the hard Ecu proposed recently by the UK, is the 'asymmetrical' (also fixed-weight) basket, which would not depreciate against even the strongest currency because quantities of the weaker currencies would be added automatically in the same proportion as they depreciate, whereas the amounts of the appreciating currencies would remain unchanged. These options were rejected at the time the Ecu was created because they would be too cumbersome for potential private market participants.

However, one might even regard the automatic increase in the weight of the stronger currencies as an advantage. Given that the future currency of the Community has to be strong, it is desirable to see the weight of the weaker currencies fall over time. That is why it has often been proposed to freeze the composition of the Ecu. This would leave the governments of the more inflationary countries with the alternatives of either seeing their currencies slowly disappear from the Ecu or adopting tougher anti-inflationary policies.

The Ecu and the EMS

The Ecu was created from the EUA when the EMS was established in 1979. Does this imply that it plays an important role in the EMS?

The EMS is an agreement among all Community central banks, but not all of them participate in the central element of the overall EMS agreement, namely the Exchange Rate Mechanism (ERM). The ERM establishes a grid of bilateral exchange rates and obliges central banks to intervene whenever exchange rates deviate by more than plus or minus 2.25 per cent from their central rates. (The UK pound and the Spanish peseta can fluctuate by 6 per cent.) For example, the present central rate for the French franc against the Deutschmark is 3.3354. The Banque de France and the Bundesbank are both obliged to intervene in unlimited amounts whenever the exchange rate in Frankfurt or Paris deviates by more than 2.25 per cent from this central rate.

The central rates which implicitly define the margins of fluctuation (±2.25 per cent for everybody except the pound and the peseta) can be changed only by common agreement through a procedure called a realignment. The need for common agreement makes realignments politically costly and ensures the stability of the EMS. In the early years of the EMS there was, on average, more than one realignment per year. This has changed, however, as the current grid of bilateral rates has been in force since early 1987 (if one excludes a technical adjustment of the Italian lira in early 1990). Moreover, the governments of all the narrow band countries have declared their intention to avoid further realignments unless forced by exceptional circumstances. This implies that about 80 per cent of the Ecu basket consists of currencies which are almost irrevocably fixed against each other.

Central banks can intervene even before the exchange rate reaches the margins of fluctuation, but there is no obligation to do so. In practice, however, most central banks intervene well before the margins are reached; the exception is the Bundesbank, which does not intervene unless it has to. This is why the EMS operates *de facto* in an asymmetric manner, although the system was designed to be symmetric. The Bundesbank acts as the leader in the EMS; if it changes its interest rates the others tend to follow unless there are special factors at work, such as the extraordinary financing requirements of German unification.[2]

When the EMS was established, the Ecu was supposed to be at the centre of the system because it has four functions in the EMS. It is:

(i) used to calculate the grid of bilateral exchange rates for the ERM. However, since the choice of the *numeraire* used to calculate the grid is completely arbitrary, this is only an accounting convention.

(ii) the basis for the divergence indicator, which was created to indicate which currency is deviating from the average. This divergence indicator is supposed to trigger corrective action in the diverging country (in practice often Germany). However, in reality it is seldom used.

(iii) the unit of account for the operations of the European Monetary Cooperation Fund (EMCF).

(iv) the means of settlement for operations arising through the financing mechanisms of the EMS.

The Ecu could therefore have played an important role in the EMS. However, the use of the Ecu in the EMS has been limited to the operations of the EMCF, so that the official Ecu has been effectively used only to settle transactions among EMS-member central banks.

The EMS agreement did not only intend to use the Ecu, but also created an additional Ecu, ie the official Ecu. Official Ecus are created because all EMS national central banks (whether or not they participate in the ERM) have to deposit 20 per cent of the approximate market value of their gold and dollar reserves with the EMCF (through automatically renewable three-monthly swaps) and receive corresponding amounts in

2. There is a vast literature on the workings of the EMS. For a recent survey see Gros and Thygesen (1991).

Ecu. These official Ecus can be held only by EMS member central banks and other officially designated institutions. The way in which these official Ecus are created shows that it is not really a currency or a reserve asset, but only a book-keeping device for exchanges of the underlying US dollar and gold reserves.

The official Ecu has never been widely used. Holdings by non-EC official institutions (mainly the Bank for International Settlements (BIS) and some smaller European central banks) have remained small. For all practical purposes, it can be considered an official unit of account that circulates only among EC central banks and cannot be exchanged against Ecu held by private agents. There are thus two separate Ecu circuits. The private Ecu is therefore the only relevant Ecu for financial markets.

The potential of the Ecu for borrowers, bankers and investors

The private Ecu is simply a contract in which the contracting parties have denominated payment obligations in Ecu and have accepted its official definition. This is the so-called 'open-basket' Ecu, which changes composition when the official composition changes. In practice, private markets have almost always used this open basket, instead of the closed basket under which the Ecu is defined as the sum of the amounts of the currencies in the basket at the time the contract is concluded. This implies that a five-year Ecu bond issue concluded before 1989, when neither the peseta nor the escudo were in the basket, has to be repaid with Ecus that contain two new currencies.

If financial markets had used the closed-basket definition, they would have eliminated the risk inherent in recompositions that can never be accurately predicted. However, with the closed basket, different Ecus would be created, which would cause confusion in the markets. The open-basket definition was thus crucial to allow a unified Ecu market to emerge (see Chapter 15).

This book contains a detailed analysis of the Ecu in different markets (bonds, banking, futures, swaps, etc). Thus only a broad picture of the development of the Ecu in the major markets is provided here.

The Ecu took off only a couple of years after the creation of the EMS. The first Ecu bond issues and bank deposits came in 1981, and the amounts involved were initially modest. Exhibit 1.5 shows how total recorded Ecu bond issues have grown since 1981. Starting from almost nothing (Ecu213 million issued in 1981), the market exploded as new Ecu bond issues increased by a factor of 60 to Ecu12,201 billion in 1985. This year proved to be exceptional, however, since it was followed by a fall in issuing activity in 1986 and 1987. Since then, there has again been an upturn in issuing activity, mainly led by some EC governments. Chapter 3 provides more detail on this development and on the size of the primary and secondary bond markets.

The use of the Ecu in the banking sector follows a similar long-run pattern. Since there is no single overall indicator that captures the importance of the Ecu in international banking, Exhibits 1.6 and 1.7

Exhibit 1.5 **Evolution of the Ecu bond market, 1981-90, International issues only**

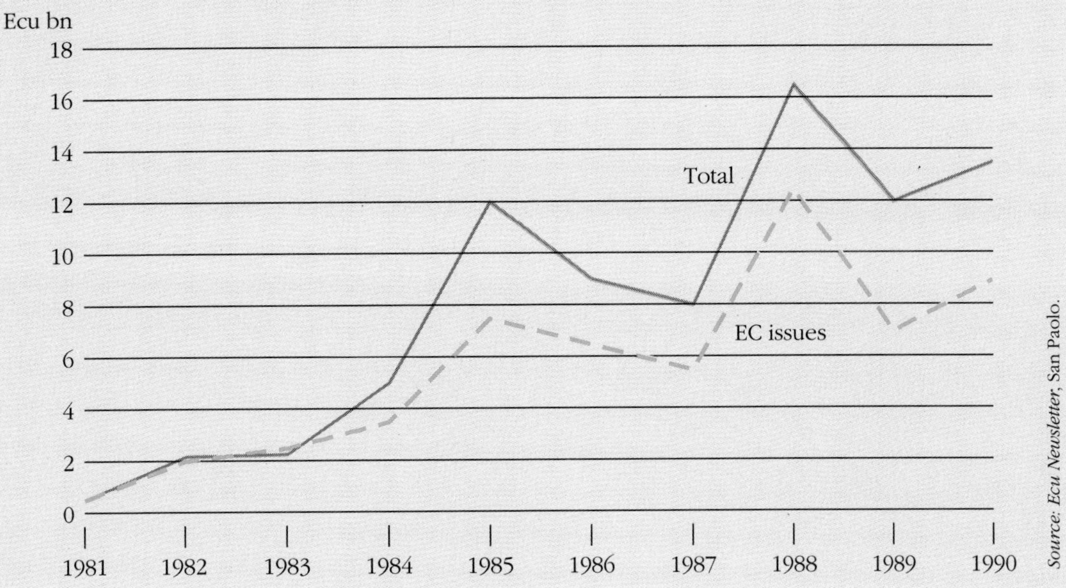

provide two different indicators. Exhibit 1.6 shows the share of the Ecu in foreign-currency positions *vis-à-vis* residents, which went from zero in early 1984 to about 3 per cent in 1985. In 1986/7 there was a small decline, but then continual slow growth, with this indicator reaching about 4 per cent in 1990. Exhibit 1.7 shows that the share of the Ecu in the overall international positions of banks followed a similar pattern. The main difference is that on this basis the Ecu seems somewhat less important, because its share reached only 3 per cent in 1990. A comparison of Exhibits

Exhibit 1.6 **Share of the Ecu in banks' foreign currency positions *vis-à-vis* residents 1984-90**

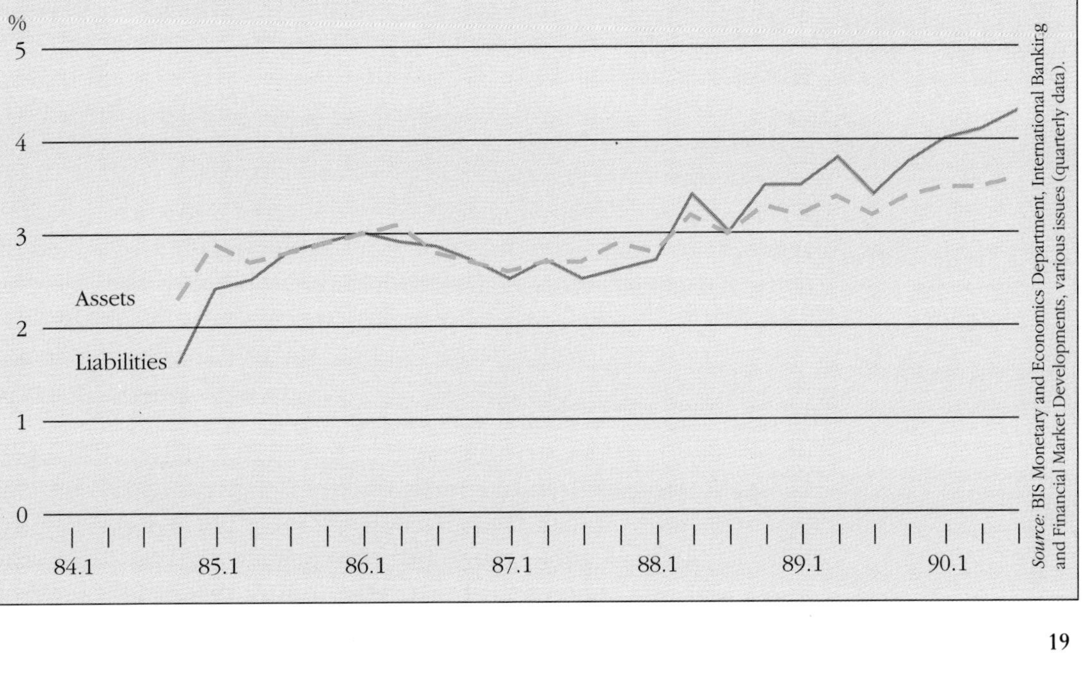

Exhibit 1.7 **Share of the Ecu in overall external positions, 1983-90**

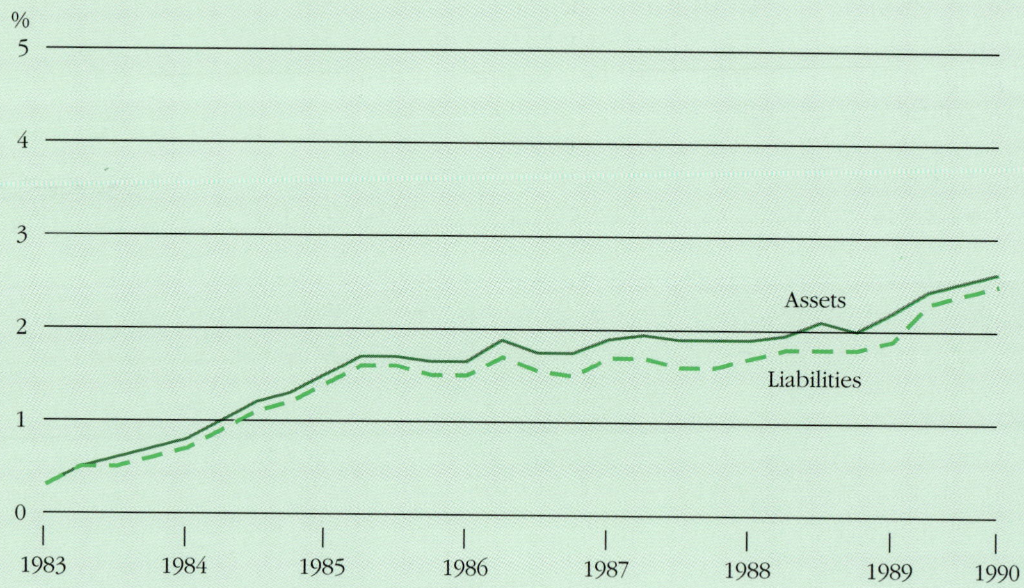

Source: BIS, Monetary and Economics Department, International Banking and Financial Market Developments.

1.6 and 1.7 with Exhibit 1.5 also shows that the market share of the Ecu is much more stable if one looks at the stocks (assets and liabilities) than if one looks at the flows (new issues). Chapters 3 and 5 provide more evidence for this.

An interesting feature of the Ecu banking market is the imbalance between assets and liabilities, shown in Exhibit 1.6. Banks can have open positions in Ecu because they can cover themselves by taking the opposite position in the individual currencies that constitute the basket. Banks always had more assets than liabilities in Ecu, but since total assets exceed total liabilities, the share of the Ecu has evolved differently for assets than for liabilities. In 1984 the share of Ecu assets in total assets was much higher than the share of Ecu liabilities in total liabilities. The situation was reversed in 1989 to 1990, so that banks now have a higher proportion of their liabilities in Ecu. (See Chapter 5 for more detail on the overall Ecu banking market, including commercial paper, medium-term notes (MTNs) and syndicated loans in Ecu.)

The use of the Ecu has not been restricted to these two basic markets segments. Since 1985 a number of derivative markets have developed which enhance the usefulness of the basic instruments denominated in Ecu. These derivative markets (including swaps, options, futures, etc) are described in Chapters 6-8 below. The Ecu markets have also become more liquid and technically more complete, attracting different classes of investor. Although less spectacular than the initial growth of the Ecu in the bond and banking markets, this widening and deepening of the Ecu markets since 1985 is crucial for the future development of the Ecu as exchange rate variability becomes less important. One sign that the Ecu is overcoming the barrier of low transaction volumes, and therefore high costs, is that the turnover in Ecu securities increased constantly in the late 1980s until, in 1990, the Ecu accounted for over 10 per cent of the total turnover in the

Euromarkets. The usefulness of the Ecu is further enhanced by the clearing system in Ecu, which operates through the Bank for International Settlements (BIS). As described in Chapter 13, this is the only European-wide system to provide same-day settlement.

This brief survey suggests that the use of the Ecu in private international financial markets, which only started in 1981, increased very rapidly until 1985 and then stagnated or increased more slowly. The Ecu has thus become a significant minor Euro currency, albeit the only one without a domestic base like the other Euro currencies. While significant, the Ecu has not yet become a major currency at the global level. In the international bond market, it ranks sixth (in terms of volume outstanding) behind the US dollar, Swiss franc, Japanese yen, Deutschmark and pound sterling. However, if compared to other EC currencies, the Ecu already occupies third place.

While the Ecu is widely used in financial markets, it is not yet an important vehicle for current transactions such as the invoicing of international trade, which is discussed more fully in Chapter 11. The Ecu is also not widely used as a unit of account in the private sector. This explains why most of the Ecu bank activity constitutes interbank business. For example, in 1990 Ecu-denominated cross-border bank assets were equal to Ecu144 billion, of which only Ecu31 billion were with non-banks. For the liabilities of banks, the predominance of interbank business was even more pronounced: cross-border Ecu deposits totalled Ecu147 billion but less than 10 per cent, ie Ecu13 billion, were held by non-banks. However, the predominance of interbank business is a general feature of the international banking market, since a similar ratio between interbank and non-bank business applies to all currencies.

What makes the Ecu so attractive for investors, bankers and borrowers? In the early 1980s, the main strong point of the Ecu was that it proved a convenient hedge against currency fluctuations. This is analysed in Chapter 10. However, as intra-EC exchange rate fluctuations are reduced through the EMS, this aspect is losing some of its initial importance. The diversification argument, while important, should also not be overestimated. Exchange rate variability among the component currencies has already been reduced to about one-third of the level reached during the early 1980s, but the Ecu has apparently maintained its attractiveness in financial markets. Other factors must therefore play a role as well.

One factor which might have been important in the past was that the Ecu received preferential treatment from the French and Italian authorities. Certain transactions that were prohibited under French and Italian capital controls could be carried out if the Ecu was used. However, this factor cannot have been important, for the use of the Ecu in these (and other) countries has actually increased even after full liberalisation of the capital markets in France and Italy. Similarly, it appears that the German prohibition of bank accounts denominated in Ecu, which was lifted in 1987, was also not very important as the use of the Ecu in the banking sector in Germany has remained very limited even after the elimination of this obstacle.[3]

The decisive factor favouring the Ecu at present must, therefore, lie

3. The restriction on the issuance of Ecu-denominated bonds was only lifted in 1990. For a survey of the legal status of the Ecu see Arthur Andersen and Ecu Banking Association (1991).

elsewhere. Many observers have argued that the Ecu continues to be attractive even as exchange rates become stable, because of the prospect of full European Monetary Union (EMU), with the Ecu as the single common currency.

Outlook: EMU and the Ecu

In the final stage of EMU one common currency will simply replace all national currencies. At present, it is certain that it will be the Ecu, even if it has been hardened in the meantime. This implies that some of the longer-term bonds, mortgages or other long-term contracts that are concluded at present in national currencies might in the end have to be fulfilled in Ecu. For example, if a German takes out a 20-year mortgage he or she can be almost certain to have to repay part of it in Ecu. British objections notwithstanding, it also seems certain that the famous "consols" will eventually be denominated in Ecu.

However, the movement towards EMU will affect the Ecu market even before the introduction of the Ecu as the common currency.[4] The creation of the single market in financial services will allow the elimination of many of the restrictions that impose the use of the national currency for large investors, such as pension funds or life insurance companies. These restrictions are no longer appropriate because intra-EC exchange rate fluctuations are slowly being eliminated by the EMS, making the Ecu a low-risk investment. A huge new market, estimated by some at Ecu800 billion,[5] will therefore open for the Ecu when regulations that impose the use of the national currency for the investments of insurance companies and pension funds can also be fulfilled by an investment in Ecu. This was proposed in a recent EC framework directive.

A second growth phase for the Ecu could therefore start well before EMU is achieved. During this phase, exchange rate variability will be progressively eliminated, so that the Ecu will not be used because of its hedging qualities but because it will be a convenient instrument to tap a European-wide capital market.

In this process, the Ecu is gradually being transformed from a basket of currencies to a currency basket.[6] One sign of this development is that the actual Ecu interest rate sometimes deviates considerably from the theoretical rate that can be obtained by investing in the bundle of currencies that constitute the Ecu. Arbitrage through bundling and unbundling limits the movements of the Ecu interest rate relative to the theoretical rate, but recent experience suggests that the transaction costs of bundling and unbundling are large enough to create some independence for the Ecu interest rate. Chapter 3 provides more evidence of this development.

EMU will not only affect the domestic (that is, European) role of the Ecu. EMU will also make the Ecu a major global currency, presumably on a par with the US dollar, for the economic potential of the EC exceeds that of the US.

What are the implications of a global role for the Ecu?[7]

Firstly, the EC will earn some seigniorage, which is the profit that

4. This chapter does not discuss the causation in the other direction, ie how the Ecu could be used to accelerate the transition to EMU. On this issue see Chapter 11 in Gros and Thygesen (1991), and Steinherr (1990).
5. see Bishop (1990).
6. This expression is due to Allen (1990) and Padoa-Schioppa (1988).
7. The following paragraphs are based on Chapter 9 in Gros and Thygesen (1991).

results from issuing coins rated above their intrinsic value. These seigniorage gains will be significant but less important than sometimes believed, because they can be earned only on Ecu assets that bear no interest, ie bank notes and coins in Ecu (that do not exist). According to some estimates, the equivalent of about Ecu30 billion in US dollar bank notes might be converted into Ecu bank notes after EMU. However, this is a once-and-for-all effect and, since this substitution can be expected to take some time, the seigniorage gain would be minor when measured as a flow over time. If full adjustment took 10 years, the benefit for the EC would be about Ecu3 billion annually, less than 0.1 per cent of its GDP.

Second, EMU should also lead to a large substitution away from US dollar into Ecu assets. These portfolio demand shifts would not yield any seigniorage revenues for the EC but they could have an effect on the Ecu/dollar exchange rate. Large portfolio shifts could be expected from both the official and the private sectors. For example, if the Ecu achieves the same share as the US dollar in foreign exchange reserves, central banks all over the world will have to exchange the equivalent of about Ecu120 billion of their dollar reserves into Ecu. Estimates of the shift in private international portfolios range from Ecu150 billion to Ecu300 billion.

Whether these portfolio shifts lead to a large appreciation of the Ecu against the dollar and other currencies depends on how fast international financial institutions react to provide sufficient Ecu-denominated instruments. At present, it seems likely that the EC will run an aggregate current account deficit during the transition to EMU. Such a deficit would represent a net supply of claims on the EC.

Thus pressures for appreciation of the Ecu might result from its growing financial role in official and private portfolios. But a large appreciation of the Ecu is not essential, especially if the Community proves willing to accept a collective current account deficit in a transitional period.

This upbeat outlook for the Ecu is therefore based on further progress towards EMU. Its role within the EC will be increasingly to represent an EC-wide capital market as exchange rate variability falls and the internal market programme creates a truly integrated European financial market. On the wider global scene, the breakthrough will come only with full EMU, ie when the Ecu becomes the single common currency. It should then become as important as the US dollar.

References

Allen, Polly Reynolds (1990). "The private Ecu markets: what they are, why they exist, and where they may go". *Journal of Banking and Finance*, **14(5)**. November.

Arthur, Andersen and Ecu Banking Association (1991). *The Ecu – making it work in Europe*. Arthur Andersen & Co and EBA. February.

Bishop, Graham (1990). *Toughening the Ecu – Practical Steps to Promote its Use*. Salmon Brothers, London. October.

Ecu Newsletter, Istituto Bancario San Paolo di Torino, Turin.

Gros, Daniel, and Thygesen, Niels (1991). *European Monetary Integration: From the EMS towards EMU*. Longman, London.

Padoa-Schioppa, Tommaso (1988). "The Ecu's coming of age", in M. Nighoff (ed.), *The Quest for National and Global Economic Stability*. Kluwer, Amsterdam.
Steinherr, Alfred (1990). "Roles for the Ecu in the process of achieving European Monetary Union". Unpublished paper for the Ecu Banking Association, European Investment Bank. December.

2

Pierre Jaillet and
Thierry Vissol
EC Commission

The Ecu and European economic and monetary union

There is a paradox between the success of the Ecu on the private markets and the lack of enthusiasm and confidence the monetary authorities have demonstrated during the 1980s towards what some of them still call "the European Currency Unit". Moreover, this "official Ecu", which was supposed to be at the centre of the European Monetary System (EMS), did not play the role it should have. Even in the Delors Report on EMU, the Ecu was assessed only in passing and without serious consideration.

The UK authorities are partly responsible for the new interest demonstrated by the member states towards the Ecu. Italy has been denominating short-term (*Buoni del Tesoro* in Euroscudo – BTEs) and long-term (*Certificati del Tesoro* in Ecu – CTEs) government securities in Ecu on a large scale since 1982. However, the British Treasury, by issuing the first Ecu Treasury Bill programme (11 October 1988), which was open without limits to international investors, stimulated other European sovereign investors to step into this market and boost the interest of private operators in Ecu. Secondly, in proposing an alternative to the Delors plan with their hard Ecu scheme for a parallel currency, the UK authorities put the Ecu at the centre of the debate about the transition towards EMU. Although this alternative has been rejected by the 11 other member states, the idea of strengthening the Ecu either by hardening its basket or freezing its composition may prove to be quite constructive.

The aim of this chapter is to describe the development of the member states' positions towards the Ecu and to present the ongoing political debate about its role in the transition and final stage of EMU.

From Bremen (July 1978) to Hanover (June 1988)

The birth: the EUA

The Ecu was officially born, under another name – UCE in French, EUA in English – on 21 April 1975. On this day, the Council, in a regulation, decided to use a unit of account defined as the sum of precise amounts of the member states' currencies in the ACP-EEC Lomé Convention and to publish in the official journal of the EC a daily exchange rate for this new European Unit of Account (EUA). Its use, still as a unit of account, spread to the European Coal and Steel Community (ECSC) in December 1975 and to the general budget of the EC in December 1977.

Even in a context of hectic exchange rate changes and disintegration of the international Bretton Woods monetary order, this new composite unit of account had no more success on the financial markets than private ones such as the EURCO, the ARCRU, the EMU, the Kredietbank UCE or even the International Monetary Fund Special Drawing Right (SDR).[1]

The transmutation of the EUA into the Ecu

It was only in July 1978, during the European Council of Bremen, when the creation of the EMS was decided, that the EUA received its new name – a name which is the same in all languages, Ecu – and the status of quasi currency. "'The European Currency Unit' (Ecu – the Ecu has the same definition as the European Unit of Account) will be at the centre of the system; in particular, it will be used as a means of settlement between EC monetary authorities."[2]

There is little doubt that its initial attractiveness to private operators can be explained by this transformation of the nature of the Ecu from the status of a unit of account to that of an official European central bank currency. This status was confirmed by the Brussels European Council Resolution of December 1978 and the agreement of 13 March 1979 between the central banks of the member states of the EC laying down the operating procedures for the EMS. Meanwhile, there were hopes that this official Ecu would become a real currency, eventually issued by a European Monetary Fund, no later than two years after the start of the scheme.[3] This never happened, and the "official" Ecu became the weakling of the EMS.

The Ecu as the weakling of the EMS

Being at the centre of the EMS, the Ecu should have had four main tasks: to be the denominator (*numeraire*) for the exchange-rate mechanism (ERM); the basis for a divergence indicator; the denominator for operations in both the intervention and the credit mechanisms; and a means of settlement between monetary authorities of the EC.[4]

Although the four points were formally put into operation, the Ecu, for several logical reasons, played only a very minor role in practice from the beginning. First, the ERM currencies should have been based on an Ecu central rate, but this central rate was only used to compute the bilateral rates and the subsequent bilateral grid. As a consequence, the various countries started to fix as an objective bilateral exchange rates, generally against the strongest currency of the system, and to intervene intra-marginally to stick to them. Thus in between realignments the Ecu central rates and the divergence indicator were useless. Moreover,

1. For an analysis of the composite currencies in the 1970s see Th. Vissol (1988).
2. Annex to the conclusions of the Presidency of the European Council, Bremen, 6 and 7 July 1978, point 1.
3. After announcing the creation of the EMS, the European Council resolution provides: "We remain firmly resolved to consolidate, no later than two years after the start of the scheme, into a final system the provisions and procedure thus created. This system will entail the creation of the European Monetary Fund as announced in the conclusions of the European Council meeting at Bremen on 6 and 7 July 1978, as well as the full utilisation of the Ecu as a reserve asset and a means of settlement. It will be based on adequate legislation at the Community as well as the national level." Resolution of the European Council of 5 December 1978 on the establishment of the CMS and related matters, point 1.4.
4. Brussels' Resolution, point 2.2. The following point 2.3 introduces the necessity to re-examine and if necessary to revise the weights of currencies in the Ecu.

interventions were made in national currencies when the intervention points defined by fluctuation margins were reached and not when the exchange rate crossed the "threshold of divergence". Credit mechanisms were denominated in Ecu, but national currencies were used. Reserves of gold and US dollars were transferred to the European Monetary Co-operation Fund (EMCF) and transformed into Ecu, but in the form of revolving three-month swaps. The credits resulting from the use of the very short-term facilities were denominated in Ecu but remunerated with an interest rate which did not correspond to the market rate. The credit lines in Ecu could not be exchanged against national currencies. The official Ecu role was then severely restricted and it was *de facto* non-convertible. Finally, the EMCF was never transformed into an EMF.

Several attempts were made to reinforce the EMS or improve its functioning and thus the "acceptability" of the Ecu. The first was in 1985, when the central banks' governors agreed to compute the interest rate of the Ecu on the basis of market rates; to accept up to 50 per cent settlements in Ecu of those financing operations falling due (in the event of a need for an intervention currency, a central bank could mobilise Ecu holdings against US dollars within certain limits);[5] and to give the status of "other holder" of Ecu to central banks or international monetary institutions which might ask for it.[6]

The second, in 1987, resulted from attacks by several member states on the asymmetry of the system. It is known as the Basle/Nyborg agreement, as it was first a political decision agreed in an Ecofin council in Nyborg which then had to be implemented by the governors. But this agreement had little significance for the Ecu because within certain limits it raised to 100 per cent the acceptability of settlements in Ecu of outstanding claims in the very short-term financing mechanism.[7] Neither of these attempts succeeded in giving the Ecu the central role it was designed for. As the Delors Report says: "Although it is an integral part of the EMS, the Ecu has for a number of reasons played only a limited role in the operating mechanisms of the EMS."[8] Similarly, propositions introduced in the late 1980s by two member states' central banks to link the official and the private Ecu did not meet with much success.

Moreover, the growing use of the Ecu in private markets gave rise among governors to their fear that it would interfere with monetary policies. So, in accordance with the rules of procedure, the Committee of Governors, in December 1985, gave a mandate to one of its sub-committees,[9] known as the Dalgaard Group, from the name of its chairman, "to follow the evolution of the private Ecu markets and report to the Committee at least once a year, or more frequently if justified by developments, for instance with regard to interventions in Ecus". As a matter of fact, the failure of the official Ecu to be used as an international currency, and the reluctance of the Bundesbank to accept holdings and interventions in Deutschmarks, led some central banks to build holdings in private Ecu and to use them for interventions on the exchange markets. In 1991 the reserves in private Ecus represent roughly 15 per cent of the foreign reserves of the European central banks. Nevertheless, none of the Dalgaard Group reports found any negative effect of the use of the Ecu either by central banks or private operators on monetary policies.

5. "Instrument relating to the agreement of 13 March 1979 between the central banks of the member states of the European Economic Community laying down the operating procedures for the European Monetary System", Basle, 10 June 1985. And Decision 17/85 of 10 June 1985 of the Board of Governors of the EMCF.
6. Decision (No. 18/85) of the Board of Governors of the EMCF of 12 November 1985 laying down the terms and conditions for acquisition, holding and use of Ecus by other holders.
7. "Instrument of 10 November 1987 relating to the agreement of 13 March 1979 between the central banks of the member states of the European Economic Community laying down the operating procedures for the EMS." Basle.
8. "Report on economic and monetary union in the European Community", committee for the study of Economic and Monetary Union, April 1989, p. 13.
9. Since June 1990 this sub-committee has been redenominated "the foreign exchange sub-committee". Its mandate was redefined in December 1990, and one of its tasks is to "monitor the development of the private Ecu".

The first attempt to introduce the Ecu in the Treaty

After some years of what was commonly described as "Europessimism", the single-market project started a new era of European dynamism which was to be represented in the Treaty. During the negotiations, it seemed to some member states that it was time to institutionalise the EMS and the Ecu as, on juridical grounds, they were no more than the outcome of an agreement between European central banks (a Council Resolution has no juridical effect). The time was not yet ripe to give the EC a real monetary capacity. The Single Act resulting from the negotiations was quite disappointing for the supporters of the Ecu and deserves to be quoted.[10] After a preamble which recalls the Bremen Conclusions and the Brussels Resolution, here are the modifications introduced in the Treaty:

> Article 20
> 1. A new chapter 1 shall be inserted in Part Three, Title II of the EEC Treaty reading as follows:
> CHAPTER 1
> CO-OPERATION IN ECONOMIC AND MONETARY POLICY (ECONOMIC AND MONETARY UNION)
> Article 102a
> 1. In order to ensure the convergence of economic and monetary policies which is necessary for the further development of the Community, Member States shall co-operate in accordance with the objectives of article 104. In doing so, they shall take in account of the experience acquired in co-operation within the framework of the European Monetary System (EMS) and in developing the Ecu, and shall respect existing powers in this field.

The disappointment of the monetary unionists was amplified by point two of article 102a, which submitted any further institutional development in the field of economic and monetary affairs to the provisions of article 236 of the Treaty, that is to say a very long and difficult procedure. It was then considered by the more pessimistic as a long-term brake on economic and monetary union. By contrast, the more optimistic immediately started to examine whether progress could be made avoiding any institutional changes. The Basle/Nyborg agreement (see above) can be considered as one such, and the Cassandras were soon contradicted.

From Hanover to Madrid (June 1989): the Delors Report

The extraordinary dynamism and hopes created by the Single Act and the Europe '92 objective were reinforced by the troubled dollar story and the first Eastern European countries' cracks and convulsions as well as the success of the EMS in introducing a stable exchange rate area in Europe in a growth context. All these factors made more urgent, necessary and possible in practice the 20-year-old project of monetary union.[11] Moreover, a single market with 12 different currencies seemed somewhat contradictory and

10. The Single European Act was signed at Luxembourg on 17 February 1986 at The Hague on 28 February 1986 and came into force on 1 July 1987.
11. The EMU was first officially mentioned in the Communique (point 8) of the conference of heads of states and governments on 1 and 2 December 1969 in The Hague, which followed the first report on a linked subject, known as Barre's report: "Memorandum de la Commission au conseil sur la co-ordination des politiques économiques et la co-opération monétaire au sein de la communauté", 12 February 1969. The Hague Council was translated into another report, the Werner Report, on the attainment by stages of Economic and Monetary Union in the Community, 8 October 1970. The conclusions of this report were adopted by the Council on 8 and 9 June 1970, and it gave rise to a "Resolution of the Council and of the Representatives of the Governments of the Member States" of 22 March 1971 on the attainment by stages of economic and monetary union in the Community.

was considered as an obstacle to the full benefits of economies of scale which might be anticipated.

So, in Hanover on 27 and 28 June 1988, the Council entrusted a committee, chaired by M. Jacques Delors, President of the European Commission, with "the task of studying and proposing concrete stages leading towards economic and monetary union". The working group, which was composed of the 12 central bank governors, on a personal basis, and three independent persons, finished its report in April 1989. Accepted unanimously by the members of the group, it was submitted to the European Council in Madrid in June 1989.

The feeling of distrust towards the Ecu was still very high. Only half a page was devoted to describing the Ecu markets and a section of just one page (the report is 42 pages long) investigates the "various aspects of the role that the Ecu might play in the process of economic and monetary integration in Europe". Apart from considering that the Ecu "had the potential" to be developed into a single common currency[12] and that "there would not be discontinuity between the Ecu and the single currency of the union", the main point of the section was to exclude any possibility of adopting a "parallel currency strategy as a means of accelerating the pace of the monetary union process".

It seemed to external observers that the despatch of the Ecu from the debate was the price to pay to reach a unanimous agreement, even if the arguments against a parallel currency were plainly justified. To compensate for this neglect, they thought that some scraps had been given to Ecu supporters by providing that "there should be no discrimination against the private use of the Ecu and that existing administrative obstacles should be removed". Therefore, among the principal steps in the monetary field during stage one, one of them would be that "all impediments to the private use of the Ecu would be removed". But once again it appears that what pessimists considered as scraps were in fact the first stepping-stones.

From Madrid to the Intergovernmental Conferences: the realisation of the Ecu's potential

Examination of what has been accomplished since the adoption by the June 1989 Council of Madrid of the Delors Report is of extreme significance. Each European Council (Strasbourg, December 1989; Dublin, June 1990; and Rome, October and December 1990) has added a stone to the monetary edifice, achieving progress in the debate and reaching major decisions. Dates for the beginning of stage one (1 July 1990) and stage two (1 January 1994) were fixed. An 11-member state consensus was reached in Rome on the overall concept of the EMU process, which directly stems from the Delors Report and its final purpose, ie a single currency, the Ecu, and a single monetary policy conducted by an independent European central bank.

As far as the Ecu is concerned, even if the debate on its role and nature

12. It must be noted that, in the Delors Report, if a single currency was considered a "desirable feature of a monetary union", it was not "necessarily required". Report. . ., op. cit. page 33, point 46.

during the transition periods has not been closed (see below), many things have been clarified.

First and most importantly, the Ecu is no longer considered as having only a "potential" to be the single currency. The aim of the EMU process is a single currency, and that currency will be the Ecu. It will no longer be a basket but a fully fledged currency issued by the European central bank, and there will be no discontinuity between the actual Ecu and that single currency. Second, the first-stage objective of levying the obstacles to the use of the Ecu has been confirmed. The Commission will make propositions to the Council in this field before the end of 1991. Third, among the tasks of the European monetary institution, which will be created at the beginning of stage two, will be "to oversee the evolution of the Ecu".

Even if the idea of strengthening the Ecu has given rise to the propositions which are examined below, this could very well be limited to freezing its basket and developing its uses, especially in international transactions. As a matter of fact, several member states (France, Italy, the UK, Belgium, Spain and soon Denmark), have developed Ecu debt programmes on a very large scale. Such an involvement of the treasuries will make them much more cautious towards plans which would modify the rules of the game. Apart from this very pragmatic argument, many other technical or theoretical ones are being deployed against the hard Ecu formulae presented by the UK and Spanish authorities and in favour of freezing its composition.

From the Intergovernmental Conferences to EMU: which Ecu for the transition?

Although the Ecu's status in the final stage of EMU is now virtually beyond dispute, member countries have still to reach agreement on its role in the transitional phase. This question is not unrelated to the monetary integration strategy officially implemented since 1 July 1990, the start of stage one, and in reality since the establishment of the EMS in 1979. According to this reasoning, the strengthening of the Ecu results from the increase in convergence and not vice versa; neither can the Ecu be a crucial issue of monetary policy, since national monetary policies will remain sovereign until stage three. In fact, the "natural" strengthening of the Ecu, a composite currency, arises from the strengthening of its constituent currencies; its attractiveness, in the eyes of economic agents and even national monetary authorities, is due to the fact that it is not an independent or competing currency, as a parallel 13th currency would be, but a common currency, collectively managed by 12 central banks working more and more closely together.

The idea of a hard Ecu launched by the UK government has, however, met with fairly widespread success in the media and with a favourable response from several member countries who were searching for a compromise solution when the Intergovernmental Conference on EMU was about to open. This idea has nevertheless confused the debate about the role which the Ecu might play during the transition. In the final analysis, three options are possible:

1. The UK plan for the hard Ecu, an abstract and parallel currency, competing with national currencies and managed according to its own criteria. This is clearly an alternative strategy to EMU.
2. The plans for a "strong basket" Ecu, ie one which cannot be devalued against any of its constituent currencies, but which would remain tied to the latter. This option creates some problems, even though it remains consistent with the Delors Report's approach.
3. A global policy of strengthening and developing the Ecu, which is very broadly in keeping with developments in the last few years (increasing convergence, removing obstacles to the use of the Ecu, etc) but also offers something new: freezing the composition of the Ecu. This solution takes the line of strengthening the Ecu, which is the wish of several member countries, but does not have the disadvantages of the first two options. It seems, moreover, that a consensus could emerge in its favour.

The UK plan for a "hard Ecu" as an alternative strategy

This proposal is a variant of the competing currencies plan proposed by the UK government in November 1989 which did not find support from the other 11 member countries (see Chapter 17). The modifications establishing a Community monetary institution ("European Monetary Fund"), introducing the co-ordination of external policies and, above all, proposing a hard Ecu which cannot be devalued, were designed to deflate some of the most serious criticisms of the earlier plan.

However, the plan cannot be limited to this proposal to harden the Ecu. The overall approach remains radically different from the one based on the Delors Report, which is the subject, among 11 member countries, of an agreement reaffirmed at the Rome European Council on 27 and 28 October 1990, as regards both the method and the objective: the proposed strategy of a hard Ecu, a parallel currency competing with national currencies, conflicts with an approach based on the progressive strengthening of monetary co-operation within Europe and the promotion of the existing basket Ecu; the end result of the plan is not clearly defined, and the UK government has recently repeated its reservations concerning a single currency, presented as the possible culmination of a long and uncertain process essentially determined by market forces. The UK plan for a hard Ecu therefore gives rise to several objections.

First, the contribution it would make to the functioning of the existing EMS is doubtful:

- With regard to monetary convergence, the EMS is an instrument which has proved its worth. For the countries belonging to the ERM, it represents a powerful constraint; it still possesses a strong anchor in the Deutschmark and has not yet shown what it is capable of (sterling and the peseta are in the wide band of 6 per cent; the drachma and the escudo have not joined the ERM). The priority is therefore to strengthen the EMS and complete it with new convergence instruments such as the multilateral surveillance which was to be set up in 1991 and is specifically designed to deal with economic and budgetary policies which drift off course.

- With regard to stability, the introduction of a parallel Ecu would represent a risk of institutional conflict and of ambiguity of leadership within the zone; moreover, the rules for managing the exchange rate of this 13th currency or its interest rate between realignments remain ill-defined. So do the criteria to be used by the EMF, as a currency board, for deciding the amount of national currencies it would keep in its balance sheet or resell to the national central banks for hard currencies.

Secondly, it is also doubtful whether it is suitable for creating an EMU:

- Demand for the hard Ecu would be of a very hypothetical and haphazard nature. This currency would have no comparative advantage in performing the functions of a *numeraire,* an instrument used in transactions, or even a store-of-value.
- The guarantee that it could not be devalued would actually operate only when realignments took place, and these are becoming rarer; in addition, in open markets the exchange risk is covered by interest rate premiums.
- The supply of hard Ecu would have to pursue two incompatible objectives: to maintain a standard for fighting inflation and to promote a common currency. The supply of hard Ecu would actually be restricted by the EMF's operating rules, which provide that national central banks would have to repurchase their currency when the EMF's holdings of this currency reach a pre-set limit.
- The scheme would entail risks for the stability of the system, EC cohesion and, in the last resort, the process of EMU, which are inherent in operating an excessively asymmetrical mechanism.

Lastly, its introduction would seriously upset the balance in the existing Ecu market. If the latter were to survive, it would only have the character of a private currency, with no institutional benchmark or future in the building of the EC. Its primary and secondary markets would be abandoned and eventually doomed to extinction.

The "strong basket" currency as an option for stage two

According to this proposal, supported by the Spanish and German governments within the Intergovernmental Conference, the Ecu would retain its composite nature throughout the transitional phase. Therefore, in theory, it would not be an abstract currency unrelated to the national currencies. At each realignment this basket would be modified so that the Ecu could not lose value against any of the system's currencies. The Spanish plan also takes up some of the provisions of the Major plan, such as the pivotal role of a European Central Bank (ECB) in managing the Ecu, the issuing of notes and coins in Ecu and the obligation for the national central banks to redeem from the ECB their own currency which had been converted by economic agents. However, it differs from the Major plan on one essential point: the Ecu would definitely be the Community's single currency in stage three of EMU.

The two major objections against the "strong basket" proposal are that it overturns the rules under which the existing Ecu operates and eventually leads to a completely new entity:

1. The composition of the Ecu would become more uncertain, and the date and scale of decisions concerning its composition would be linked to the date and scale of realignments; any strain in the EMS would lead operators to expect a modification of the basket, thus increasing the volatility of the Ecu's short-term interest rate and the risks involved in its use. Because of that uncertainty, the short-term interest rate of the Ecu would be higher than that of the best currency in the system.
2. Because of the exchange rate guarantee given to the Ecu, its medium- and long-term interest rates would be significantly different from the theoretical rates calculated as the average of the component currency interest rates and would normally be lower than those of the best currency. Therefore, the yield curve of the Ecu would be structurally reversed, which would greatly complicate the arbitrages of banking operators who lend long-term and hedge short-term. The Ecu would *de facto* become an abstract currency which would have to be managed by the ECB according to its own criteria (this comes back to the disadvantages of the British "hard Ecu"). It should also be stressed that the German monetary authorities are always expressing their permanent opposition to the development of an abstract currency of this kind.

A global policy of strengthening the Ecu

This position is based on three prior observations:
1. It is necessary to build on past achievements: since 1987, the basket Ecu has become a stable currency, particularly against the Deutschmark. It is gaining naturally in strength and credibility as a result of the improvement in convergence between the member states; the strengthening of the Ecu is first and foremost the result of the convergence process.
2. The creation of an abstract hard Ecu (or a strong basket Ecu) would signify a break for present operators in the Ecu markets, and a change in strategy for EMU. It would make the management of the transitional phase more complex and would involve conducting an independent policy for the Ecu which is still opposed by 11 out of the 12 member countries.
3. The move to the single currency will be even faster and less traumatic if economic agents are already familiar with all of the Ecu's uses.

The Commission as well as some member countries therefore advocate a global and coherent policy designed to strengthen the Ecu and enlarge its market. Five guiding principles can be identified:
1. Make continued progress towards convergence, as a result of the new instruments available in stage one of EMU (multilateral surveillance); all currencies become members of the narrow band of the ERM.
2. Remove all technical and legal obstacles to the use of the Ecu.
3. Involve further the national monetary authorities and managers of the public debt in promoting and regulating the Ecu market.
4. Prepare for the move to the single currency (interlinking of markets and payment networks and designing of new monetary symbols, etc); this will be one of the principal tasks of the common monetary institution as soon as it is created in 1994.
5. Definitively freeze the composition of the Ecu. This measure would enable the existing basket Ecu to strengthen further without changing its

definition or altering the rules under which it operates. Definitively fixing the amounts of each currency in the Ecu (which are now subject to revision every five years) would be tantamount to allowing the percentage weights of the various currencies to evolve: the weight of the appreciating currencies increases and that of the depreciating currencies falls. This natural drift of weights penalises any failure in convergence. Thus, if this drift is no longer corrected, the value of the Ecu would tend towards that of the strongest currencies in the system. The natural hardening of an Ecu, the composition of which would be definitively fixed, can be assessed by comparing the evolution of the theoretical exchange rate and interest rate of an unrevised Ecu over the period 1979-90 with the actual rates of the real Ecu revised in 1984 and 1989. This comparison brings out several important points:

- the exchange rate of the unrevised Ecu would have strengthened by about 2 per cent against the Deutschmark (by convention taken here as the benchmark);
- the interest rate of the unrevised Ecu would have moved closer to that of the Deutschmark; at the end of the period, the interest rate differential between the unrevised Ecu and the Deutschmark would be one point (instead of 1.9 points for the real Ecu);
- the behaviour of the unrevised Ecu, in terms of volatility or variability, would be similar to that of the real Ecu.

In addition to this automatic strengthening, the advantage of fixing the Ecu's composition would be to remove the uncertainty surrounding the Ecu market, particularly in the long-term segment of the market, but also in the other segments as the revision dates approached. In fact, the rules determining the calculation of the new weights are imprecise and uncertain; the scale of the revisions cannot be anticipated with certainty; currencies which have relatively higher interest rates (and are therefore riskier) can be given greater weights; and other currencies may be introduced into the Ecu, which would alter its characteristics, etc. All these uncertainties would finally be removed if the composition of the Ecu was frozen. So would any danger of discontinuity between the basket Ecu, the common currency and the single currency of the EMU.

Appendix: The main EC legislation on the Ecu[13]

Council decision of 21 April 1975 on the definition and conversion of the EUA for expressing the amounts of aid mentioned in article 42 of the ACP-EEC Lomé Convention (75/250/EEC). This is the text which created the Ecu.

Decision no. 3289/75/ECSC of the Commission of 18 December 1975 on the definition and conversion of the unit of account to be used in decisions, recommendations, opinions and communications for the purpose of the Treaty establishing the European Coal and Steel Community.

Article 10 of the Financial Regulation of 21 December 1977 applicable to the general budget of the EC.

Annex to the Conclusions of the Presidency of the European Council, Bremen, 6 and 7 July 1978.

Resolution of the European Council on the establishment of the EMS and related matters, Brussels, 5 December 1978. Article 2 defines the functions of the Ecu and article 2.3 creates the principle of five-year re-examinations of the weights

[13] These texts have been published in *De Pecunia*, vol. i, no. 0 and no. 2.

of currency in the Ecu. It also provides that the weights would be re-examined for the first time six months after the entry into force of the system. This was done in September 1979: the system started in March 1979 (see below).

Council Regulation (EEC) no. 3180/78 of 18 December 1978, changing the value of the unit of account used by the EMCF. (Introduces the Ecu as unit of account.)

Council Regulation (EEC) no. 3181/78 of 18 December 1978, relating to the EMS. (Empowers the EMCF to issue Ecu against monetary reserves and the use of the Ecu as a means of settlement and for transaction between central banks and the EMCF.)

Memorandum concerning the calculation methods necessary to implement articles 3 and 4 of the agreement between the central banks of the member states of the EEC laying down the operating procedures for the EMS. Committee of governors of the central banks of the member states of the EEC, 12 February 1979. (Gives the methodology for computing the Ecu central rates and the divergence indicator.)

Agreement of 13 March 1979 between the central banks of the member states of the EEC laying down the operating procedures for the EMS. (This is the reference text for the EMS.)

Communication on the calculation of the equivalents of the Ecu and on the EUA published by the Commission, *Official Journal of the European Communities*, no. C69/4, 13 March 1979. (Gives the methodology followed to compute the exchange rates of the Ecu.)

Council Regulation (EEC) no. 2626/84 of 15 September 1984, amending article 1 of Regulation (EEC) no. 3180/78 amending the value of the unit of account used by the EMCF. (First revision of the Ecu composition and introduction of the drachma in the basket.)

Council Regulation (EEC) no. 3066/85 of 28 October 1985, *OJ of the EC*, no. L 290, 1 November 1985. (Modifies the C.R. (EEC) no. 3181/78, to introduce in article 2 the status of "other holders" of Ecu.)

Joint declaration on the inclusion of the peseta and the escudo in Ecu, *OJ of the EC*, 15 November 1985. (Gives the conditions for the peseta and the escudo to be included in the Ecu basket.)

Decision no. 18/85 of the board of governors of the EMCF, laying down the terms and conditions for acquisition, holding and use of Ecu's by other holders, 19 November 1985.

Council regulation (EEC) no. 1971/89 of June 1989, amending article 1 of Regulation (EEC) no. 3180/78, which itself amended the value of the unit of account used by the EMCF. (Second revision of the Ecu composition and introduction of the escudo and the peseta; it announced the new weights and the date of the revision: 20 September 1989.)

Information of the Commission, new composition of the Ecu (89/C 241/01), *OJ of the EC*, no. C 241/1, 21 September 1989. (Gives the new monetary amounts resulting from the Council Regulation (EC) no. 1971/89.)

References

Artis, M. (1990). *Delors and the hard Ecu: transition to EMU.* Manchester University, September.

Bishop, G. (1990). *Toughening the Ecu: practical steps to promote It.* Salomon Brothers International Ltd, October.

Duisenberg, W. F. (1989). "The Ecu as a parallel currency". Annex to the Delors Report, OPDOCE.

EC (1989). "Report on Economic and Monetary Union (Delors Report)", OPDOCE, April.
HM Treasury (1990). "UK proposals for a European Monetary Fund and a hard Ecu", August.
Jaillet, P. (1990). "La proposition britannique d'un Ecu fort: une Stratégle alternative vers l'UEM", *De Pecunia* vol. III, no. 1, March.
Major, J. (1990). "Economic and monetary union beyond stage 1", Chancellor's speech to German Industry forum, June.
Ministerio de Economia y Hacienda (1991). "The Ecu and the ESCB during stage 2". January.
Padoa-Schioppa, T. (1990). "Monetary union and competition: notes for a debate", *Politica Economica,* no. 3/90.
Pezet, J. L. (1990). "Hard Ecu, variation on a theme", Crédit Lyonnais Capital Markets Group, October.
Pöhl, K. O. (1989). "The further development of the EMS". Annex to the Delors Report, OPDOCE.
Vissol, T. (1988). "Les monnaies composites: innovation financière, innovation monétaire", in Ph. Kahn (ed.), *Droit et Monnaie: Etat et espace monétaire transnational.* Litec-CNRS.
Vissol, T. (1990). "Why firms should adopt the Ecu now". *De Pecunia,* vol. iii, no. 1, March.
Vissol, T. (1989). "La révision du panier de l'écu de Juin-Septembre 1989 et ses enseignements". *Revue Ecu,* no. 9.
Young, J. (1990). "The British approach to European Monetary Union". *De Pecunia,* vol. iii, no. 1, March.

3

Jennifer Schofield
Deutsche Bank Group

Ecu bond markets and their operations

The Ecu primary market

Introduction

The Ecu bond market comprises mainly Eurobonds and domestic issues, with few "international" bonds. Eurobonds are denominated in any currency issued outside the borrower's domestic market by international banks and sold to international investors; foreign/international bonds are issued by a foreign borrower in another country's domestic market and often sold to foreign investors; domestic bonds are issued by a borrower in his own domestic market and mainly sold to domestic investors. However, for the Ecu the distinctions between the bond types are somewhat blurred. Some bonds structured as Eurobonds are primarily targeted at domestic investors; some domestic issues are targeted at both domestic and foreign buyers. In this chapter, reference made to the "Ecu bond market" should be taken to cover the Eurobonds and those large benchmark government issues from countries such as France which are traded on the international markets alongside Eurobonds, unless specific note is made of domestic bonds.

The background and development of the market

The early Ecu issues were Eurobonds. In April 1981 the first Ecu Eurobond was launched for SOFTE, the Italian telecommunications company (Ecu35 million, 13 per cent coupon, issue price 100, maturity 1987). Before this, other composite currencies such as the European Unit of Account (EUA), the European Composite Unit (EURCO) and the Special Drawing Right (SDR) had been used by non-US dollar borrowers. However, political support for the EMS and the Ecu ensured that this was the composite currency which gained prominence. Over the years since its inception, the Ecu bond market has developed rapidly into one of the world's major financial sectors. The total outstanding volume of Ecu bonds on the Euro and international capital markets stood at Ecu76 billion by the end of March 1991. In the first few years, the Ecu bond market underwent dramatic growth, accounting for around 4.5 per cent of total annual issue volume on the Euro and international capital markets by 1985. The annual market share of Ecu bonds increased during the decade to reach nearly 11 per cent by the end of 1990. If the Ecu *obligations assimilables du Trésor* (OATs) from France's and Spain's debut Ecu issue in April 1990 are included, the total issue volume on the Ecu bond market in 1990 was the third highest after US dollars and Japanese yen. Large-issue volumes in the first quarter of 1991 saw the Ecu market share rise to over 20 per cent of total issuance, second only to the US dollar. The increase in the average size of Ecu bonds is further evidence of the swiftness of the development (see Exhibit 3.1).

Various reasons lie behind the swift expansion of the market:

1. The drive to European Economic and Monetary Union (EMU), especially over the last couple of years. Governments identified the cheaper and diversified funding available in Ecu and the access through this market to a wider investor base. This was especially applicable to EMS member countries with higher domestic interest rates than in the Ecu sector. Funding in Ecu has been seen more recently as a political support mechanism to accelerate progress towards EMU and the development of the Ecu as a single European currency. France has issued Ecu-denominated government bonds (OATs), despite the fact that funding costs would have been lower in domestic currency, as part of the French government's commitment to EMU. The UK issued its first Ecu-denominated government bond in February 1991.
2. The natural need for Ecu by EC supranational institutions as an accounting and financing unit.
3. Balance sheet rebalancing by commercial banks which had extended Ecu credits to their clients and had been left with mismatched currency positions.
4. The increasing use of the Ecu as a reserve currency and for foreign exchange intervention to ease tension within the ERM.

Exhibit 3.1 **Annual Ecu issue volume (left axis) and average issue size (right axis)**

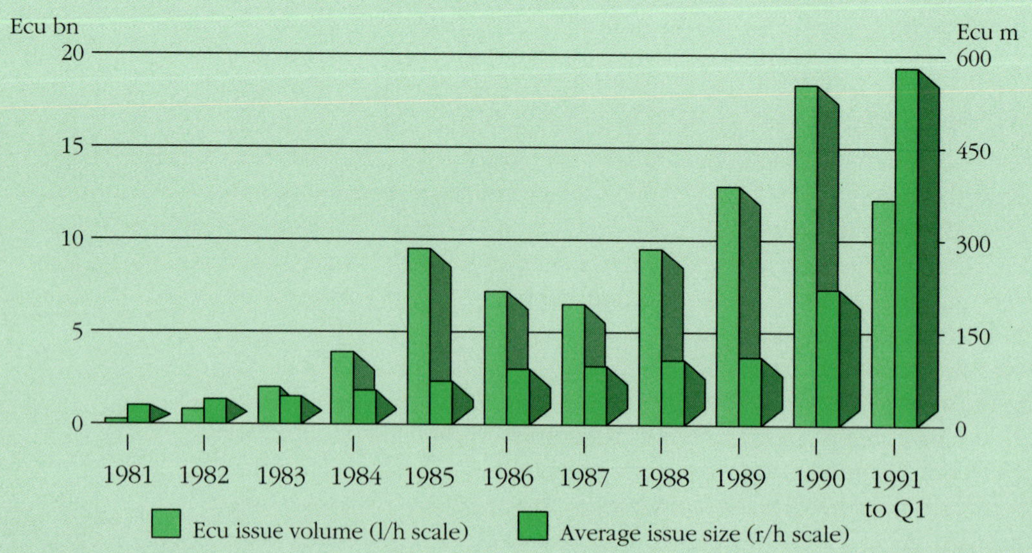

The data has been adjusted to include the Ecu OATs from france as well as the Spanish debut Ecu issue in April 1990.

Source: Euromoney Bondware.

5. The growth in corporate Ecu borrowing, increasing name recognition in the Euromarket or taking advantage of attractive funding levels in Ecu via the deepening swap market.

As the Ecu sector has matured, it has increasingly come to be used as just another bond market for a wide range of borrowing needs. Issuance activity has become less sporadic and disruptive to the secondary market. The market is less reliant on short-lived bursts of retail interest followed by a long period of gradual absorption. Attractive swap opportunities can encourage new issues which then pull in new investors and lead to more active switching activity between outstanding and new offerings, helping the liquidity of the secondary bond market.

A more efficient investor base is being created as Ecu issues find a wider audience. Thus the traditional small retail investors in Ecu, the Swiss and those from the Benelux countries, many of whom could not buy primary paper, or were even precluded from buying any Ecu issues until they were included in selected portfolio recommendations, have been joined by larger, institutional accounts. These large accounts were attracted by liquid issues with a European flavour (the Ecu currency), which offer increasing currency stability, given the workings of the ERM, and a yield advantage over the main European bond markets of Germany and France.

Characteristics of Ecu issues

Eurobonds

Ecu Eurobonds are typical Eurobonds, mostly distributed through an international syndicate and placed with a wide variety of institutional and private investors.

The fixed price re-offer system of launching new issues (which originated in the Eurodollar market) is now often used in the Ecu sector. This generally is held to offer smoother placement of the bonds as well as reducing syndication risk. There are few regulations restricting the market and no registration or queuing system.

There is free choice of which country's governing law and listing requirements are to be applicable. Most bonds are listed in Luxembourg. Any bank can be lead manager. Issue documentation includes the normal Euromarket provisions of negative pledge, cross default and *force majeure*. Interest payments on Eurobonds are free of withholding tax.

Since the Ecu is an artificial currency basket, the prospectus allows for the eventuality that the Ecu no longer exists at the bond's maturity, although this is thought to be increasingly unlikely as moves towards EMU progress. In this case the documentation generally lays down a specific method by which the bond can be redeemed at maturity. This involves calculation of an equivalent of the Ecu's value at the time of redemption by taking the currency amounts of each component of the Ecu as they existed whenever the Ecu was used last. Other eventualities, such as an alteration of any component currency of the Ecu which could change the composition of the basket, are also covered by normal issue documentation.

Types of issues. Among the Ecu Eurobonds issued, there have been a number of variations to the classical "straight" bonds (ie those with no special features attached which are always redeemed with one payment at maturity). Thus zero coupon bonds, floating rate notes (FRNs), bonds with calls and puts, partly-paid issues, deals with warrants attached and convertibles have all been brought to the market. Nevertheless, straight bonds have dominated Ecu issuing activity, with FRNs and equity-linked instruments remaining underdeveloped in comparison with the other international capital markets. Ecu FRN instruments have lacked a natural investor base because European banks have their balance sheets in one of the currencies of the Ecu and have been reluctant to accept the foreign-exchange exposure on an FRN, which should be a low-risk, asset/liability matching position. A similar problem exists for equity-linked bonds: there are no shares denominated in Ecu and consequently the natural linkage in the same currency is lacking.

Ecu domestic bonds

This sector is growing rapidly as more governments identify the opportunities offered by Ecu funding. Issue conditions differ, depending on the country and borrower in question. The bonds are usually issued via the country's traditional method of government bond issuance. However, French Ecu OATs have been issued both by the traditional method of issuing French franc-denominated OATs (Dutch auctions) and for the first time in November 1990 via an international syndicate to ensure that the desired volume could be sold and that placement would be wider. Interest is paid in the same way as for Ffr OATs, ie actual/365 annual coupon. An international syndicate was also the issue procedure used by the UK for its debut Ecu deal in February 1991. Spain's first Ecu issue, launched in April 1990, was a quasi-domestic bond (targeted and sold mainly to domestic investors) although issued via an international syndicate as in the Euromarket and paying interest using Euromarket conventions.

Lead managers

Historically, the use of the Ecu bond for issues grew up in Belgium and France in the days of restrictions on capital flows in Europe. Patronage of the Ecu by these countries is reflected in the league table of lead managers of Ecu bonds, where French banks have a disproportionate share of new issue business (see Exhibit 3.2). Additional European, US and most recently Japanese banks have joined the ranks of lead managers, demonstrating the changing profile of Ecu investors, as well as a recognition by investment houses of the great potential of the Ecu bond market.

Pricing of new issues

In most other major bond markets, new bonds are priced at a yield spread over the relevant government benchmark issue. The return on government bonds is seen as the lowest risk rate available in each currency and non-government issuers have to pay a premium over this rate, the size of which depends on their credit quality. Because there is no natural underlying government bond market for the Ecu, pricing of new issues is

Exhibit 3.2

League table of lead managers, total Ecu market (1981 to end Q1 1991)

		Lead managed		
Position	*Manager or group*	*Amount (Ecu m)*	*Number of issues*	*Share (%)*
1	Banque Paribas	18,073.08	130	23.75
2	Morgan Stanley International	5,370.00	17	7.06
3	Credit Suisse First Boston/ Credit Suisse	4,345.00	34	5.71
4	Crédit Lyonnais	4,305.00	46	5.66
5	Kredietbank NV	3,143.01	55	4.13
6	Union Bank of Switzerland	2,947.00	21	3.87
7	Swiss Bank Corporation	2,781.00	23	3.65
8	Deutsche Bank AG	2,640.00	20	3.47
9	Bankers Trust International Ltd	2,575.00	22	3.38
10	Banque Nationale de Paris	2,525.54	34	3.32
11	Sociéte Générale	2.347.80	33	3.09
12	Crédit Commercial de France	2,287.26	31	3.01
13	Merrill Lynch Capital Markets	1,900.00	20	2.50
14	Banco Di Roma	1,800.00	4	2.37
15	J P Morgan	1,685.00	17	2.21
16	Istituto Bancario San Paolo Di Torino	1,508.00	6	1.98
17	Nomura Securities Co Limited	1,320.00	11	1.73
18	Generale Bank	1,102.50	21	1.45
19	Mitsubishi Bank Ltd	1,000.54	10	1.31
20	Industrial Bank of Japan	970.00	12	1.27
	Total of issues used in the table	76,092.46	723	100.00

Source: Euromoney Bondware.

somewhat more complicated. New issues are usually priced with reference to secondary market yields. The emergence of Ecu-denominated French government bonds from April 1989 meant that, from 1990, these issues began to be widely used as benchmarks for pricing new paper. As more governments have tapped the Ecu market, particularly during the early part of 1991, these bonds too will gain status as benchmarks along much of the yield curve and are likely to be used for new issue pricing over time. Pricing procedures may still differ between those used for "jumbo" issues from sovereign or supranational borrowers and those for smaller corporate or agency deals. Depending on the borrower, even the large issues may be priced for coupon acceptability or name recognition rather than as active trading instruments. The role of the swap market in new issue pricing is dealt with in more detail later in this book.

Borrowers and investors in the Ecu market

There has been a significant change in both borrower and investor profiles since the early days of the Ecu bond markets. At first, the Ecu was almost exclusively used for borrowing by French and Belgian banks, state-guaranteed entities from these countries and supranationals. Subsequently, it has also been tapped by private sector borrowers from an

Exhibit 3.3 **Ecu borrowers by areas in 1991 (to Q1 1991)**

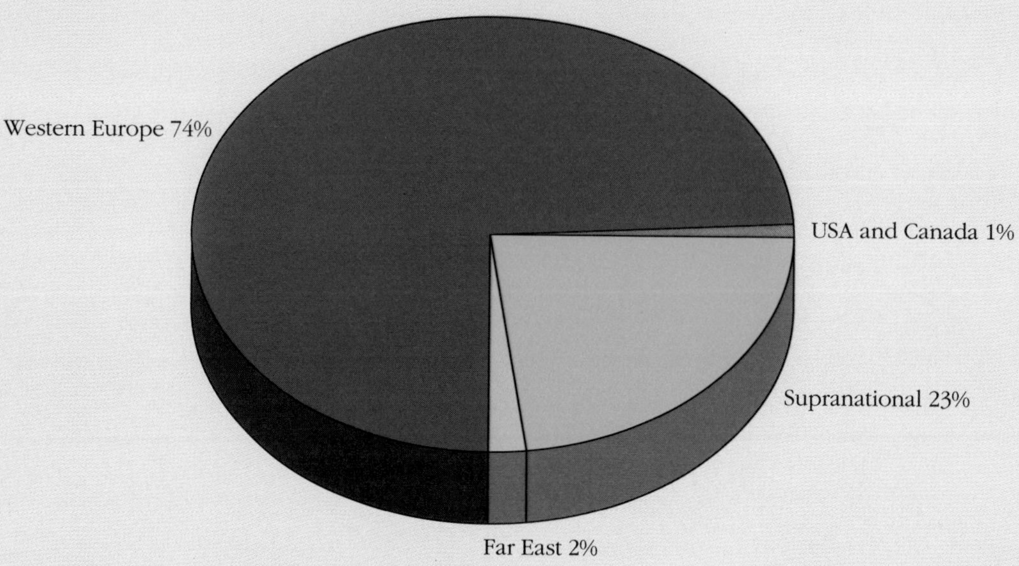

The data has been adjusted to include the Ecu OATs from France

Source: Euromoney Bondware.

increasing number of different countries. However, a large share of total Ecu issue volume is still made up of sovereign and supranational issuers. Indeed, the Ecu market is becoming a market of government bonds as these issues provide the liquidity demanded by institutional investors. Thus, a high proportion of Ecu paper is triple A rated by the two main credit-rating agencies, Standard & Poor's and Moody's.

For the placement of Ecu paper, the following trends have been observed:

Exhibit 3.4 **Ecu borrowers in 1991 (to Q1 1991)**

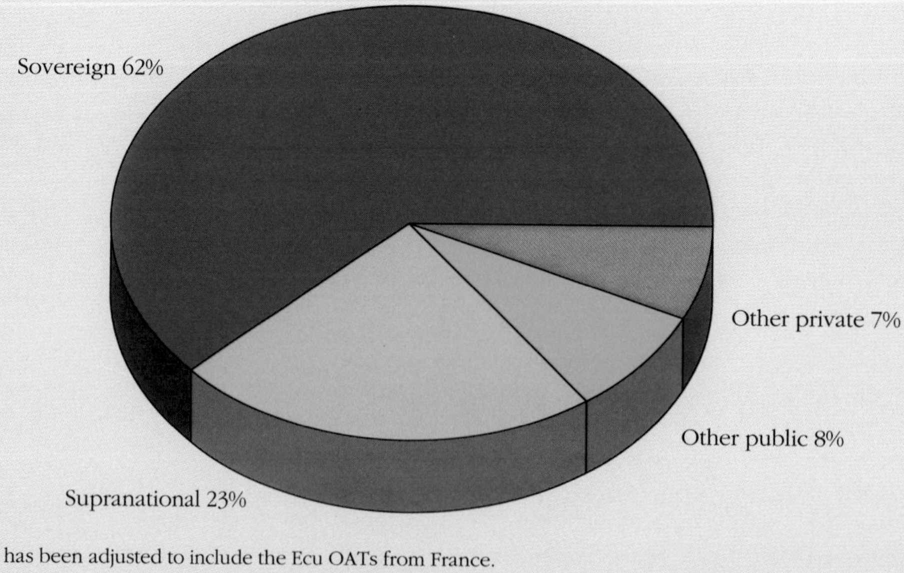

The data has been adjusted to include the Ecu OATs from France.

Source: Euromoney Bondware.

Exhibit 3.5 **Ecu borrowers in 1986**

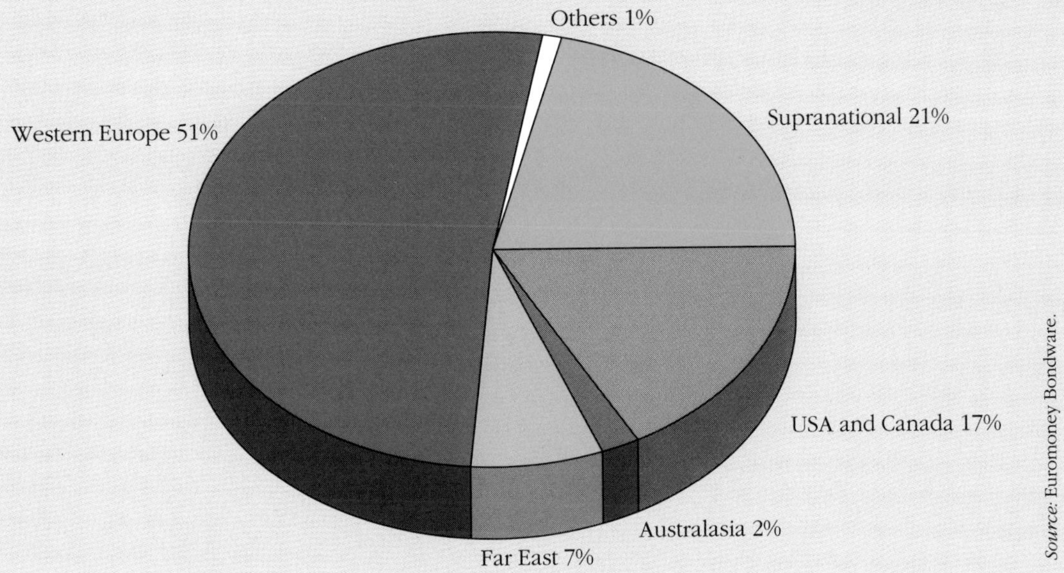

Active buyers of Ecu paper are still found among the traditional small-account retail investor base, "the Belgian dentists" (rich investors looking for a safe investment for their savings) and the Swiss and Benelux accounts. The first group of investors tends to exhibit steady demand for specific names or maturities. The latter two groups are often private and discretionary funds which frequently adhere to buy recommendation lists. The currency is seen to offer limited risk, with a yield above that of Deutschmark bonds.

Exhibit 3.6 **Ecu borrowers in 1986**

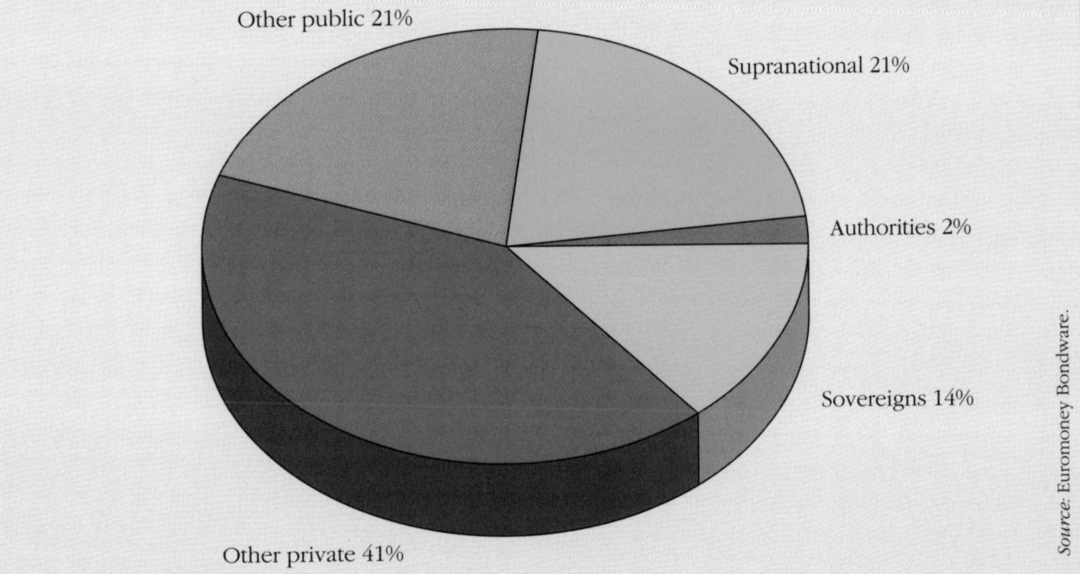

The investor base has now been widened by larger institutional funds. In December 1990, the Intergovernmental Conference (IGC) on EMU began. During 1991, EC finance ministers will debate economic union and the development of a single currency, aiming to agree amendments to the EC's founding treaty. The perception that the process of EMU is being accelerated and the desire to participate in the future single European currency have encouraged many more funds to allocate assets to Ecu. The greater sovereign and supranational support for the Ecu, as witnessed by an increasing number of new issues from these borrowers, has also raised the profile of this sector.

French investor demand has increased, especially in response to the OAT issues. France has also supported the Ecu market in founding the first long-dated Ecu futures contract on the MATIF in Paris in October 1990.

The Far East, the Middle East and the United States are emerging as powerful investor bases. Demand is accelerating rapidly as issues available become more liquid and investors see the potential of the Ecu as a major bond market, thus identifying a need to incorporate the Ecu in their portfolios. These investors often see the Ecu bond market as a way of participating in the European bond markets and having a view on "Europe" versus Japan and the United States without personal allocation criteria for individual countries. The Ecu is perceived as offering diversification with minimal risk due to ERM stability. In addition, it is a way of participating in higher-yielding markets where direct investment may increase transaction costs and/or suitable paper may not always be available.

Spanish investors have recently been introduced to Ecu bonds with Spain's own Ecu deal. Italian demand is generally channelled into domestic Ecu paper (CTEs) or confined to supranational Ecu Eurobond issues (tax advantages). Scandinavian investor interest is steady with potential to increase as these countries show interest in tying their currencies to the Ecu (eg Norway) and discussions continue about the Scandinavian countries joining the EC.

The secondary market

Trading

The secondary market in Ecu bonds is continually developing as more Ecu-denominated paper becomes available. A burst of issuance in the early months of 1991 gave a strong impetus to secondary trading of Ecu bonds, with higher liquidity enhancing tradability. There are currently over 700 issues outstanding in the Ecu market, the majority of which are straight Eurobonds. Most trading books are arranged in the following manner.

There is a "liquid" book of around 60 issues, with approximately eight of these having benchmark status for their particular maturities (sovereign and supranational names). The benchmarks trade on a very narrow spread of 10 cents, and ticket sizes are often Ecu5 million between dealers. These issues are used for spread trading and futures-related arbitrage. The other liquid issues are traded on a spread of between 20 cents, ⅜ to ½ point; normal ticket size is Ecu2 million.

Exhibit 3.7

Total Ecu turnover (US$bn equivalent)

1986[1]	179.48	1989	375.44
1987	243.38	1990	722.14
1988	268.34		

[1] 1986 is the first year for which records are available. Cedel's and Euroclear's figures capture most of Ecu turnover although not the Ecu OATs cleared through SICOVAM, the French domestic clearing system.

Source: Cedel and Euroclear.

There is an "illiquid" book, of growing importance for retail clients, on which two-way prices are usually made. Supply and demand, however, depend on outstanding positions and also on Ecu swap rates, because bonds are sometimes traded against swaps.

There are currently over 35 market-makers in five major European countries (UK, France, Belgium, Luxembourg and Italy), but the number is expected to increase as the market expands. Over the last two years there has been an increase in the number of Japanese market-makers, reflecting the greater interest of Far Eastern investors in Ecu bonds. There is also a broker market. Greater manpower is generally being invested by each house on running Ecu books. "Street" trading (between investment houses) is increasing and with it turnover. New types of client are using the Ecu to diversify currency risks and are trading the bonds at a spread off both other Ecu issues and bonds in other currencies. Major institutional accounts are being attracted into the largest, most liquid issues and trade these actively. The rise in turnover is shown by the figures from the two European clearing houses, Cedel and Euroclear.

Cedel has always had a larger share of total Ecu clearing volume than its rival, Euroclear. Its market share reached around 60 per cent of total Ecu turnover by 1990. It saw a dramatic rise (63 per cent) in Ecu turnover in 1990 over the previous year.

Evaluation of Ecu bonds; development of the theoretical yield concept

The lack of an underlying domestic government bond market as a benchmark to trade and evaluate arbitrage opportunities inhibited the growth of the Ecu bond market in its early stages. A substitute for a government bond yield curve has been necessary in order to have some means of measuring the value of the various outstanding bonds as well as of new Ecu issues. A rough guide is provided by the German and French government bonds (statistical analysis shows that Ecu bonds are highly correlated with both markets, ie movements in both Deutschmark and French franc yields explain a great deal (over 80 per cent) of the movement in Ecu yields; in addition, the Deutschmark and the French franc make up nearly 50 per cent of the Ecu currency basket) or by Ecu issues from supranational entities. However, these approaches are still imperfect from the point of view of hedging risk. As a result of this, various ways of measuring Ecu bonds against all the bond markets which make up the Ecu currency basket have been undertaken. One of the most common methods is to create a so-called "theoretical" Ecu government bond yield curve, which then represents a substitute benchmark to assess the relative attractiveness of Ecu bonds.

Two models for calculating the theoretical Ecu yield curve are widely accepted among market professionals. One method breaks the Ecu cash flows down into their constituent components and uses the zero coupon yield curve in the component currencies to determine the net present value of all the cash flows and consequently the theoretical yield. The second, easier method is to take a portfolio of benchmark government bonds in the component currencies of the Ecu. The yield on each maturity in the portfolio is the weighted average of each of the individual component bonds (ie the yields on the most representative domestic government bonds are weighted by the present weight of that country's currency in the Ecu basket).

As for the actual Ecu-denominated bonds, due to the individual fluctuations of Ecu bonds, it has been more appropriate to consider a simple average Ecu yield of a basket of the most liquid supranational and government Ecu issues rather than taking one specific bond in each maturity as the benchmark yield. Individual Ecu issues have been subject to fluctuations due to the relatively small size of the market, and an average Ecu yield for each maturity has been shown in the past to be a more representative indication of Ecu yield levels. The yield spread between the theoretical and actual Ecu yields is observed over time as a substitute for the spread, in other capital markets, between the Euro and domestic bond markets.

In most major bond markets yield spreads are positive for non-domestic bonds (eg Eurodollar bonds trade at a certain premium to US Treasuries) unless there are specific tax situations which cause most investment to be made in the non-domestic bonds, thus pushing these yields below government yields. On the other hand, actual Ecu bond yields for the highest-quality Ecu bonds should generally be lower than the theoretical yields in the corresponding maturities. The main reasons for this yield relationship are as follows:

There are advantages in buying actual Ecu bonds rather than putting together a corresponding theoretical Ecu yield by buying all the domestic bonds which make up the Ecu basket. Transaction costs are lower for those choosing to buy an Ecu bond rather than bonds in 12 different domestic markets, if indeed this is even possible for the smaller component markets of the Ecu. Over time, this advantage will be reduced as European capital markets are liberalised. There is also no withholding tax on Ecu Eurobonds, as opposed to some government bonds.

Some of the European domestic markets (eg Portugal, Greece) are still too inefficient or too small to allow liquid trading conditions. In addition, there may be a lack of relevant instruments (eg until March 1991 there were no fixed-rate 10-year Italian government bonds). The loosening of regulatory control during moves towards a single European market, plus specific government measures to offer a wider range of investment products, will also reduce this problem.

Exhibit 3.8 **10-year Ecu yield spread (theoretical minus actual yield)**

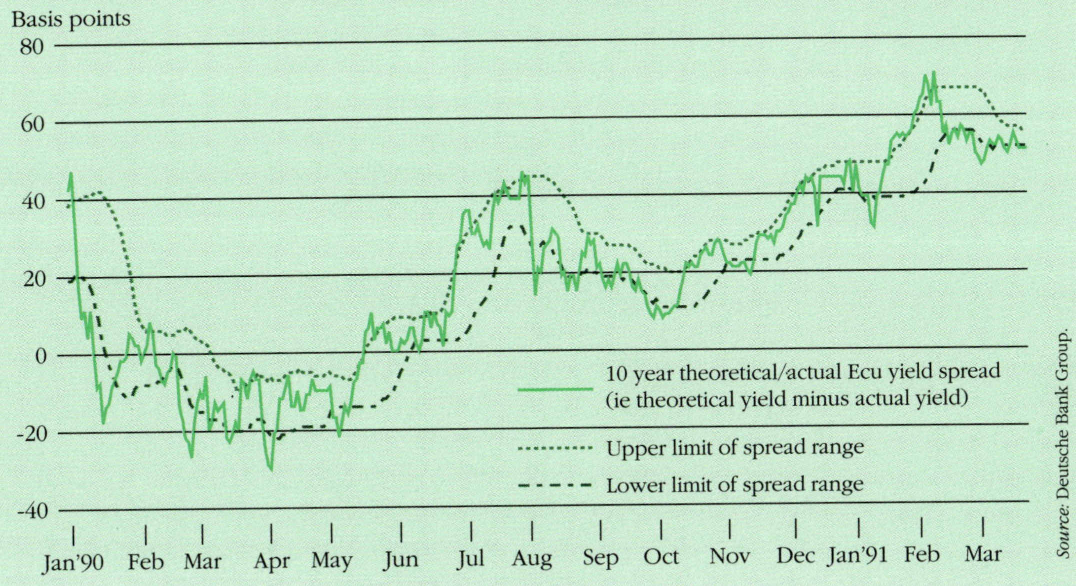

The use of the theoretical/actual Ecu yield spread for trading purposes

The movement of the spread between actual and theoretical yields over time, especially in relation to the general movement of European interest rates, indicates buying and selling opportunities. Using simple statistical techniques, a model of the expected movement in the spread (a spread range in each maturity) can be set up. When the spread attains the upper or lower limits of the given ranges, the attractive buying or selling opportunities are reached. The graph of this movement indicates that much of the spread movement is captured by the spread ranges (dotted lines) and that a breakout above or below the ranges leads to a correction of the spread through moves in prices and yields. Spreads at the shorter maturities are generally wider on average than spreads of longer-dated Ecu bonds because, for several reasons (such as the existence of long-dated futures contracts), Ecu bond issuance tends to be skewed towards the long end of the maturity spectrum. In the past the relative illiquidity of the short end has meant unnaturally low Ecu yields compared to the theoretical.

In a bear market (rising European interest rates), Ecu bonds have traditionally underperformed the underlying domestic markets, ie Ecu actual yields rise faster than theoretical, and the spread narrows (as actual yields move up nearer to theoretical levels). When the spread is extremely tight (Ecu bond yields are close to the theoretical curve) compared to historic levels, Ecu bonds are attractive versus the underlying markets, and arbitrage buying/market-maker price adjustments will generally bring Ecu prices back into line. At times the speed of this process has been hindered by an over-supply of swap-driven new issues into thin markets, the existence of which weighed on Ecu prices. In a bull market, Ecu bonds have out-performed domestic bonds and the spreads between actual and theoretical yields have widened (Ecu yields far below the theoretical curve).

Factors affecting the spread

Historically, the lower liquidity of Ecu bonds compared to the major domestic markets (Germany, France) meant higher Ecu price volatility during large interest rate movements. In addition, periodic influxes of new paper generated by favourable swap opportunities (eg Spring 1989), even at times of limited retail interest, have rapidly impacted on yields in the secondary market. As the sector gains liquidity and depth, the impact is less dramatic due to new investors coming in to absorb the larger issues.

Domestic market factors can also influence the theoretical/actual spread. The proposal in 1988 by the German government to impose withholding tax on domestic interest income caused German Bund yields to rise sharply, which also led to an increase in the Ecu theoretical yields.

A repeal of the 12.5 per cent withholding tax on Italian government bonds, when it comes, should lower Italian government bond yields to equate the net yields available in alternative markets, and the theoretical yields will fall somewhat (the Italian lira has a weight of just under 10 per cent in the Ecu basket).

The sharp sell-off suffered by German Bunds early in 1990 as fears about the costs of German reunification took hold was reflected in an even more precipitous fall in Ecu bond prices, which meant that, for a time, Ecu bonds traded above theoretical yields.

The effect of changes in the Ecu currency on Ecu bond yields

The anticipation of a revision in the Ecu basket, implying a reduction in the weight of the currencies with lower interest rates and an increase in the

Exhibit 3.9 **Factors affecting the theoretical/actual yield spread**

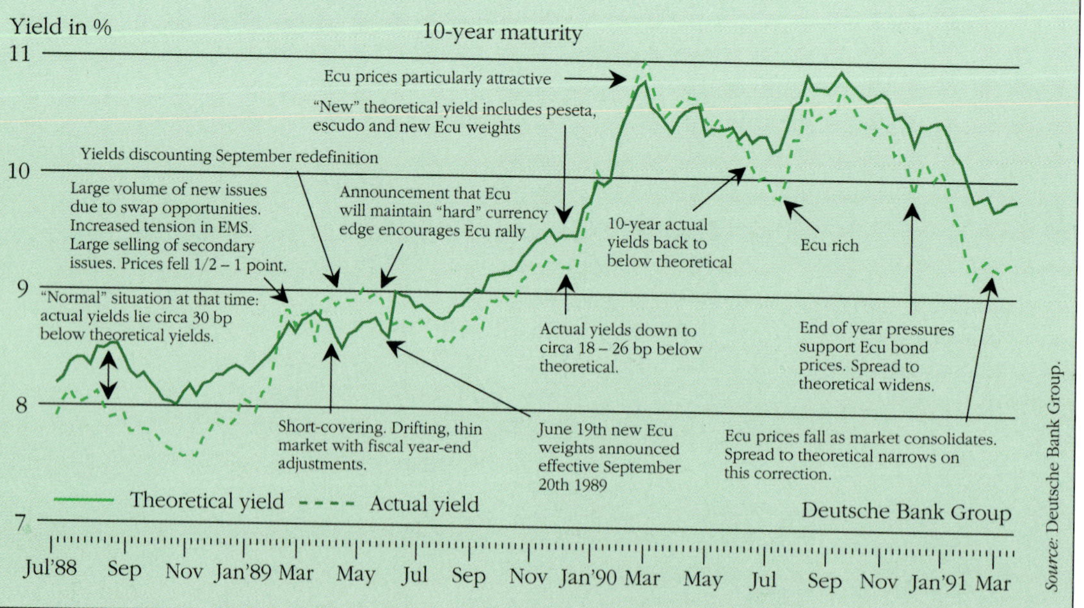

Source: Deutsche Bank Group.

currencies with higher interest rates, has in the past caused actual Ecu yields to rise several months ahead. This occurred in early 1989 (see Exhibit 3.9), causing actual Ecu yields to rise above theoreticals as participants anticipated the inclusion of the high-yielding Spanish peseta and Portuguese escudo into the basket. In fact, EC finance ministers tried to avoid a sudden shock to Ecu rates by overweighting the Deutschmark at the revision which took effect in September 1989. However, as the European currencies become less volatile and move towards a fixed exchange-rate system under the scheme for EMU, a revision will become purely technical and will not cause market distortions.

The anticipation of a full Ecu realignment (ie changes in the central bilateral exchange rates to the Ecu) may lead participants to sell Ecu bonds and buy the appreciating currencies (those which are causing strains within the ERM grid and are likely to force a realignment). A realignment caused by, for argument's sake, Deutschmark strength would increase weight of the Deutschmark in the Ecu basket; the Ecu would "harden". Thus, the realignment itself should have a positive effect on Ecu bond prices, because the devaluation of "soft", high-yielding currencies reduces the contribution of these currencies to the level of Ecu yields. As negotiations between the European partners on the shape of EMU continue and economic convergence in Europe becomes more pronounced, there is a decreasing likelihood of realignments. There have already been suggestions that the current Ecu should be "hardened". The "hard" currency core of the Ecu could then increase in weight to the disadvantage of the softer, high yielders. This would mean that Ecu bond yields would eventually converge towards the lowest European yields.

The attractions of Ecu bonds

The Ecu is a means of diversifying into the bond markets of all of the EMS countries. Instant currency diversification is achieved through one transaction.

The convergence of European inflation and interest rates increases the stability of Ecu bonds and reduces currency fluctuations. Thus, although high-yielding sectors may out-perform, the higher return may potentially be offset by currency losses. As fluctuations in the ERM diminish and the Ecu itself hardens (see above), currency risk on Ecu bonds is reduced. Yet with the inclusion of some European high yielders in the Ecu currency basket, Ecu bonds still offer an advantage over the "hard" European currencies. For example, the 10-year French Ecu OAT has out-performed the 10-year German Deutschmark Bund. (See Exhibit 3.10).

Ecu bonds provide an opportunity for investors to access European bond markets without requiring a personal detailed knowledge and allocation strategy.

The volume of new issues in liquid, tradeable sizes has grown rapidly in 1991. Portfolio managers will therefore further increase their participation in the Ecu market. Additionally, as Monetary Union and a single currency approaches and the commercial use of the Ecu expands, funds will need to match assets to liabilities. At some future date, bonds denominated in other European currencies will be converted into Ecu.

Exhibit 3.10 **Relative performance in DM**

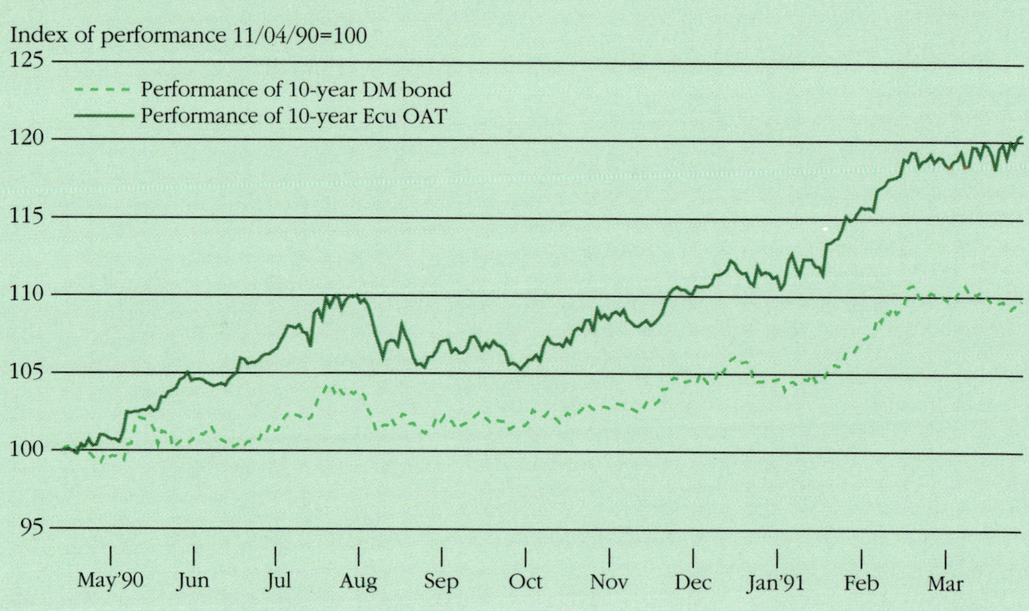

Source: Deutsche Bank Group.

Greater government support for the Ecu is driving the development of the Ecu sector. The first two months of 1991 saw a dramatic increase in the issuance of Ecu-denominated government bonds. Other European countries are expected to launch Ecu issues ahead of EMU both to show a political presence in the sector and to match future Ecu liabilities. For the investor, a greater volume of sovereign Ecu paper makes the sector more attractive and, as European interest rates converge, the development of an Ecu government yield curve will increase the transparency of the sector and eventually obviate the need for a theoretical yield curve. There are currently liquid sovereign issues in five-, seven- and 10-year maturities, plus the UK Treasury-bill programme at the short end of the curve.

The existence of two Ecu long-dated futures contracts on the MATIF and LIFFE should provide the first effective hedging instruments in the Ecu sector. To date, the use of substitute bonds and markets, such as a combination of the futures contracts in the four major component markets of the Ecu, using adjusted Ecu weights, in an attempt to hedge Ecu positions has been imperfect, at times impractical and relatively expensive. It is not yet clear which of the two contracts will gain more liquidity but the existence of efficient futures contracts will increase the attractions of the Ecu sector.

Conclusion

The growing political consensus for European Economic and Monetary Union in a form such as that set out in the Delors plan, and the development of a single European currency, suggest that heightened investor interest in Ecu will drive the further maturing of the sector. Progress towards EMU is likely to encourage more official and business transactions to be conducted in Ecu. This will then mean the creation of more Ecu assets and liabilities which will support the Ecu swap market. Better hedging instruments are being developed through bond futures contracts on the MATIF in Paris and LIFFE in London which should underpin the cash market. The burst of Ecu-denominated government bonds in early 1991 has been undertaken as EC governments strive to enhance their "European" status. France has announced that 15 per cent of total net borrowing in 1991 will be raised in Ecu. Other governments are lining up to launch Ecu bonds later this year. European finance ministers are being heard arguing their country's case for holding the position of the main Ecu trading centre, recognising the currency's future importance in Europe. As European economic convergence continues, the Ecu market has the potential to become the developed world's largest non-US dollar bond sector.

4 Users of Ecu bond markets

Graham Bishop
Salomon Brothers

The development of the Ecu bond market can be split into two phases. The first phase began in 1981 and lasted until about the middle of 1990. The second phase has existed since then. This transition is shown clearly in Exhibit 4.1. In the first quarter of 1991, the average maturity of Ecu Eurobonds lengthened by a third from that seen between 1988 and 1990, while the average issue size quadrupled and annualised issue volume more than tripled compared to 1990.

Exhibit 4.1
The Ecu Eurobond[1] market, 1981–89

	New issue volume (Ecu m)	*Average issue size (Ecu m)*	*Average maturity at issue (years)*	*Number of issues*			
				Central government	*Supranational institutions*	*Other public sector*	*Other private sector*
1981	280	31.1	7.0	–	2	5	2
1982	815	40.7	7.8	3	5	10	2
1983	2,007	43.6	8.5	3	15	17	11
1984	3,457	54.9	8.1	6	20	17	20
1985	8,794	70.9	7.6	6	18	28	72
1986	7,216	93.7	8.1	7	14	17	39
1987	6,541	93.4	6.1	5	15	21	29
1988	9,157	101.8	4.9	5	20	24	41
1989	11,151	97.0	4.9	9	20	34	52
1990	14,081	167.6	4.9	6	10	39	29
Q1 1991	11,395	633.1	6.6	4	6	5	3

[1] Domestic bonds, such as French OATs and Italian CTEs, are excluded from this definition.
Source: Euromoney Bondware.

The characteristics of the "new" market – large, liquid issues with longer maturities – demonstrate powerfully that some EC governments, responsible for 60 per cent of Ecu Eurobond issuance in the first quarter of 1991, have decided to take a lead in sponsoring the development of the Ecu bond markets. They clearly intend to make investors familiar with the Ecu as the new money of the future by enabling them to use Ecu assets as a store of value for long-term savings. Governments now dominate Ecu bond issuance and are likely to remain the largest users, by far, for the foreseeable future, although private sector use should rise progressively as the day of a single European currency approaches. Exhibit 4.2 analyses outstanding Ecu bonds by issuer category and includes both domestic and Eurobonds.

Exhibit 4.2

Outstanding Ecu bonds by category of issuer, end-March 1991 (Ecu bn)

Within the EC		*Outside the EC*	
Governments		Governments	
Belgium	2.0	EFTA[3]	1.9
Denmark	1.1	Other	0.7
France, OAT[1]	6.1		
Ireland	0.4		
Italy, Eurobonds	6.5		
Italy, GTE[2]	25.4		
Portugal	0.2		
Spain	0.5		
UK	2.8		
Subtotal	45.0		
Supranational institutions	11.0	Supranational institutions	3.3
Public sector	11.1	Public sector	4.9
Private sector	9.8	Private sector	10.5
Outstandings within the EC	76.9	Outstandings outside the EC	21.3
		Total Outstandings	98.2

[1] OAT Obligations ássimilables du Trésor.
[2] CTE Certificati del Tesoro in Euroscudi.
[3] EFTA European Free Trade Association.
Source: Association of International Bond Dealers (AIBD).

Ultimate scale of the Ecu bond market of the EC governments

When a single currency – the Ecu – replaces existing national currencies, all existing contracts, such as bonds, will have to be rewritten in Ecu. This process should not create windfall gains or losses, because the process of interest rate convergence is already well under way – driven by market anticipation. Indeed, the German EMU Treaty draft explicitly sets reasonable convergence of capital market yields as a test for the timing of the initial move to irrevocably locked exchange rates. Once that locking has occurred, there will be strong pressure to move to the ultimate goal – a single currency – as the only really credible form of "irrevocably" fixed exchange rates. All the debts (including bonds) of EC governments will then be denominated in Ecu. This implies the eventual existence of a massive bond market. Exhibit 4.3 shows the relative size of existing debts.

Exhibit 4.3
Total debts and bonds[1] of EC member states (Ecu bn), end-1990

Country	*Total debt*	*Central government bonds*	*Percentage of total debt*
Belgium	198	103	52
Denmark	64	30	47
France	337	132	39
Germany	511	203	40
Greece	48	NA	NA
Ireland	34	14	41
Italy	862	149	17
		221[2]	26[2]
Luxembourg	0.5	0.1	17
Netherlands	169	89	53
Portugal	31	NA	NA
Spain	172	37	21
UK	330	134	41
Total	**2,756.5**	**1,112.1**	**39.4**

[1] Fixed-rate public debt, maturity over one year, domestic currency.
[2] *Certificati di Credito del Tesoro* (CCTs): floating coupon, five- to 10-year maturity.
NA Not available.
Sources: EC services, central bank bulletins, OECD, Salomon Brothers estimates.

The world's largest bond market?

The size of a government bond market is simply a reflection of that government's accumulated fiscal deficit. For many years, the US has been criticised for the scale of its budget deficit, but the EC governments, collectively, have run even larger deficits. As a result, their accumulated debts now rival those of the US. Coincidentally, publicly issued government bonds represent about 40 per cent of the government debt of both blocs.

Exhibit 4.4 shows the relative size of the total debts and bond markets of the US, EC and Japan. The scale of the EC bond markets already rivals that of the US Treasury market. A greater reliance on market discipline to control excessive budget deficits (see below) will require EC governments to raise the proportion of their debt in marketable instruments; the EC government Ecu bond market should eventually become clearly the world's largest.

Exhibit 4.4
Size of government bond markets at end-1990 (Ecu bn)

	Total government debt	*Central government bonds*
EC	2,757	1,106
US	2,449	933
Japan	1,191	414

Sources: European Commission, US Federal Reserve, Bank of Japan, Salomon Brothers estimates.

The transition from national currencies to Ecu

The transition from national currencies to the Ecu began at the start of the "new" Ecu bond market during 1990. The speed of the changeover will be dictated by the political commitment to rapid progress on EMU. There is no reason why some governments should not make the transition more rapidly than others. A government's speed of conversion will send a clear signal to that country's private sector about the need to begin to adjust to Ecu-denominated finance.

The first hurdle is the acceptance of the Ecu as the equivalent of national money. With its powerful commitment to the "*franc fort*" policy, the French government has shown no hesitation in stating publicly that it will fund between 15 and 20 per cent of its new debt requirements in Ecu. These must be converted into French francs to settle domestic obligations – with the effective result that the Ecu is looked upon as domestic money. As the EMU process develops, it is quite conceivable that the French authorities could push the Ecu proportion of funding rapidly higher.

At the other end of the spectrum is Germany. The commitment to EMU is undoubted, yet the Ecu is unlikely to feature significantly in German funding plans, for the simple reason that it will cost more. In the past, the German authorities have opposed the use of the Ecu because they believed it was little more than an indexation mechanism that could trigger inflation. That attitude has softened, but the heavy costs of funding German unification suggest that any political gesture of borrowing in Ecu may be modest, and delayed, because of the higher interest costs. Nevertheless, the image of the Ecu as Europe's future currency will be completed when Germany borrows in Ecu.

The UK attitude towards the Ecu is towards the German end of the spectrum. As reservations about a single currency diminish with time, a powerful mechanism for reducing longer-term sterling interest rates will be provided by a shift in the British government's funding programme towards the Ecu – following the French. The government made it clear that its Ecu issue in February 1991 was just to increase the foreign exchange reserves, thus avoiding any implicit commitment to a single currency. Nonetheless, the UK's Ecu issue probably marked a turning-point in the development of the Ecu bond market. The symbolism of the sceptical UK government demonstrating a belief in the Ecu's future triggered a wave of issuance, catapulting the Ecu bond market out of its infancy and into adolescence.

For many other European governments, a decision to borrow in Ecu, or not, may be much more pragmatic. Once they have signed the monetary union treaty – hopefully by the end of 1991 – and their parliaments have ratified the plan to move to a single currency, then a decision to borrow in Ecu may well be based on little more than the cost-saving. Exhibit 4.5 shows the comparison between Ecu bond yields and those of domestic currency bonds – an indicator of the likely use of the Ecu market. Some of the largest borrowers would reduce funding costs by issuing in Ecu at 9 per cent yields, rather than continuing to issue in domestic currency at yields ranging from 10 to 13 per cent or more. By itself, each such decision will help promote the convergence of interest rates – accelerating the approach of a single currency.

Exhibit 4.5

Winners and losers from Ecu bond issuance – long-term bond yields and central government bond markets, 1990-91 (Ecu bn)

	Long-term bond yields (%) 22 April 1991	*Central government bonds end-1990*
The winners – cost saving		
Italy	13.3	370.2
Spain	11.8	36.9
Sweden[1]	11.4	31.0
UK	10.2	133.7
The neutrals – little difference		
Ireland	9.2	13.8
Denmark	9.2	30.4
Belgium	9.1	102.7
Ecu	9.0	–
France	8.9	132.0
The losers – cost disadvantage		
Netherlands	8.6	88.6
Austria[1]	8.4	22.7
Germany	8.4	202.8
Switzerland[1]	6.9[2]	6.0

[1] Member of the European Free Trade Association (EFTA). [2] Swap rate

Note: Total net borrowing of the European Communities and the European Investment Bank was Ecu57 billion equivalent at end-1989.

Non-EC governments: EFTA

Exhibit 4.5 includes some European Free Trade Association (EFTA) countries. Austria has already formally applied to join the EC and Sweden has decided to apply. If the current negotiations on a European Economic Area – co-operation between the EC and EFTA – fail, then the other members of EFTA will have little alternative but to join the EC. This is the probable outcome and could occur on a similar timescale to that of the transition to a single currency. This would add a further substantial category of users to the Ecu bond market. EFTA governments have already used the Ecu bond markets but they only account for about 2 per cent of Ecu bonds outstanding.

Non-EC governments: Central and Eastern Europe

The need in Central and Eastern Europe for stable currencies that can be trusted by the people has been highlighted by German monetary unification. A currency's attractiveness as a store-of-value is the key to making savings worthwhile. The Ecu bond market can play several roles in this process.

Several Central and Eastern European countries have already expressed interest in EC membership, although their perceived timescale may be shorter than the EC's. Accordingly, they are shaping their financial legislation to make it compatible with the EC's evolving framework. However, they will clearly not have a sophisticated financial market, with all the legal and technical back-up, for several years. As this will deter foreign inward investment, there seems every reason to piggy-back developments in the West and "borrow" the financial power that Western Europe will assemble over the next few years.

Once the scale and liquidity of the EC governments' Ecu bond market is established, it should be possible for Eastern European governments to issue bonds at a yield spread over those of the EC. The divergence would reflect creditworthiness alone; the uncertainty of new market systems would be avoided, because all the dealing and settlement systems would be well established.

The risk attached to a large-scale "foreign" borrowing lies in the possibility of devaluation. It is conceivable, indeed probable, that some countries may choose to peg their currency to the EC by using the Ecu. This plan has obvious logic for countries with EC membership as an ultimate ambition, because they would then be well placed to join a European monetary union in due course. The question of whether their economies can adjust to such a link is no different in principle from the problems faced by, for example, the UK enduring the upheaval necessary to adjust from a 10 per cent inflation rate to the desired EMU rate of perhaps 2 per cent.

Initially, Eastern European bonds would undoubtedly trade at substantial yield premiums to those of the EC. However, the second component of the exercise is to ensure that the citizens of the issuing country have the freedom to use the Ecu bond market as a "store-of-value" in which they can invest their money with confidence. Initially, that confidence might be placed in the bonds of EC governments, but money is fungible, and other funds would be available to find the higher-yielding opportunities represented by Eastern European government bonds.

Over time, if the issuing countries successfully created a democratic and healthy economy there is little doubt that their own citizens would be the first to recognise the evolution. At that stage, and acting rationally, they would sell their EC government bonds and reinvest in the higher-yielding issues of their own governments. With domestic savings then being freely channelled into domestic uses via the government's indebtedness, the cycle would be complete and yield levels would fall. The size of the yield premium would serve as one simple test of the readiness of these economies to join EMU.

This approach would also allow Eastern European countries to build their financial services capability by participating progressively in the EC's system and developing state-of-the-art expertise.

Should bonds be a higher proportion of government debt?

At present, publicly traded bonds only account for about 40 per cent of the debts of EC governments. There are good reasons for this proportion to rise substantially – with dramatic implications for the ultimate use of the Ecu bond markets. These reasons stem directly from the move towards monetary union and the measures necessary to ensure that member states are fiscally responsible.

The rationale for such a policy shift springs from the "no-bail-out" rule. This will be enshrined in the Treaty and will ensure that neither the Community, nor its members, assume collective responsibility for the debts of any of the members. The attempts to encourage fiscal discipline by peer pressure will be buttressed by a prohibition on the European central bank providing credit to any government and by the removal of "privileged access" by governments to the financial markets. These privileges take many forms – taxation, accounting practices, special uses (eg rediscount facilities at the central bank), mandatory investment rules for financial institutions, etc.

The elimination of these financing possibilities will force governments to compete in the open market with all other borrowers. Investors no longer adopt a "buy and hold" strategy and they have demonstrated a desire for liquidity in the secondary market if primary yields are to be minimised. Many governments in Europe have recognised this need and responded – the creation by the French authorities of the *obligations assimilables du Trésor* (OAT) market in 1985 signalled the beginning of this trend. The recent leap forward in the Ecu market, as jumbo issues of Ecu1 billion to Ecu2 billion were issued, illustrate the fact again. Thus, governments that have to give up other sources of privileged "cheap" funding are likely to turn to an efficient public bond market as the "next cheapest" source.

The independence of the proposed European central bank is one of the crucial points in the debate about monetary union. This, it is argued, will free the central bank from the tyranny of Treasury pressure to fund expenditure with money creation. There is a corollary – the national Treasuries will be free to pursue an optimal debt-management strategy rather than assist the central bank's monetary management. The German Treaty draft proposes that the "golden rule of finance" be in the Treaty itself – borrowing should not exceed investment spending. Over time, such a condition should bias debt maturities towards the longer-term – matching the assets being financed. Many EC governments – especially the most heavily indebted – have relatively short debt maturities and are consciously trying to lengthen them to remove any risk of a liquidity crisis. Both these factors point towards increased reliance on long-term debt markets.

The EC has a public policy interest in encouraging greater use of public bonds – the markets' assessment of the creditworthiness of individual governments should be absolutely transparent. Public bond issues make the scale of debt creation abundantly clear. If this is excessive, then a deterioration in the credit standing of the issuer should be reflected in a rise in relative yields. A vital mechanism to enforce market discipline on profligate governments is the requirement that all financial institutions value government debt at the current market price. Losses will induce – or force – the lenders to cut off new supplies of credit. This is the mechanistic discipline of the market – effective discipline is unlikely to be exerted by a rise in yields inducing governments to moderate their spending and thus borrowing. Such a rise is a preliminary phase, prior to the ultimate sanction: the markets may no longer be willing to provide credit at any reasonable price.

A credit risk will exist once governments give up the power to print the money with which they repay bonds. Although this will usually be very small, the normal principles of prudential regulation of financial institutions should be applied. In particular, there should be limits on the maximum exposure to the obligations of any group of debtors – a "large exposure" limit. This will protect the financial system against the domino effects of any default. As an excessive borrower finds institutions are unable to lend more, then a credit spread will inevitably begin to open up. The mark-to-market procedure will reinforce the unwillingness of potential lenders to lend – thus completing the exercise of the market's discipline through the ultimate sanction of withdrawing new credit supplies.

The greater the proportion of debt that is issued publicly in the bond market, the more transparent this process will be. Moreover, there can be no argument – on the grounds of a "small market"– that the market price does not reflect a proper evaluation of the credit risk. These arguments amount to a powerful reason to fund *all* debt in the bond markets – unless there is a specific social reason to do otherwise, for example by providing a vehicle for small-scale savings deposits that would not be commercially viable. Such a policy would have a profound impact on the ultimate size of the Ecu bond markets – perhaps doubling it from the current prospective size.

The speed of the transition

A clear limit on the speed of the transition will be imposed by the willingness and ability of investors to purchase the volume of bonds potentially available. Many institutional investors are still subject to restrictions on the purchase of non-domestic currency bonds. These restrictions should be eased – as part of the review of prudential regulation – by the advent of the single European market. This occurs for most institutions only at the beginning of 1993 – although it is open to governments to accelerate the liberalisation process if they wish. The next hurdle will be the ability of these institutions to sell financial products to the public. Prudently, they can then hold Ecu assets as the counterpart to their liabilities to customers. Customer willingness to purchase a rising proportion of Ecu-denominated financial products will be the factor which finally controls the pace of the move towards the Ecu as the single currency.

Having ensured that the investor base exists to purchase Ecu bonds, it would be surprising if most EC states did not institute a formal policy corresponding to the French policy of issuing 15-20 per cent of new debt in Ecu. Once a treaty has been signed, and especially after ratification by national parliaments, it would almost be inconsistent not to have such a policy. As most EC government debt has an average life of under five years, a "20 per cent of debt in Ecu" rule would produce an Ecu market of Ecu200 billion or more by the mid-1990s as existing debt was rolled over. The EC's aggregate budget deficit is about 4 per cent of GNP, so a corresponding policy towards financing new deficits would produce further Ecu issuance of about Ecu20 billion annually. (Such figures assume that Germany, in particular, adopts this policy. Moreover, the proportion of "private placement" debt would reduce the growth of the Ecu market correspondingly.) Such calculations reveal the potential for the EC governments' Ecu bond market to grow from Ecu45 billion now to perhaps Ecu300 billion in the mid-1990s, *en route* to over Ecu1,000 billion on the day of the "single currency".

Private sector users – multinational corporations

The Ecu ought to be an ideal source of finance for a pan-European multinational corporation (MNC). Exhibit 4.1 shows they have been consistent users of the market, but non-financial corporations only account for about Ecu12 billion worth of bonds – about 11 per cent of the market.

Given the scale of activity of MNCs, this volume of issuance does not represent a major source of funding. Chapter 11 discusses the reasons why the Ecu has not satisfactorily fulfilled the needs of MNCs. In summary, national legal restrictions have the effect of constraining the Ecu's use as a unit of account. Nor is the "means of payment" monetary function sufficiently developed that Ecu funding would be useful for working capital purposes. Few companies would have assets that approximately match the Ecu's basket composition, so hedging would not be perfect, either. Accordingly, the principal attraction lies in opportunities to arbitrage cheap funding sources.

This set of constraints is unlikely to disappear rapidly. It may be necessary for virtually all the impediments to Ecu usage to be removed before MNCs become large issuers of Ecu bonds. This may be quite close to the beginning of stage three of EMU in the mid-to-late 1990s, so MNC use of the Ecu bond market, although growing steadily, is unlikely to match the explosive growth expected in the government sector.

Private sector users – domestic EC corporations

Use of the Ecu bond market by non-financial EC corporations has been small – about 5 per cent of total bonds outstanding – and most of these bonds fall squarely within the MNC category. All the problems facing

MNCs also affect domestic companies, but without even the possible hedging benefits. However, some domestic corporations in "high interest rate" countries may be prepared to anticipate an effective locking-in of exchange rates even before the formal date for establishing a single currency.

Once the government component of the market is fully established, there could be substantial attractions for domestic companies in countries where there is no effective corporate bond market. This would give them direct access to the long-term capital markets of the entire Community, rather than leaving them wholly reliant on their domestic banking system.

The travails of the banking system may, in fact, play a critical role in spurring use of the Ecu capital markets. The new capital adequacy requirements, developed by the Bank for International Settlements (BIS) and given legal status by the EC's Solvency Ratio Directive, have pushed up the amount of capital needed by banks. Shareholders are also looking for a higher return on their investment – putting extra pressure on banks to widen profit margins. A key element of the single market in financial services is the concept of a level playing field. For banks, one of the critical aspects will be additional competition for retail deposits. Depositors have already shown, in the UK and Spain, for example, that they are rational and will respond to attractive deposit yields – thus raising the effective cost of funds to the banking system. The banks will seek to recoup that lost margin from their borrowers, whose rational response will be to bypass the banks and access the capital market direct – which may well be the Ecu market.

This phenomenon could extend to consumer credit markets – especially where residential mortgages can collateralise the capital market borrowing. Although securitisation of residential mortgages, credit cards and car loans seems likely to spread rapidly from the US as the "single market" effects are felt, the use of the Ecu may grow more slowly for such securitisation deals – depending on the consumer's willingness to be involved in Ecu transactions (see Chapter 12).

Conclusion

If EC governments carry through to a logical conclusion the implications of the treaty they seem about to sign, then the government component of the Ecu bond market should see explosive growth in the next few years. Many technical obstacles have to be identified and removed before the private sector increases its activity correspondingly. However, the biggest impetus for private use could result from the banking system's efforts to improve profitability – indirectly pushing customers towards the capital markets. With governments setting a powerful example, the private sector might then begin to use the Ecu markets on a reasonable scale.

Taken together, it is possible to envisage the Ecu bonds outstanding rising from the current Ecu98 billion to Ecu400-500 billion in the mid-1990s – establishing it as the largest European financial market. Whether the path is one of steady progress, a dramatic initial surge or a late catch-up will be determined by the EC governments' actions. If this target proves to be a mirage, then so will EMU.

5

Dominique Rambure
Ecu Banking Association

Ecu banking and short-term markets

The Ecu market's initial development has taken place at both ends of the maturity scale, with both the interbank Ecu deposit market and the Ecu-denominated bond market emerging together in the early 1980s. Technically, the two sides of the market, short- and long-term, are closely connected with each other. The Ecu bond market could not have developed as fast as it did without the backing of a strong, liquid, self-sustaining deposit market. The market has thus been expanding in two directions: on the one hand, it has progressively filled the gap between the short-term and long-term range of market instruments; on the other, it has progressively moved from an interbank and sovereign risk market to the corporate area. The interaction between the two markets has led to an increased sophistication, such as the trading of futures contracts based on one end (the three-month deposit) or the other (the eight- to 10-year French Treasury OAT).

This chapter describes Ecu banking and the short-term markets and shows how the Ecu has become more popular and more widely used over the past few years. It covers Ecu banking activity within the Bank for International Settlements (BIS); the Ecu deposit market; syndicated Ecu loans; short-term Ecu notes; Ecu mortgages; Euro commercial paper; and the prospects for the future.

Ecu banking activity within the BIS

The range of Ecu banking products has developed enormously over the last few years. Besides activity linked with the bond market, banks also offer their customers many kinds of transactions, including demand and time deposits, commercial paper, Treasury bonds, Ecu-denominated funds, Ecu-denominated securities, syndicated bank loans and other Ecu loans or financing.

International Ecu-denominated assets of banks in the BIS reporting area rose sharply from Ecu7 billion at the end of 1982, the earliest date for which figures are available, to Ecu145 billion at the end of September 1990. In 1990, Ecu banking activity continued to expand alongside the introduction of Ecu-denominated interest rate futures on London

International Financial Futures Exchange (LIFFE) and successful issues of Ecu Treasury bills by the UK and Italian governments.

About 84 per cent of Ecu banking activity within the BIS reporting area has been concentrated in five European financial centres: France, Luxembourg, Belgium, Italy and the UK. However, banking activity in Ecu is gradually becoming more widespread.

The Ecu banking market within the BIS reporting area is mainly interbank. This accounts for over 76 per cent of all lending denominated in Ecu, and some 88 per cent of Ecu deposits taken (see Exhibit 5.1). Whereas the Ecu interbank market continued to be buoyant throughout 1989 and 1990, the growth of Ecu business with non-banks was relatively slow. Exhibit 5.1 shows the overall size of the Ecu money market at the end of 1990.

The Ecu money market is about 10 per cent larger than the total of outstanding Ecu bonds, both Euro and domestic. Not surprisingly, bank liabilities represent more than 88 per cent of the total.[1] According to BIS banking statistics, between December 1987 and June 1990 Ecu bank liabilities rose 99 per cent, while total non-US dollar liabilities in the Euro deposit market grew by 41 per cent in the same period.

The deposit market

The Ecu deposit market is the most important segment of the Ecu money market, accounting for approximately 88 per cent. The Ecu deposit market is now the fifth largest Eurodeposit market after the US dollar, the Deutschmark, the Swiss franc and the Japanese yen.

Looking at the figures by depositor, the Ecu remains mainly an interbank market: only 12 per cent of total bank liabilities are with the non-financial sector. In fact, although corporate interest is growing, the general pattern has not changed substantially in recent years. Corporates do not hold short-term Ecu assets for cash management purposes and generally do not redeposit in the banking system the Ecu they borrow from the banks, but instead swap them to take advantage of arbitrage opportunities. Ecu deposit rates are still the benchmark for the pricing of

Exhibit 5.1

Dimensions of the Ecu market, end-1990

Money market	*Ecu m*	*(%)*
Bank liabilities	92,141	88.6
MTNs	952	0.91
CDs	280	0.27
CP	3,707	3.53
UK T-bills	2,900	2.76
BTEs	4,964	4.47
Total	**104,994**	**100.00**
Bond market	93,336	
Off-balance sheet	2,569	

Sources: BIS, Webster Communications Int., *Ecu Newsletter*.

[1] See Namor, E. (1991). "The money market", *De Pecunia*. CEPIME.

Ecu money market instruments. Besides deposits, European banks have developed their financing activity. Lending in Ecu to non-banks by banks in the BIS reporting area increased from Ecu27 billion at the end of December 1988 to Ecu34 billion at the end of September 1990. The largest lenders in Ecu to domestic non-bank residents are banks in Italy, France and the UK.

Ecu loans can be in various forms, among them financing for enterprises either as syndicated bank loans or as trade financing.

International financial credits can be divided into two main categories: syndicated Ecu loans and the facilities which are a formal guarantee for short-term bond issues.

Syndicated Ecu loans

The banker's approach to composite currencies has been cautious. In fact, it was not until the beginning of this decade that the bank credit market took its first tentative steps towards the use of composite currencies in syndicated loans.

The first composite currency to make its debut in the syndicated loan market was the Special Drawing Right (SDR), albeit with a lack of sustained enthusiasm, and not the Ecu.

In contrast with the SDR, the Ecu had firmer foundations on which to build in the syndicated loans market. It was a natural complement to trade flows and, in some countries, a quasi-domestic currency. The EC Commission also gave strong support to wider private use of the Ecu and money market rates and a settlement system were available.

The first transaction in Ecu was in mid-1981 and the first Ecu syndicated loan followed soon after. The gradual development of a market for syndicated lending in Ecu was part of the wider trend since 1983 towards lending in currencies other than the US dollar. This trend led to a significant increase in loans denominated in yen, sterling and Ecu. In 1990, the Ecu accounted for over 8 per cent of new external bank loans, compared with just 0.3 per cent in 1982, and thus became the third most widely used currency in the market. Exhibit 5.2 compares syndicated loan activity in Ecu with the total market.

Syndicated Ecu loans have maturities from five to 10 years. The reference rate for interest payments is the rate at which funds are offered in the international interbank market (Libor), with different spreads (from ½ to ¾ of a percentage point) according to different credit maturities. Lenders and borrowers come from different countries and continents.

Japanese and American banks are among the top 100 lead managers in Ecu-syndicated loans. European banks are often more interested in participating in Ecu loans than in US dollar facilities for similar borrowers. In many cases the smaller banks express greater confidence about funding in Ecu than in US dollars.

Ecu syndicated loans are, in terms of mechanism and structure, otherwise identical to conventional US dollar syndicated loans. This homogeneity has been instrumental in the Ecu's successful acceptance into the market. The syndicated loan market in Ecu has accordingly achieved a

Exhibit 5.2
New syndicated loans

Year	No of deals	Ecu market Volume (US$ bn)	Total market Volume (US$ bn)
1982	8	0.35	146.6
1983	23	1.05	95.3
1984	54	2.08	189.6
1985	56	2.04	156.1
1986	21	1.26	52.4
1987	39	4.58	91.7
1988	44	4.33	125.5
1989	56	4.85	121.1
1990	48	5.60	118.2

Sources: Euromoney, Ecu Newsletter.

maturity and sophistication comparable with all sectors of the market. Of crucial significance to the development of the syndicated loan market has been an effective underlying market for bank deposits. Generally, Ecu assets have been larger than liabilities.

The picture for the future is unclear. However, new markets provide a perfect opportunity for increased use of the Ecu. In parallel with the shift away from the US dollar and into such currencies as the yen, sterling and the Ecu, the structure of the capital markets has also changed with the move towards securitisation or disintermediation.

Ecu short-term notes

Ecu short-term note facilities include: (a) Underwritten facilities, such as Euronote facilities, note issue facilities, CDs, etc; under these facilities, the borrower is able to issue short-term (ie up to six months) bearer notes which are either sold to third-party investors or taken on the books of the underwriting banks. (b) Non-underwritten facilities, usually known as commercial paper programmes. In this case, the borrower can issue short-term (up to 365 days) bearer notes which are sold by one or more dealers to third-party investors. The dealers do not initially undertake to place any particular volume of paper or obtain any particular price from the market.[2]

Securitisation has led to growth in the volume of all kinds of short-term note facilities, mainly at the expense of the traditional syndicated loan. Whereas the growth of the bond markets has been spectacular, borrowers also became interested in shifting floating rate funding away from syndicated bank borrowing and towards various forms of short-term note facility. This has had consequences for the Ecu. Many central banks were unwilling to see the development of a major offshore market for short-term paper denominated in currencies for which they were responsible. Consequently, although many borrowers would no doubt have wished to issue notes, their choice of currency was effectively limited to two: the US dollar and the Ecu.

In 1990, a number of technical measures were taken by major countries

[2] See Causer, C. "Syndicated Ecu loans and note facilities", in Levich, R.M. (ed.), *Ecu*, Euromoney Publications, London, 1987.

which should contribute to the growth of the Euro commercial paper (ECP) and medium-term note (MTN) markets. In reviewing the regulations on issuance of commercial paper, Japan permitted domestic firms to issue ECP from April 1990. The MTN market was also expected to benefit from a new US rule which relaxed restrictions on the resale of privately placed securities to qualified investors. Changes in English law have allowed the development of a sterling commercial-paper market and domestic commercial paper markets exist in almost every European country. However, borrowers have so far found it simpler to use the US dollar and the Ecu if they want to issue paper under a short-term note facility with a minimum of formalities.

It is relatively uncommon for a borrower to set up a facility which is solely denominated in Ecu; more usually, the option to issue Ecu notes will form just one part of a more complex (US dollar-denominated) transaction. The introduction in 1981 of Euronotes – short-term notes with a syndicated bank guarantee – constituted a big innovation. Euronotes have been created for operators seeking short-term investments. The development of these kind of activities has contributed to the development of the Ecu money market.

Among tradeable instruments, Ecu-denominated MTNs are one of the sectors which showed the highest growth in 1990. Exhibit 5.3 shows that, at the end of 1990, outstanding MTNs in Ecu ranked in third place after the US dollar, and just after the Japanese yen, with 8.4 per cent of all paper outstanding.

MTNs generally represent an intermediate segment between the money and the bond markets, as tranches are issued between one and nine years.[3] In the case of Ecu MTNs, however, 67.2 per cent of the tranches issued in 1990 had an original maturity not exceeding two years. In particular, instruments with an original maturity of one year accounted for 40.5 per cent of the market, putting them in direct competition with shorter instruments, such as CDs and commercial paper. In 1990, 61 different tranches worth Ecu850.25 million were placed by 10 different issuers. Most are European, primarily French, but the market has been tapped by at least two US borrowers. The two most active borrowers in 1990 were the Council of Europe (Ecu285 million) and Spain.

The prime reason for the explosive growth of the Euronote market is

Exhibit 5.3

Total outstanding MTN issues (US$m equivalent)

	US$m	*(%)*
US$	10,965	68.8
Yen	1,407	8.8
Ecu	1,339	8.4
UK£	965	6.0
A$	746	4.7
Lira	264	1.7
Skr	238	1.5
Total	**15,925**	**100.0**

Sources: Webster Communication Int., Medium-term Notes "Notebook".

[3] See Namor, E., op. cit.

the general movement towards securitisation that has affected the capital markets as a whole. But there is a combination of factors that explains the success of Ecu MTNs. Euronotes offer certain advantages to both the issuer and the investor which are not found to such a degree elsewhere. For the issuer, the great flexibility of MTNs is certainly an advantage.

Another positive factor is the possibility of exploiting the arbitrage opportunities created by the differences between the short and long end of the yield curve. For the investor, Euronotes usually offer higher yields than those in the short-term money market, and considerably higher than those on US Treasury bills. Growth in the volumes traded on the Euronote and Eurocommercial paper market can improve liquidity, which is very important for potential investors. There are also structural reasons. The composite currency nature of the Ecu gives it an exchange and interest rate stability that is generally greater than that for national currencies. For many borrowers, the currency risk on the Ecu is likely to prove more acceptable than that associated with other currencies. For example, US borrowers find the Ecu a natural currency in which to diversify their funding.

Another category of bank credits are those used directly to finance specific purposes such as Ecu mortgages.

Ecu mortgages

The first Ecu mortgage, indexed to the Ecu, was launched in Italy, by Istituto Bancario San Paolo di Torino, in 1983. This kind of operation usually has a 10-year maturity, with the interest rate reviewed every six months.

Ecu mortgages were initially offered only to public operators. The exchange rate risk was entirely taken by the customer, for whom it was less convenient to be indebted in Ecu. Some banks have created new instruments to protect customers from currency risk: San Paolo introduced mortgages with amortisation plans and Abbey National created a product with a fixed rate based on an interest rate swap between an Ecu variable interest rate and a lira fixed interest rate.

These new products have been successful. For example, in 1989 the BNL dedicated nearly 80 per cent of its global mortgages to Ecu mortgages for households. The percentage of Ecu mortgages granted by other banks is also high. In 1990, Ecu mortgages granted by Italian banks totalled nearly Ecu4 billion, or more than 10 per cent of total mortgages issued by the Italian banking system. The same percentage applies to total Ecu mortgages issued by mortgage banks. In 1990, San Paolo, the largest mortgage lender in Italy, provided 40 per cent of all domestic mortgages denominated in Ecu. Borrowers enjoy lower interest rates without too great a risk, due to the Italian currency being part of the ERM. Other lenders have subsequently followed San Paolo in launching Ecu mortgage schemes in Italy.

The stability of the exchange rate, combined with the interest rate saving on the Ecu loan, makes it a highly attractive and viable method of borrowing for mortgage purposes. Generally, the Ecu mortgage is indexed either to the Ecu exchange rate or the Ecu interbank interest rates in the

London market. Higher international interest rates can make Ecu mortgages more expensive, but in Italy and the UK Ecu interest rates have historically always been lower than domestic rates. The exchange risk means Ecu mortgages are convenient only for countries with very high domestic rates, such as Italy, the UK and Spain at the end of the 1980s.

San Paolo was the first bank to launch an Ecu mortgage scheme in the UK, on 7 February 1989. The scheme was aimed at borrowers with a knowledge of economics and the financial markets. Here too Ecu borrowers could enjoy an interest rate substantially lower than sterling borrowers.

However, some borrowers who took out Ecu mortgages in the 1980s were seduced by the argument that converting their mortgage debt would cut their monthly payments by the difference between sterling and Ecu interest rates. With sterling's entry into the ERM in October 1990, home-owners were locked into an arrangement where the benefits disappeared in administrative costs.

Now the pound movement in the ERM band is limited but, while mortgage rates in the UK are around the base rate, if you borrow in foreign currency you always pay a 1-2 per cent premium over the local market plus the bank's fee to switch a mortgage from one currency to another, and further hidden costs in the form of wide exchange-rate spreads. Perhaps only members of the European Parliament, who get paid in Ecu, would find Ecu mortgages really suitable.

Among the various banking activities are loans typical of the money market, such as short-term credits for financing imports and exports.

Eurocommercial paper

Commercial paper (CP) is a negotiable monetary bearer instrument, and is less costly than a normal credit, even if issued without a guarantee. The first users of Euro Commercial Paper (ECP) have been Italian banks and the Ecu has suddenly become one of the main denominations for ECP. In fact, even if there are actually domestic commercial paper markets nearly everywhere in Europe, one can visualise a corporate treasurer based in any European country being able to obtain quotes for multicurrency ECP. CP denominated in a single, rather than multi-, currency basket with high interest rates and stable exchange rates, could be more advantageous. 1990 was a good year for corporates who wanted to raise short-term money in the CP markets. The inverted yield curve in most European markets encouraged investors to buy money market instruments instead of equities or bonds.

After stagnating in 1989, the ECP market grew to $92 billion at the end of 1990, if Euronotes are included. Having been overshadowed by the departure of several banks and by three defaults in 1989, it seemed that ECP was at last developing into a mature and liquid market in its own right, even if European corporates are unlikely to rely on the ECP market as their sole source of short-term funding.

Although official data on the size of the market are not available, at the end of 1990 there was Ecu3.7 billion of outstanding Ecu CP, compared with a total of Ecu280 billion of all CP issued. Ecu CP represented approximately 7 per cent of all ECP programmes outstanding. Taken together, these two segments account for almost 4 per cent of the Ecu money market.[4]

Even if the market has recently been developing gradually, its secondary market is not liquid enough. The market is, in fact, mainly demand-driven, which is a disadvantage compared with the most developed markets, which are regulated by the institutions. Nevertheless, a growing number of corporates are interested in short-term Ecu liabilities, even if most issues of Ecu CDs and CP are accompanied by foreign exchange transactions which transform the Ecu exposure into other currencies. Ecu CDs and CP are generally issued with multicurrency facilities which provide maximum flexibility for borrowers. The buyers are mainly institutional investors: corporates do not seem to be very active yet.

Prospects for the future

The perception that the Ecu will one day become the currency of Europe is attracting serious interest in the Ecu money market from a growing number of players, including financial institutions willing to position strategically in the new market and end-users keen to become familiar with the currency. Further support comes from the stability of the ERM and the approach of stage two of the Delors Plan in 1994, when exchange rates should be locked (although there are several obstacles to the development of EMU).

The daily operations of market players (banks, companies, customers, etc) will foster the role of the Ecu as a European currency, thus supporting the Delors Report's "institutional approach" with a "market approach" towards EMU. An expansion of Ecu deposits should remain the leading force behind the growth of the market. Corporates are also likely to be more active both as issuers of short-term instrument, and in terms of cash management. In fact, dealing in Ecu makes foreign currency cash management easier and safer for firms heavily involved in international transactions. In the long term, however, the full development of the Ecu money market is clearly linked to the progress of EMU.

A currency is not just a market product depending exclusively on the forces of supply and demand. A currency needs a central bank to regulate the settlement system, be the lender of last resort and implement monetary policy. The market will never develop its full potential until the Ecu is extensively used as a means of payment and a European Central Bank starts operating in the open market and guarantees order.

[4] See Namor E., op. cit.

6 The Ecu swaps and options market

Jim Durrant
Paribas Capital Markets

Introduction

This chapter reviews the development of Ecu swaps and options markets and shows how the conflicting demands of borrowers and investors, risk managers and speculators and the arbitrating role of banking intermediaries combine to produce one of the fastest growing markets for swaps and options.

Covered in this section are the classical currency and interest-rate swaps. Focus is placed on innovative structures involving taxation arbitrage with CTEs (Italian Certificates of the Treasury in Ecus: see Chapter 18 – Italy). The second part looks at developments in the interest-rate option market which, although not as large as the swaps market, offers diverse means of managing interest-rate risk exposure. In conclusion the direction of future market growth is forecast and an attempt is made to understand how the new Ecu derivative markets on LIFFE and the MATIF will affect these developments.

Cross-currency swap market

The growth of the Ecu swaps market happened as a natural consequence of the growth and diversification of the international financial markets and the increased emphasis on asset/liability management within the large corporations and public institutions around the world.

The increase in volume of currency swaps was initially driven by classical financial arbitrage. Borrowers would issue in fixed rate non-dollar denominations and swap into floating rate dollars at a lower funding cost than they could achieve by borrowing directly in floating rate dollars.

More recently, increasing global capability of banking intermediaries has meant that borrowers can swap into the currency of their choice without going through an intermediate dollar stage, and today one-third of all cross-currency swaps do not involve dollars (see Exhibit 6.1).

This form of borrower-driven swap arbitrage is extremely common in the Ecu market, which depends more on primary market swaps than the US or UK markets. The growth of this market has somewhat mirrored the

Exhibit 6.1 **Non-dollar currency swaps as % of total, 1987-90**

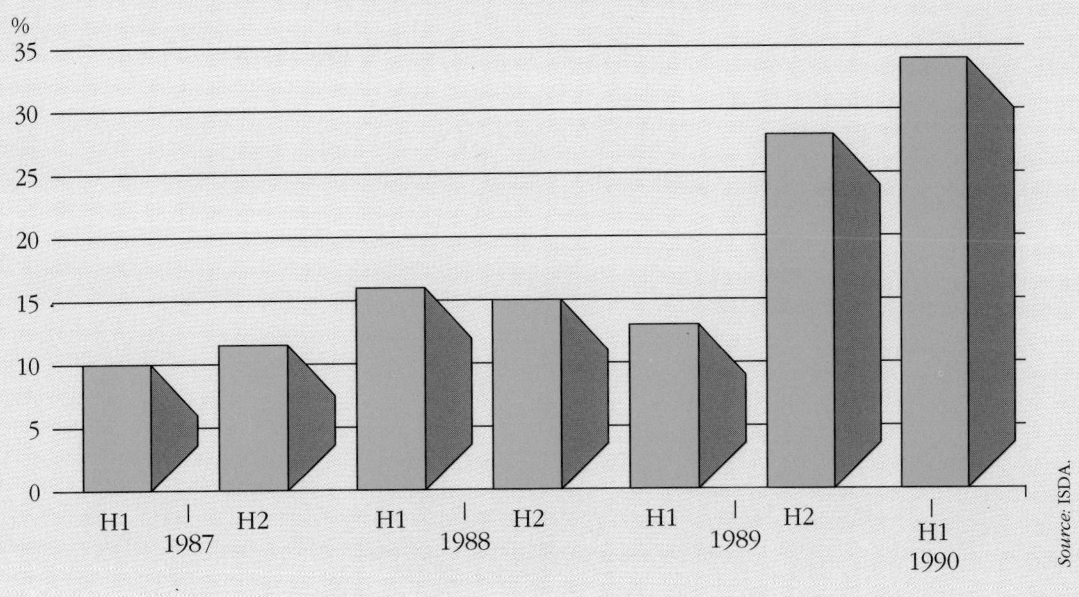

growth in the Ecu new issue market, but the volume of cross-currency Ecu swaps has now declined (see Exhibit 6.2).

There are three major reasons for this. The first is the reduced access by multinational corporations and banks to the Ecu new issue market due to "crowding out" by enormous government issues. The second is the imposition of higher-risk weighted credit margins on cross-currency swaps by banks. The third is that more institutions are happy to leave their funding costs in Ecu as the rates may be way below those in their own

Exhibit 6.2 **Ecu new issues and cross-currency Ecu swap volume (US$ bn)**

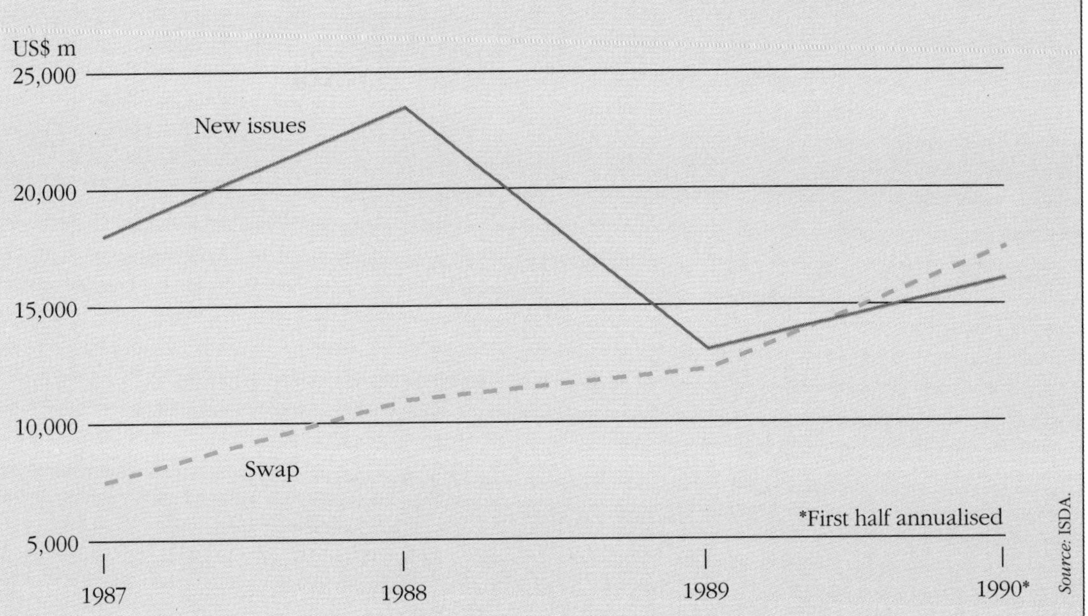

currency. As a consequence, the dollar has reduced in importance in cross-currency Ecu swaps and recent data show that in only half the cases is the dollar the other currency, with Deutschmark (13 per cent), yen (10 per cent), Swiss franc (9 per cent) and French franc (8 per cent) assuming increasing importance.

What circumstances make the cross-currency primary market swap attractive? There has to be demand from investors for fixed-rate Ecu paper. This tends to come from "hard" currency countries like Benelux and Switzerland and more recently from Japanese, UK and US funds wanting high coupon "safe" currency investments. The swap rate should be high in comparison with the bond rate so that sub-Libor funding is possible. This generally happens when banks believe interest rates will rise (see Exhibit 6.3). This leaves the bank exposed to the risk of Ecu rates falling. If the swap was in dollars or sterling rather than Ecu this would not pose a major problem. The bank could hedge its position by buying government securities or bond futures and just take a spread risk (swap rate–government bond yield) rather than the absolute rate risk.

Unfortunately, until mid-1990 there was insufficient liquidity in the Ecu bond market to hedge, and even the new futures contracts on MATIF and LIFFE lack the volume to hedge large swap positions.

Some houses chose to hedge with proxy baskets of swaps (eg

Exhibit 6.3 **Swap spread and interest rate history, 1987–1991**

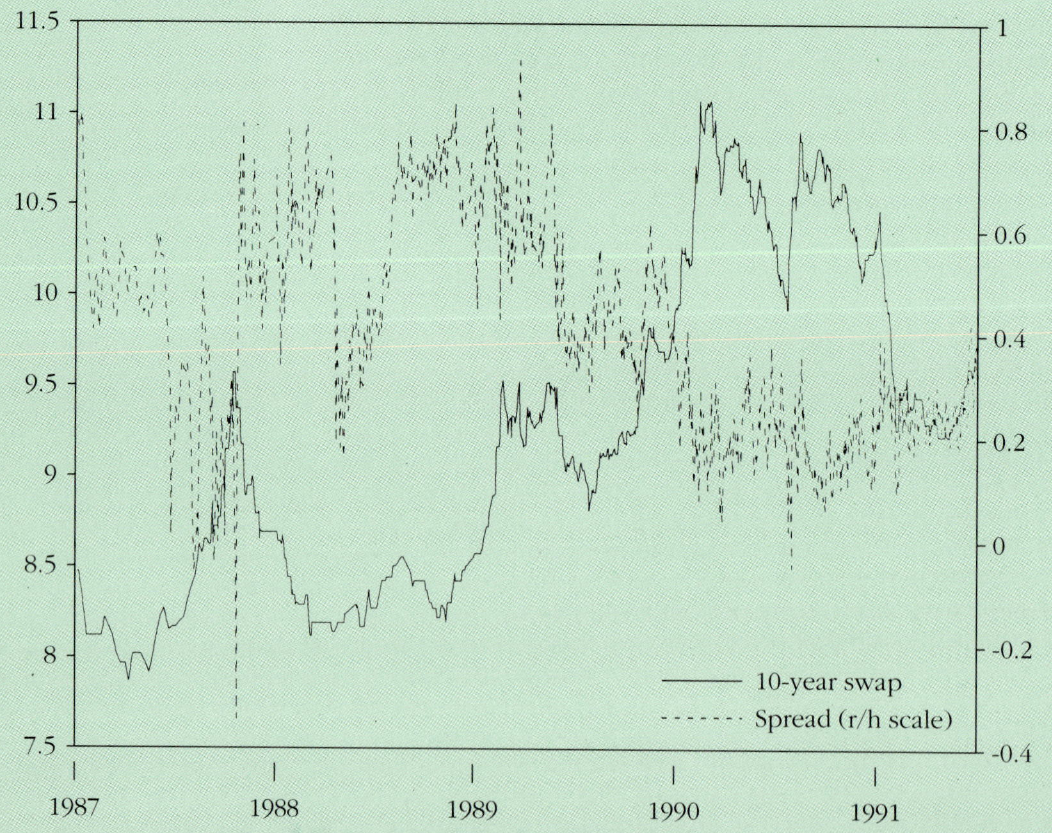

Source: Parisbas.

Exhibit 6.4 **Swap end-user business location**

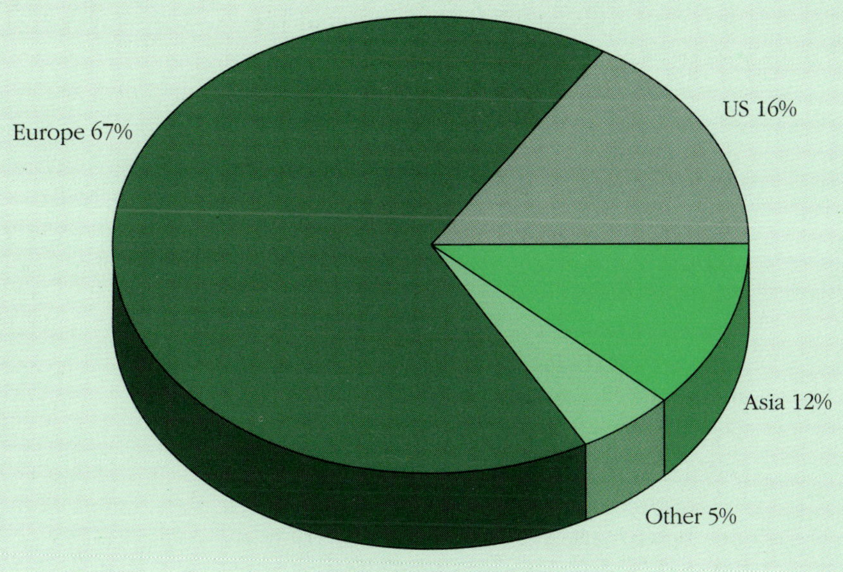

Deutschmark, sterling and Franch franc) or with futures contracts involving LIFFE Bund futures, long gilt futures and MATIF's *notionnel* with varying degrees of success. However, more often the swap transactions to pay fixed rate Ecu for floating dollars would be part of a bank's strategy to square a warehouse position which was long of receiving fixed rate Ecu and had been built up over the previous weeks.

Other more speculative banks would swap the new issues and either remain unhedged, awaiting a rise in Ecu rates, or attempt to find fixed rate Ecu payers in the market to square the book.

There are few natural payers of fixed rate Ecu, for example corporates matching assets with liabilities. The only significant group has been sophisticated European liability managers who use secondary swap markets to swap from yen or dollar exposure into a currency more related to their own or that of a significant proportion of their assets. In so doing, they lower the currency risk of their debt portfolio. This restructuring of debt portfolios is both highly analytical and opportunistic, because the swaps are not related to specific bond issues. The benefits of reducing the risk of the debt swaps are not related to specific bond issues. The benefits of reducing the risk of the debt portfolio will apply only to European institutions; North American and Japanese liability managers would increase currency risk exposure by swapping into Ecu, because their base currencies have low correlations with those in Europe.

Exhibit 6.4 confirms that the cross-currency Ecu swap market is still dominated by European entities.

The group of institutions which paid fixed rate Ecu was never large, and without fixed rate payers there was reluctance on the part of the banks to take open positions on the swap book. However, with the momentum towards a single European currency picking up, demand for Ecu bonds increased solidly through the period 1987-90, and it was the financial engineers and the Italian government who came to the rescue.

The first development was the CTE asset swap market, which will be covered in the section on asset swaps. The second was the launch in early 1990 of the Ecu1 billion "jumbo" issue by the Italian government, which marked the change in the nature of the Ecu bond market from retail-driven to institutional investor-driven. As liquidity in large government bond issues rose, the swap houses were at last in a position to use these bonds as hedges for their swap books, eliminating gross position risk and leaving just swap spread risk. Indeed, today sophisticated swap houses can actually deliberately mismatch the maturities of their swap and hedge in taking a view on future yield curve movements.

Interest rate swaps

The Ecu interest rate swap market has grown dramatically over the last few years. This growth can be attributed to four major factors:

- The interbank market, where banks lay off risks on their Ecu warehouse, which has both currency and interest rate swaps within. The number of banks that make prices in Ecu swaps has grown dramatically, thereby enhancing the liquidity of the interbank business. Today approximately 80 per cent of Ecu interest rate swaps involve financial institutions.
- The growth of Ecu interest rate swaps associated with asset swapping CTEs (see next section).
- There is growing use of Ecu interest swaps among fund managers who use the market to hedge their bond positions against the threat of interest rates rising. This approach has advantages over using Ecu bond futures, because the maturity of the bond portfolio and the maturity of the swap can be matched (or more ideally the modified durations), and the swap market is still more liquid than the infant futures markets.
- The other relevant feature of swaps markets is that, when markets first begin, a high proportion of the business is in currency swaps because the fledgling market is not fully arbitraged. However, as the markets increase in size the interest rate swap becomes a critical instrument in interbank positioning and the ratio of interest rate to currency swap business increases dramatically (see Exhibit 6.5).

Asset swaps

In 1982, the Italian government began issuing fixed rate Ecu bonds initially aimed at Italian domestic accounts, but small amounts of the issues were syndicated on the Euromarket. Initially, there was strong demand for this paper domestically because it provided protection against a devaluing lira. However, as the lira stabilised within the exchange rate mechanism (ERM) and following imposition of 12.5 per cent withholding tax on the coupon of Italian government debt, the securities became unattractive.

As yields rose due to falling demand, asset managers found they could create synthetic government securities with attractive returns. The withholding tax problem was sidestepped due to bilateral tax treaties

Exhibit 6.5 **Increasing importance of Ecu interest-rate swaps**

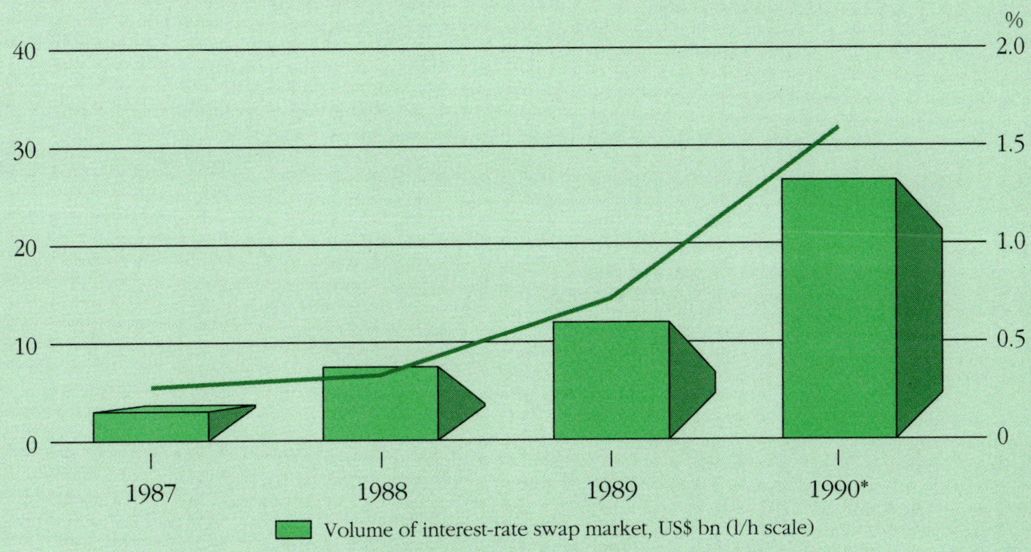

**H1 1990 annualised*

Source: ISDA.

between Italy and the investor's domicile, and the Bank for International Settlements (BIS) rules made holding sovereign paper attractive since it is not necessary to set aside tier two capital against it.

The swap itself can be structured in a number of ways in order to create a synthetic asset denominated in a large choice of currencies to suit the investor's requirement and to receive floating rate at a very substantial margin over Libor. Alternatively, the swap could be structured to create a synthetic fixed rate asset, either bullet, zero or level payment.

The basic concept underlying asset swaps is to tie up the purchase of a security (the asset, in this case CTEs) with a swap transaction which results in creating an asset swap in any of a number of currencies, paying fixed or floating rate at high spread levels. An Ecu fixed rate CTE, for example, could be changed into a US dollar floating rate synthetic government security or a yen fixed rate synthetic government security, paying a high spread over Libor or government bonds but carrying the risk of a triple A sovereign issuer (the Republic of Italy). The structure can be seen in Exhibit 6.6.

The life of the asset swap is always equal to the life of the asset itself, ie the CTE, so that the investor paying par for the bond on the issue of the CTE will receive his original investment back at the end of the asset swap when the bonds are redeemed. When the swap involves a different currency, the investor will pass on the capital redeemed in Ecu by Italy to the bank, which conversely will pay the initial capital in the second currency under the swap to the investor. With the opportunity for the investor to select a different currency to Ecu, the asset swap enables him to invest in a floating rate investment in the currency of his choice, with all the principal payments guaranteed by the collateral of the asset held, ie the CTE.

The fixed rate Ecu payment made by the investor to the bank is equal

Exhibit 6.6 **Typical asset swap structure Ecu fixed-rate into floating US dollars**

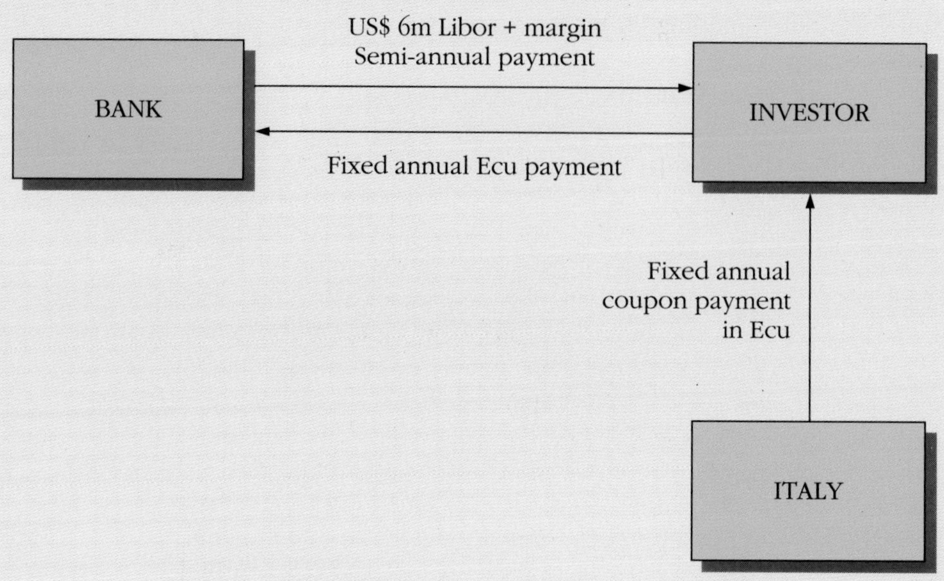

Source: Parisbas.

to the gross coupon of the CTEs. However, the investor will receive a net coupon, as Italy pays interest net of the 12.5 per cent withholding tax. Therefore the investor will have to reclaim the withholding tax if he is entitled to and will fund the difference, be it in Ecu or in his local currency, until it is offset. Assuming that the investor recoups the withholding tax in his own country through an offsettable tax credit, the structure then looks like Exhibit 6.7.

Currently, CTE coupon payments match only 87.5 per cent of the

Exhibit 6.7 **Typical CTE asset swap structure Ecu fixed-rate into floating US dollars**

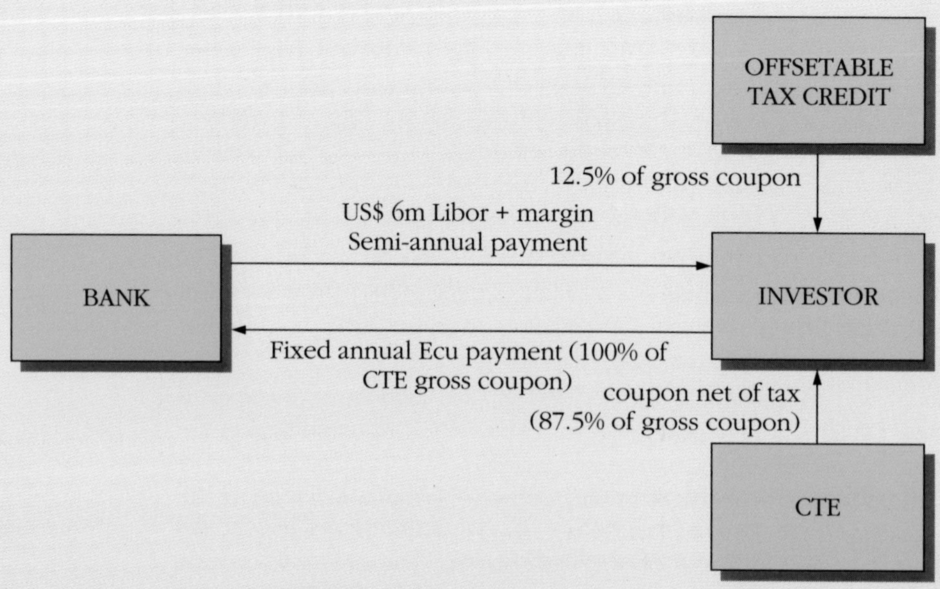

Source: Parisbas.

fixed payment to the bank. However, the tax credit received from the tax authorities will be offsettable only after the end of the tax year, when the taxes for the current tax period fall due. This delay entails a certain cost of carry for the investor, depending on the amount of taxes withheld and the financing costs.

The driving force for these arbitrages has been the major Ecu new issue houses which have purchased the securities, swapped from Ecu into floating US dollars or Ecu and picked up as much as Libor plus 40 basis points. This swap position can then be used to bring new issues in Ecu which the issuer wishes to swap into floating Ecu, US dollars or any other currency. The practice led to bursts of new issue activity following each Italian Treasury new-issue auction. Auctions occur roughly every two months with Ecu1 billion at each auction. So popular was the arbitrage that at times the subsequent launch of fixed rate Ecu issues after each auction swamped investor demand.

As with all arbitrages, the spreads on the trade have narrowed considerably over the last two years as more institutions have used the route to establish a presence in the Ecu market. Investing institutions have also reached their investment limits with Italy as issuer. It is quite possible therefore that this route for receiving Ecu on the swaps may have a limited life.

Caps and floors

The growth of interest rate protection products began in the US, where clients initially wanted protection against rising rates but wanted to take advantage of falling rates. It was not long before borrowers in other currencies required similar products.

Demand for this form of interest rate protection for the floating rate Ecu borrower is small due to the limited number of floating rate liabilities. However, fixed rate Ecu fund managers have been purchasers of caps which offer long-term protection against rising rates and are available to those institutions which cannot enter into a swap because of insufficient credit standing.

Fund managers are also the major purchasers of floors to hedge floating rate asset positions for the same reasons.

However, with increasing liquidity in the Ecu bond futures contracts in London and Paris it is probable that this demand for cap products will diminish somewhat as fixed rate bond managers use the futures markets and options on futures to hedge their positions, and credit standing poses no problem to their use.

Interest rate swaptions

The main problem associated with the cap as a hedge for a long bond position is the maturity mismatch between the two instruments, leaving the hedger at risk to a steepening of the yield curve. The obvious solution would be the purchase of a put option on a bond, but this market has never been highly liquid. The alternative is the purchase of a payer swaption with a maturity or duration of the underlying swap equivalent to that of the bond portfolio.

This offers the ideal hedge for fixed rate assets: it enables the holder to exercise the option should interest rates rise while allowing the fund manager to benefit from any fall in interest rates. Further, with no maturity or duration mismatch the hedge should perform well against yield curve twists.

If the purchaser of the swaption does not have sufficient credit standing to enter into a swap transaction upon exercise, the two counterparties can agree in advance to receive a cash settlement at that date if the swaption is exercised in-the-money.

There are two main types of swaption. The payer swaption allows the holder to pay fixed rate and receive floating rate for a set period commencing at the exercise date. The option exercise is normally European style (ie the swaption can only be exercised at the end of the option period). These are attractive to those with a view that rates will rise, and therefore provide good hedges for fixed rate funds.

The second type is the receiver swaption, allowing the holder to receive fixed rate and pay floating rate. Again, these are normally European options which rise in value when rates fall and are consequently useful to hedge floating rate funds or fixed rate borrowings.

These swaptions have been used to some extent to monetise the implicit value of the call option on callable bond issues. Exhibit 6.8 illustrates the approach.

Exhibit 6.8

Callable bond issue combined with a receiver swaption

Terms of the bond		*Terms of receiver swaption*	
Currency:	Ecu	Maturity:	18/4/2000
Issue date:	18/4/1990	10-year swap rate:	10.75
Maturity:	18/4/2000	Swaption premium:	M (amortised)
Coupon:	10.45	Exercise date:	18/4/1995
Call provision:	At par on 18/4/1995 and every year thereafter		
Issue price:	Ecu100		

Source: Paribas.

Exhibit 6.9 illustrates the typical cash flows for this structure where the option premium is generally amortised over the life of the issue. In this case we have let the amortised annual premium be M.

Note that the borrower is selling a bank an option on a five-year swap exercisable in five years, allowing the bank to receive at a predetermined fixed rate (a receiver swaption). If the margin M paid is 25 basis points (bp) then the bank effectively pays a higher rate on the swaption at 11 per cent (10.75 per cent + 25 basis points) than on the swap without the receiver swaption, which only pays 10.75 per cent and the borrower's all-in cost is Ecu Libor −55 basis points. If interest rates fall over the next five years, the borrower will call the issue, and the bank will exercise the swaption,

Exhibit 6.9

Typical cash flows for Exhibit 6.8

	Issue		Swap		Swaption		Net Cash Flow	
	Called	Non-call					Called	Non-called
18/04/90	100	100	−100	100			100	100
18/04/91	−10.45	−10.45	10.75	−(Libor−M)			−(Libor−.30−M)	−(Libor−.30−M)
18/04/92	−10.45	−10.45	10.75	−(Libor−M)			−(Libor−.30−M)	−(Libor−.30−M)
18/04/93	−10.45	−10.45	10.75	−(Libor−M)			−(Libor−.30−M)	−(Libor−.30−M)
18/04/94	−10.45	−10.45	10.75	−(Libor-M)			−(Libor−.30−M)	−(Libor−.30−M)
18/04/95	−110.45	−10.45	10.75	−(Libor−M)	100	−10C	−100−(Libor−.30−M)	−(Libor−.30−M)
18/04/96		−10.45	10.75	−(Libor−M)	−10.75	+Libor−M		−(Libor−.30−M)
18/04/97		−10.45	10.75	−(Libor−M)	−10.75	+Libor−M		−(Libor−.30−M)
18/04/98		−10.45	10.75	−(Libor−M)	−10.75	+Libor−M		−(Libor−.30−M)
18/04/99		−10.45	10.75	−(Libor−M)	−10.75	+L.bor−M		−(Libor−.30−M)
18/04/00		−110.45	110.75	−100−(Libor-M)	−110.75	100+Libor−M		−100−(Libor−.30−M)

Source: Paribas.

resulting in the simultaneous termination of the bond and the swap. This can be seen in the second column from the right in Exhibit 6.9. If, on the other hand, interest rates rise the issuer is highly unlikely to call the bond and the bank is equally unlikely to exercise the swaption. Exhibit 6.10 shows the cash flows for this structure diagrammatically.

Contingent swaptions

Contingent swaptions are one of the newest option products, having only been introduced in Ecu in the latter half of 1989. They are designed to capture the residual option value lost when monetarising a callable bond and receiver swaption, as we showed in the example given above. Note that in this example the bond has a call provision every year following 18 April 1995, but the receiver swaption has only one exercise date on 18 April 1995. If a borrower sells a receiver swaption for each of the bond call dates, there is a risk that the call on the bond and swaption will both be exercised on 18 April 1995, leaving the borrower exposed to the four remaining receiver swaptions without an underlying bond to offset the transactions. On the other hand, the borrower could sell a receiver swaption with exercise on 18 April 1995 and a series of four contingent receiver swaptions which are exercisable each year following 18 April 1995 if, and only if, the preceding receiver swaptions have not already been exercised. From this example, it is clear that the option is called a contingent swaption because its value is contingent on the outcome of another event, such as the exercise of another option. By using this structure, the borrower receives maximum benefit from all the options on the bond without exposure to naked receiver swaptions; the value of the additional options is reflected in the higher margin premium paid on the swaption, as seen in Exhibits 6.11 and 6.12 ie 40 basis points versus 25 basis points for the conventional swaption.

Exhibit 6.10 **Callable bond with receiver swaption**

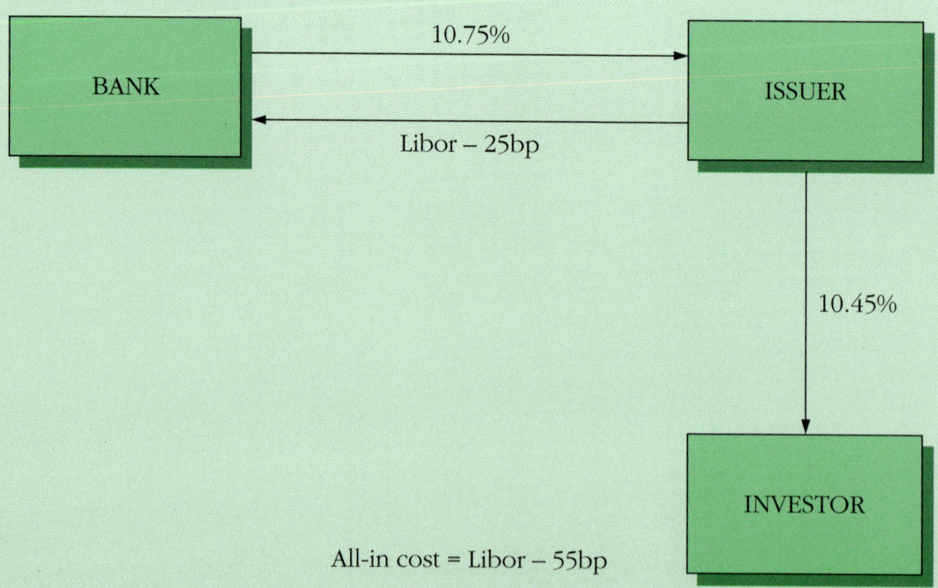

Source: Parisbas.

Exhibit 6.11

Callable bond combined with contingent receiver swaption

Terms of the bond		*Terms of receiver swaption*	
Currency:	Ecu	Maturity:	18/4/2000
Issue date:	18/4/1990	10-year swap rate:	10.75
Maturity	18/4/2000	Swaption premium:	40 basis points per annum
Coupon:	10.45	Exercise dates:	18/4/1995 and every year thereafter
Call provision:	At par on 18/4/1995 and every year thereafter.		
Issue price:	100 Ecu		

Source: Paribas.

Cross-currency swaptions

In 1985, the first currency swaption was created in which the issuer launched a floating rate US dollar note with an investor option to switch to a fixed rate Ecu issue. At the same time, a contingent swap was written with a second counterparty wishing to borrow Ecu against US dollar Libor. The swap would be exercised if the investor option on the issue was invoked, and the second counterparty would pay the coupon on the Ecu issue.

The investors paid a premium for their option, which was distributed between both issuer and the second counterparty so that the issuer would receive sub-Libor funds whether the investor option was exercised or not, while the second counterparty would raise fixed-rate Ecu funds below market rates on the simultaneous exercise of the investor option and the cross-currency swaption. Exhibit 6.13 illustrates a similar structure.

Exhibit 6.12 **Callable bond with contigent receiver swaption**

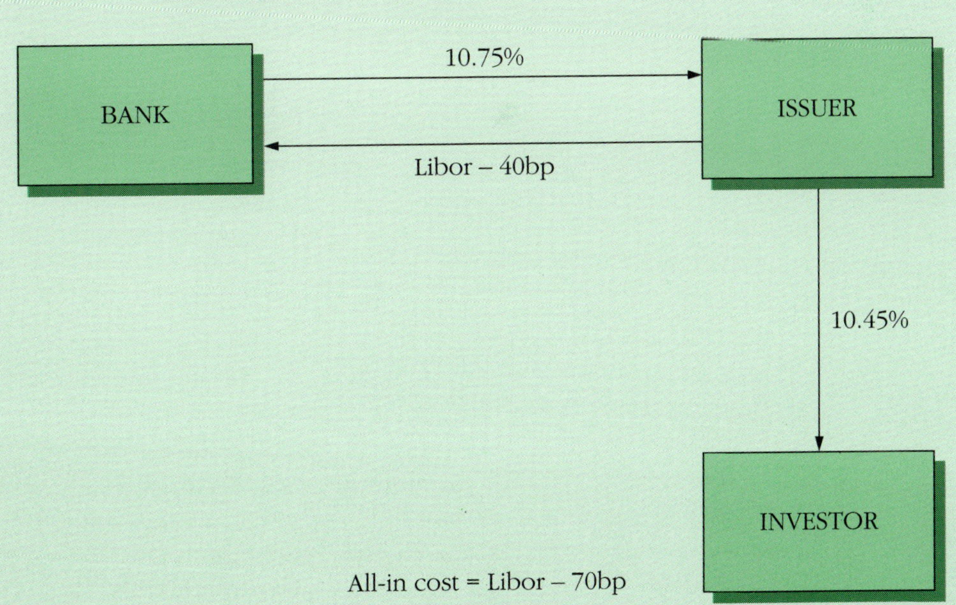

Source: Paribas.

Exhibit 6.13 **Cross currency swaption**

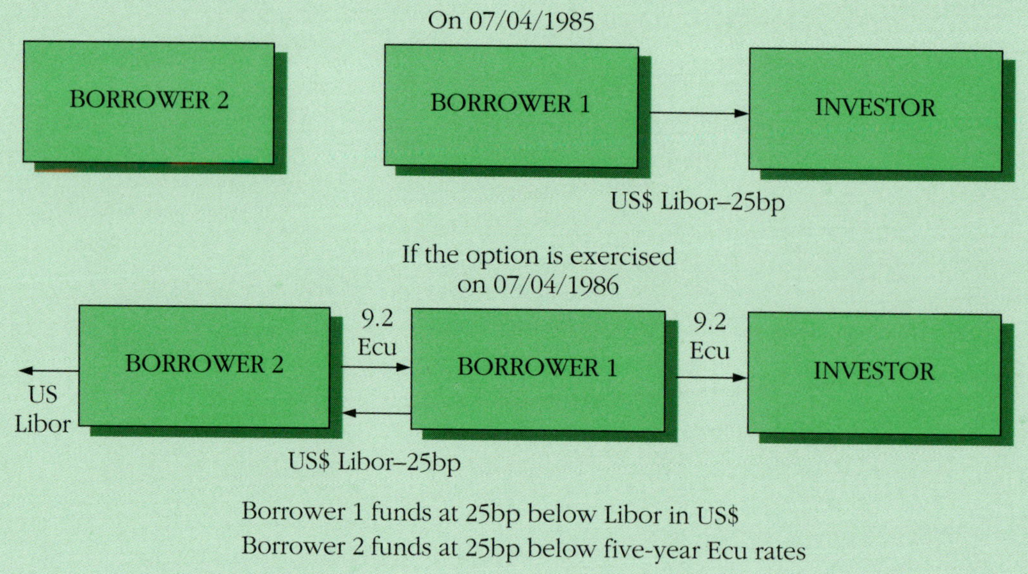

Source: Parisbas.

Although the cross-currency swaption market is relatively new, there has been a great deal of interest generated by the potential to purchase an option on interest rate spreads between currencies which are closely linked to each other. For example, if the spread between Ecu rates and Deutschmark rates is unusually wide an issuer could purchase an option to receive in Ecu and to pay in Deutschmark at a further date when the spread is likely to narrow. As the spread narrows, the option holder issues an Ecu bond and swaps it into Deutschmark at rates significantly lower than the Deutschmark market rates. The example in Exhibits 6.14 and 6.15 shows how below-market funding is achieved.

Exhibit 6.14

Below-market funding with spread options

Market conditions on 1/5/1991	*Market conditions on 1/11/1991*	
Ecu five-year forward swap rate: 10.90% (6 months forward)	Ecu five-year swap rate:	10.40%
DM five-year forward swap rate: 9.00% (6 months forward)	DM five-year swap rate:	8.90%
Premium on option to receive Ecu and pay DM: 15 bp per annum	Five-year issue yields in Ecu:	10.00%
	Five-year issue yields on DM:	8.60%

Source: Paribas.

Today it is possible to purchase a cross-currency option with or without a pre-agreed exchange of principal at the beginning of the cross-currency swap. In the example above the issuer would agree to exchange principals if, in their view, the Ecu was a weak currency which was bound to depreciate against the Deutschmark between 1 May and 1

Exhibit 6.15 **Cross currency spread option**

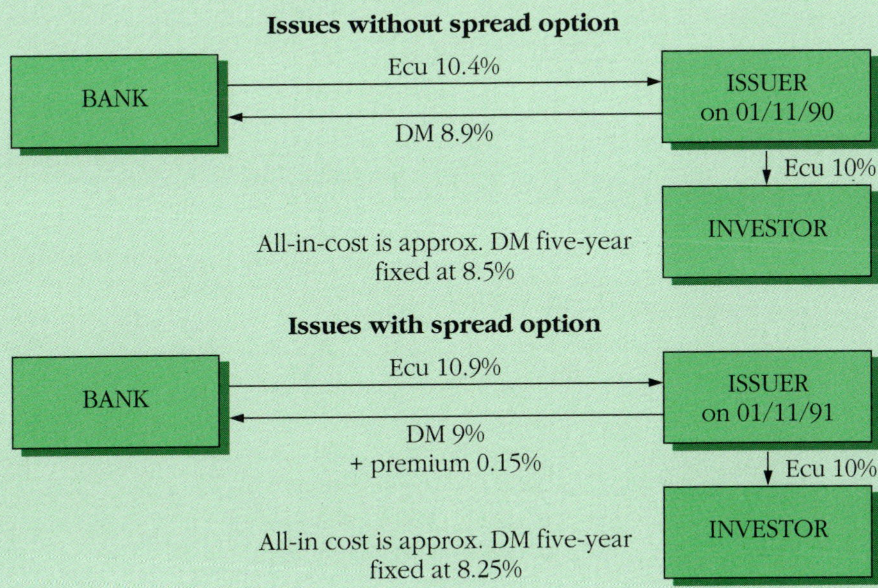

Source: Parisbas.

November. In effect, the exchange of principal at the beginning of the swap is an option to put the Ecu and call the Deutschmark.

As already mentioned, these option structures are comparatively new and usually only used by very sophisticated borrowers who have had previous experience in using options.

Bond options

The Ecu bond option market has only been in existence since the launch of the "jumbo" issues. There is supply from fund managers of large Ecu bond portfolios, who write call options on liquid government issues from France, UK, Italy or European Investment Bank (EIB), using the premium received to enhance the return of their portfolios; the implied volatility on the options tends to be lower than that of the comparable Bund options market, due to the innate relative price stability of Ecu bonds.

The option market coverage is increasing with each large issue, and the recent futures markets have made hedging the positions somewhat easier. Long-dated options on the future have already been launched in the OTC market and the MATIF has proposed options on its Ecu bond futures which will help traders hedge their gamma risk, assuming the contracts are liquid enough.

Conclusion

As the countries of the EC move inexorably towards monetary union, it seems that many governments have already chosen the final currency of union: the Ecu. With the underlying bond market increasing rapidly in size and liquidity, we can look forward to a pan-European Ecu bond market which will rival the US bond market in size. Inevitably, the derivative markets will respond to this growth as asset and liability managers in Europe become as familiar with swaps, swaptions, caps and floors as their North American counterparts.

The swaps market itself will become dominated by interest rate swaps as the interbank market increases in liquidity, while currency swaps will remain restricted to the clients of banks. Asset swaps will be relegated to a minor position as arbitrage becomes steadily less attractive.

The big growth areas will be in the use of option products where and when demand rises above a base level, bid-offer spreads shrink and liquidity increases exponentially. In all the major currency markets the initial period of slow growth in the use of option products has been followed by a dramatic increase in popularity and utilisation.

The success of the swaps and options markets around the world has primarily relied on the entrepreneurship and risk-taking of bankers and futures market participants. The growth of the Ecu derivatives markets will depend also on these two factors but will be impaired by turf battles between different financial centres in Europe. These have a tendency to reduce the liquidity of the hedging instruments. Looking at the growth of the dollar swap volumes and the comparable position of the Ecu shows the potential for this market, assuming that co-operation overcomes competition.

7

Neil Rogers
UBS Phillips & Drew

The Ecu futures market

Overview

The creation of a successful Ecu futures market is an essential step in the development of the Ecu into a major investment and trading currency.

In anticipation of the Ecu becoming the single European currency, futures exchanges are developing Ecu contracts to establish trading in their respective financial centres. The number of exchange-traded Ecu futures contracts has grown rapidly in recent years. Contracts are now available on bonds, three-month interest rates and the Ecu/US dollar exchange rate.

Trading is based on three separate exchanges (see Chapter 8). They are: FINEX, the Financial Instrument Exchange of the New York Cotton Exchange; LIFFE, the London International Financial Futures Exchange; and MATIF, the Marché à Terme International de France in Paris.

The growth of the underlying financial instruments has been centred largely around the Ecu capital market and it is here that futures activity is likely to be most active. Only when the Ecu begins to be used as a currency in its own right will commercial use increase strongly.

At present, the relatively small number of underlying Ecu instruments means that liquidity in the Ecu futures contracts is still well below that of the major contracts based on currencies such as the US dollar, the Deutschmark and the Japanese yen. However, the possible eventual adoption of the Ecu as the single European currency would overnight turn Ecu futures into some of the most actively traded in the world.

Despite the risk diversification qualities implicit within a currency basket, the volatility of actual Ecu instruments at times matches that of any other major currency, underlining the need for well-developed Ecu hedging instruments. In addition to the futures contracts mentioned here, other derivative instruments are being developed. An option on the Ecu/US dollar exchange rate will soon be supplemented by an option on the MATIF's long-term Ecu bond contract.

What are Ecu futures?

Futures contracts based on Ecu-denominated instruments work in exactly the same way as those based on any other currency. The only difference is that, because the Ecu is made up from a basket of currencies, additional trading opportunities can arise to trade the Ecu against its components.

A financial future is an agreement to buy or sell a stated quantity of a specific financial instrument (or foreign currency) at a pre-determined future date at an agreed price. Hence the price of a futures contract is directly related to the movements of the underlying financial instruments. Exchange-traded futures are standardised in the sense that all the terms and conditions of the contracts are fixed except for the price.

These financial futures enable money managers to fix exchange rates for a currency; interest rates for borrowing or lending; or returns on a fixed interest investment or disinvestment where the actual transaction will take place at a future date.

A futures contract imposes an obligation on both parties. The nominal contract size (for example, Ecu1 million per contract in the case of the LIFFE three-month interest rate future) is not paid or received. Instead, an initial margin is placed with the broker acting on the client's behalf when the futures contract is first bought. Subsequently, a variation margin is debited or credited to the client's account when the futures contract is revalued at the closing price each day.

Since their inception in the US in the early 1970s, the use of financial futures has grown rapidly because of the opportunities they present.

For traders

Financial futures can be traded by those who are willing to assume price risk in order to profit from the rises or falls they expect to occur in interest rates or exchange rates. Because the underlying financial instruments do not have to be purchased or sold, the leverage in futures contracts allows the establishment of a long or outright short position without requiring a large investment of capital.

In particular, financial futures offer traders the ability to go short when they expect interest rates to rise or a currency's value to fall.

For hedgers

The risk of loss through adverse price movements can be eliminated by taking a position that is equal and opposite to an existing or anticipated position.

For example, take a fixed-income fund manager. At the end of August he anticipates that in three months' time he will purchase 10-year Ecu bonds for a long-term investment. (He is unwilling or unable to borrow in order to buy the bonds now.)

To avoid the possibility of yields falling (and thus Ecu bond prices rising) between now and the end of November, the fund manager locks in today's rate by buying Ecu bond futures contracts for delivery in December.

If Ecu yields fall, the fund manager will still have to pay the higher price for the Ecu bonds, but this will be offset by the increase in value of the Ecu futures contracts, thus preserving the return on the funds.

If, on the other hand, Ecu yields rise, the loss on the futures contract will offset the gains in the cash market which result from being able to buy the Ecu bonds at a lower price. The use of futures, therefore, locks the fund manager into current rates. The foregone cash market profits are the price of insulation from volatility in interest rates.

Futures prices reflect only the movements in price of the underlying instruments and do not take into account the accrued interest that would be received while holding cash bonds.

EMS realignments and Ecu recompositions

Official changes to the European Monetary System (EMS) and Ecu recompositions can have major effects on the underlying Ecu instruments. Ecu futures contracts can be used to take hedging or trading positions in anticipation of these alterations.

During an EMS realignment, the official Ecu central rates of ERM currencies are changed. The immediate effect on the Ecu/US dollar exchange rate will tend to be fairly small, as most European spot rates will remain largely unchanged. Over the longer term, the new currency divergence limits will allow the weights of the components to move away from their previous limits, affecting individual currencies' weights within the Ecu and hence the Ecu/US dollar exchange rate and interest rates/bond yields.

By comparison, Ecu recompositions tends to have a large one-off effect on Ecu interest rates and bond yields. When the Ecu basket is recomposed, usually every five years, new currencies may be added and the fixed amounts of each currency in the Ecu may be changed. The Ecu/US dollar exchange rate is always maintained but, because all assets and liabilities are payable at the new rate, changes in the relative weights of hard and soft currencies will affect theoretical yields and interest rates. (Because the Ecu is composed of a basket of currencies, a theoretical fair value can be calculated from underlying currencies that constitute the Ecu.)

For instance, at the last recomposition in September 1989, the addition of a weak currency (the peseta) with a relatively large weight and the wish to reduce the Deutschmark weight (because of previous EMS realignments) caused 10-year simple theoretical bond yields to rise 42 basis points on the day (see Exhibit 7.1).

The different Ecu futures contracts

The Ecus/US dollar exchange rate contract

The Ecu/US dollar exchange rate contract has been trading on FINEX since January 1986, offering investors and commerce the ability to hedge exposure to Ecu/US dollar currency movements. This contract can also be combined with others to hedge exposure to any currency that has a futures contract against the dollar.

Membership of the exchange rate mechanism (ERM) has reduced the volatility of most European currencies against the Ecu, especially those in the narrow band. Following the entry of sterling in October 1990, some 98.5 per cent of the Ecu's component currencies are now within the

Exhibit 7.1 **Actual and theoretical 10-year yields during recomposition**

Source: UBS Phillips & Drew.

mechanism. Furthermore, the ERM will continue to move towards a fixed-exchange rate system as all countries move to the narrow band and existing narrow-band members announce tighter pegs to the Deutschmark along the lines of the Netherlands and Belgium. However, while the basket nature of the Ecu means that it will rarely perform as badly as its worst component currency, or as well as its best component, volatility between the Ecu and non-ERM currencies remains high (see Exhibit 7.2).

As well as offering the ability to hedge exposure to Ecu-specific risk,

Exhibit 7.2 **Ecu currency movements**

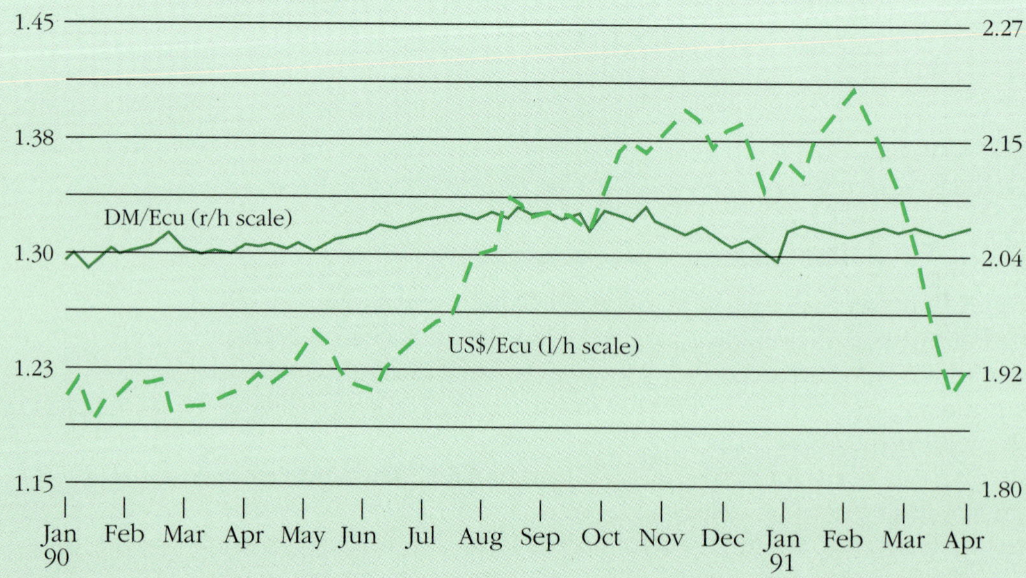

such as a holding of Ecu-based investments, the contract can also be used to hedge broad-based currency risk in Europe and exposures to ERM currencies which do not have a futures contract of their own.

The use of the Ecu as a transaction medium by private organisations is small (only around 2 per cent of European trade is denominated in Ecu). Until this changes, commercial use of Ecu/US dollar futures for hedging will remain limited.

Three-month Ecu interest rate contract

The three-month interest rate future, launched on LIFFE in October 1989, can be used to hedge a wide variety of short-dated Ecu instruments.

Despite its basket status, actual Ecu interest rate volatility has proved much higher than the theoretical rate calculated from the component currencies, even though the relationship can be easily arbitraged (see Exhibit 7.3).

The LIFFE three-month interest rate contract can be used for both hedging and trading.

Hedging

For example, if a manager needs to borrow Ecu to pay for a project in three months' time, but does not wish to assume the risk of rising borrowing costs, the current rate on the futures contract can be fixed by selling three-month Ecu futures contracts.

If the current rate is 10 per cent, Ecu futures would be sold at 90.00, guaranteeing a rate of 10 per cent on Ecu1 million nominal per contract. (With three-month interest rate futures, prices move in the opposite direction to market interest rates. This is because they are quoted on the exchange as 100 – the implied rate of interest.)

If rates fall to 9 per cent the manager buys back futures at 91.00 and makes a loss of Ecu100,000 ((90.00−91.00) × Ecu1 million) which is added to the 9 per cent borrowing cost. If rates rise to 11 per cent the manager buys back futures at 89.00 and makes a profit of Ecu100,000 ((90.00−89.00) × Ecu1 million) which is deducted from 11 per cent.

Trading

As well as simply speculating about moves in interest rates by holding a long or short position, traders can also take offsetting positions in the cash and the futures market. They can also take offsetting positions in different months, thereby taking a view about when, as well as if, rates will move.

The Ecu contract also enables the user to speculate on moves in short-term European rates, while reducing exposure to a monetary policy shock affecting a single currency, and to profit from anomalies arising between actual and theoretical three-month interest rates.

Trading Ecu anomalies

The advantage of using futures to trade the actual Ecu against the basket when it deviates to a level where it can be arbitraged is that the capital required is much lower than in the cash market. However, unlike carrying out the trade in, say, the forward currency market, it does not offer the

Exhibit 7.3 **Three-month interest rate volatility**

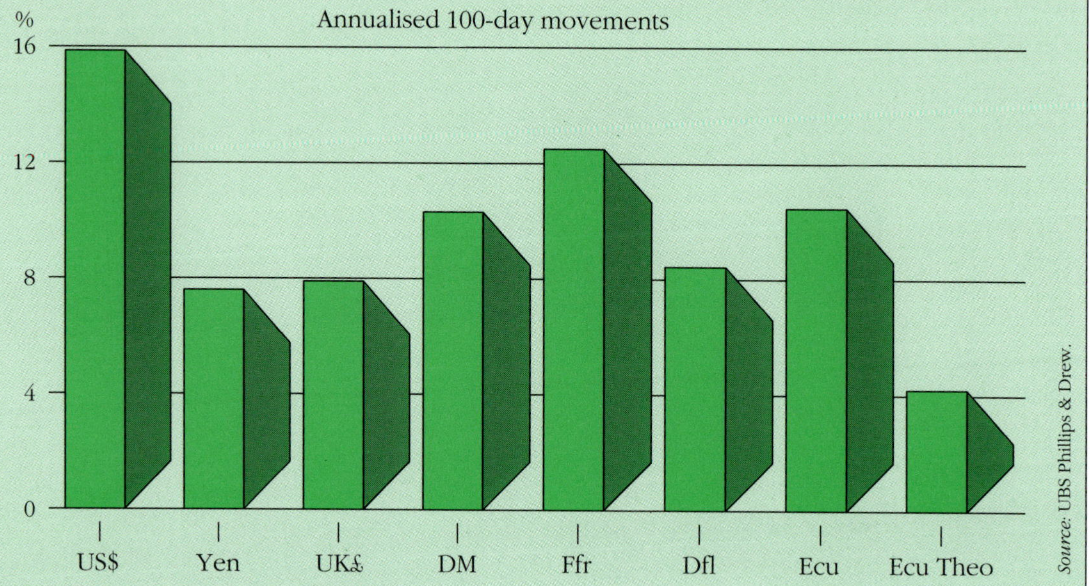

same arbitrage benefits of accruing interest. Hence, the risk remains that the anomaly will continue, or even worsen.

For example, in the middle of March 1991 the three-month Ecu deposit rate traded between 0.8 per cent and 1 per cent below the rate implied by the constituent parts of the Ecu. As a result, three-month Ecu rates at times traded just 3/16 of a percentage point above German rates.

Exhibit 7.5 shows the currency weights and three-month interest rates of each EC currency. The theoretical three-month deposit rate, calculated according to the weights given in the table, is 10.10 per cent and the current three-month Ecu deposit rate is 9.25 per cent Libid (London Interbank bid rate), giving a differential of −0.85 per cent.

Exhibit 7.6 shows how the relatively stable relationship between actual and theoretical rates was broken in mid-February 1991, when actual Ecu rates fell sharply.

Exhibit 7.4

Three-month deposit volatilities[1] (%)

US	15.87
Japan	7.62
UK	7.88
Germany	10.29
France	12.49
Netherlands	8.65
Ecu	10.46
Ecu theoretical	4.20
100 days, annualised	

[1] Actual Ecu volatility of 10.46% is considerably higher than the 4.2% volatility on theoretical interest rates.

Source: UBS Phillips & Drew.

Exhibit 7.5

Three-month deposit rates bid, 19 March 1991 London close (%)

Currency type	*Interest rate*	*Ecu weight*
Germany	8.85	30.43
France	9.19	19.05
UK	12.19	12.49
Italy	12.50	9.92
Netherlands	9.20	9.50
Belgium	9.38	7.84
Spain	12.95	5.39
Denmark	9.75	2.51
Ireland	10.50	1.11
Greece	19.00	0.65
Portugal	13.25	0.78
Luxembourg	9.38	0.31
Theoretical Ecu	10.10	
Actual Ecu	9.25	
Theoretical differential	−0.85	

Source: UBS Phillips & Drew.

There are several ways the actual/theoretical Ecu deposit rate differential can be traded using the Ecu futures contract.

One example involves selling, or buying, Ecu futures against a basket of European futures.

Although contracts are not available for all underlying currencies, a basket covering about 80 per cent of the Ecu can be constructed. The close link between German rates and those in the Benelux countries means that the Deutschmark weight can be scaled up to reflect the Deutschmark bloc as a whole. This is achieved by adding DM30.43, Dfl9.50, Bfr7.84 and Lfr0.31, taking the total to 48.08 per cent of the Ecu composition.

Exhibit 7.6 **Three-month actual/theoretical Ecu deposit rate – differential, January 1990 – March 1991**

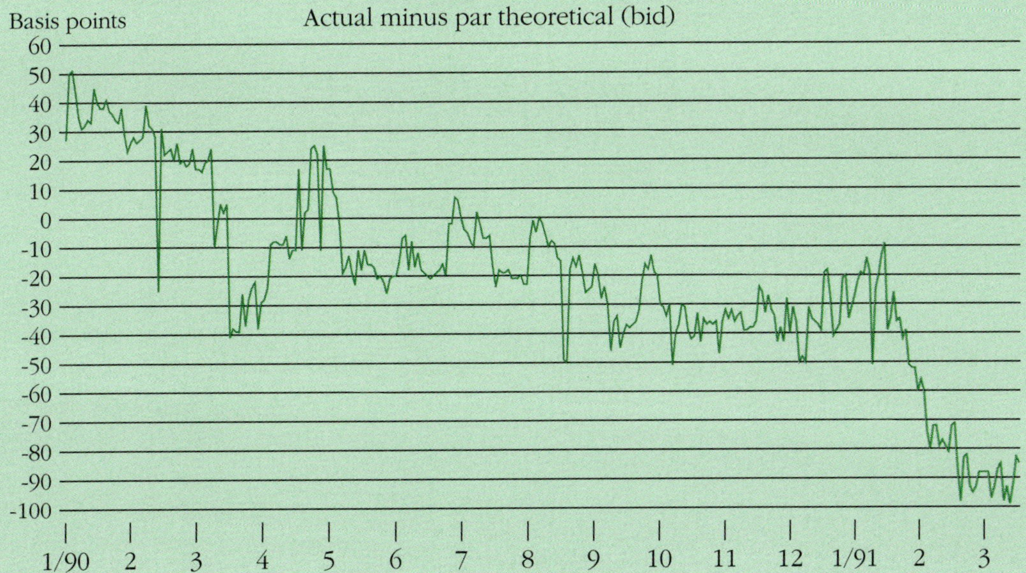

Combining this with the weighting for the pound (12.43 per cent) and the Ffr (19.09 per cent), 79.6 per cent of the Ecu basket can be represented by futures contracts.

If Ecu rates are below the theoretical deposit rate, the strategy involves selling the LIFFE Ecu deposit future against buying a basket of MATIF Pibor, LIFFE short sterling and LIFFE Euro Deutschmark, specifically: sell 100 Ecu and buy a basket of 105 Euromarks, 27 short sterling and 42 Pibor.

The risk in using an incomplete basket as a proxy for the Ecu is that the anomaly could correct itself as a result of changes in interest rates in currencies omitted from the futures basket.

Another way of exploiting the actual/theoretical Ecu deposit rate differential is to trade the spread between three-month Ecu and three-month Euromark futures. Although simpler to carry out, this method exposes the trader to the greater risk that the anomaly corrects itself due to movements in European interest rates outside Gemany.

Ecu bond futures

The dramatic growth of the Ecu bond market in recent years (see Exhibit 7.8) has led to the introduction of two Ecu bond futures contracts. The first, launched by the MATIF in October 1990, was quickly followed by LIFFE in March 1991.

Growth of the Ecu bond market is likely to remain buoyant as EC sovereigns compete to establish themselves as benchmark borrowers. In the first quarter of 1991, this led to Ecu Eurobond new-issue volume approaching that for US dollars. The arrival of large liquid benchmarks, and the move from being a private to an institutional market, has dramatically boosted Ecu turnover. Benchmark issues are now often

Exhibit 7.7 **Three-month Ecu deposit – three-month DM Eurodeposit**

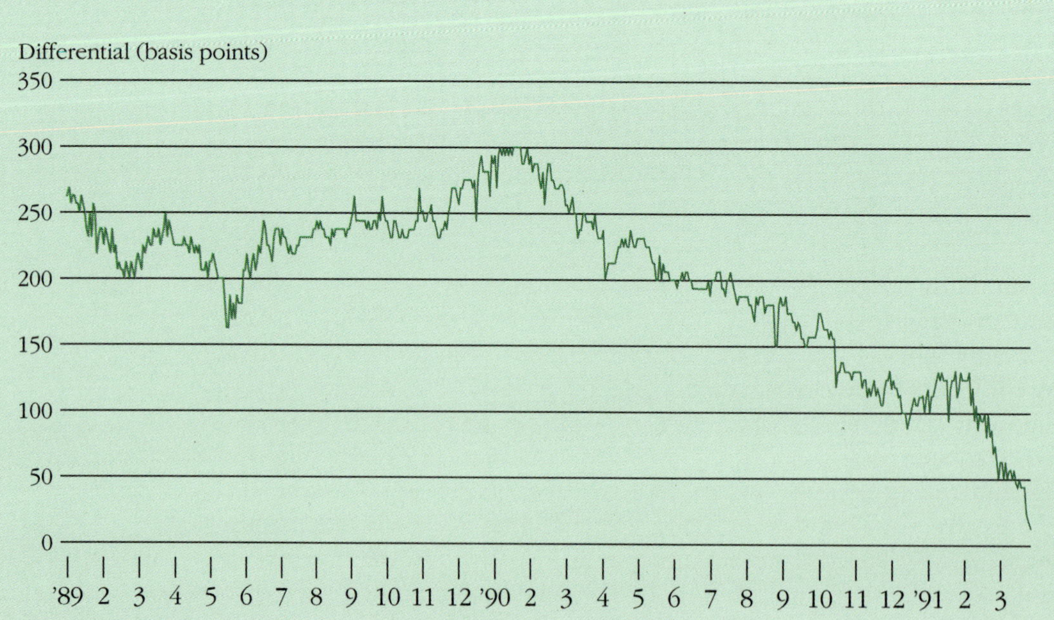

Exhibit 7.8 **Ecu new issue volume, 1981–90 (Ecu bn)**

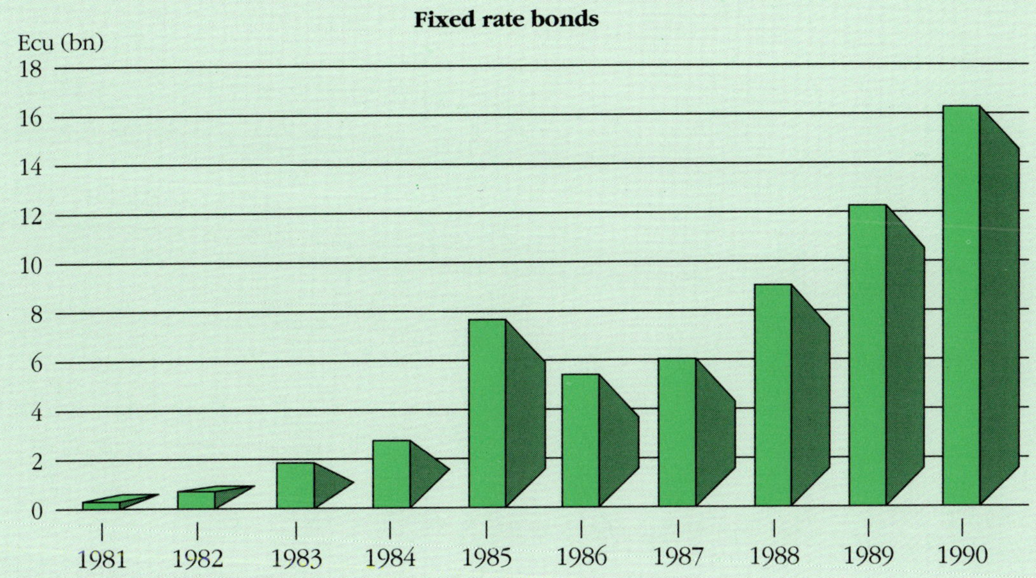

Source: UBS Phillips & Drew.

among the most actively traded of any Euro or domestic bonds at Cedel. This can only be positive for the growth of Ecu bond futures trading.

The development of Ecu bond futures contracts has greatly enhanced the cash bond market in the following ways:

- bond positions can now easily be hedged; previously, swaps or a basket of futures based on the underlying currencies had to be used;
- fund managers can carry out asset allocation decisions quickly, prior to choosing which specific bonds to buy or sell longer-term; and
- the ability to go short of Ecu by using the Ecu bond future is a major advantage; for most participants it is difficult to establish a short position in the cash market for Ecu bonds.

At present, participation by locals (individuals who trade for their own account on the exchange) in Ecu contracts is still small, reflecting the relatively low level of volume compared with the major currencies. This means it can be difficult to trade in large amounts without moving the market, and more liquid contracts will continue to draw greater speculative trading activity.

Ecu bond price volatility

Despite the Ecu's basket nature, Ecu bonds are not noticeably less volatile than bonds denominated in other major currencies. Whereas volatility on a theoretical Ecu bond will always be lower than the average of its components, the volatility of actual Ecu bonds can deviate wildly from that of the synthetic basket.

Exhibit 7.9 compares volatility on actual and theoretical 10-year bonds. It shows that the volatility of actual Ecu bonds is high when there is a systemic shock. Indeed, at times of general market uncertainty (such as during Iraq's invasion of Kuwait in August 1990), actual Ecu bond volatility tends to be among the highest of any currency. The benefits of

Exhibit 7.9 **10-year Ecu bond volatility (one-month annualised)**

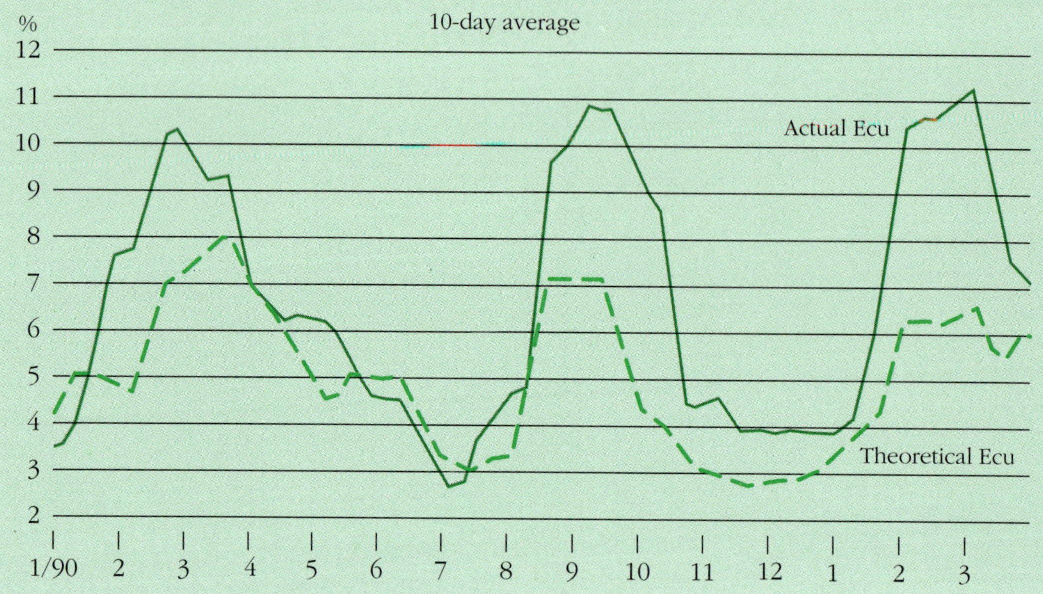

risk diversification thus only apply when a shock is limited to a specific component currency.

Contract differences

Both Ecu bond futures contracts cover a range of high-quality, fixed rate Ecu bonds. However, although the contracts are very similar, technical differences, and variations in the way the contract specifications are applied (eg eligibility), mean that the two contracts trade differently.

Both contracts cover fixed rate bonds which are issued by AAA-rated sovereign and supranational bodies; are Ecu1 billion or more in size; and have a maturity of between six and 10 years.

The major differences occur in the nominal coupon and delivery basket (see Exhibit 7.12).

Exhibit 7.10

Benchmark volatilities[1] (%)

US Treasuries	7.99
Japanese JGBs	9.67
UK gilts	8.23
German Bunds	5.56
French OATs	7.04
Dutch DSLs	4.08
Ecu (OAT 2000)	6.53
Ecu theoretical	4.61
100 days, annualised	

[1] Actual Ecu benchmark volatility (6.53% on the Ecu OAT 2000) is higher than volatility on a portfolio of bonds constructed from the underlying component bonds (4.61%).

Source: UBS Phillips & Drew.

Nominal coupon

The duration and convexity of bonds on the two futures contracts differ because the price factors are calculated on different yield levels. The MATIF has a 10 per cent nominal coupon, while the LIFFE contract has a 9 per cent nominal coupon.

Price factors are set for each bond to equalise the different coupons and maturity dates so that they yield the same as the national bond underlying the contract. For instance, in LIFFE the price factor is the price per Ecu1 nominal at which the Ecu bond would yield 9 per cent, and is directly reflected in the potential invoicing amount for each Ecu bond at delivery.

For the LIFFE contract, setting the futures base price at a higher level of duration implies that the contract is less price/yield sensitive. It will therefore require a greater proportion of contracts, relative to the nominal value, to hedge a particular bond in London than in Paris. However, because the LIFFE contract is twice the nominal size of the MATIF contract, at Ecu200,000, a hedge will be cheaper to establish in London because of the lower level of commission.

For example, using the price factors in each case to calculate hedge ratios for the OAT 9.5 per cent 2000 implies 5.146 LIFFE contracts to 9.709 MATIF contracts. This would give a MATIF/LIFFE ratio of only 1.887:1 contract, rather than 2:1.

In addition to the normal price factor, MATIF plannned to make a further adjustment to take account of differences in relative value between the different issuers. So far this has not been invoked, and in practice the difficulty of establishing a fair adjustment means that it may well be deemed unnecessary.

Deliverability

The terms of both the MATIF and LIFFE long bond futures contracts

Exhibit 7.11 **10-year bond volatility**

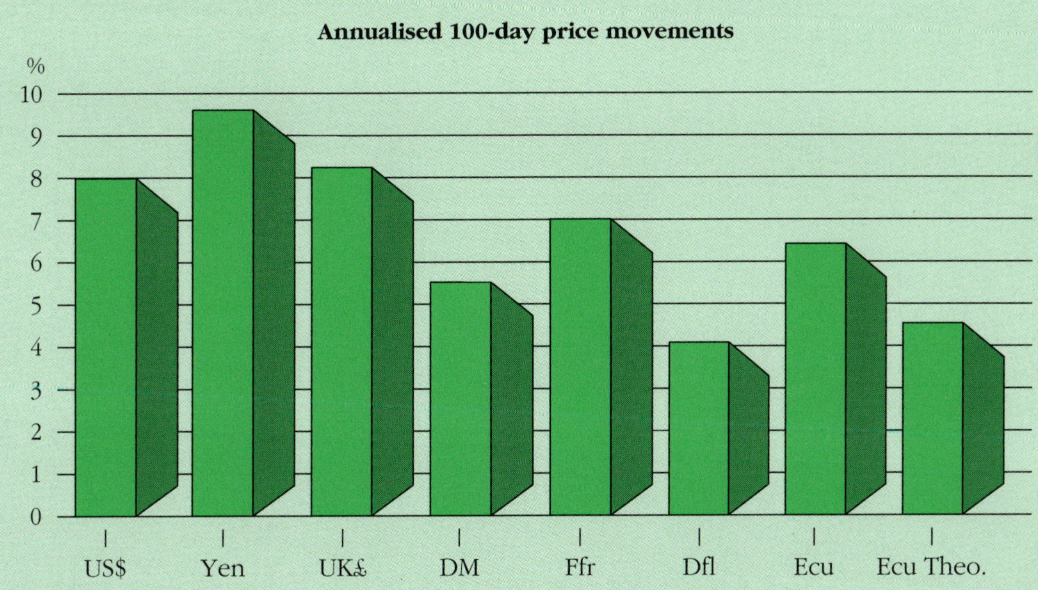

Source: UBS Phillips & Drew.

Exhibit 7.12
Contract specifications

	bond futures LIFFE	bond futures MATIF	3-mth interest rate future LIFFE	Ecu/$ future FINEX
Underlying instrument	6–10 year bond 9% coupon	6–10 year bond 10% coupon	3-month Ecu interbank deposit	Ecu/$ exchange rate
Unit of trading	Ecu200,000 nominal	Ecu100,000 nominal	Ecu1m	Ecu100,000
Quotation	Per Ecu 100 nominal	Per Ecu100 nominal	100.00 minus implied rate of interest	US cents per Ecu
Minimum price movement (tick size and value)	Ecu0.01 (Ecu20)	Ecu0.02 (Ecu20)	Ecu0.01 (Ecu25)	0.01cent/Ecu (US$10)
Trading hours	08.00-16.15 London time	09.00-16.00 Paris time	08.05-16.05 London time	08.00-13.00 New York time
Delivery months	Mar, Jun, Sep, Dec	Mar, Jun, Sep, Dec	Mar, Jun, Sep, Dec	Mar, Jun, Sept, Dec
Delivery day	20th calendar day	20th calendar day	First business day after last trading day	Third Thursday of expiring contract month
Last trading day	11am (Brussels time) same last day as Bund contract	Four business days prior to last business day in delivery month	11am 2 business days prior to the 3rd Wednesday of the delivery month	Two business days prior to 3rd Wednesday of expiring contract month
Quote	Reuters LECU Telerate 993	Reuters ECUM Telerate 3218	Reuters LFCA Telerate 997	Reuters ECNE/EC61 Telerate 907
Settlement	6–10 year eligible bonds	6–10 year eligible bonds	Cash	Physical delivery of Ecu

Source: LIFFE, MATIFF, FINEX.

allow a range of bonds to be delivered with different maturities and different coupon rates. The contracts are a major departure from most traditional futures contracts in that they allow delivery of both government and non-government bonds.

The eligibility criteria for both contracts are essentially the same, but the process of how bonds are selected varies. At LIFFE, bonds that meet the set criteria are more or less automatically included in the contract delivery basket. This is different from the MATIF contract where a panel meets to give final approval. At present, MATIF has decided not to allow Republic of Italy Eurobonds to be delivered despite the fact that they meet the set criteria.

The cheapest deliverable bond on a delivery day is that which can be bought in the cash market and sold via the futures market with the maximum profit or minimum loss. According to the invoicing amount formula, the cheapest deliverable bond on a given delivery day is that bond for which the following expression is maximum:

(futures settlement price) × (price factor) − (clean price of bond)

Exhibits 7.13 and 7.14 show the eligible bonds for delivery into the June contract for both MATIF and LIFFE, ranked in order of how cheap they would be to deliver.

In this instance, the OAT 9.5 per cent 2000 is the cheapest to deliver (CTD) in the MATIF contract while at LIFFE it is the EIB 10 per cent 2001.

Prior to delivery day, the bond which can be bought in the cash market and sold in the futures market with the maximum profit, and after taking into account the cost of financing the purchase of the cash instrument, will be the CTD.

The cheapest deliverable bond can be approximately identified as that which maximises the expression:

$$(\text{current futures price}) \times (\text{price factor}) + (\text{cost of carry}) - (\text{clean price of bond})$$

The cost of carry is equal to the difference between the interest earned on the cash bond and the cost of financing it.

The CTD is also affected by moves in the shape of the yield curve. When the curve is inverted, a six-year issue is more likely to be the CTD. When it is positive, a 10-year issue is more likely. The CTD will be the bond that the contract most closely tracks and which is potentially most easily arbitraged.

Exhibit 7.13

Cheapest to deliver – LIFFE Ecu bond contract, June 1991

Issue	*%*		*(1) Clean price*	*(2) Price factor*	*(3) Futures price*	*(4)=2×3 Implied cash price*	*(4–1) Profit*
EIB	10.00	24/1/01	104.33	1.0614714	98.29	104.33	0.00
Italy	10.75	18/4/00	108.62	1.1029241	98.29	108.41	−0.21
OAT	9.50	25/4/00	101.42	1.0291127	98.29	101.15	−0.27
OAT	10.00	26/2/01	104.90	1.0619508	98.29	104.38	−0.52
Italy	10.38	09/7/97	104.97	1.0618684	98.29	104.37	−0.60
UK	9.13	21/2/01	99.60	1.0069868	98.29	98.98	−0.62

Source: UBS Phillips & Drew.

Exhibit 7.14

Cheapest to deliver – MATIF Ecu bond contract, June 1991

Issue	*%*		*(1) Clean price*	*(2) Price factor*	*(3) Futures price*	*(4)=2×3 Implied cash price*	*(4–1) Profit*
OAT	9.50	25/4/00	101.42	0.9709198	104.46	101.42	0.00
OAT	10.00	26/2/01	104.90	0.9989542	104.46	104.35	−0.55
UK	9.13	21/2/01	99.60	0.9463895	104.46	98.86	−0.74

Source: UBS Phillips & Drew.

Using the futures contracts

Trading outright positions

The leverage available in the Ecu futures contract provides the opportunity to establish a long or outright short position with a relatively low investment of capital, if long-term interest rates are expected to fall or rise. (The minimum initial margin of Ecu4,000 represents 2 per cent of the Ecu200,000 face value of the LIFFE contract.)

Trading straddles

The price relationships between the different delivery months of the Ecu contract are determined by the net cost of carry. The implied interest rate deducted from a straddle in the long Ecu futures contract can be related to the forward-forward interest rate in the deposit market or to the implied rate deducted from the three-month Ecu interest rate futures contract. These rates are very sensitive to changes in money market yield curves. Opportunities for straddles arise when the rate implied by the three-month Ecu futures contract deviates from the relevant money market rates, or if a change in the level or shape of the money market yield curve is expected.

Trading spreads to other markets

Spreads to other markets are traded by simultaneously going long and short in different but related contracts. For example, long Ecu versus Bunds can be used to take a position on yield convergence within Europe.

In setting up spreads involving other futures, allowances need to be made for differences in contract size and different currencies.

Hedging

The futures contract can be used to hedge all long-dated Ecu bonds, not just those eligible for delivery into the contracts. In the case of smaller, illiquid bonds, the hedge will not be as good, due to differences in the way liquid and illiquid bonds trade.

Even for deliverable bonds, a futures contract is not a perfect hedge. The difference between the profit from the futures and cash market loss arises from the change in value of the basis. (Basis is the difference between the clean price on the bond and the multiple of the futures price and price factor.)

The contracts can be used to:

- Protect the value of a portfolio of Ecu bonds when long term interest rates seem likely to rise.
- Lock in the current yield level, in anticipation of investing future cash receipts in Ecu bonds when long-term interest rates seem likely to fall.
- Avoid an increase in the cost of a planned bond issue when long-term interest rates are expected to rise. A company planning to hedge a debt issue would need to adjust the number of contracts it sold by using a price factor calculated for the coupon and maturity its own debt issue would carry.

8 The major derivatives markets

FINEX and the Ecu

Steven Warren Jones
FINEX

The Ecu is a necessity for the growth of European business. As the issuance of short-term Ecu securities mounts, more emphasis will be put on the Ecu's spot and forward markets. Europe's commitment to unification, and the economic potential of such a commitment, will continue to ignite the interest of the global investor.

As the economic ties between the US and Europe intensify, the constant monitoring of the Ecu/US dollar exchange rate at the corporate and personal level will be exceedingly important to international, US dollar-based business.

FINEX (Financial Investment Exchange), a division of the New York Cotton Exchange, realised the great need for the Ecu in the derivatives market. On 7 January 1986, FINEX introduced the first Ecu/US dollar currency rate contract to the futures industry.

Ecu futures are priced to reflect a single future settlement date. There are four contract months listed for trading.

FINEX's Ecu futures contract specifications

Trading hours
8.00 am to 3.00 pm New York time. On the last trading day, trading in the spot month ceases at 10.00 am.

Contract size Ecu100,000.

Contract months March, June, September and December.

Ticker symbol EU

Price quotation
The Ecu futures contract is quoted in US cents and hundredths of a US cent per Ecu, with each cent representing US$1,000 per futures contract.

Minimum price fluctuation
The minimum price fluctuation, or tick, is .01 of a cent per Ecu, which is equivalent to $10.00 per futures contract.

Daily limit on price movement
200 ticks above and below prior day's settlement, except during the last 30 minutes of trading when no limit applies. Should the price reach the limit and remain within 100 ticks of the limit for 15 minutes, then new limits will be established 200 ticks above and below that price limit.

Last day of trading
Two business days prior to third Wednesday of expiring contract month.

Settlement
Physical delivery of Ecu.

Ecu management

More international US dollar-based firms will realise their need to manage Ecu risk as they acquire European holdings. Futures markets provide an avenue for investors to transfer risk. The more institutions possess debt or investments denominated in Ecu, the more they are exposed to Ecu risk *vis-à-vis* their own sovereign currency. Since it has been the function of futures to help the risk-averse investor manage his exposure, Ecu currency risk management was one of the major reasons for the contract's development.

As many US dollar-based businesses continue to amass broad European holdings, they enhance their exposure to two forms of risk:

- local: the local or intra-country performance of an investment or group of holdings; and
- currency: the performance of the currency in which an investment or group of holdings share in common.

Whatever the criteria for European investment, whether it is based on local or currency return, or both, international business directly or indirectly invests in Ecu. FINEX's Ecu currency futures contract serves as a vehicle that can assist the international manager in neutralising or enhancing his Ecu exposure.

A US dollar-based investor, who is more concerned with garnering equity return rather than currency or foreign exchange return, can isolate the European currency component of his portfolio in two ways:

1. By stripping out the foreign exchange (FX) return of his investments currency by currency using individual currency derivatives that reflect each currency exposure (ie the Deutschmark, French franc or sterling, etc).
2. By taking an offsetting position in an Ecu currency derivative which reflects accurately broad-based European exposure.

The Morgan Stanley Capital International "Europe" (MSCI Europe) is a capitalisation-weighted index of 618 companies denominated in 13 different European currencies, eight of which (italics) are in the Ecu: the *UK, Germany, France,* Switzerland, *Italy, The Netherlands, Spain,* Sweden, *Belgium, Denmark,* Norway, Austria and Finland.

Exhibit 8.1 shows that the FX return of a portfolio based on the MSCI Europe index *vis-à-vis* the US dollar correlates 98.9 per cent of the time to Ecu/US dollar return.

From 1986 to 1991 both MSCI Europe and Ecu's FX returns are so similar with a correlation of 98.9 per cent that a chief financial officer could have neutralised his European currency exposure during this period by offsetting his position using Ecu currency futures.

Ecu futures trading

Ecu futures provides not only an opportunity for individuals to manage the risk associated with pan-European investment but also to trade this very important currency.

The futures industry is a medium that can bring the Ecu into the hands of more people. Not everyone who wishes to take a position in the Ecu has access to the interbank cash market. The futures industry, which is rapidly expanding, in part because of the accessibility of its products, now offers all the major currencies to the currency futures trading public.

The Ecu futures industry provides immediate price discovery. Futures markets fulfill this vital function by concentrating all buying and selling in a central trading location. All buy-and-sell orders are routed to the entire market through the open outcry system, which generates a key source of market information. This is further enhanced by the market's ability to provide complete time and sales data.

Futures also provide protection against counterparty credit risk. All futures trades are ultimately executed at the clearing-house level, which ameliorates counterparty credit risk and upholds the ultimate integrity of the futures market.

Exhibit 8.1 **Ecu vs. FX return of MSCI Europe, January 1986 to December 1990**

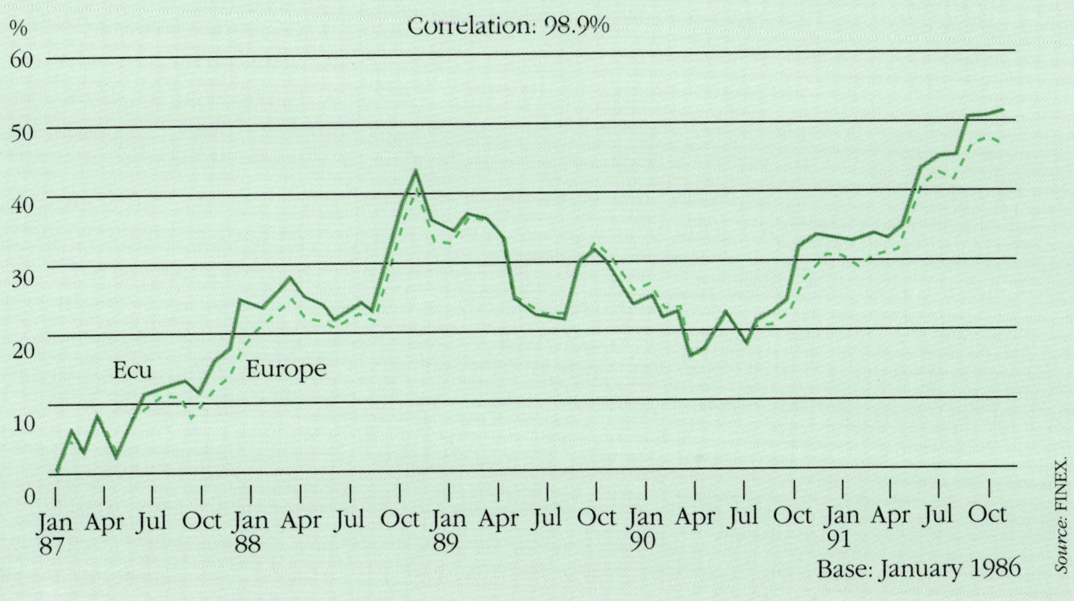

There has never been a default in the 121-year history of the New York Cotton Exchange's clearing-house.

Moreover, because the clearing-house is the counterparty to each buyer and seller, an institutional customer or bank trader can use futures with a greater degree of anonymity.

The growth of the currency futures market

Multinationals are increasingly monitoring currency risk on a 24-hour basis as well as developing strategies which can combat or harness their currency risk. Thus more and more banks are finding it lucrative to provide 24-hour foreign exchange markets to the corporate community.

Corporates and banks have been increasingly big players in the spot and forward currency markets as the business community becomes more global and aware of exchange rate volatility. In conjunction with the variety of individuals in the market place, derivatives such as currency futures have provided successful secondary markets for the currency trader.

The managed futures sector of the industry, where institutional investment is found, had approximately $1 billion in total assets invested in 1984. Managed futures now have over $12 billion and are growing. Among the most important contributors to this substantial growth were corporate institutions, which began to accept currency futures as a strategic investment or hedge against currency risk. This new institutional activity has made currency futures one of the most prominent derivatives markets for the cash currencies.

FINEX and the Ecu's future

FINEX's long-standing commitment to providing an Ecu currency futures market to the world has been prudent, given that the Ecu financial market has grown to well over US$13 billion by 1991.

FINEX have included the Ecu into the derivatives market to provide a secondary market place for both institutions and individuals. They are now more optimistic about the future growth of the Ecu and their Ecu contract. As the Ecu's applications and uses grow more evident in a global context, the need for Ecu currency futures as a vehicle for investment and risk management will be a necessity.

LIFFE and the Ecu

Philip Bruce
LIFFE

The exchange and its contracts

The London International Financial Futures Exchange (LIFFE) was established in 1982 to provide its members, and their clients, with a means of hedging financial exposure brought about by movements in fluid and changing currencies, interest rates and stock markets.

Since that time, LIFFE has developed into a highly efficient market place in which hedging and trading activity takes place in 17 different contracts – 11 futures contracts and six options contracts. These are denominated in sterling, Deutschmarks, Ecus, Swiss francs, US dollars and Japanese yen. Average daily turnover of these instruments in nominal value amounted to the equivalent of £34 billion in the year ending Februry 1991.

LIFFE's membership has also broadened and now encompasses 180 members drawn from 22 different countries, including 39 from the US, 37 from Japan and 94 from the UK and the rest of Europe (these figures indicate the geographical location of the parent companies of members).

LIFFE's European focus

From its birth, LIFFE has always focussed on becoming the principal trading centre for futures and options within the European time zone. Its success in doing this is linked to the major successes that have come from the exchange's development of European-related products – particularly those denominated in sterling and Deutschmarks. Among its product range, LIFFE now boasts five international bond contracts (three of which are European) and five short-term instruments related to the money market (four of which are European).

Developments in the Ecu market

LIFFE first became interested in the Ecu as a currency and commenced research into the listing of Ecu-related products in 1988. The rest of this section describes the background to this interest and the practical developments that have sprung from it.

Most people would have still described the Ecu as a rather "exotic" currency in 1988. Its usefulness in providing some protection against intraEuropean exchange rate volatility was beginning to be recognised. Yet despite the fact that the Republic of Italy was well into its programme of funding in Ecu, the money markets and capital markets still regarded the Ecu as a currency to be swapped out of, hopefully with an arbitrage gain, rather than a "proper" investment currency.

In 1988, the Ecu markets lacked instruments with sufficient homogenity and liquidity to warrant the attention of institutional investors. It was on 11 October 1988 that the Bank of England began to show the money market the way by commencing an issuing programme of Ecu-denominated one-month, three-month and six-month Treasury bills.

The three-month Ecu interest rate contract

LIFFE responded to this by listing a three-month Ecu interest rate futures contract on 26 October 1989. The purpose of this contract was to provide participants in the Ecu T-bill and money markets with an exchange-traded hedging vehicle.

Three-month interest rate contracts enable institutions to manage the risk associated with interest rate movement on both the liability side (where the exposure is to interest rates rising) and the asset side (where the exposure is to interest rates falling) by protecting a future, or forward, rate.

In brief, LIFFE's three-month Ecu interest rate contract has a nominal value of Ecu1 million, is listed for standard quarterly maturities and is based on the anticipated level of the British Bankers' Association Interest Settlement Rate (BBAISR) for three-month Ecu deposits as published on fixed quarterly dates. All positions that remain open in the contract at each quarterly maturity are revalued to the BBAISR for three-month Ecu deposits on that day and a final adjustment of differences is made in cash.

Simultaneously with the launch of the contract, LIFFE initiated a market-maker scheme for three-month Ecu futures. The purpose of this scheme is to ensure that there is always a narrow dealing spread for a specified transaction size in the contract in order to maintain and develop liquidity. The scheme is still running and continues to provide the cash market with certainty of its ability to lay off its interest rate risk.

Between its inception and the end of February 1991, the three-month Ecu contract turned over Ecu93.8 billion (monthly average, Ecu 5.5 billion) and had recorded a maximum end-of-month open interest (an indication of the degree to which the contract is being used for hedging purposes on any given day) of Ecu4.9 billion. The long-term prospects for the three-month Ecu contract look promising. Additionally, its availability together with the other European money market instruments listed by LIFFE (Euro Swiss franc, Eurodeutschmark and short sterling) provides LIFFE's members and their clients with further spread trading opportunities.

Research into an Ecu bond contract

During 1989, and while LIFFE was concluding its research into the three-month Ecu interest-rate contract, the exchange commenced an examination into the potential for an Ecu-denominated hedging instrument that would be useful for participants in the fixed income capital markets, better known as an Ecu bond futures contract. As opposed to the three-month Ecu contract described above, which is finally settled in cash, an Ecu bond futures contract would be settled by the physical delivery of Ecu bonds themselves.

One of the prerequisites of the design of any potentially successful bond futures contract is the existence of a sizeable, homogeneous and liquid underlying cash market. In 1989, these particular qualities were lacking: the secondary market consisted of a wide range of small issues of varying credit quality and liquidity. Development of an Ecu bond futures contract was temporarily shelved.

However, 1990 proved to be a watershed for the development of the Ecu and the international Ecu bond markets. Since the beginning of 1990, sovereign issuance has increased dramatically. Sovereign borrowers are not necessarily natural users of Ecu, but they have become large borrowers partly because of political decisions to promote the Ecu in the approach to EMU. Liquid "jumbo-size" benchmark issues from Belgium, France, Italy, Spain and the UK are now actively traded in the secondary market. European supranational borrowers, such as the EIB, have also increased their Ecu borrowings and the new European Bank for Reconstruction and Development is expected to raise funds principally denominated in Ecu.

LIFFE's international membership responded to these rapid developments in the Ecu cash markets by requesting that LIFFE launch an Ecu bond futures contract to meet their new hedging and trading requirements.

Launch of an Ecu bond contract

On 6 March 1991, LIFFE launched its innovative Ecu bond futures contract.

The form of the contract is similar, in principle, to LIFFE's other deliverable bond futures contracts. It is based on a notional Ecu bond of nominal value Ecu200,000 with a 9 per cent annual coupon. Holders of open positions at each quarterly maturity of the contract are obliged to make/take physical delivery of Ecu bonds through the international clearing houses, Euroclear and/or Cedel. The invoicing amount payable in respect of each contract delivered is calculated by the so-called price factor system (a mechanism which brings the maturity and coupon of various Ecu bonds onto a common base), and adjustment is made for full coupon interest that has accrued.

Perhaps the most innovative aspect of the contract's design is that there is a set of rules that objectively determines the deliverability of Ecu bonds into the contract. This publicly available set of rules allows issuers, underwriters and participants in the secondary market to determine a new issue's deliverability as soon as the issue is announced. A full description of the rules for inclusion is beyond the scope of this article but, in summary, an Ecu bond must be issued by a sovereign or supranational, have an outstanding amount of at least Ecu1 billion, have a remaining maturity of between six and 10 years, have the highest credit rating and be a "straight" issue in order to qualify for inclusion.

MATIF and the Ecu

Jacques Werren

MATIF

After only five years but already 94,318,410 contracts traded, the Marché à Terme International de France (MATIF) is a market to reckon with in the futures and options industry (see Exhibit 8.2).

The MATIF market share in futures and options trading activity worldwide has regularly increased, from 5.79 per cent in 1988 to 7.94 per cent in 1989 and 8.09 per cent in 1990. After witnessing exponential growth in its early years (33 per cent in 1988 and 55 per cent in 1989), the MATIF currently shows a pattern of regular growth, with a 10 per cent increase in 1990. Activity for the first months of 1991 has been very strong.

European top contracts

MATIF star contracts are the notional bond futures and its options – the notional futures being the first contract to be launched on the MATIF in

February 1986. For three years since 1988, the turnover in these two contracts has been surpassing the volume of any other long-term contract in Europe and coming second after the volume in the Chicago T-bond. Total volume for 1988 was 15,788,033 contracts, 1989: 22,154,460 and 1990: 23,406,401, making up around 80 per cent of the total volume in the MATIF in 1990.

Other contracts are also remarkable for their growth. Among them, the Computerised Continuation Quotation (CAC 40), which jumped 184 per cent in activity in 1990. Because it is the perfect hedging instrument against stock index variation, as well as a very liquid contract, it became a most attractive instrument for investors and portfolio managers. In MATIF's successful contracts, liquidity usually prevails right from the beginning. In futures contracts, locals have been providing extra liquidity since the implementation of a locals scheme in January 1989. In 1990, locals accounted for 15.7 per cent of the total volume in the notional bond futures contract and 15 per cent in the CAC 40.

The market markers' plus

MATIF option contracts are now considered the Paris market place's forte. The MATIF listed option contracts for the notional bond futures in January 1988, the three-month Paris interbank offered at (Pibor) in March 1990 and the Ecu bond futures contract in April 1991. Traders in Paris have clearly developed an expertise in these mathematically complex tools. They propose and implement sophisticated strategies for house and customer accounts.

An international comparison of the ratio of options traded as compared with the underlying futures underscores the wide use and the success of these products: the notional option/notional futures ratio is

Exhibit 8.2 **MATIF financial contracts, traded volumes since opening**

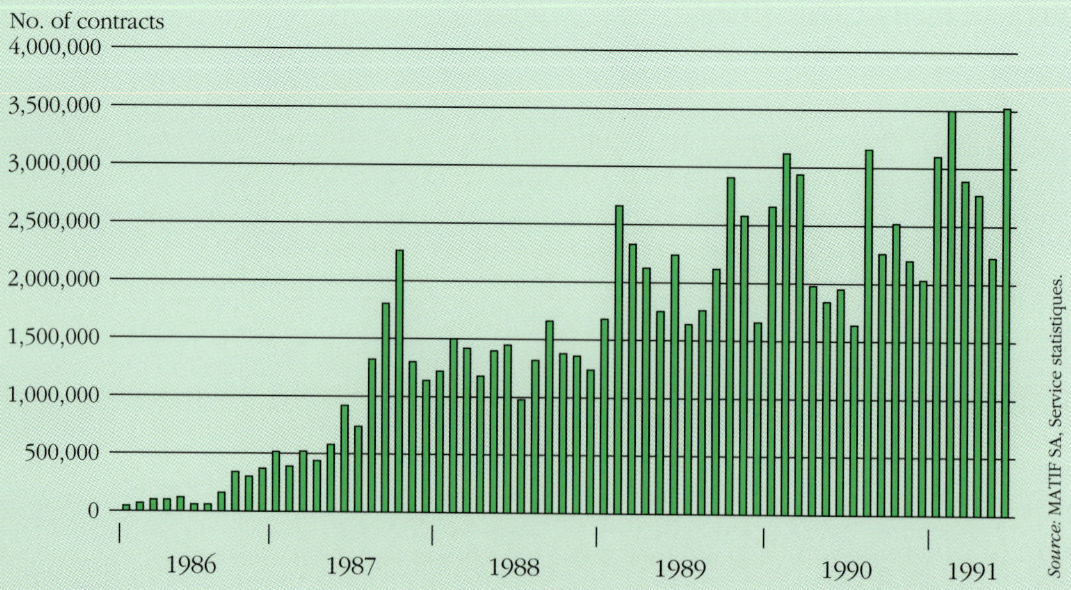

Exhibit 8.3 **Total traded volume on MATIF contracts: 20/2/86 to 28/6/91**

Contracts	*1986*	*1987*	*1988*	*1989*	*1990*	*1991*	*Total*
Notional bond	1,663,961	11,911,434	12,357,118	15,004,901	15,996,096	10,335,670	67,269,180
90-day T-bill	50,117	106,856	15,973	–	–	–	172,946
3-month Pibor			452,374	2,296,359	1,900,851	1,351,572	6,001,156
CAC 40 Index			64,688	581,473	1,641,398	1,029,527	3,317,086
3-month Eurodem				613,748	393,850	285	1,007,883
4-year BTAN				84,628	27,866	–	112,494
Ecu bond					56,292	262,343	318,635
Financial futures	1,714,078	12,018,290	12,890,153	18,581,109	20,016,353	12,979,397	78,199,380
Notional option			3,430,915	7,149,559	7,410,305	4,429,500	22,420,279
Pibor option					709,736	606,239	1,315,975
Eurodem option					109,445	400	109,845
Ecu option						6,004	6,004
Financial options			3,430,915	7,149,559	8,229,486	5,042,143	23,852,103
Financial total	1,714,078	12,018,290	16,321,068	25,730,668	28,245,839	18,021,540	102,051,483
Sugar Ffr			160,441	321,463	255,978	45	737,927
Sugar US$					46,930	104,545	152,475
Coffee			3,383	2,826	1,799	291	8,299
Cocoa			2,336	167	–	–	2,503
Potato 40mm			700	606	23	–	1,329
Potato 50mm			7,838	30,983	37,165	19,221	95,207
Commodities total			174,698	356,045	341,895	124,102	996,740
MATIF total	1,714,078	12,018,290	16,495,766	26,086,713	28,587,734	18,145,642	103,048,223

about 50 per cent, while it is generally about 25 per cent in the US for similar types of products.

The constant presence of experienced market-makers provides further liquidity in options. MATIF members who are selected by MATIF SA to become market-makers must, during official market hours, be prepared to always propose bid and ask quotes on all delivery months, for minimum amounts of 20 (notional options) to 50 contracts (Pibor options) with a maximum spread between bid and ask. The end-user consequently enjoys the benefits of tight price spreads which are often for amounts superior to the minimum required by MATIF SA's market-making scheme.

Total security for operations

MATIF members and end-users also enjoy a rare level of security for their MATIF operations, for MATIF SA is not only the organiser of the market's everyday operations and contracts' research and development, it is also the MATIF's clearing house. Consequently it guarantees the counterparty risk of each transaction that takes place in the MATIF and the sound performance of operations. The MATIF clearing house, MATIF SA, has over Ffr600 million in assets.

A highly capitalised and international membership

In order to reinforce every link of the security chain, MATIF SA and its regulating authority, the Conseil du Marché à Terme (CMT), requires a large amount of capital from the MATIF's members. General clearing members (Adhérents Compensateurs Généraux) have to have a net worth of at least Ffr750 million. They are among the most highly capitalised in the world, since the French authorities rightly considered that the market members are the first level of guarantee *vis-à-vis* the end-users. In fact, the MATIF is the only market in the world which relieves the final customer of complete counterparty risk should a MATIF member be insolvent.

MATIF SA intends to ensure the international prospects of the French futures and options market, with an increasingly international membership: one-third of the MATIF membership is now composed of non-French institutions. The strategy of membership internationalisation was set from the very outset and has borne fruit. In 1990, the four new members of the MATIF were all top foreign institutions. Foreigners play a growing role in the MATIF turnover, representing 25 per cent of overall activity. They are specifically concentrated in the notional contracts (futures and options), the CAC 40 and the newly-launched Ecu contract, which is *per se* international.

As early as 1989, MATIF SA signed on Globex, the global electronic trading system initiated by the Chicago Mercantile Exchange and Reuters. The MATIF saw this partnership as the way to secure a truly international role for itself with their notional bond and Pibor contracts to be listed on the system in 1992.

The challenge the MATIF faces is to maintain the rank and recognition it has obtained in the futures and options industry worldwide. MATIF SA will do so by proposing attractive new international products, with a competitive and low-cost service for the members and hence their clients, and the same level of extreme security.

The Ecu bond futures contract embodies the MATIF's position in terms of international policy as well as its anticipation of a united Europe with a single currency. Naturally, the MATIF will co-operate with other exchanges, in Europe and in the rest of the world, to provide comprehensive hedging products to market players who are more than ever in need of such tools to face the volatility of the markets.

Philadelphia Stock Exchange

Robert Prior

Timber Hill Inc

The first securities exchange in the US, the Philadelphia Stock Exchange (PHLX), founded in 1790, was also the first exchange in the world to create and introduce listed options on foreign currencies. Exchange-traded currency options, similar to options on common stock, provide a versatile and well leveraged investment vehicle with a known and limited risk. The PHLX is committed to providing its membership and the whole financial community with a market place which responds to the increasingly sophisticated, international needs of securities dealers. The PHLX currently trades over 1,900 equities, 166 equity options and eight foreign currencies.

In the late 1940s, the PHLX transformed itself into a major international force. A series of smaller regional exchanges, including the Baltimore and Washington Stock Exchanges, merged with the Philadelphia Stock Exchange. In 1975, the PHLX helped pioneer an unproven idea for the trading and hedging of stocks – listed stock options. Now an important element of the exchange's business, these equity instruments proved to be one of the most crucial innovations in the history of equities trading.

In 1981, the PHLX became the first exchange to trade the now popular foreign currency options. Foreign currency options were introduced to help the international financial community respond to more volatile currency markets. Reflecting the growth in international demand for these contracts, the PHLX undertook its third extension of trading hours in three years by adding six-and-a-half hours to its trading day in 1990. At 20½ hours, it is by far the longest trading day of any exchange in the world and covers all key time zones, serving the needs of market participants around the world. The PHLX trading day now runs from 6.00 pm EST (7.00 pm EDT) until 2.30 pm (EST/EDT) the following day.

In 1990, the PHLX filed with the Securities and Exchange Commission (SEC) for approval to trade an innovative new type of foreign currency option: cross-rate options. Beginning with options on the rates of sterling against the Deutschmark, sterling against the Japanese yen and Deutschmark against the Japanese yen, the PHLX will once again break new ground by becoming the first US exchange to offer an investment product denominated and settled in a currency other than the US dollar.

The PHLX is the only exchange in the US to offer foreign currency spot-delivered options and futures on eight major currencies *vis-à-vis* the US dollar. These are based on the Australian dollar, sterling, Canadian dollar, Deutschmark, Ecu, French franc, Japanese yen and Swiss franc. Trading volume for 1990 in the PHLX's eight foreign currencies equalled 10,122,918 contracts representing approximately US$455 billion in underlying volume.

The Ecu

The Ecu options contract offered on the PHLX is an instrument settled for spot delivery which provides the holder, upon exercise, the right to buy or sell Ecu62,500 for a specific Ecu/US dollar cross-rate. The unique spot-settlement feature of this contract makes it especially useful for hedging forward delivery risk. Option premium is paid in US dollars, with a minimum charge of $6.25 per contract. A premium bid of 1.90 would be equal to an actual dollar cost of $1,187.50. For instance, an exercise of the 124 Ecu call would require the holder to tender approximately $50,000 in exchange for Ecu62,500. The Ecu contract is traded in exercise price intervals of $.02 and, in addition to the standard quarterly expirations, is also traded in the two near-term months. Average daily volume for 1990 in nominal Ecu contract value was Ecu6.25 million, with an open interest equal to Ecu6.25 million. Narrow spread differentials are required by the exchange and are supported by the combination of specialist and market-makers who can accommodate virtually any size of trade with little disruption to the market place.

As a listed securities exchange, the PHLX offers several advantages not found in other trading environments. Option integrity is guaranteed by the Options Clearing Corporation (OCC), a clearing agency regulated by the SEC, which has issued and guaranteed all options traded on US securities exchanges since 1973. Margin must be posted on options written on the PHLX, thereby assuring contract fulfilment, as opposed to the OTC market, which requires only an open credit line with the counterparty. Contract fulfilment in the OTC market is guaranteed only by the trading counterparty's solvency.

Another advantage of exchange-based trading is the standardisation of contract size, maturity and quotation. This is important to the potential Ecu contract trader because it guarantees the presence of a constant market place in which to sell or repurchase options in positions already held. Since the PHLX uses a specialist/market-maker system to support its markets, a fair and reasonable market is guaranteed at all times for all listed options. The bid and offer quotation for each option traded on the exchange, in addition to last trade date, is posted and publicly disseminated by the specialist, who is usually willing to accommodate trades of all sizes. This system makes trading and monitoring PHLX Ecu options a much easier task that in other market places where a quote is only available upon request, and then only when the other participants are willing.

9 Investment in Ecu

Alfred Steinherr and
Eric Peree
European Investment Bank

The first section of this chapter establishes the share of Ecu securities in optimally structured portfolios. This approach ignores transaction and information costs (an argument in favour of the Ecu) and the variety of available instruments (an argument not in favour of the Ecu in relation to the two to four major currencies). The second section discusses the Ecu yield curve as a basis for pricing and arbitrage strategies. The conclusions summarise the main findings.

The Ecu in optimally diversified portfolios

The rapid growth of the Ecu bond market is frequently explained by referring to the basket nature of the Ecu. The basket construction is responsible for returns that are between the lowest and the highest in the basket and an exchange rate performance that also contains a hedge. Therefore, Ecu bonds initially appear well suited to risk-averse investors. However, there are problems, because risk-averse investors with a national habitat will usually have lower risk in investments in their domestic currency. For short- and long-term securities with "reasonable" volatilities, the exchange rate dominates the interest rate risk, rendering investments in domestic currencies more attractive than investments in Ecu. This argument applies to all foreign currencies. The Ecu is a special case only because it has no preferential habitat base. In any case, risk aversion does not apply to Ecu investments.

This view is supported by the fact that the Ecu is not strictly necessary for diversifying risk. An investor can achieve better risk diversification by investing in different currencies. Investment in Ecu as a standard cocktail would, in this view, result from transaction cost savings. Alternatively, this chapter develops the argument that the Ecu is not identical to a basket replication. In this view, Ecu instruments are linearly independent of instruments in basket currencies.

To further test the attraction of the Ecu for investors, a mean-variance approach is taken with shares not constrained to be non-negative.[1] Because the exchange rate is habitat specific, the efficiency frontier varies across habitats. Habitats within and outside the EMS are retained and a (futuristic) European habitat is postulated whose currency is the Ecu.

The investment horizon is assumed to be three months, and

1. For basics see Markowitz (1970).

investments are confined to three-month money market instruments. The main justification for this restrictive choice is the homogeneity and comparability of three-month instruments in relation to long-term bonds.

The period for the computations is the fourth quarter of 1984 to the fourth quarter of 1990. This period corresponds roughly to that of a depreciating dollar. The preceding period, from 1979 to 1984, characterised by an appreciating dollar, is covered in Hamui (1984) and Masera (1987), and their results are congruent with those here.

What can one possibly learn from a mean-variance approach? Adding an additional currency in which securities are denominated should always contribute to better risk diversification. Inclusion of the Ecu in an optimally constructed portfolio would therefore not be surprising.

However, the Ecu is unlike any other currency. One must face the question whether the Ecu can be exactly replicated or not. If it can be (and if transaction costs are ignored), then addition of the Ecu to a universe of component currencies should not add anything: each investor constructs a portfolio of component currencies according to his own preferences.

By contrast, if the Ecu is not replicable then it is interesting to check if this depends on choice of habitat or on time period. If the share is small across all habitats, then the Ecu is not a useful addition.

The hypothesis here is that the Ecu is not replicable. This hypothesis will be further analysed in the next chapter by comparing Ecu and basket yields. For the portfolio analysis, only four basket currencies are retained: Deutschmark, guilder, sterling, French franc. These currencies represent the most liquid and liberalised markets, with a weight of more than 70 per cent of the basket. The remaining currencies cannot be replicated as they lack appropriate instruments, liquidity or free access. To these basket currencies are added the US dollar and Japanese yen. If the Ecu plays a prominent role in this universe, then it can be concluded that it is not redundant and even exhibits features that make it an important innovation.

What does the notion of "important innovation" mean? Compared to security holdings in national currencies, the Ecu necessarily plays an insignificant role because it is a foreign currency and is not used in national payment systems. Therefore, it is preferable to examine portfolios restricted to foreign currency securities before examining portfolios which include domestic currency securities.

Foreign exchange asset management

To isolate the Ecu's attraction among foreign currencies, a portfolio of foreign currency securities is first constructed. This portfolio corresponds when an investor proceeds with a two-step optimisation. First, a decision is made about the size of funds in foreign currency instruments and then the allocation over individual currencies is determined. Examples include management of foreign exchange reserves or foreign currency investment funds.

As demonstrated in Steinherr and Girard (1989), any point along the efficiency frontier represents a combination of the minimum variance portfolio (MVP) and a pure-risk portfolio (PRP), with the optimal weight of the latter increasing inversely with the degree of risk aversion of the investor. The PRP is a portfolio with the sum of asset shares constrained to zero. The MVP and the PRP can be shown to be uncorrelated and uniquely determined and along the efficiency frontier only their mix varies. Because the PRP has no net investment position, its return is proportional to risk, and because its composition is constant and more risk is only generated by scalar multiplication, the price of pure risk (return on the PRP) is a constant and corresponds to a ray through the origin in return-risk space. To describe all efficient portfolios fully, it suffices, therefore, to determine MVP and PRP.

Exhibit 9.1 summarises the composition of the foreign currency MVP for the various habitats. Ecu assets are held long (their share is positive) in most habitats, most notably (in terms of large shares) in habitats not in the ERM, such as the US and UK. Returns on the foreign currency portfolio are generally higher than on domestic currency investments, at the cost of increased risk. The exception is the Ecu, where returns are higher than those of the foreign currency portfolio, while risk for Ecu investments remains lower. This is important because, even if the Ecu proved not to be an important addition to portfolios in national habitats, it is a most important addition to the European habitat. There, Ecu securities beat diversified foreign currency portfolios both in terms of return and risk.

It is clear that results are predominantly influenced by exchange rate

Exhibit 9.1

Minimum variance portfolios constrained to foreign-currency assets

A. Q4 1984 – Q4 1989

Share of	*Currency of habitat*						
	JPY	*US$*	*DM*	*Dfl*	*Ffr*	*GBP*	*Ecu*
			a. *Minimum variance portfolio***				
JPY		−0.22	0.04	0.00	−0.06	−0.02	0.02
US$	−0.04		0.01	0.00	0.01	−0.06	0.04
DM	1.76	−0.70		0.52	0.36	−2.52	0.31
Dfl	−5.12	−8.97	0.73		−1.25	−1.88	0.39
Ffr	−1.98	−0.62	0.02	−0.21		−0.74	0.07
GBP	−0.32	−1.47	−0.08	−0.06	−0.21		0.14
Ecu	6.71	13.00	0.25	0.75	2.15	6.24	
Return*	1.88	6.13	1.39	1.37	2.11	3.93	1.72
Risk*	3.50	5.00	0.29	0.27	0.65	1.29	0.21
			b. *Pure-risk portfolio***				
JPY		−0.03	−0.13	−0.04	−0.03	−0.03	0.04
US$	−0.09		−0.20	−0.09	−0.09	−0.14	−0.10
DM	−2.31	−3.31		−2.36	−2.26	−2.76	−3.38
Dfl	−0.17	0.76	−3.50		−0.09	2.17	2.70
Ffr	−0.07	−0.13	−0.51	−0.08		0.64	0.84
GBP	−0.52	−0.60	−0.60	−0.49	−0.48		−0.15
Ecu	3.16	3.31	4.96	3.07	2.98	0.13	
Return*	1.00	1.00	1.00	1.00	1.00	1.00	1.00
Risk*	0.69	0.92	1.08	0.70	0.70	1.19	1.10

* On a quarterly basis

** Due to rounding, the sum of currency shares may not add up to the constraints (i.e. 1 for MVP and 0 for PRP).

Exhibit 9.1 (continued)

Minimum variance portfolios constrained to foreign currency assets

Q4 1984 – Q4 1990

Share of	*Currency of habitat*						
	JPY	*US$*	*DM*	*Dfl*	*Ffr*	*GBP*	*Ecu*
			a. *Minimum variance portfolio***				
JPY		−0.05	0.03	−0.02	0.01	0.02	0.01
US$	0.07		0.01	−0.02	0.01	−0.10	0.02
DM	4.68	0.47		0.58	0.32	−1.61	0.08
Dfl	−3.01	−7.36	0.82		−1.05	−2.52	0.57
Ffr	−1.51	−0.35	0.06	−0.13		−0.79	0.17
GBP	0.62	−1.04	−0.07	−0.06	−0.21		0.13
Ecu	0.14	9.34	0.13	0.66	1.96	6.01	
Return*	1.07	5.94	1.49	1.58	2.16	3.92	1.90
Risk*	4.01	4.85	0.34	0.46	0.69	1.46	0.29
			b. *Pure-risk portfolio***				
JPY		−0.02	−0.11	−0.04	−0.04	−0.08	−0.04
US$	−0.15		−0.20	−0.14	−0.15	−0.18	−0.18
DM	−1.57	−3.77		−1.77	−1.35	−1.45	−2.06
Dfl	−0.54	1.24	−2.29		−0.74	0.66	1.58
Ffr	−0.09	−0.16	−0.27	−0.00		0.36	0.71
GBP	−0.41	−0.59	−0.36	−0.34	−0.35		−0.00
Ecu	2.78	3.31	3.24	2.31	2.65	0.71	
Return*	1.00	1.00	1.00	1.00	1.00	1.00	1.00
Risk*	0.87	1.27	1.08	0.88	0.89	1.15	1.18

* On a quarterly basis

** Due to rounding, the sum of currency shares may not add up to the constraints (i.e. 1 for MVP and 0 for PRP).

movements rather than by interest rate differentials, which are of less magnitude. As a consequence, returns on foreign currency portfolios are highest in countries with a strongly depreciating currency during the period of analysis: the US and the UK. High risk, as measured by the portfolios' standard deviation, is not concentrated on depreciating currencies but, as one would expect, on those currencies with strong exchange rate movements in either direction, ie those of Japan, the US and the UK. Habitats of the Deutschmark zone (Germany, the Netherlands) are an exception because there international portfolio risk is the lowest. This is because, with a long position in Deutschmark, Ecu or both, returns in domestic currencies are not greatly affected by exchange rate variations.

For any habitat except Germany, the Ecu is the most important investment currency. Results are quite stable over time, with the exception of the Ecu's share in the Japanese habitat.

International portfolio management

It is worthwhile comparing the results in Exhibit 9.1 with those in Exhibit 9.2, where investors in each habitat choose a portfolio of securities in a variety of currencies, including their home currency (called the "international portfolio"). One might expect that the minimum variance property of the Ecu would diminish its attractiveness for such a portfolio, as opposed to one where the choice is restricted to foreign currencies. Exhibit 9.2 shows this is right, but only in a restricted sense. For MVP, the Ecu regularly occupies the most important share after the domestic currency, even in habitats outside the ERM. However, virtually all Ecu positions, except in the Ecu habitat, are now short.

Comparing returns and risks of the international portfolio with those on domestic assets, an unambiguous result emerges for all habitats; the risk of the international portfolio is smaller than that of the domestic portfolio at the cost of smaller returns. These results are exactly the opposite of those obtained in the previous comparision of a foreign currency portfolio with a domestic portfolio.

Exhibit 9.2

Summary of optimal international portfolios

A. Q4 1984 – Q4 1989

	Currency of habitat						
Share of	*JPY*	*US$*	*DM*	*Dfl*	*Ffr*	*GBP*	*Ecu*
			a. *Minimum variance portfolio***				
JPY	0.98	0.00	0.04	0.02	0.01	0.03	0.02
US$	0.03	1.01	0.02	0.02	0.02	0.03	0.03
DM	0.27	0.22	0.94	0.03	0.10	0.25	0.21
Dfl	0.10	0.05	0.25	1.05	0.13	0.26	0.23
Ffr	−0.04	−0.03	−0.00	−0.03	0.89	−0.01	0.02
GBP	0.08	0.04	0.03	0.02	0.02	1.10	0.08
Ecu	−0.42	−0.30	−0.29	−0.13	−0.19	−0.68	0.38
Return*	1.01	1.74	1.13	1.33	1.99	2.46	1.80
Risk*	0.20	0.19	0.18	0.13	0.17	0.32	0.20
			b. *Pure-risk portfolio***				
JPY	−0.03	−0.04	−0.04	−0.04	−0.04	−0.04	−0.04
US$	−0.09	−0.09	−0.09	−0.09	−0.09	−0.09	−0.09
DM	−2.19	−2.07	−2.18	−2.19	−2.18	−2.18	−2.18
Dfl	−0.33	−0.35	−0.32	−0.31	−0.30	−0.24	−0.30
Ffr	−0.13	−0.13	−0.13	−0.13	−0.13	−0.11	−0.13
GBP	−0.52	−0.50	−0.51	−0.51	−0.51	−0.50	0.51
Ecu	3.31	3.20	3.30	3.30	3.28	3.18	3.28
Return*	1.00	1.00	1.00	1.00	1.00	1.00	
Risk*	0.68	0.71	0.69	0.69	0.69	0.69	0.69
			c. *Efficient portfolio with same risk as habitat***				
JPY	0.98	0.00	0.02	0.01	0.00	0.02	0.01
US$	0.00	0.99	−0.00	−0.00	0.00	0.00	0.01
DM	−0.25	−0.06	0.33	−0.52	−0.38	−0.52	−0.38
Dfl	0.02	0.00	0.16	0.97	0.06	0.17	0.14
Ffr	−0.07	−0.05	−0.04	−0.07	0.86	−0.05	−0.01
GBP	−0.04	−0.02	−0.11	−0.11	−0.09	0.92	−0.05
Ecu	0.36	0.14	0.23	0.72	0.55	0.44	1.28
Return Port.*	1.25	1.88	1.41	1.59	2.21	2.82	2.07
Return Dom.*	1.18	1.85	1.23	1.43	2.10	2.70	2.00
Differ.	0.06	0.02	0.18	0.16	0.11	0.11	0.07
Risk*	0.25	0.21	0.26	0.22	0.23	0.40	0.27

* On a quarterly basis

** Due to rounding, the sum of currency shares may not add up to the constraints (ie 0 for the PRP and 1 for the MVP and the efficient portfolio).

Exhibit 9.2 (continued)

Summary of optimal international portfolios

Q4 1984 – Q4 1990

	Currency of habitat						
Share of	*JPY*	*US$*	*DM*	*Dfl*	*Ffr*	*GBP*	*Ecu*
			a. *Minimum variance portfolio***				
JPY	0.99	0.00	0.05	0.04	0.02	0.04	0.03
US$	0.03	1.00	0.03	0.03	0.02	0.04	0.04
DM	−0.10	0.10	0.51	−0.26	−0.11	−0.28	−0.08
Dfl	0.26	0.02	0.53	1.32	0.28	0.57	0.40
Ffr	−0.01	−0.04	0.02	0.00	0.92	0.02	0.04
GBP	0.01	0.01	−0.02	−0.01	−0.00	1.02	0.04
Ecu	−0.19	−0.11	−0.13	−0.12	−0.13	−0.42	0.53
Return*	1.16	1.80	1.30	1.44	2.08	2.69	1.92
Risk*	0.25	0.18	0.27	0.22	0.20	0.40	0.23
			b. *Pure-risk portfolio***				
JPY	0.00	−0.01	−0.01	−0.01	−0.01	−0.01	−0.01
US$	−0.13	−0.13	−0.13	−0.13	−0.13	−0.13	−0.13
DM	−1.86	−1.68	−1.85	−1.85	−1.84	−1.85	−1.84
Dfl	−0.29	−0.39	−0.32	−0.30	−0.31	−0.28	−0.31
Ffr	−0.11	−0.11	−0.11	−0.10	−0.11	−0.10	−0.11
GBP	−0.43	−0.41	−0.43	−0.43	−0.43	−0.42	−0.43
Ecu	2.83	2.75	2.85	2.85	2.85	2.81	2.84
Return*	1.00	1.00	1.00	1.00	1.00	1.00	1.00
Risk*	0.86	0.86	0.86	0.86	0.85	0.85	0.85
			c. *Efficient portfolio with same risk as habitat**				
JPY	0.99	0.00	0.05	0.04	0.02	0.05	0.03
US$	0.05	1.02	0.07	0.06	0.05	0.08	0.07
DM	0.20	0.26	1.07	0.21	0.28	0.33	0.38
Dfl	0.31	0.06	0.62	1.40	0.35	0.66	0.48
Ffr	0.00	−0.03	0.06	0.02	0.95	0.05	0.06
GBP	0.09	0.05	0.10	0.10	0.08	1.16	0.15
Ecu	−0.65	−0.36	−0.99	−0.85	−0.76	−1.35	−0.19
Return Port.*	1.33	1.89	1.60	1.70	2.29	3.02	2.17
Return Dom.*	1.25	1.86	1.36	1.53	2.18	2.85	2.09
Differ.	0.07	0.02	0.24	0.16	0.11	0.17	0.08
Risk*	0.29	0.20	0.37	0.31	0.27	0.49	0.32

* On a quarterly basis

** Due to rounding, the sum of currency shares may not add up to the constraints (ie 0 for the PRP and 1 for the MVP and the efficient portfolio).

One might have expected that when the foreign currency yields higher returns and higher risk than the domestic portfolio, then combining both portfolios should still yield higher returns and higher risk. Thus, why are return and risk now lower compared to the purely domestic MVP? This occurs because the portfolio manager must select the portfolio with the smallest variance. If the international portfolio does not have a smaller variance than the domestic one, he simply picks the domestic portfolio.

From Exhibits 9.1 and 9.2, it can be seen that the Ecu is not only of interest for investors based in EMS currencies. Habitats with more volatile Ecu exchange rates (Japanese yen, sterling, US dollar) should, in fact, make optimally greater use of the Ecu.

In Exhibit 9.2 the share of the Ecu in the MVP of the Ecu habitat is positive and increasing, thereby reinforcing similar conclusions obtained from Exhibit 9.1. This confirms the belief that the Ecu has very desirable characteristics for the integrated European market. As the EC gets closer to the single-market objective, the importance of national habitat loses ground. Companies will become increasingly European and measure their performance on a European scale, particularly when ownership spreads beyond national boundaries. It should be recalled that the above results are obtained from purely financial considerations and independently of the role of the Ecu as a transaction currency.

Pure risk portfolios

MVPs are useful benchmarks, but the composition of the portfolio along the efficiency frontier is of more general interest.

As argued above, a knowledge of the composition of MVP and PRP is sufficient for the determination of any efficient point. Exhibits 9.1 and 9.2 also provide the composition of PRP for both the foreign and international portfolios, with quarterly returns normalised at unity. This normalisation does not affect relative shares, but facilitates the comparison of the price of risk across habitats. For the international portfolio, the choice set is the same for all habitats and therefore the PRP are virtually invariant across habitats.

The price of risk – that is, the standard deviation of returns in relation to average returns – is also invariant across habitats. In Exhibit 9.1, where domestic currency is excluded, the PRP and the price of risk vary across habitats. The dominant feature in all habitats is a long position in Ecu and a short position in Deutschmark (or guilders for German investors), exploiting the yield differential and the high exchange rate correlation between Ecu and Deutschmark.

In both PRP, with and without domestic currency, the share of the Ecu is positive and largely dominant. This implies that, in all habitats, portfolios moving outwards along the efficiency frontier exhibit rising long shares in Ecu. Thus, the assumption that Ecu assets are only suited to investors pursuing minimum risk is not sustainable. It is particularly worth noting the extreme sensitivity of the composition of the portfolio along the efficiency frontier at its beginning, near the MVP. This simple fact explains why, despite its negative share of the international portfolio MVP, Ecu shares increase very rapidly to a positive contribution in the efficient portfolios. Consequently, previous judgments about the relation between low-risk investment strategies and shares of the Ecu should be tempered.

What actually accounts for increasing, positive Ecu shares along the efficiency frontier? From traditional portfolio theory, we know that any point on the efficiency frontier can be replicated with a combination of a MVP and a market portfolio. As the Ecu, among the different currencies, is closest to the notion of a market portfolio, it is natural that it figures predominantly in the PRP.

To demonstrate the ambiguity of a judgment based solely on the composition of MVP, Exhibit 9.2 also gives the composition of an efficient international portfolio. This includes domestic currency, which would exhibit exactly the same risk level as the habitat currency, but a higher return. The Ecu's share is generally the largest (in absolute value) of all foreign currencies, demonstrating two fundamental features: first, the advantage of international diversification; second, the strong role of the Ecu. On average, the international portfolio generates a net gain on returns of 50 basis points per year for the same level of risk as the domestic portfolio. This gain was particularly pronounced in 1990 and is consistently highest for the Deutschmark habitat.

While the sign of the Ecu share in the efficient portfolio based on the experience of the fourth quarter of 1984 to the fourth quarter of 1989 is positive for all habitat currencies, it is uniformly negative when estimated over the period of the fourth quarter of 1984 to the fourth quarter of 1990. This sign reversal also holds true for the Deutschmark, but in the opposite direction. This kind of instability is not uncommon in the application of the portfolio approach, and, in this particular case, can be rationalised as follows. Because of the structural links existing between the Ecu and the EMS currencies, inclusion of the Ecu in a portfolio increases the possibility of arbitrage between the Ecu and other European currencies. As the interest rate differential between the Ecu and the Deutschmark/guilder has narrowed strongly, the efficient policy has shifted from investments in Ecu and guilders of funds borrowed in Deutschmark to investments in Deutschmark and guilder and financed in Ecu.

It is noteworthy that, while returns on MVP are dominated by exchange rate movements, returns on PRP, and hence the movement along the efficiency frontier, are dominated by interest-rate differentials. As shown in Steinherr and Girard (1989), only exchange rate movements among the reference currencies, but not those involving the habitat currency, which are by far the largest, have an impact on PRP. Another consequence is that the price of pure risk is the same for all habitats as long as the domesic currency is included in the portfolio.

The role of the Ecu in theoretically contracted optimal portfolios heavily exceeds actual shares. For example, a German investor could achieve as low a risk as with a pure Deutschmark investment but a 100 basis points higher return with an internationally diversified portfolio. In the light of the generally less diversified structure of portfolios, it seems that information and transaction costs are too high to break down established investment patterns. The fact that these computations benefit from hindsight may also contribute a partial, but certainly not a fully satisfactory, explanation, as the Ecu's share in the optimal portfolio structure is relatively stable. An investor who had based his portfolio allocation for 1990 on the ex-post computation up to end-1989 would have been near the optimum.

The optimal share of the Ecu in 1990 has not increased in all habitats. Yet investors still bought many more Ecu securities in 1990 (and above all in 1991) than in 1989. The explanation appears to be that actual shares are far below optimal ones, and the difference has been narrowing in 1991. The fact that optimal shares did not increase in 1990 should be related to tighter Ecu yields, reflecting lower premiums for reduced risks not considered explicitly in the portfolio balance approach. The question of Ecu pricing is pursued in the next section.

Ecu yield curves, bond pricing and arbitrage

For a long time, the Ecu market suffered from two imperfections, typical of a young market: first, issues were relatively small in size and, consequently, institutional investors were lacking; and, second, the maturities of bond issues were concentrated at the shorter end of the market, with only a few issues having maturities up to 10 years. Starting in June 1988 with the European Coal and Steel Community (ECSC) issue of Ecu500 million and an initial maturity of six years, establishment of true benchmarks along the yield curve has proliferated.

Because the Ecu bond market is unique in that it lacks a clean-cut domestic counterpart in which government bonds normally set benchmarks, the development of benchmarks is particularly crucial. Once benchmarks exist, the pricing of a newly issued bond (or the assessing of the value of a bond in the secondary market) is made more objective and transparent when determined as a spread over the current benchmark yield.

In a study of comparative market liquidity and effiency, Grammatikos and Steinherr (1990) show that up to early 1990 bid–ask spreads in Ecu markets, even for the larger benchmark issues, compare unfavourably with those observed in liquid national markets like the US, UK and Japan. In these markets spreads are typically less than 10 basis points and half as wide as the bid–ask spreads for Ecu benchmarks. This situation has greatly improved since then, and the most liquid benchmark spreads are as low as 10 basis points, but the Ecu market has not yet fully caught up with the most liquid national markets.

By contrasts, Ecu markets compare more favourably in terms of efficiency. Grammatikos and Steinherr use the random walk hypothesis as an efficiency benchmark to test the speed of adjustment of prices to their new level when unexpected information is released in the market. Their results suggest that the highest efficiency is observed in government bond markets of the US, UK and Germany, followed by Ecu benchmarks. This ranking has not been upset in the meantime, but efficiency in Ecu markets has increased.

Since February 1991, government and EIB issues provide a full range of highly liquid benchmarks from four to 20 years. The largest and most spectacular issues were those by the governments of Italy, by amount and maturity (20 years), UK, France and Italy, by the amounts in the seven- to 10 years maturity range, and Spain and Belgium, in the four- to five-years maturity range. The 20-year benchmark is particularly important because it offers institutional investors liquidity in a section of the European bond market which was liquid only in France. US and Japanese fund managers with long duration targets can now shift into European currencies. Some of this demand could have benefited the Deutschmark if such long maturities had been available.

In our view the Italian issue will set the pace for other long-dated Ecu bonds by providing a benchmark and satisfying investors' demand, for which there are far too few alternatives (US dollar and French franc). Furthermore, due to its basket structure and, therefore, very low exchange risk, the Ecu is ideally suited to long maturities. Recent political initiatives have discussed "hardening" the Ecu, either by stopping recompositions at five-year intervals or by introducing a multiple option on the Ecu by not devaluing it in terms of any component currency. As shown in Steinherr and Girard (1989), the risk premium necessary to compensate investors for the risk of recomposition (ie the risk of capital losses as recomposition tends to lower the weight of hard and therefore low-yield currencies and thus increases the Ecu interest) rises with the maturity of the bond. Thus what stimulates the current trend in favour of longer issues is the reduced long-term risk of the Ecu, namely recomposition or political oblivion. Hardening would lower Ecu yields and therefore make it more attractive to investors. For an analysis of the various proposals for hardening the Ecu, see Steinherr (1990). Hardening the Ecu with a multiple currency option would, of course, increase the value of outstanding Ecu bonds. CSFB (1990) estimate, on the basis of the stocks of Ecu bonds outstanding on 3 December 1990, the transfer of wealth from bond issues to investors is equal to Ecu1.8 billion. This amount has substantially increased and it now appears unlikely that the "hardening option" will be implemented.

Under current market conditions, Ecu pricing in primary markets has become much easier and similar to pricing in developed national markets. Spreads to benchmarks mainly reflect credit risk and liquidity premiums.

In the secondary market three compartments have emerged.[2] Within the first tier, composed of benchmark issues, bid–offer spreads are as low as 20 basis points, and market efficiency is higher than in any other European market except the Deutschmark. This efficiency is measured by a regression of daily price changes on their lags.

The second tier is composed of relatively liquid bonds without benchmark character. The spreads fluctuate widely among themselves. When a bond ceases to be liquid and joins the third tier, then dramatic yield changes are common. Illiquid bonds, therefore, have very variable spreads compared to the second tier (even for the same issuer) but quite stable spreads to the swap curve. Investors not concerned with liquidity can pick up to 80 basis points in yield increases by switching between liquid and illiquid Ecu sectors.

The illiquid sector uses the swap market as a "floor" with second-tier bonds having a spread from zero up to 75 basis points. While the top tier hardly uses the swap market (issuers are usually end users of Ecu), the second tier is strongly related to it. Until recently, the third tier also participated strongly in the swap market but during the last two years supply has dried up.

Because the Ecu is a basket, it is natural to compare its yields with a weighted average of the component yields. The latter is called the theoretic or synthetic Ecu yield. Synthetic yield curves were particularly useful when no market benchmarks existed. Even now they are appreciated as an indication of whether Ecu issues, inclusive of benchmarks, are properly priced.

However, great care is needed in constructing synthetic yield curves.[3] There are manageable theoretical and problematical empirical problems. The theoretical issues concern weighting of yields derived from zero coupon bonds and the fact that current Ecu weights are not adequate for future maturities as long as exchange rates are not definitely fixed. Hence, it becomes necessary to project expected exchange rates and thus weights. A

2. See McCree (1991).
3. For such constructions, see CSFB Research (1988), Paribas (1988) and Steinherr and Girard (1989).

logical approach involves using implied interest-rate parity. This may not always be correct: during periods when realignments are considered imminent, the theoretical rate could decline more strongly.

Steinherr and Girard show that properly weighted synthetic yields can be as much as 10 basis points below the simple weighted average. On the basis of interest-rate parity, low-yield currencies are expected to appreciate, increasing their weights and lowering the average yield.

The empirical issues mainly pertain to the available data. On numerous European markets, liquid, high-quality zero coupon-bonds do not exist and even coupon-bond yields exist only for a limited number of maturities. Where a sufficient number of maturities can be observed, the solution generally adopted involves using polynominal regression. This approximation affects the estimate of the zero-coupon bond yield curve, with the error increasing in magnitude with maturity. The magnitude of observational error is likely to be five to 10 basis points.

As Ecu bonds are Eurobonds, having securities in component currencies of identical maturity, liquidity and credit risk in the Euromarket would be ideal. However, such instruments do not exist. Therefore, securities in internal markets where yields are influenced by regulatory and tax treatments are used. Hence the empirical approximation is rather crude.

Exhibit 9.3 shows the evolution of the spread since the beginning of 1990 between actual and theoretical rates as computed by Paribas. Spreads have been volatile over time, predominantly positive until early 1990 and declining and negative since then. Therefore something has changed in the market which now pays a premium for Ecu bonds. The change is particularly due to the reduced political risk of the Ecu and the support given to the various proposals for hardening the Ecu.

Spreads as large as those in Exhibit 9.3 raise the question of the role of arbitrage between the basket and the Ecu. Possible measurement errors

Exhibit 9.3 **Spreads of market minus theoretical Ecu yields, month-end observations from June 1988 to June 1991**

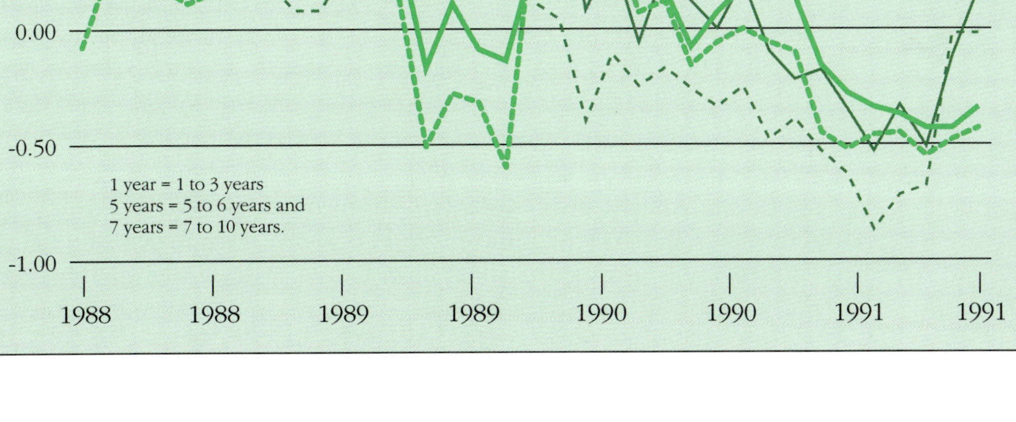

Source: DATASTREAM interest rates are computed for a pool of most liquid issues which change over time, maturity bands illustrated.

should bias the theoretical rate upwards or downwards and therefore cannot explain away the problem, as the spread has changed sign. During 1990 and 1991, the maximum between positive and negative spreads is about 100 basis points for all maturities. As spreads were more positive before 1990, the long-term movement of the spread is even more pronounced. Given that the cost of bundling or unbundling is estimated to be around 20 to 30 basis points, how are spreads as high as 100 basis points explained? A partial explanation is that the cost of unbundling underestimates the arbitrage cost, because counterparty risk in several EC markets is high and instruments are lacking.

The main reason, however, is that the Ecu and its underlying basket are not the same thing, ie the Ecu is to some extent independent of the basket. It should also be noted that there is no legal convertibility obligation of the Ecu into the basket and vice versa. The basket only served as a useful definitional device during the infancy stage. A complete decoupling from the basket is perfectly feasible, particularly at a later stage, when the transaction role of the Ecu becomes more important. This independence from the basket is demonstrated most clearly by the recomposition risk which affects the Ecu and not the basket. For the basket interest rate, one need not project exchange rate movements to find its average interest rate. Hence even with zero transaction costs one should not expect arbitrate to equalise actual and theoretical rates.

As a consequence of the Ecu's improved perspectives as an independent currency, the net asset position of Ecu banking intermediation has been drastically reduced. According to Bank for International Settlements (BIS) statistics, total net Ecu assets have declined from Ecu14 billion in 1988 (Q2) to Ecu3 billion in 1990 (Q2) and Ecu0.7 billion in 1990 (Q3).[4] It seems logical that the premium charged by banks for holding excess assets has diminished with dwindling excess asset holdings. This is likely to be the reason behind the very pronounced decline in the spread of money market instruments.

As argued before, liquidity and efficiency have improved dramatically during 1990 and 1991. Hence measures of Ecu yields are not comparable over time. An index of liquid Ecu bonds now contains more liquid issues (with a lower credit risk because all benchmark issues are government or EIB issues) than previously. Therefore observed market yields are necessarily lower, *cet. par.*, and contribute to a larger negative spread. In addition to the recent spate of benchmark issues, the availability of an Ecu bond futures contract on the MATIF (and another one on LIFFE since March 1991) contributed further to the reduction in the liquidity premium. Four months after its launching in October 1990, more than 100 financial institutions have traded the Ecu bond futures contract. At the end of February 1991, the open interest position exceeded 4,000 contracts and daily trading activity exceeded 4,000 contracts on several sessions. These contracts facilitate hedging of interest rate risk for long-dated Ecu securities and allow trading of the futures, instead of the occasionally illiquid cash position. This makes holding any Ecu issues, even when illiquid, more attractive. In comparison, short-term Ecu futures and options available on LIFFE have been unsuccessful because the exchange-rate risk on the Ecu is already minimal due to its basket construction.

4. Committee of governors (1991).

Clearly, the theoretical rate is not a solid basis for arbitrage operations and can, at best, only suggest the market's changing evaluation of the Ecu's attractiveness and independence.

Conclusions

Theoretical considerations based on return and risk give prominence to Ecu securities in optimally diversified international portfolios. This prominence is not confined to European habitats and is just as pronounced overseas. Moreover, Ecu securities are not only appealing to risk-averse investors. In the absence of diversification they are indeed attractive for their low risk. However, in a diversified portfolio the share of Ecu investments increases with the desired risk of the investor.

The Ecu is an increasingly independent investment vehicle. As the Ecu market grows, its definition as a basket of currencies loses relevance. The Ecu was always different from a basket and not tied to it by a convertibility clause, making arbitrage between the two costly and imperfect.

Thus the theoretic yield curve of the Ecu is a crude approximation, being based on the basket. Happily, the need for a theoretic benchmark has declined as large government issues and a long-term futures market have established market benchmarks along the yield curve up to 20 years. Liquidity and efficiency in the top tier of the Ecu market are now only surpassed by those in US dollar or Deutschmark markets.

References

Committee of governors of the central banks of the member states of the EC (1991). *Recent developments in the use of the private Ecu: statistical review.* February.

CSFB Research (1988). *Ecu recomposition and the true synthetic yield.* September.

– (1990). *European Monetary Union: What value Ecu bonds?* December.

Grammatikos, Harry, and Steinherr, Alfred (1990). *Liquidity and efficiency in the Ecu bond market.* EIB.

Hamui, Rony (1984). "Lo sviluppo dei mercati finanziari in Ecu: una prima valutazione su rischi e rendimenti". *Bancaria*, May.

Markowitz, Harry M. (1970). *Portfolio selection.* Yale University Press.

Masera, Rainer S. (1987). *L'unificazione monetaria e lo SME.* Il Mulino, Bologna.

McCree, Julian (1991). *The Ecu bond market technical aspects.* Greenwell Montagu Gilt-Edged.

Paribas (1988). *The Ecu bond market.* October.

Steinherr, Alfred (1990). "Roles for the Ecu in the process of achieving European Monetary Union". *The Journal of International Securities Markets.* Winter.

Steinherr, Alfred, and Girard, Jacques (1989). "*The Ecu: a currency unlike any other*". EIB Papers.

Steinherr, Alfred, and Girard, Jacques (1991). "*Ecu financial markets: recent evolution and perspectives*". Université Catholique de Louvain, W. P. 8907, 1989; to appear in A. Steinherr and D. Weiserbs (eds.), *Evolution of international and regional monetary systems – essays in honour of Robert Triffin.* Macmillan, London.

10

William Ledward,
Liisa Salojarvi and
Akira Yasuoka
Nomura Research Institute Europe Ltd.

Investors in Ecu: the case of Japan

Macroeconomic incentives

During the early years of the Ecu, in the late 1970s and the early 1980s, the macroeconomic incentives for Japanese investment in Ecu instruments were not great. The main reason was that EC member states responded to the second oil shock of 1979-80 in a variety of unco-ordinated ways, generated primarily by national rather than Community objectives. The result was frequent European Monetary System (EMS) realignments, strengthening of controls on international capital movements, divergent economic performances, widening inflation differentials, etc. Inasmuch as Japanese investors wanted to invest in European currencies at all, they looked to the least risky and most stable economy, Germany.

The strongest reason for investing in Ecu bonds during this period was one of risk reduction. Because interest rates in the 12 (from 1981) member states of the EC were not moving in tandem – indeed, sometimes they were moving in the opposite direction – interest rates on Ecu instruments were substantially less volatile than interest rates in the Ecu's 12 component currencies. As a result the volatility of returns was substantially lower for Ecu bonds than for Deutschmark, French franc or sterling bonds. However, this did not motivate Japanese investors, for whom the relative volatility between European bond markets was a minor question compared to the future movement of the yen against European currencies.

The Ecu bond market's resurgence in the early 1990s followed from the renewed drive towards Economic and Monetary Union (EMU) within the EC. The implications of the April 1989 Delors Report for the Ecu and the Ecu bond market are profound. As far as the Ecu is concerned, there was a commitment that it would become a much stronger currency than hitherto – that it would, in time, become as strong as the Deutschmark. This impression was given added impetus when the European Council, meeting to consider the Delors Report, made a formal announcement that the Ecu would be the future single European currency. The assurance that the Ecu would be a currency with a life of its own, in the care of an institution in the image of the Bundesbank, undoubtedly increased its attractiveness for Japanese investors.

Exhibit 10.1 **Deutschmark/Ecu exchange rate, 1984–91**

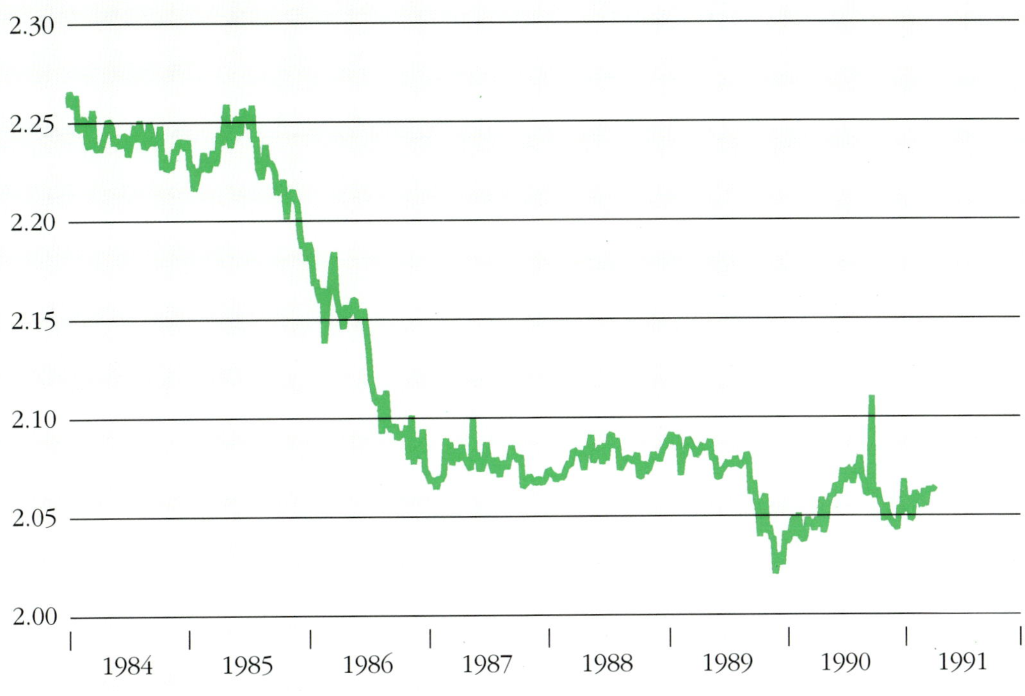

In theory, interest rates on Ecu instruments are an average of interest rates on its 12 component currencies, although it requires some complexity to work out what is the correct theoretical level. Ecu interest rates have always been much higher than German interest rates, a reflection of the

Exhibit 10.2 **Deutschmark and Ecu bond yields, 1984–91**

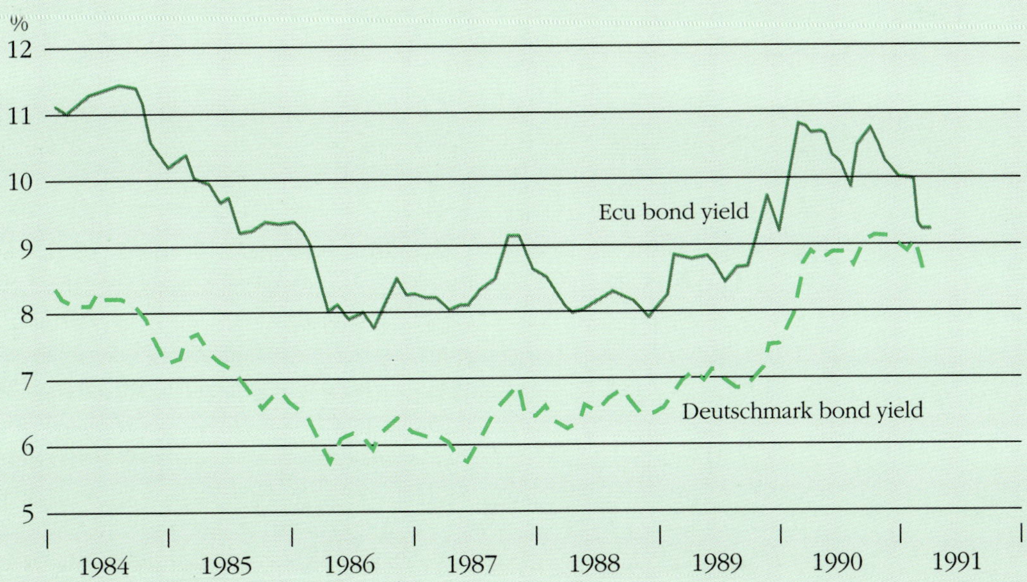

Source: Datastream.

higher interest rates available in some of the component currencies (for example, sterling, the peseta and the lira). These higher interest rates reflect the market's expectation that these currencies would depreciate against the Deutschmark in the longer term. Therefore the higher level of Ecu interest rates reflected the extent to which the market thought that the Ecu would depreciate against the Deutschmark.

The Delors Report led the market to reconsider to what extent the "weaker" EMS currencies, and hence the Ecu, would depreciate against the Deutschmark in the run-up to monetary union. Some depreciation was to be expected, but would it really be as much as the market was expecting in late 1989? The answer was no, and from then until mid-1991 there was a redirection of international capital away from the lower-yielding German and Dutch markets to the higher-yielding French, British and, eventually, Spanish and Italian markets. The Ecu market has benefited from this trend as well. Japanese investors have played a part in this movement but because of lack of knowledge have preferred the Ecu market.

Japanese investors' international bond investments

Japanese investors' foreign securities investments

In order to put Japanese investors' involvement in Ecu bonds into context, it is necessary broadly to review developments in Japanese investments abroad in recent years.

Japanese investors have been permitted to purchase foreign securities freely since December 1980, when the Japanese government began to liberalise international capital flows. Previously, certain investors, such as

Exhibit 10.3 **Japanese investors' net purchases of foreign bonds, 1986–90**

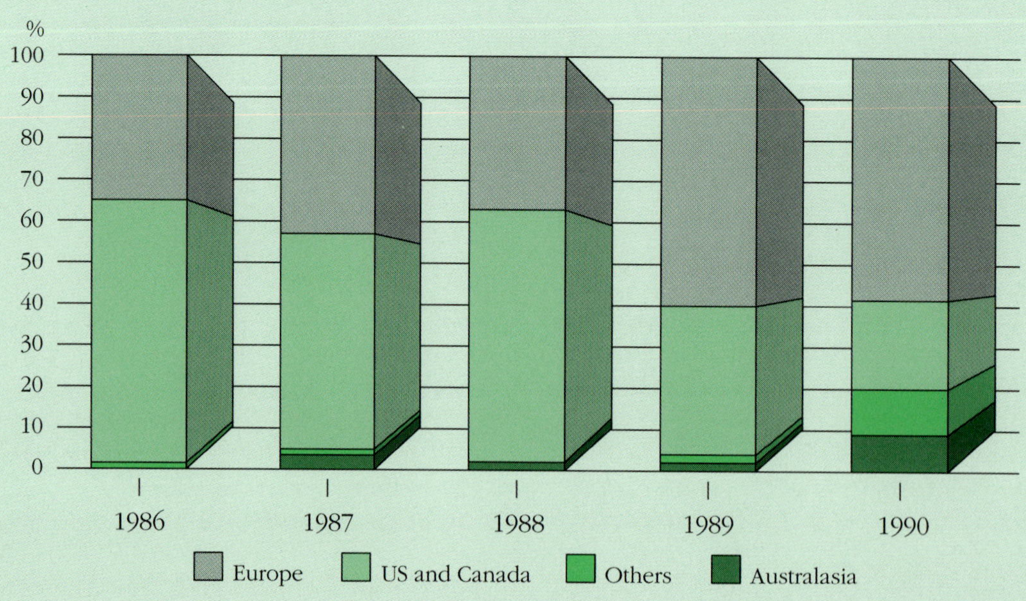

Source: Datastream.

life insurance companies and security investment trusts, were allowed to buy foreign securities, but only within a certain (low) limit. This restrictive system, and favourable domestic investment opportunities, particularly in the stock market, meant that investments in foreign securities were small. When Japanese institutions were suddenly allowed to invest abroad, there was a large and rapid increase in investment in foreign securities, due mainly to the lack of profitable investment opportunities domestically in Japan, and higher rates of return abroad. Initially the funds went mainly to the US, strengthening the dollar relative to the yen.

Exhibit 10.4 shows net purchases of foreign securities by Japanese investors since 1985, broken down by country, as published by the Ministry of Finance (MOF).

Exhibit 10.4 includes purchases of bonds and equities. It shows some important developments in Japanese investors' foreign securities purchases: total investments moved from a low level at the beginning of the 1980s to over US$55 billion in 1985. It then doubled to around US$100 billion in 1986 and stayed roughly at that level until 1990. In 1990, a considerable and historic change took place, as foreign investments fell by 65 per cent compared to 1989.

This fall was due to the historically unusual situation of a net sale of securities in major markets such as the US, Germany and Australia and a reduction of net purchases in the UK and Canada. Some countries did, however, at the same time experience an increase. One example is France, suggesting that a certain amount of switching out of Germany into France took place in the wake of German reunification. Switzerland and the group of "other" countries also experienced an increase. The others include mainly the smaller European bond markets and Ecu-denominated bonds. The entry for Luxembourg includes Eurodollar bonds, Euroyen bonds, Euro-equity warrants, and convertible bonds issued by Japanese companies, which are usually listed in either Luxembourg or London.

Portfolio outflows from Japan have traditionally been dominated by bond flows, and, according to data from the Japanese Securities Dealers

Exhibit 10.4

Geographic distribution of Japanese net purchases of securities abroad, 1985–91

%	*1985*	*1986*	*1987*	*1988*	*1989*	*1990*
US	56	49	41	41	23	−41
Canada	4	7	3	2	4	2
Germany	1	3	6	7	4	−5
Netherlands	0	0	1	1	0	0
France	0	0	1	1	3	14
Luxembourg	21	24	30	29	42	82
Switzerland	1	0	0	1	1	5
UK	11	13	10	12	10	5
Australia	2	0	3	2	1	−3
Others (incl. Ecu)	3	4	5	6	10	40
Total (US$ millions)	55,405	101,026	90,610	88,908	113,670	39,455

Source: Japanese Ministry of Finance.

Association (JSDA), purchases of foreign equities were less than 10 per cent and, in some years, almost insignificant. Exhibit 10.5 shows the outflows year by year, broken down between equities and bonds.

These data do not correspond exactly with the data from the MOF, for they capture only transactions by members of the Japanese Securities Dealers Association and thus do not include transactions conducted through banks and brokers based outside Japan.

As most Japanese purchases of foreign securities are bonds, it is possible to generalise by looking at the reasons for the fall in foreign bond purchases in 1990.

First, Japan's current account surplus, and with it the long-term capital account deficit (historically substantially larger than the current account), has fallen from a record high in 1987.

Second, Japanese interest rates, both long-term and short-term, were on an upward trend during 1990. The official discount rate (ODR) was increased twice, from 4.25 per cent to 6 per cent by the Bank of Japan (BOJ), in order to keep inflation under control, and other rates followed. This was in contrast to the US, where short-term rates were on a downward trend and long-term rates stayed roughly unchanged, resulting in a widening of the US/Japanese interest rate spread. At the same time, the US dollar weakened substantially against the yen, leaving yen-based investors with currency losses on US dollar assets. The relative attractiveness of investing at home, rather than abroad, therefore increased during this period.

Third, losses on domestic securities, both bonds and shares, prompted some selective selling of foreign securities which could generate profits to cover these losses. Particularly during periods where the US dollar was strong, there was significant Japanese profit-taking on US securities.

Fourth, the implementation of Bank for International Settlements (BIS) capital requirements by Japanese banks meant they were competing in the domestic market for capital that might otherwise have gone abroad. Also, interest rates on bank deposits were deregulated so that banks are now paying a much higher rate of interest on savings deposits, another factor limiting the incentive to give the money to insurance companies, who are more likely to move the funds abroad.

Finally, the Gulf crisis (sparked by Iraq's invasion of Kuwait) for a time clouded the outlook for international financial markets in general in

Exhibit 10.5

Analysis of Japanese net foreign securities purchases, 1986–90

	Bonds %	*Equities* %	*Total (US$m)*
1986	96	4	59,960
1987	95	5	68,878
1988	98	2	66,581
1989	95	5	77,011
1990	98	2	43,070

Includes only foreign currency denominated securities.
Source: Japanese Securities Dealers Association.

the latter part of 1990, dampening activity and increasing risk aversion in international financial markets.

Another factor, which presumably will not have any long-term effect, was the request around May 1990 by the MOF to life insurance companies and pension trusts not to buy US dollar securities to the same extent as was the historic norm. The worry was that this continued "over-financing" of Japan's current account surplus with the US would have a depressing effect on the yen against the US dollar, and also give rise to increasing protectionist sentiments in the US Congress, since a weak yen makes Japanese exports more competitive. However, it is a difficult task to put a stop to this outflow of capital, which is due in part to a continued lack of sufficiently profitable domestic investment opportunities, without the reintroduction of capital controls, which is clearly not in everybody's best interest.

Japanese investments in European bonds

Historically, Japanese investors have mainly been involved in US dollar-denominated bonds, first and foremost US Treasuries. Exhibit 10.6 shows the geographical distribution of net bond purchases as published by the JSDA. It can be seen that the purchase of US Treasury bonds was about 50 per cent of total bond purchases in the 1986–88 period, but has been on a downward trend since then, falling to 34 per cent in 1989 and to a low of 20 per cent last year (the data shown are not comparable with those in Exhibit 10.4 as they include only transactions done through members of the JSDA). The gap has been taken up partly by an increase in the purchase of bonds listed in Luxembourg, of which a significant percentage is likely to be Eurodollar and other Eurobonds. Investment in French bonds also rose markedly, as did that in Switzerland and the "others", at the expense of German bonds, a market in which Japanese investors were net sellers in 1990. They will include Ecu bonds, as well as "minor" European markets such as Denmark, Sweden, etc.

Japanese institutional investors' foreign bond strategy

In Japan there are three main groups of institutional investors, who have slightly different investment strategies:

- institutional investors such as insurance companies, securities investment trusts and pension trusts;
- non-financial corporations; and
- banks.

Japanese non-financial corporations have periodically invested large amounts in foreign securities, but a lack of data makes this difficult to quantify. At one point, before the fall in the Japanese stock market, Japanese companies would borrow money relatively cheaply via issues of convertible bonds and warrants and partly invest the proceeds in foreign securities, an activity called "Zaitech" operations, derived from the Japanese word for "corporate finance".

Japanese banks, on the other hand (as opposed to life insurance companies), are only permitted to hold a very small part of their foreign

Exhibit 10.6
Geographic distribution of net purchases of bonds abroad, 1986–90

%	*1986*	*1987*	*1988*	*1989*	*1990*
US	55.1	49.9	58.0	33.9	20.0
Canada	8.3	2.3	3.0	2.7	1.6
UK	6.4	6.7	9.0	9.9	1.7
Germany	0.8	4.4	3.6	0.2	−1.5
Luxembourg	25.3	27.8	20.4	42.7	48.5
Netherlands	0.1	0.3	0.5	−0.1	−0.3
France	0.4	0.9	0.9	2.3	5.6
Switzerland	−0.1	0.1	0.4	0.3	2.9
Belgium	2.1	3.1	2.5	3.7	2.0
Italy	0.2	0.0	0.0	0.4	−0.4
Hong Kong	0.1	0.1	0.5	1.3	4.3
Singapore	0.0	0.0	0.0	0.0	2.3
Australia	−0.1	2.1	1.4	0.7	2.8
New Zealand	−0.2	1.0	−0.3	−0.2	−0.1
Others (incl. Ecu)	1.6	1.5	0.3	2.2	10.8
Total (US$ million)	57,619	65,117	65,219	73,480	42,190

Includes only foreign currency denominated bonds
Source: Japanese Securities Dealers Association.

securities with the currency exposure unhedged. Thus for banks the movement of exchange rates, as well as the higher short-term interest rates available abroad, is made irrelevant by the required hedge transaction. It is therefore attractive for banks to invest in foreign securities only if they offer a yield advantage over domestic securities or if they are bullish about bond prices or the equity market.

In our study of Japanese foreign investments, we have concentrated on the institutional investors of the first category.

Life insurance companies: long-investment horizon

Japanese life insurance companies have gradually increased their holdings of foreign securities, and these nearly doubled between the fiscal years 1987 and 1989.

These companies all have the same three main objectives, which they seek to achieve in designing their foreign portfolio investment strategy:

1. *Yield.* Higher yield than on domestic investments. Traditionally, Japanese insurance companies' main investment objective has been related to current yield (coupon) because of the accounting treatment of capital gains. Total return does play a role as well, although a less prominent one. The degree of acceptable exchange-rate risk depends on the yield advantage in the foreign market.

2. *Liquidity.* Ideally, markets should be at least as liquid as the domestic bond market. It should be easy to trade in relatively large size,

without affecting the price adversely. This is the major reason why Japanese institutional investors have been so heavily involved in the US Treasury market.

3. *Cost*. The cost-effectiveness also plays a major part. This includes portfolio managers' and traders' salaries, research, transaction costs, etc. As individual European markets are quite small by international comparison, costly information gathering is required on the individual differences in these markets' products, currencies, tax systems, etc. This is where the Ecu bond market has an advantage in being a pan-European market, because it includes the 12 EC currencies in one.

The aims above are generally met by larger, "high-yielding" markets, and tend to generate a concentration on a few major markets, as shown in Exhibit 10.8. Life insurance companies are to a much lesser extent concerned with the benefits from investment diversification and the resulting reduction in portfolio risk.

Exhibit 10.8 shows that there has recently been a shift away from the heavy bias towards US and Canadian dollar-denominated assets in favour of European bond markets. The percentage held in US dollar assets was reduced from 75 per cent in 1986 to 64 per cent in 1990.

To provide a first-hand impression of Japanese life insurance companies' foreign investment strategy, there follow a number of statements made by representatives from these companies in a survey conducted by Nomura Research Institute in Tokyo.

Life Insurance company "A"

The slow-down in the growth of funds available for investment, coupled with increased domestic loan demand, has seen the surge in external portfolio investments run out of steam, and consequently Japanese institutions were net sellers of US Treasury bonds in 1990. However, the main part of our external investment portfolios are still US dollar-denominated, and primarily these are US domestic instruments rather than low-liquidity Eurodollar securities.

We will basically follow the same course in future. However, should the size of our portfolio increase, we will have to consider currency diversification as a means of reducing exchange rate risk. Over the last five years, the portfolio share of US dollar-denominated

Exhibit 10.7

Life insurance companies foreign assets, 1985–90

% (*fiscal year*)	*1985*	*1986*	*1987*	*1988*	*1989*
Equities	10	11	16	17	19
Government Bonds	32	43	43	41	42
Local Govt. Bonds	7	4	3	3	2
Corporate Bonds	50	41	35	35	32
Others	1	1	3	4	5
Total (Yen bn)	4,668	7,525	9,803	13,596	17,790

Source: Japanese Life Insurance Company Association.

Exhibit 10.8

Geographic distribution of life insurance companies' assets, 1986 and 1990

%	*1986*	*1990*
US	54	51
Canada	21	13
UK	4	6
Germany	2	4
France	1	4
Australia	4	6
Ecu	3	3
Other	11	13
Total (Yen bn)	**7,525**	**17,790**

Source: Nomura Research Institute, Tokyo.

products has dropped from 70 per cent to less than 60 per cent, with the gap being filled by European currency products.

Life insurance company "B"

While our external portfolio investments are unlikely to increase much in monetary terms this year and next, my own view is that we will have to maintain external portfolio investments at a certain level in the medium term. Fund management competition is so intense that we have to keep investing in assets with a yield higher than domestic rates. The question of how much, in terms of new funds, to commit to foreign investments must take into account exchange rate risk and other factors. Personally, I would set our ceiling for new fund injections at around 20 per cent.

A case can be made for Japanese investors to increase their involvement in Ecu bonds but, as yet, investments have been small. This partly reflects the small overall size of the market, although its share of the new issues market has been increasing, and the resulting low degree of liquidity. The yield motive usually stated as a reason for investing in Ecu instruments coincides with Japanese life insurance companies' general investment objectives. Ecu bonds have a higher yield than Deutschmark, French franc and guilder bonds, although not as high as UK gilts. They also yield more than both US dollar and Japanese yen bonds, making them attractive in comparison.

Liquidity has slowly been improving in the Ecu bond market, with several large benchmark issues by sovereign or supranational borrowers in various maturities in the Euromarket, all the way out to 20 years. Domestic French Ecu OATs offer a reasonably liquid alternative. The emergence of Ecu bond futures has been another positive factor.

The time and cost involved in following and investing in individual European bond markets, some of which are very small by international standards, can be a deterrent. The Ecu, on the other hand, as a weighed average of all 12 EC currencies, offers exposure to all these markets at the same time. It is therefore ideal for Japanese investors who want exposure to European bond markets, but require a slightly higher yield than that

Exhibit 10.9 **Comparison of international bond yields**

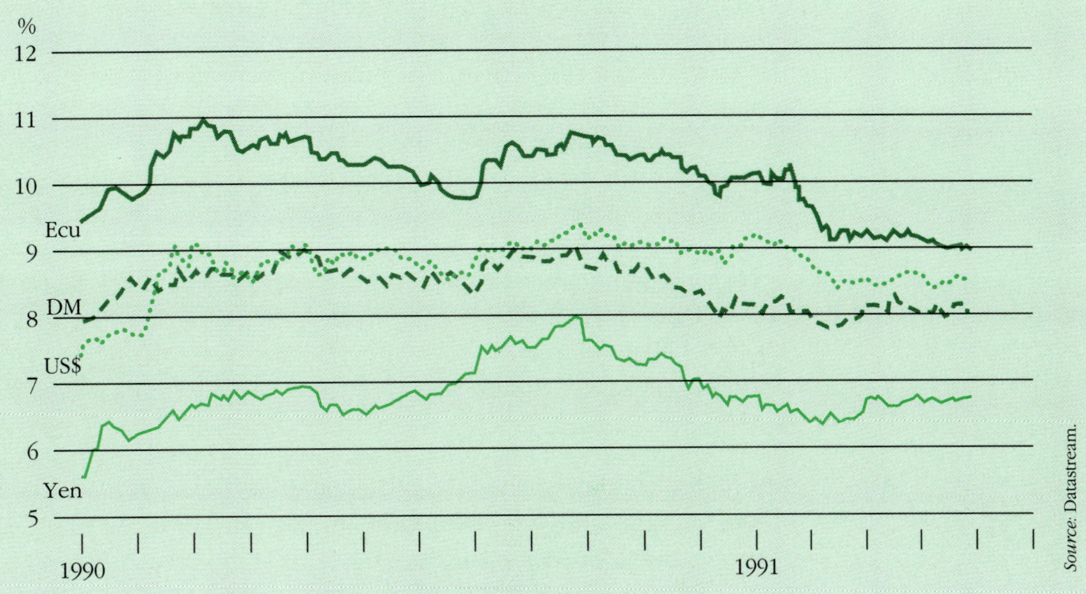

available on, for instance, Deutschmark bonds. Japanese investors probably put less emphasis on the risk reduction from diversification which is obtained by investing in the Ecu market, although it is an added advantage. This effect is, of course, going to become increasingly less important in future as the correlation between European currencies and bond markets continues to increase. Since sterling joined the EMS, the UK market, which historically has had a lower correlation with the rest of the European markets, has started moving more in line.

On the theme of Ecu investments, some Japanese life insurance companies made the following statements in our survey:

Life insurance company "C"

DM-denominated bonds are not very attractive in yield terms, given the large number of higher-yielding European currencies. Since our income goal is around 10 per cent per annum, we favour Ecu-denominated bonds. Last year's Ecu appreciation makes this kind of investment ideal. We have a substantial amount of Ecu-denominated floating-rate notes with puts, recently a popular product.

Unlisted bonds are desirable from an accounting point of view (as these bonds can be valued according to cost price rather than current market price). Currently the multicurrency MTN (medium-term note) programme is popular, pegged to Ecu rates. We prefer a rating of AA or better and, as far as corporate bonds are concerned, we are looking more to European than US issuers at the moment; given the US recession, there is just too much uncertainty and credit risk. In short, we prefer sovereign and supranational issuers.

Life insurance company "D"

Our Ecu-linked investments have grown, particularly in the first half of 1990. The Ecu-denominated assets that we hold are mostly in the form of floating rate notes. Our past experience leads us to favour products with put options, as a means of compensating for any lack of liquidity. Exercising the put ensures the return of the principal, leaving mainly exchange rate risk, which means that exchange rate gains can also be targeted. The "floater with put option" combination is in our opinion essential for the viability of Ecu-denominated products.

The Ecu's merit as a currency is its adaptability to packaging: buying a ready-made package comprising various markets is simpler and cheaper than scrutinising individual markets. In my experience, it is difficult to examine each currency on its own merits, and buying into separate denominations is not quantitatively efficient. The Ecu is also an effective cushion against DM fluctuations.

If I had to choose a single European currency, though, it would have to be the Deutschmark. DM bonds can be safely held for a number of years. However, it is difficult to be too bullish about the Deutschmark at present, given the anxieties concerning reunification, the Soviet Union and the Eastern European situation. Buying Ecu and French franc products can therefore act as close substitutes for Deutschmark investments.

Securities investment trusts: short-investment horizon

Securities investment trusts reduced their foreign assets substantially between 1989 and 1990. This was achieved by selling off principally US dollar assets, so the proportion in other assets increased, boosting exposure

Exhibit 10.10

Foreign-currency assets of largest insurance companies, September 1990

%	*Nippon*	*Dai-Ichi*	*Sumitomo*	*Meiji*	*Asahi*	*Yasuda*	*Chiyoda*	*Total (Yen bn)*	*Average %*
US$	57	66	44	55	49	51	53	9,306	54
C$	14	10	15	19	24	13	10	2,489	15
A$	9	3	7	8	10	4	7	1,182	7
UK£	5	8	10	2	11	8	6	1,193	7
DM	5	1	6	3	1	0	8	592	3
Ffr	4	7	0	8	4	3	11	783	5
Others	6	5	19	6	3	20	5	1,543	9
Ecu	3	2	6	3	1	4	0	500	3
FIM	0	–	–	–	0	0	0	–	–
NZ$	0	–	–	–	0	4	0	–	–
Sfr	0	–	–	–	0	0	0	–	–
Lit	1	–	–	–	0	0	0	–	–
Pta	0	–	–	–	0	0	0	–	–
Dfl	0	–	–	–	0	0	0	–	–
HK$	0	–	–	–	0	0	0	–	–
Others	1	3	–	3	2	13	5	440	3
Total	4,639	3,312	3,286	1,894	1,800	1,308	849	17,088	100

Note: (Yen bn) – means data not available

Source: Annual reports, Nomura Research Institute, Tokyo.

Exhibit 10.11
Foreign assets of securities investment trusts, 1985–90 (net asset values)

%	*1985*	*1986*	*1987*	*1988*	*1989*	*1990 (Nov.)*
US	97.4	89.9	80.7	87.5	86.8	75.0
Canada	0.3	6.6	6.5	4.9	3.2	3.6
Germany	0.3	0.9	3.5	1.5	2.6	3.6
Netherlands	0.1	0.1	0.3	0.3	0.2	0.8
France	0.4	0.1	0.9	0.6	0.8	3.8
UK	1.4	0.5	3.0	1.9	1.4	1.9
Switzerland	0.3	0.1	0.1	0.1	0.2	0.6
Ecu	0.2	0.7	1.2	0.9	0.5	0.6
Australia	0.1	0.5	2.1	1.2	1.5	1.6
Japanese yen	0.0	0.3	0.8	0.4	0.7	1.5
Others	0.0	0.2	0.8	0.9	2.3	7.1
Total (yen bn)	1,593	4,096	3,469	4,698	5,316	2,978

Source: Securities Investment Trust Association.

Exhibit 10.12
Analysis of foreign assets of pension trusts, March 1990

	Types	%	*Currencies*	%
	Yen assets	6	Yen	6
	Equities	44	US$	74
	Bonds	42	DM	6
	Other	8	Lit	5
Total (Yen bn)		**3,445**	Ffr	3
			C$	2
			Other (incl. Ecu)	3
		Total (Yen bn)		**3,445**

Source: Bank of Japan, Nomura Research Institute, Tokyo, estimates.

particularly to European bond markets, although the proportion in Ecu bonds remains small.

Pension trusts: long-investment horizon

As there are no publicly available statistics providing details of the trends in the foreign portfolio investments of corporate pension funds managed by trust banks, it is hard to get any clear impression of the composition. However, the information available is detailed in Exhibit 10.11. The foreign portfolio investment objectives of these trusts are very close to that of life insurance companies, as they are the main competitors in the corporate pension management market. They seek high income, ie a high yield on bonds, in a cost-effective way and put emphasis on liquidity. As pension trusts have not been investing in foreign assets for quite as long as life insurance companies, they tend to adopt a more conservative policy.

They have a much higher concentration in US dollar assets than the life companies, and also a much higher proportion of equities.

Trust bank "A"
Our main aim in investing in foreign bonds is to earn interest. While some of our funds are set aside for capital gains purposes, working assets as a whole are too large for this sort of operation, so we concentrate on interest return. Accordingly, our foreign bond investments depend on both the yield spread to domestic bonds and the exchange rate risk we are willing to take. Current US yields are not very attractive, following the easing of monetary policy by the Fed. We have therefore shifted our foreign bond acquisitions to some extent to European bond markets.

Trust bank "B"
Given the lower performance of pension trusts compared with life insurance companies, many trust banks are seeing an erosion of their pension fund management share. The growth rate of new funds has slowed and the flow of trust bank funds into foreign portfolio investments is less than brisk, both in terms of the market environment and volume of funds committed.

We have recently increased our European currency assets at the expense of US dollar-denominated assets. The proportion of US securities in our foreign security portfolio has been reduced from 90 per cent in April 1989 to 70 per cent currently. We have also reduced the share of bonds within our US dollar-denominated holdings from 50 per cent to 40 per cent. In terms of new funds, we feel that an allocation of less than 10 per cent to foreign securities is an appropriate level.

Up to now, the lack of our own back-office has limited our investments in foreign currency products to all but the major currencies. We are short of portfolio managers – we have only four staff handling ¥500 billion-worth of investments, two for equities and one for bonds, while I myself deal with cash positions and foreign exchange.

Trust bank "C" (on the subject of Ecu investments in particular):
We tend to concentrate on the Ecu rather than on individual EC currencies, which require too much research. The Ecu provides both an effective, all-round substitute for individual EC currency movements and reasonably high yields. Given the recent increase in Ecu issues, growth in market size has enhanced their attractiveness.

Our core strategy for Ecu bond management is to hold the short- and medium-term instruments – up to five years – to maturity. As long as foreign exchange losses do not bring the return below 7 per cent, their performance against domestic rates is still favourable.

Our favoured issuers are governments, supranationals and Japanese corporations, because researching foreign companies is rather complex. The Ecu bonds we have been holding up to now have been floating rate notes (FRNs). Although we will probably go into fixed-interest products in the future, we are satisfied at the moment with our concentration on FRNs with put options. We are also interested in an FRN with a put option, which is convertible into other currencies, now available on European markets. We are prepared to invest in this product, even if it is issued below Libor. We tend to buy Ecu bonds in Ecu50 million lots, rather than make massive Ecu100–200 million purchases all at once.

Conclusion

In the early 1980s Japanese investors did not get too involved in the Ecu bond market, but continued to look to German bonds because Germany had the least risky and most stable economy. Since it became clear that the Ecu might become the common currency of the EC in the care of a central bank based on the Bundesbank model, Ecu bonds have without doubt become more attractive to Japanese investors. They have increasingly become involved in the "higher-yielding" bond markets such as those in French francs, sterling and Ecu and, more recently, Spain and Italy.

Japanese investment in foreign securities, traditionally dominated by bonds, particularly US Treasuries, fell dramatically between 1989 and 1990, and net purchases were increasingly directed towards European bond markets. This was mainly due to developments in Japan and the relatively high interest rates available in the domestic market compared to the US. In their investment strategy, Japanese institutional investors put emphasis on the yield, liquidity and costs of investing in foreign markets. Based on yield, Ecu bonds compared quite favourably with other bond markets in mid-1991, with a higher yield than US dollar and yen bonds, although not as high as that on UK gilts and some of the smaller European bond markets. Liquidity in the Ecu market has improved, with several large high-quality issues, and an impressive share of the Eurobond new issue market by mid-1991. However, the market is still quite small by international standards, making it hard to trade very large amounts. The elements of cost is in favour of Ecu bond investments, as Japanese investors can gain exposure to European bonds without having to gather information about each individual market. Ecu bonds were in fourth position in terms of popularity among European bond markets in mid-1991, following Germany, France and the UK. There is, nevertheless, room for increased interest from Japanese investors in Ecu bonds as the market grows in size and liquidity improves further.

11

Roger Lomax
B.A.T

Commercial applications

By contrast with the growing prominence of the Ecu in the capital and credit markets, its use for commercial transactions has been much more limited. Essentially, in a commercial deal a businessman will normally wish to express a sales contract and receive settlement in the currency of the country in which he operates and in which the majority of his costs are denominated. This approach has tended to minimise transaction costs and exchange rate risks.

The main exceptions to this general principle are:

(a) where by convention goods or services are priced in the currency of a third country. Examples are the aircraft and aero-engine industries, whose products are priced in US dollars, largely because of the dominance of US companies both as suppliers and operators of aircraft; and

(b) sales to overseas markets where the main competition is from locally manufactured items.

Experience shows that suppliers are generally not able to specify the currency of their choice where the customer wishes to price in a different currency and alternative sources of supply are available. Thus, while it might suit the European Airbus consortium to price its products in Ecu to reduce the exchange risk from trading, it is unlikely that the management of their potential customers (the airlines) would be willing to contract on this basis. This is because the airlines' revenues tend to be related to the US dollar and to assume liabilities, and hence costs, denominated in Ecu would involve a longer-term trading exchange risk. A switch to the Ecu or another EC currency by a supplier would be practicable only in circumstances where there was a considerable degree of market dominance and price leadership.

Circumstances where use of the Ecu, as opposed to the national currency of the buyer or seller, could be attractive are:

(a) where there is a price advantage in terms of transaction costs;

(b) where the component currencies of the Ecu are reasonably closely matched with the revenues of the buyer, the costs of the seller or both; and

(c) where the buyer or seller believe that the exchange risks between entering a transaction and its settlement are less than in using an alternative currency, after making due allowance for interest-rate differentials. Since the Ecu as it is presently defined has the character of an average, it follows that its exchange rate is likely to be less volatile than those of its individual component currencies.

Against these possible advantages are a number of significant potential drawbacks which together account for the as yet limited use of the Ecu except as a financing medium. The main disadvantages are:

(a) transaction costs are higher than for payment in the domestic currency of the buyer or seller, because the whole amount has to be changed into another currency (except where the Ecu is used as a clearing or netting medium – see below), and

(b) the absence of a clearing system for high-volume Ecu transactions. The clearing system operated by the Bank for International Settlements (BIS) in Basle, in conjunction with the Ecu Banking Association, is suitable for high-value low-volume items. No guarantee of settlement is provided. While the system has coped well with the demands made on it so far, it would require considerable development before it was able to handle large volumes of commercial payments. Responsibility for the Ecu clearing system, if and when it becomes the single currency of the EC, has not yet been decided. (See Chapter 13 for further details.)

There are nevertheless signs of a growing awareness in business of the potential advantages which the use of the Ecu can bring. A survey in 1990 by San Paolo of Turin showed that 15 per cent of the sample of companies used the Ecu regularly while 47 per cent said they would consider using it in the near future. The main advantages seen by firms were the:

(a) greater inherent stability of the Ecu basket compared with using a national currency;

(b) potential for simplifying pricing and accounting;

(c) use of the Ecu in place of the US dollar, which can help producers and consumers to eliminate the risk from US dollar fluctuations – especially in regard to trading in commodities; and

(d) currency management may be simplified and the need for hedging reduced.

Among the growing number of commercial applications for the Ecu are:

Trade with Central/Eastern Europe

Sales of capital goods to Eastern European countries have been made and financed in Ecu. The attractions from the point of view of the customer are said to be the 'political neutrality' of the Ecu and that, as a basket, it is inherently likely to exhibit greater stability than any single component currency. It is not, however, clear how the possible hardening of the Ecu – effectively a scheme to tie its value to that of the strongest currency in the basket – would affect its attractiveness to buyers.

Intra-group settlement by multinationals

Several large multinational companies based in the EC have found it advantageous to express transactions between group companies in Ecu.

Price lists for intra-company sales and purchases are fixed in Ecu and the resultant transactions are netted periodically with settlements between companies being made in Ecu. The main advantages are:

(a) reduced risk, because the Ecu, as an average, is likely to enjoy a more stable effective exchange rate than national currencies;

(b) the greater stability of the Ecu should reduce or eliminate the need for hedging, simplifying groups' treasury operations and leading to lower costs; and

(c) simplification of intra-company accounting and payment systems with the implementation of a central clearing system.

The main disadvantage is that each entity needs to convert its net Ecu receipts or payments under the system into national currencies, because it would have little need for Ecu to complete transactions with third parties: suppliers, wages and taxes are invariably paid in national currency. The savings in hedging and administration would therefore have to outweigh the transaction costs to the group of the purchase and sale of Ecu to make its use as a medium of account a commercial proposition.

The Ecu is used by Fiat, the Italian car company, as the basis of settling intra-group accounts. Alcatel, the French telecommunication group, is also considering implementing such a system, in which they see considerable advantages. Alcatel's Italian subsidiary invoices a significant proportion of its export sales in Ecu, mainly transactions linked to finance by international development banks or the Italian overseas aid programme.

Accounting

So far, only in the UK, the Netherlands and Greece are companies able to prepare their statutory financial statements in Ecu. However, a growing number of large companies based in the EC are preparing their financial statements in Ecu as well as the currency of their domicile (see Chapter 14). A smaller number of companies, including Alcatel, have also switched to denominating their budgets and monthly internal management reporting systems in Ecu. At Alcatel, all operating units report their accounting data in Ecu at two different rates of exchange:

(a) the rate which will be used for the purpose of the published financial statements; and

(b) a rate fixed in advance for the year so that the underlying operating performance of each subsidiary can be assessed.

Clearing house operations

An obvious application for a common currency is settlement between utilities which operate a clearing-house arrangement. Potential applications include transportation (airlines and railways) and telecommunication.

From September 1990, some members of the European Conference for Posts and Telecommunications have agreed that settlement between them will be made in Ecu. Accounting is carried out centrally by the system, which computes each month the net amount owing to or from each country. In the first instance, the balances are calculated every three months in Special Drawing Rights (SDR). The SDR balance is converted into Ecu at the average exchange rate for the previous three years published by the European Commission. Experience of the system to date has yielded savings in costs which would have arisen as a result of fluctuations in the exchange rate between the SDR and national currencies.

Purchases of commodities

Certain commodities, including wood pulp, are priced in Ecu as well as in other major currencies. A significant amount of business is transacted in Ecu. Companies with purchasing programmes compare quoted prices in both US and Ecu and accept whichever appears the more advantageous, taking into account a judgment as to the likely course of exchange rates up to the time of delivery and payment. They are attracted by the stability of the Ecu when there is a general expectation that the US dollar will strengthen.

Financial services

Development of insurance and other financial service products denominated in Ecu is constrained by regulations in various EC countries which require insurance companies to match assets and liabilities in the same currency. To meet a demand for Ecu denominated policies would require corresponding insurance funds to be invested mainly in securities denominated in Ecu. While a range of such securities (other than equities) is now available, a critical mass would be required before it became economic to constitute separate Ecu-based funds.

A significant demand for Ecu-based products exists, notably from customers who favour it as a hedging medium. An example is expatriate employees who have not decided where to retire and may not wish their pensions and other benefits to be denominated in the currency of any one country. It would be impractical or very expensive for such individuals to have a series of policies each payable in a different currency, and an Ecu-based contract can provide a hedge at no additional cost.

In general insurance a number of areas can be identified where Ecu-denominated business has been written:

(a) the leading Italian insurance company, Generali, markets a business interruption insurance policy for hotels which depend for their revenues on travellers from other EC countries;

(b) insurance of satellite ventures. The European Space Agency's insurances, which were previously arranged in US dollars, are now denominated in Ecu, which matches its own internal accounting and also corresponds more closely with the Agency's pattern of procurement. Expressing sums insured in Ecu, rather than a national currency, matches the Agency's risk profile more closely;

(c) some policies have been issued in Ecu for multinationals; and

(d) one UK corporation is said to be considering switching to Ecu-denominated policies to maintain the real value of its policy limits. This is of particular relevance where the assets covered by the policy are located in the EC.

In life assurance a number of applications have been identified:

(a) companies with pan-European operations and mobile personnel may find it convenient for benefits under the contract to be denominated in Ecu as a protection against exchange risks (though such risks should diminish as progress is made towards full monetary union and the exchange rate mechanism (ERM) fluctuation bands are progressively narrowed); and

(b) geographically mobile individuals may wish to have their retirement contracts or policies denominated in Ecu as a protection against exchange risk.

At present, growth in demand for Ecu-denominated policies is limited by laws which require pension benefits to be paid in the currency of the country of residence. Taking out Ecu policies to match liabilities in a national currency would result in an exchange risk.

Examples of Ecu-based products include:

(a) savings products offered by Generali of Italy;

(b) Swiss Life gives all policyholders an option to conduct business in Ecu; and

(c) American Express offers life policies denominated in Ecu to its credit-card holders.

The UK company, Eagle Star, has for many years offered life policies denominated in a composite currency – the Eagle – made up of sterling, US dollars, Deutschmarks and yen. The policy has been sold largely to expatriates and demonstrates the attractiveness of a basket currency as a hedging instrument in the retail market.

However, the scope for growth of Ecu-based insurance business will be limited until changes are made in supervisory and social security regulations and the currency has become used more widely in commercial transactions.

Fund raising

In contrast to the limited, and somewhat specialised, use of the Ecu in commercial transactions, a large volume of financing takes place in the currency, both from banks and in the bond markets. However, Ecu borrowing is not greatly used as a primary source of funding by companies. The majority of borrowing by the private sector has been undertaken either as a means of hedging balance sheet exposures by broadly matching assets in the underlying currencies or to swap into another currency to take advantage of a favourable market opportunity.

The Ecu market is estimated at about Ecu130 billion in outstandings at the end of September 1990, according to the committee of governors of the central banks of member states of the EC. It is fairly evenly divided between final bank lending (Ecu49 billion, reduced from a gross Ecu145 billion if redepositing among banks is excluded), international bonds (Ecu54 billion), and domestic securities (Ecu40 billion). There is some overlap between categories. The Ecu bond markets remain dominated by governments, supranational bodies and banks as issuers, although private-sector companies now account for about 27 per cent of outstanding issues, the large majority by non-financial firms. French, US and Japanese firms account for the bulk of private sector borrowing activity in the markets. Issues by the private sector have been predominantly straight bonds, with only a small proportion having equity conversion rights attached. There have been only a small number of equity issues denominated in Ecu, none by UK firms. This possibly reflects legal impediments in most EC countries to the denomination of capital and preparation of published financial statements in currencies other than the national currency.

The market has not been used extensively by business for financing, partly because there is an imbalance in the maturity range and it lacks liquidity in some maturities. It is therefore difficult for a company to have a full range of treasury management activities in Ecu. The majority of issues have traditionally been medium/long-dated stocks with a relative shortage of short- and long-dated issues. However, extra liquidity and volume, particularly at the short end, has been provided by recent large government issues, including UK Ecu-denominated Treasury bills and gilts (see Chapter 18).

The main factor limiting the development of the market and its use by companies for financing has been the absence of a commercial end-use of the Ecu. It is, however, likely that UK companies will become increasingly attracted to borrowing in Ecu at the favourable interest rates which have started to prevail in the market once they are convinced that ERM entry and moves towards a single currency have reduced the risk of sterling depreciating relative to other ERM currencies. The volatility of the Deutschmark may also add to the attraction of borrowing in a more stable medium.

Balance sheet management

Companies typically do not hedge fully their balance sheet exposure in overseas countries. Hedging is normally confined to:

(a) protecting trading cash flows across the exchanges in respect of imports, exports and inter-company dividends through a combination of forward sales and purchases and currency options; and

(b) ensuring that borrowings in foreign currencies are broadly matched with assets in the same currency. This limits the potential effect on the balance-sheet, in terms of debt/equity ratio, from movements in parities.

A large proportion of Ecu borrowing has been undertaken for balance sheet hedging by companies with substantial assets in EC countries.

Future developments

While the commercial use of the Ecu has so far been modest, there is strong evidence that firms expect to use it much more extensively and to derive significant benefits from it. Companies involved in extensive cross-border trading within the EC clearly stand to make the largest savings in transaction costs if or when the Ecu becomes widely accepted as a means of payment and the necessary clearing and money transmission infrastructure is in place. Moreover, a survey in 1990 by Ernst & Young and the National Institute for Social and Economic Research (*A Strategy for the Ecu*, Kogan Page) showed that more than half of a sample of EC companies believed that a European currency would have a positive effect on exports, sourcing,

Exhibit 11.1 **Effect of the Ecu as a parallel currency on different aspects of business strategy**

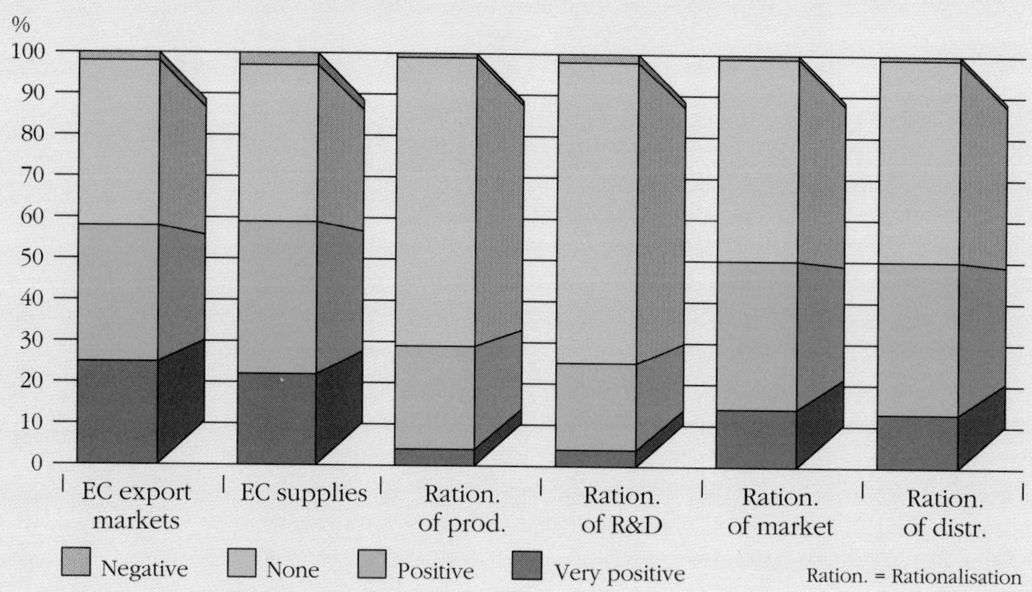

marketing and distribution strategies. The potential impact of the Ecu as a single currency was thought to be significantly more favourable than if it remained essentially a parallel currency. The companies' responses are detailed in Exhibits 11.1 and 11.2.

Much depends, however, on the shape of future developments and in particular whether the Ecu remains a parallel currency or becomes a single currency throughout most of the EC as decided at the European Council in Rome in October 1990.

Exhibit 11.2 **Effect of the Ecu as a single currency on different aspects of business strategy**

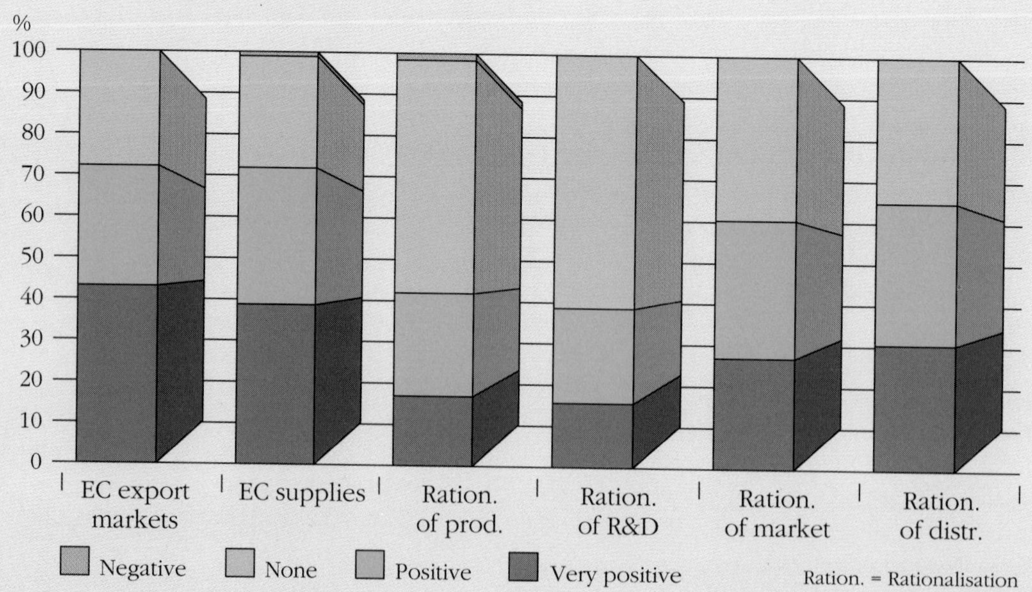

12

Didier Cahen
Association Eurocitoyen

The Ecu and the consumer

Introduction

As preceding chapters have shown, the Ecu has a comprehensive banking and financial infrastructure and has become one of the most recognised currencies. This is remarkable, because the rise of the Ecu in private transactions has been quick, spontaneous and unanticipated by the founders of the EMS. The use of the Ecu by individuals is just beginning. Even if there are still no notes or coins in Ecu, except for collectors, various methods of payment in it are already available to the European citizen:

1. Any citizen of the Ecu, unless he is Portuguese or Greek, may open an account in Ecu, write a cheque on a current account in Ecu or carry out transfers abroad from this account.

2. Travellers' cheques for sums of Ecu50 and Ecu100 issued by Thomas Cook are available to the European tourist. These travellers' cheques are accepted as payment without any problems in the Benelux countries but much less in other regions of the EC.

3. The traveller may also use Eurocheques in Ecu.

4. Any citizen may make a payment in Ecu by letter of credit (LC) from his ordinary account in national currency.

In order for the Ecu to become a currency used by everyone in Europe, it is essential to:

- make the use of the Ecu available to everyone on a European scale by means of more promotional campaigns for it along the lines of that carried out in Luxembourg in November 1989;

- limit charges made by European banks on individuals' payments made in Ecu;

- consider introduction of the Ecu into electronic point-of-sale terminals; and

- promote the use of the Ecu in sectors linked with tourism.

Before returning to these points, the attitude of Europeans towards the replacement of their currencies must be analysed.

The attitude of Europeans towards the replacement of their national currencies by the Ecu

A survey on this subject was carried out at the request of the Association for the Monetary Union of Europe in the 12 countries of the EC, using a sample of 6,049 persons aged 15 and over. These are nationwide samples in Belgium, Denmark, Germany, France, Italy, Luxembourg, the Netherlands and the UK, and samples from large urban areas in Greece, Spain, Ireland and Portugal. The survey was carried out between 26 September and 9 October 1990 by EOS-GALLUP Europe, and co-ordinated by *Faits et Opinions*, Paris. The results shown for the EC are for totals weighted by the actual population of each country.

Out of the 6,049 people questioned, 61 per cent declared themselves in favour and 39 per cent against this change within the next five to six years. A large majority showed itself to be in favour in nine countries, a narrow majority in Germany and a large minority in the UK and Denmark. The enthusiasm of the French, Spaniards and Italians (73 per cent, 75 per cent and 66 per cent in favour) contrasts with an obvious "wavering" on the part of the Germans (51 per cent for, 49 per cent against) and the marked reluctance of the British (37 per cent in favour, 63 per cent opposed).

When invited to give their opinion on the importance they attached to the various consequences of adopting a single currency, those questioned put the positive and strategic consequences at the forefront: monetary stability, the strengthening of the EC and the single market. It was only afterwards that any mention was made of their advantages as consumers: easier travel, savings on exchange costs.

The attachment to national sovereignty was referred to only as the last item on the list, even in the UK where this subject is at the heart of the debate. The possible establishment of a European central bank (ECB), linking together the national institutions, was approved by 76 per cent of those who expressed a clear opinion (80 per cent in France, 89 per cent in Italy, 73 per cent in Germany). Even in the UK, 58 per cent of those polled agreed to the setting up of this bank.

Mobile freelance interpreters, who work for EC institutions in one country or another, as well as experts sent on secondment from national governments to the EC, have concluded that for them Ecu could be a preferable solution, on average, to the alternative of one particular currency. The salaries of these interpreters and experts, the contributions they pay to insurance companies for medical coverage and pensions and the benefits they receive from these organisations, are made out and paid in Ecu. The European Commission has also suggested that its employees be paid in Ecu.

It is possible today to envisage the setting-up of cultural or sports events which largely or even exclusively make use of the Ecu. The example of the European piano competition illustrates this. The takings from this event (registration fees, subsidies, entrance tickets, etc) are denominated and often paid in Ecu, and the expenses (awards, telephone costs, payment of the jury, salaries, etc) are all settled in Ecu.

The Month of Europe

The use of the Ecu by the individual may quickly become more generalised if the "Month of Europe" campaign, carried out in November 1989 in Luxembourg, were to be repeated in other EC countries.

The monetary interest of this campaign centred on the Ecu was that it introduced a double posting of prices in Ecu and in Luxembourg francs and, for the first time in the history of European monetary construction, enabled citizens (whether resident or not) to make ordinary payments in Ecu. On this occasion, the Ecu fulfilled two roles: that of a unit of account or, strictly speaking, price quotations; and that of a means of payment for those wishing it.

The means of payment in Ecu were those currently available:

- the Eurocheque;
- the cheque;
- the travellers' cheque;
- the Visa credit card in Ecu which enables Luxembourgers with accounts in Ecu to have them debited in Ecu; and
- credit cards: those holding a credit or charge card, Visa, Eurocard, American Express and Diners, were able to settle their bills in Ecu and be debited in the currency in which their card was issued.

During this event, residents of Luxembourg were able to settle their bills in Ecu without charge, since the domestic banking sector fully supported the event. Primarily designed to publicise the Ecu by making it accessible, this initiative, which was thought up and put into effect by the Association Eurocitoyen, was reasonably successful. Indeed, during the campaign, about six to 10 per cent of shops' turnover was in Ecu.

Monetary advances achieved in the context of the Month of Europe

1. The banks issuing the Eurocheque system (more than 8,000) have extended their guarantee to Eurocheques made out up to Ecu170. They have also set up a payment system for these Eurocheques which authorises transactions to be made in Ecu by this means.
2. The Ecu has become an instrument of payment and official transaction within both Visa International and Eurocard International. In practise, this means that the international network handling Visa and Eurocard can now handle payments and settlements in Ecu.

European banks issuing Visa or Eurocard-Mastercard may start or continue to issue cards in Ecu. This also means that more than 1.5 million shops which accept Visa or Eurocard-Mastercard may henceforth accept payments in Ecu.

No fractional or paper currency was in circulation during this Month of Europe, so the use of the Ecu by individuals on this occasion was a source neither of monetary creation nor of difficulties for domestic economic policy. This shows that a community can manage its transactions autonomously in a currency other than its national currency. It is therefore now appropriate to increase these types of initiative in Europe and, if possible, make them permanent, since they will allow the individual to become familiar with the use of the Ecu in his daily business.

The problem of Ecu banknotes

Despite these various endeavours, it is clear that Europeans will only think of the Ecu concretely when they can use Ecu banknotes to make payments. The banknote, at least in Europe, represents the most familiar form of currency and the one commonly used by individuals daily. The issue of Ecu notes would thus have a clear symbolic value. This would give the public at large a clear awareness of the existence of the Ecu. This leads us to ask why there are no Ecu banknotes, and what would be the conditions under which these could be issued.

Historically, currencies have always progressed from the most concrete form (metal coinage) to the more abstract (deposit money), passing through the intermediate form which in this instance is represented by paper currency. The Ecu, on the contrary, was set up from the outset in the more abstract form, as a unit of account and a means of payment: first, only between central banks as the official use of the Ecu; then between private agents (commercial banks, businesses, etc) as the private use of the Ecu. Its establishment in an abstract form is narrowly linked to the definition of the Ecu as a basket currency.

If this definition of a composite currency is conceivable for purely deposit money, which is only used through book entries, one must acknowledge that it does not seem compatible with the status of a printed currency, circulating in the form of banknotes. Some symbolic endeavours have nevertheless been made to give the Ecu a material form (see Chapter 19).

The issue of Ecu notes for general use by commercial banks would increasingly come up against the central banks' monopoly of the note issue. Of course, commercial banks do have the power to create currency in the form of deposits. The monopoly of the note issue enjoyed by the central banks in all countries is the result of historical circumstances. These national authorities would probably have difficulty today in accepting the circulation of banknotes issued by private banks, which might default, on their territory. The issue of notes by banking consortia could be explored, but this would involve legal changes in every country. The issue of banknotes in Ecu by national central banks is also conceivable.

Currently, the central banks of the EC are those which originally created the official Ecu, since these are issued by the European Fund for Monetary Co-operation (EFMC) in return for the contribution by the central banks of 20 per cent of their reserves in gold or US dollars. The national central banks also intervene on the exchange markets. Nevertheless, each of them is issuing its own currency and ensuring that its value is maintained, and they would probably not agree to issue notes made out in another currency. They would emphasise the difficulty of having several deposit monies coexisting on the same territory, whatever the degree of exchange rate stability.

Without strong political will, the circulation of Ecu banknotes in these conditions risks remaining narrowly linked to the establishment of EMU. At the end of the anticipated transition period, when the rates of exchange have finally been fixed, the adoption of a single currency by the EC should follow. As shown in the Delors Report, the Ecu will become this single currency, circulating not only in its current deposit money form but also as banknotes. At this final stage of EMU, an ECB will have been set up. It will be responsible for issuing the Ecu in the "central bank" form of monetary issue, ie the fiduciary form. According to the Delors process, we shall then see Ecu notes circulating throughout Europe.

Limitation of charges by European Banks on individual Ecu payments

For a European individual, making payments in Ecu involves costs which cannot be ignored. The following examples quote the charges made by French banks on payments by individuals in Ecu.

Payment by cheque made out in Ecu between two individuals holding accounts in Ecu

1. The bank on which the cheque is drawn receives a transfer commission of 0.1 per cent minimum, and the minimum commission is, depending on the bank, between Ffr40 and Ffr70 (+18.6 per cent VAT).
2. The bank into which the cheque is paid charges the same commission for collection.

Payment by cheque made out in Ecu between two individuals holding accounts in national currency

1. The bank on which the cheque is drawn will apply the selling rate of the Ecu (and will benefit from the gap between the buying and selling rate of the Ecu), charging not only a transfer commission (see above) but also an exchange commission equal to 0.05 per cent. The minimum commission, depending on the bank, is between Ffr42 and Ffr55 (+ VAT).
2. The bank into which the cheque is paid will apply the buying rate of the Ecu (and will benefit from the gap between the buying and selling rate of the Ecu), charging not only an exchange commission (as above) but also a commission for collection (that is, 0.1 per cent (+ VAT), as above).

Payment by transfer in Ecu

The above commissions are also applicable, with the exception of the commission for collection, which is not charged by French banks in this type of operation.

Reduction of the delay in individuals' payments in Ecu

Even if transfers of Ecu carried out by the clearing system are at same-day value, individuals still face delays in their Ecu payments (the minimum delay being six working days) for the following reasons:

- banks' foreign department staff are not always familiar with the Ecu clearing system;
- the bank branch does not usually make payments in foreign currency;
- there may be one or two days' additional delay, depending on whether the bank on which the cheque is drawn is the head office.

There may be an additional delay depending on whether the banks making the payments in Ecu belong to the clearing system (which includes nearly 90 banks).

Finally, a delay in payment will occur in cases where the bank in which the cheque is drawn does not know the Ecu correspondent of the bank into which the cheque is being paid.

Most of these problems of cost and delay when individuals make payments in Ecu are identical to those which arise where foreign currency operations are concerned.

Nevertheless, for the European individual to want to use the Ecu, it is necessary for it to be treated in a preferential manner by banks, which should place a special limit on Ecu payment charges.

Introducing the Ecu into sectors linked with tourism

Initiatives should be made to encourage the international hotel and restaurant chains, European tour operators and travel agencies to advertise the Ecu within their establishment, publish their prices in Ecu and accept payments in it.

Indeed, the use of the Ecu has advantages for tourism, in terms of stability, simplicity and clarity.

Stability of the Ecu

Companies in the international tourism business offer services with long validity periods. Thus, the stability of the Ecu (which arises from its basket nature and the existence of the EMS) would enable these companies to work out stable prices and resort less frequently to price review clauses. It would facilitate and lend credibility to their forward planning and simplify their management of exchange risk.

Simplicity of the Ecu

Companies in the tourism industry operate in several European countries and advertise to potential customers by means of brochures.

These businesses would simplify their pricing systems if they adopted a uniform price. Moreover, a single price in Ecu is a solution likely to be more attractive to a customer base in several countries than a price shown in several of the national currencies which all buyers would have to stick to.

However, before publishing their price in Ecu alone, these companies should first familiarise their customers with the Ecu. To begin with, these companies should add the Ecu to the list of foreign currencies used in their brochures.

To implement these advantages of the Ecu and thus achieve the objectives of this study, an attempt should be made to overcome the technical and financial obstacles. To advance beyond simple posting of the Ecu rate in the large hotel and restaurant chains in Europe and encourage the growth of Ecu payments in these sectors, the reduction of the following two types of costs should be considered:

- the banking charges for intra-community payments made by the individual; and

– the commissions charged by international payment companies on these same payments.

Technical obstacles

Approaches should be made to builders of electronic point-of-sale terminals to enable these machines to handle the Ecu, which the majority cannot yet do.

These approaches should be made jointly by the Ecu Banking Association, the Association for the Monetary Union of Europe, the Committee for the Monetary Union of Europe, the European Commission, Visa International, Eurocard International and Eurocheque International.

The development of private uses of the Ecu is a permanent feature of international financial markets. Thanks to the diversification of instruments, the increase in its users and the variety of its functions, the Ecu has become one of the most recognised currencies.

This rise of the Ecu in private transactions, moreover, is crystallising European monetary policy and developing monetary awareness of Europe. The transition towards EMU will require the abandonment of sovereignty and therefore an enormous common political will.

In democracies, there is much will when public opinion demands change. It is therefore necessary to get public opinion interested in monetary Europe with the use of the Ecu the most visible symbol of EMU. The road towards a common currency is therefore still long but must be started on immediately.

13

Malcolm Levitt
National Institute of Economic and Social Research

The Ecu clearing system

The Ecu clearing system is an electronic system for clearing interbank debit and credit Ecu balances on a same-day-value basis. It involves the netting of positions among a group of 45 Ecu clearing banks. The average daily volume of transactions is approximately 5,000 and involves an average daily turnover of Ecu30 billion (1991).

Although encouraged by the Commission of the EC, its evolution primarily represents private sector initiatives. As cross-border payments in Ecu grow, especially under the stimulus of the transition to EMU, the amount cleared and the demands on the system will expand.

Brief history

The origins of the Ecu clearing system lie in the initiation of a Mutual Ecu Settlement Account (MESA) system in 1983, when a group of banks opened "mutual" Ecu accounts with one another. The group included Kredietbank (Brussels), Lloyds, Crédit Lyonnais, Générale Bank, Kredietbank (Luxembourg), Banque Bèlge Pour l'Industrie and Istituto Bancario San Paolo di Torino.

The MESA system developed because there was no centralised, multilateral system for handling the growing volume and value of payments in Ecus between Europe's banks. Unlike clearing within a single country, there was no facility for netting interbank debits and credits and final settlement across accounts held at a pan-European central bank. The MESA banks had two functions. They were to act, in effect, as "correspondent" bank for all other banks dealing in Ecus and to act as a multilateral netting and clearing organisation. In the latter capacity each MESA bank took turns (monthly) assembling the gross debits and credits of the MESA banks with one another and establishing net positions, which were then settled in component currencies. The efficiency of the new system was greater than the numerous preceding bilateral arrangements, because the number of interbank transactions was reduced. However, settlement was in nine component national currencies, which involved costly bundling and unbundling. Since September 1986, settlement has been in Ecus.

The Ecu Banking Association (EBA) was established in 1985 with the responsibility for the daily management of the Ecu clearing system and its improvement. There are currently about 90 members of the EBA, of which 45 are members of the Ecu clearing system. Clearing members of the EBA are appointed on the basis of objective criteria relating to the amount and value of their Ecu transactions.

Clearing members of the system act as correspondent banks for all other banks making or receiving Ecu payments. Firms and individuals can make payments via their own banks, which will be either Ecu clearing banks or will have a correspondent relationship with a clearer. In principle each member state of the EC has a right to have at least one of its clearing banks as a member of the Ecu clearing system, and it is likely that one bank from both Greece and Portugal will be admitted soon. The Ecu clearing system also involves the Bank for International Settlements (BIS) and SWIFT (Society for Worldwide Interbank Financial Telecommunication).

Transactions take place across accounts held at the BIS, which helps to operate the system but is not a regulator or supervisor of the system nor is it a lender of last resort. Its role is simply that of an agent. SWIFT provides the transmission mechanism for payment messages, and its netting computer produces the balances, positive or negative, of each bank *vis-à-vis* the others.

Operations of the system

SWIFT, on behalf of the EBA, transmits, records, stores and nets all payment messages denominated in Ecu, informing each member of the Ecu clearing system of its balances. The system is "closed" in that the total of all balances is zero, although individual banks may have credit or debit balances, which they must settle. The system is multilateral; banks with positive balances are required to lend them overnight to banks with negative balances and not simply to the specific bank with which they have a credit balance, so that by the end of the clearing day all balances are squared-off at zero. Thus, unlike bilateral netting, they may be required to provide credit to banks with which they have had no dealings. Interest on all overnight loans is charged at a uniform rate by all members of the clearing system.

Banks involved in Ecu transactions which are not members of the clearing system pass their payments through an Ecu clearing bank. Ecu payments are for same-day-value, that is, debit and credit transfers are executed the same day the payment order is given, provided it is made before the SWIFT system deadline.

Ecu payment orders are passed through the SWIFT network, with a cut-off at 2 pm Brussels time. Payment orders are automatically copied into a netting computer managed by SWIFT. At 2 pm, the netting centre establishes a preliminary overall credit or debit balance for each Ecu clearing bank. This is communicated to each bank and to the BIS. The BIS then indicates on Reuters screens the positive or negative position of each bank but not the amounts. Debit or credit balances greater than Ecu1 million are indicated by – and + signs respectively; balances in excess of Ecu100 million are shown by – – and + +.

The Ecu clearing banks have until the final cut-off time, 3.15 pm Brussels time, to try to reduce their balances below Ecu1 million. Those with credit balances then lend Ecus to debtor clearing banks; the netting computer calculates and transmits the final balances. The further phase, between 3.15 pm and 3.45 pm, is a period when debtor positions remaining above Ecu1 million are reduced. By 3.45 pm, each member of the clearing system confirms its final netting balance to the BIS, authorising it to balance its clearing account by debiting or crediting its Ecu sight account with an amount not exceeding Ecu1 million; sight accounts must remain in credit. It is only then that banks, which have received messages paying them Ecus, can really know they can effect their own payments. Under the agreement with the BIS, the BIS can withdraw up to Ecu1 million from the sight accounts of creditor banks (provided that their accounts are not put into overdraft) and credit this amount to a debtor bank as an automatic credit facility. However, any bank with a debit balance over Ecu1 million after such a BIS transfer has to seek special transfers from the other Ecu clearing banks themselves.

If a particular bank has an especially large credit balance, whereas another bank has a particularly large debit balance, the former might theoretically be unwilling to provide the entire credit needed by the latter; in such circumstances it is likely to make credit available to each of the other members of the system and they, in turn, provide credit to the bank needing substantial credit. This procedure reduces the exposure of each individual bank extending credit to the risk of default by the debit bank. The members of the Ecu clearing system have agreed to provide, in principle but not unconditionally, Ecu5 million credit to each of the others, making a total standby facility of Ecu220 million.

Although it has never happened, it is conceivable that creditor banks may be unwilling to extend the necessary credit to debtor banks by the daily deadline. A number of options for coping with this possibility have been discussed. One is for all Ecu clearing banks to deposit collateral (with their home-country national central bank or possibly the BIS). Against this collateral, creditor banks should be prepared to lend to the debtor bank up to the amount of the latter's collateral; this development does not confront the possibility that the debtor bank's credit needs may exceed its collateral. Another option, proposed by the Bank of England and the Banque de France, is for these two central banks to guarantee the clearing by extending credit to banks which need it against the security of Ecu Treasury bills; until recently the volume of Ecu bills was insufficient to provide the basis for a significant extension of credit, and other EC national central banks may possibly join with the Bank of England and the Banque de France in developing this idea.

Credit risk and systemic risk

The Ecu clearing banks include some of Europe's larger as well as smaller banks. Some of the larger banks are concerned about the risk that some of the smaller ones might not always be in a position to meet their liabilities.

In the circumstances systemic risk exists. That is to say the failure of one bank to meet its liabilities would have repercussions throughout the multilateral Ecu clearing system. It operates without a lender of last resort.

The agreement among the members of the clearing system theoretically makes provision for a situation where one bank cannot find sufficient funds to square-off its position. All payments made by that bank would be unwound, and the bank taken out of the system. This would create severe problems for the other banks; some believe that payment messages sent by SWIFT are, in any case, irrevocable, so that the option is not practical.

There are several options for avoiding this situation:

1. The gross liabilities of each bank would be limited to their gross credits plus collateral (deposited with the national central bank or the BIS). However, this would slow down clearing operations enormously.

2. The "home country" central bank of each clearing bank would act as lender of last resort, but it is unclear whether any of them would take on this responsibility.

3. A European central bank (ECB) would accept this responsibility, but one does not exist at present. Although discussions on the development of a System of European central banking are under way, it is unclear at this point what lender of last resort features will emerge.

The concept of the "home country" central bank would mean that the national central banks, where the subsidiaries of non-EC banks are based in the EC, would be required to guarantee their positions as Ecu clearing banks, insofar as they are accepted as such by the Ecu clearing system. It seems unlikely that all EC national central banks would be willing to help guarantee the system without stronger involvement in its management than they have had so far; as indicated below, such involvement – whether or not it is associated with a lender of last resort role – will probably be a feature of Ecu clearing in future.

The BIS has drawn attention to the risks present in multilateral netting systems. Although neither the Ecu clearing system nor any other was named, some of the concerns may be relevant to Ecu clearing. In the Angell Report (*Report On Clearing Systems*, BIS, February 1989) the potential efficiency of multilateral netting for reduced transaction costs was noted. But concern was expressed about the potential for liquidity risks (failure to settle on the due date) and credit risks (failure to settle in full), the possible absence of supervision by any central banking or government authority, and the uncertain legal basis for netting agreements. In November 1990 the BIS produced the Lamfalussy Report (*Report of the Committee on Interbank Netting Schemes of the Central Banks of the Group of Ten Councils*) which, building on the Angell Report, made several recommendations, including:

- effective central bank oversight;
- a well-founded legal basis in all relevant countries;
- well-founded procedures for the management of risks, including limits on credit exposure;
- the capability for timely completion of the daily settlement in the event of inability to settle by the largest net debtor;
- public, objective criteria for membership; and

– reliable technical systems, including back-up facilities.

In future the Ecu clearing system, which has largely been a matter for private sector initiatives, should probably expect greater involvement by the authorities. A catalyst will be the transition to European Monetary Union (EMU) with a single currency.

A single currency

In 1991 an Intergovernmental Conference (IGC) of the member states is discussing the transition to EMU. EMU would involve a single currency, presumed to be called the Ecu, a single monetary policy and a system of central banking. The outcome of the IGC will set the framework for transition to EMU within which the financial services industry will need to develop its plans; although several important issues, particularly the time frame for the creation of EMU, need to be resolved, there is little doubt about the eventual scale and scope of the initiative. Some of the implications of EMU for monetary policy and the operation of markets are discussed in other chapters; here the focus is on the logistics of a single currency for the financial service industry.

In order to understand these implications it is necessary to consider the effects of the adoption of a single currency, including those relevant to cross-border transactions and domestic operations.

Regarding cross-border transactions the effects include:

- the abolition of exchange risks attached to payments between countries belonging to the EMU;
- a reduction in transaction costs for cross-border intra-European trade and investment, which are estimated by the European Commission at Ecu15 billion (1990) and represent fees and other charges to banks;
- partly as a result of the above, the reinforcement of the effects of the single-market stimulus to cross-border payments between firms (associated with purchases of supplies, investment in production and distribution facilities, marketing and sales efforts), individuals (such as remittances by geographically mobile workers to their home countries), from firms to individuals (such as employees and pensioners), from individuals to firms (for purchases) and from governments to firms and individuals (such as suppliers of services and pensioners located abroad); and
- the use of the Ecu by EC institutions in their revenue-raising and expenditure functions, such as the common agricultural policy and programmes of regional systems.

Thus, the Ecu will be substituted for existing currencies in the large, and growing, volume of cross-border retail and wholesale payments.

Regarding domestic operations the effects include:

- the Ecu being substituted for national currencies in all transactions between individuals, firms and government agencies; and
- the rebasing of interbank payment and clearing systems on an Ecu base will be required;

For firms, whether involved in domestic or cross-border activities in the financial services or other sectors, there will be the need to adapt the

Ecu for all aspects of accounting (including statutory reporting, management accounts and book-keeping), payments to suppliers, employees, pensioners and tax authorities and pricing (including transfer pricing) and invoicing. If a transition phase was adopted by the IGC, banks and their clients would benefit from a learning process. During this time, the Ecu would exist in parallel to existing currencies for either cross-border payments or domestic transactions or both. Banks and their clients would then familiarise themselves with the Ecu but with much more complexity than presently exists where a single, national currency is used.

Apart from the need to replace revenue associated with the loss of existing European currency exchange services and Treasury operations, the financial services sector will be required to develop and implement plans in order to:

- meet new and growing customer demands;
- develop new Ecu-based operating and financial systems; and
- respond to the pressure for faster and more efficient Ecu-based cross-border European payment systems capable of coping with the greatly expanded use of the Ecu in all retail and wholesale transactions.

Bank corporate and personal customers will need to be able to transact payments in Ecu (perhaps initially for cross-border transactions if such a transition arrangement were to be adopted), and they will expect their banks to provide the necessary services and advise them on Ecu operations. Because of the relatively low current use of the Ecu outside wholesale financial markets, banks do not have the necessary expertise in their branch network to service a massive increase in client interest in the Ecu. Consequently, a training programme will need to be put in place.

Bank operating and financial systems will need to be adapted to the new Ecu basis of their business. For example, all customer accounting information, currently denominated in national currencies, will need to be rebased on the Ecu. Although this may not seem a difficult operation, the practical scale of the operation will be very large indeed and needs to be planned well in advance; some banks might need to close down their systems for several days while the changes are made, although most are likely to adopt parallel computer processing systems involving the simultaneous use of both the Ecu and the national currency, for a limited period up to a "big bang" when everything is changed over to the Ecu. If, during a transitional period, the Ecu were to be used as a parellel currency alongside existing currencies, many clients will need both Ecu and national currency accounts with a facility for easy transfer between the two. Banks are presently accustomed to operating foreign accounts for customers, but this need during the transition could be huge and particularly complicated if the Ecu were to be used as a parallel currency for domestic payments prior to its adoption as a single currency replacing all existing national currencies.

Major changes are necessary for cross-border payment and clearing systems. All cross-border payments, whether retail or wholesale, after EMU will be in Ecu, implying a huge increase in the volume and value of Ecu-denominated payments. The existing Ecu clearing system is concerned with large, wholesale interbank operations, but the combination of the single market with the adoption of the Ecu as a single currency will mean an explosion in the number and value of cross-border retail payments in Ecu. Existing cross-border retail payment services have been criticised by the Commission of the EC, especially where low-value and irregular retail payments are concerned. Criticisms are that the services concerned are too costly and subject to excessive delay, fees for customers are unclear and there is excessive uncertainty about the date on which value will be received and the amount which will be credited to recipients.

To improve matters, the Commission has proposed that fee and cost structures should be clear and that the delays and costs associated with different payment systems around the EC should be overcome by developing a pan-European automated clearing house network, involving electronic linkages between existing national payment systems. This approach would involve the adoption of common standards, formats and codes but would require massive investment in the necessary new software and hardware.

To facilitate the introduction and operation of EMU and the use of the Ecu as Europe's currency, the Commission has included draft articles in its proposed Treaty on European Economic and Monetary Union giving the proposed new ECB "responsibility for the Ecu bank clearing system".

At the same time, the Group of Ten, acting via the BIS, is concerned about the extent of systemic risk in cross-border netting systems and has proposed much closer central bank supervision and a clearer, firmer legal basis for such netting systems. For all these reasons, it seems inevitable that major changes are pending for cross-border payments within Europe.

However, many commercial bankers are unhappy with the notion that the alleged inefficiencies in existing cross-border retail systems and the adoption of the Ecu as a single currency require major changes in existing cross-border payment arrangements, while accepting some increased role for central bank supervisors. They concede that, where small and irregular retail payments are concerned, criticisms of existing services have some force. They argued nonetheless that where high costs or lengthy delays arise they often reflect problems within certain countries where domestic payment systems need to be reformed because payment messages between countries pass extremely quickly via SWIFT. Several favour the wider use of Eurocheques and cards, to be made available to corporate clients, with payments in Ecu. Many believe that banks' fee structures and procedures, developed in the past for large payments, should be reformed and adapted to small and irregular payments. It is not necessarily the case that existing systems are inefficient but that they are not always appropriate for low-value payments. However, the proposed linkage of automated clearing houses is regarded with concern because of the lengthy delays which would be required before common standards are adopted, the considerable expense associated with the related investments and because many banks are already investing heavily in new competitive services and systems.

The volume and value of Ecu-denominated cross-border payments would be much greater under EMU than at present, and there is doubt whether the Ecu clearing system could be expanded to cope. A number of options are under discussion. One, favoured by some, is to expand the existing Ecu clearing system as a joint venture by some commercial banks, with little involvement by central banks; those who favour this approach argue that it is well tried, membership criteria are strict and numbers will grow when market demand warrants it, while indirect access to non-members is available by correspondent banking arrangements. However, some central and commercial bankers are concerned with systemic risk in the Ecu clearing system, which they believe constrains its potential growth. However, the risk might be less if, as proposed by the European Commission, the ECB or some other system of European central banking took over the running of the Ecu clearing system.

Another option would be for all EC clearing banks to become members of an EC-wide electronic clearing house system, in effect replicating, but on a very large scale, existing national automated clearing house systems; this pan-European system would be complicated to design and expensive to implement. An alternative is to create a hierarchy of local, national and European netting and settlement, to be organised by the European central banking system. Local and national netting/settlement among national banks would be undertaken across accounts held with the national central bank, with residual netting/final settlement being undertaken across accounts held by national central banks with the proposed ECB.

Another option would be for Europe's automated clearing houses to themselves organise all the necessary netting, although their final settlement would need to be across accounts held at central banks.

The question of access to pan-European payment systems arises. One proposal under discussion is to extend the "single passport" concept embodied in the Second Banking Directive (to be implemented on 1 January 1993) whereby a bank licensed to operate in one member state of the EC has a right to establish branches and provide services throughout the EC; in this instance it might mean giving the banks of any single national clearing network rights of access throughout Europe. Commercial bankers argue that as they bear the risk they should control access. If banks throughout Europe were to have access to automated clearing houses throughout Europe – whether through electronic linkages between national systems or through "single passport" rights of membership – systemic risk would explode. They are concerned that EC institutions might enforce open access without being prepared to accept responsibility for the ultimate risks; however, if EC institutions, including the proposed central bank, were to enforce open access, then these institutions should logically bear ultimate liability for risk.

In the circumstances, many commercial bankers and several central bankers favour a pragmatic approach which will allow several competitive solutions to emerge, offering choice to users and suppliers, responsiveness to changing needs, flexibility in adapting to new technological opportunities and maximum efficiency.

14

John Chown
J F Chown & Co Ltd

The accounting and tax treatment of Ecu transactions

Introduction

This chapter examines the accounting and tax consequences of the growing use of the Ecu as a secondary currency for commercial and investment transactions. Most of the problems considered here will disappear or become irrelevant if the Ecu ever becomes the single legal tender currency of the EC. In summary, there are three key points:

1. The Ecu is not legal tender in any EC country except (in a purely technical case) in Belgium.

2. The Ecu is treated *de facto* if not *de jure* as a "foreign currency" in most of these countries.

3. The tax and accounting treatment of all foreign currencies (including the Ecu) is complex, confused and very unsatisfactory. The UK Inland Revenue published a consultative document in March 1991. If and when its recommendations are enacted, it could remove a "tax fragmentation" booby-trap which has cost large but badly advised UK companies hundreds of millions of pounds of unnecessary tax in the last 20 years.

International tax analysts, particularly those concerned with foreign exchange and modern financial instruments, need to be even more precise than accountants in pinning down the exact economic and legal implications of complex transactions. The first part of this chapter looks more closely at points (1) and (2) above, and the following sections look at the problems of accounting and calculating tax liabilities in foreign currencies like the Ecu.

What is an Ecu?

The "basket Ecu" is a weighted average of EC currencies (see Chapter 1 and Exhibit 1.1). It is defined as so many units of each national currency per Ecu. The percentage weightings are derived from these figures and can vary with exchange rates.

It is not at present "legal tender", but this does not matter in practice. There is a historical distinction between the "intrinsic" and "fiat" value of coins,[1] and, historically, banknotes became acceptable long before they were legal tender. Scottish banknotes are not legal tender, even in Scotland, but what Scot would insist on a "real" English one? "Not all money is legal tender, but all legal tender is money."[2]

Although its legal tender status may be a red herring, it may be more important to ask whether the Ecu is legally a "foreign currency". Some writers (eg Mehnert[3] in an excellent overview of the legal issues) labour the point that, in each country, part of the Ecu is domestic currency. This had some practical implications in the days of exchange control but is now irrelevant. Sir Joseph Gold[4] pointed out in 1984 that "to clear the way for the use of the Ecu as a unit of account, and also as a means of payment, most members of the EC [had, even then] taken steps to ensure that, notwithstanding the domestic component, it could be regarded as a Eurocurrency and could be shown as such in the accounting returns ... by financial operators."

J. Trevor Brown[5] discusses the Miliangos case,[6] which established the principle that a UK court can express a judgment in foreign currency. The judgment debtor then has the option to pay in the currency of judgment or in sterling at the exchange rate prevailing at the date of actual payment instead of the date of breach. He argues that the Ecu "cannot be held by anyone other than the member states of central banks" (*sic*) and the European Monetary Co-operation Fund (EMCF).[7] "Hence the Ecus used privately are, like the Special Drawing Rights (SDRs) similarly used, units of value created by the parties with reference to the Ecu."

It appears that national courts have not yet given judgment in an Ecu case. It is possible, though unlikely, that they could do so without specific legislative authority, but the latter would undoubtedly help. There are no legal obstacles to the more widespread use of the Ecu in the UK or most other member states.

What of the "hard Ecu"? It does not presently exist, and its legal status and that of the issuing authority would have to be determined. It would probably then be treated, for the purposes of Section III, at least as favourably as the present Ecu.

Accounting and taxation consequences

Can we account in Ecu?

There is already a proposed EC Directive[8] which would permit companies to make up accounts in Ecu:

> *Article 51a*
> Companies may draw up and publish their accounts in Ecu at the exchange rate prevailing on the balance-sheet date. The method to be used for conversion into Ecu is described in the notes to the accounts.

This begs a lot of questions, and is, at this stage, little more than a statement of intent. Setting accountancy standards for foreign currency is very difficult even at a national level.

Meanwhile, most member states require accounts to be prepared in

1. See, for instance, Harry A Miskimin, "The enforcement of Gresham's law" and "Money, the law and legal tender", in *Cash, credit and crisis in Europe, 1300-1600.* Variorum Reprints, London, 1989.
2. F. A. Mann, *Legal aspects of money*, p. 186. Oxford, 1982.
3. Ralph J. Mehnert, "The European currency unit – the Ecu – currency for the United States of Europe". *George Washington Journal of International Law and Economics*, 23(2), 1989, p. 400.
4. Sir Joseph Gold, *Legal and institutional aspects of the international monetary system: selected essays*. Vol. ii, pp. 702-5. 1984.
5. J. Trevor Brown, "The private Ecu and composite currencies: their legal nature". *International Business Lawyer*, 18(5), p. 203, May 1990.
6. Miliangos *v.* George Frank (Textiles) Ltd (1976), AC 443.
7. Since 1985, the monetary authorities of non-EC countries and international monetary institutions may be authorised to hold Ecu. See Sir Joseph Gold, *Exchange rates in international law and organisation*.
8. Com/89 561 final. SYN 158. 29 November, 1989.

domestic currency. The requirement seems absolute in Belgium, Denmark, France, Germany, Italy and Spain. Companies incorporated in the UK and Ireland can legally make up their accounts in any currency and, particularly where tax is not in question, frequently do. Luxembourg requires accounts to be in the currency in which the company's capital is denominated (see below). This can be any currency, and the Ecu is often used. Portugal also has no formal currency requirement regarding accounts.

Greece normally requires drachma accounting, but there are specific exceptions for shipping and offshore companies set up with foreign capital.

Since 1988, Dutch companies have been permitted to account and submit financial statements in a foreign currency. At least one company (Alcatel NV) has chosen to report in Ecu.

Can capital be denominated in Ecu?

UK, Irish and Luxembourg companies can denominate their share capital in any currency, including the Ecu. Luxembourg holding companies and investment funds, exempt from Luxembourg tax on profits, can and do use the Ecu in this way. It used to be possible to form UK incorporated non-resident companies for tax purposes. These companies were required to, and often did, denominate their capital in a currency other than sterling in the days of exchange control. Since the changes in the UK rules on corporate residence, similar companies can be incorporated in Ireland.

Although UK practice had permitted foreign currency capital for many years, the Scandinavian Bank case (1987)[9] looked at whether capital could be denominated in more than one currency. The bank, a UK company, then owned by a consortium of foreign banks, found it convenient, for regulatory purposes, to do so in a mixture of foreign currencies. This was held by the court to be within the requirement of Section 2(5)(a) Companies Act 1985 that the company's memorandum must "state the amount of the share capital ... and the division of the share capital into shares of a fixed amount." The singular includes the plural, and the capital structure was approved. Luxembourg requires accounts to be kept in the currency of the registered capital.

Taxation

Introduction

As seen above, a company can, with a few restrictions, transact its business in Ecu and may, in certain circumstances, make up its accounts or register its capital in Ecu. It does not follow that such accounts will be accepted by tax authorities.

In the English-speaking countries the tax treatment of foreign exchange gains and losses has been disastrous. Many companies have been the victims of "tax fragmentation", a term coined by Jill Pagan.[10]

If a British company raises a long-term dollar loan to buy a long-term American asset, a foreign exchange gain realised on disposing of the asset will be subject to capital gains tax. There will be no corresponding

9. 2 WLR 752.
10. Inner Temple. Author of *Taxation aspects of currency fluctuations*. Butterworths, 1983, new edition due 1991.

relief for the exactly equivalent loss on the other side of the balance-sheet.

Apparently "cheap" borrowing of hard currency may prove disastrously expensive when the company belatedly discovers higher sterling cost of repayment of a strong currency is not deductible.

An apparently attractive cross-currency swap offering a 20 basis points advantage may result in a loss of 2 or 3 percentage points if the tax planning goes wrong.

This has all been well documented[11] but the traps continue to work. A few companies have sophisticated Treasury departments which work in close liaison with specialist tax advisers and manage to play the system backwards to their own advantage.

Continental European countries have a rather different approach to taxation, historically paying less attention to the revenue/capital divide. These problems are seldom material, at least in their extreme form.

Since 1986, the US has had the most comprehensive and complicated set of rules for dealing with the tax treatment of foreign exchange. Australia and New Zealand have nearly got it right, while Canada is halfway there.

The UK lags behind. In spite of a long history of consultative documents and working groups, the law remains messy. On 19 March 1991 the Inland Revenue produced a consultative document[12] which may possibly result in legislation in 1992. It will require a rethink of the accounting provisions of SSAP 20. Any changes needed to rationalise the accounting treatment of foreign currency are likely to be in the direction of Continental usage and should favour the use of the Ecu.

What does this mean in practical terms to companies wanting to do business in Ecu? This question has to be considered at three levels: commercial transactions, capital market transactions and accounting.

The tax treatment of commercial transactions in Ecu

The US legislation refers to a company or a "qualifying business unit" (QBU – eg a branch) as having a "functional currency". In the US case this may be the US dollar, in which it keeps its accounts for tax purposes.

The first step in making the tax computation is to look at transactions in a non-fundamental currency (NFC). The US terminology is convenient and used in the UK consultative document.

Companies using a domestic currency as their functional currency may transact their business in Ecu. Providing the transactions are on trading account, there is usually no major tax problem. The payments or receipts would be converted into domestic currency and taken into account for tax purposes in the normal way.

The only problem is likely to be timing. The amount due might first be converted into domestic currency at the exchange rate ruling on invoice date. If the exchange rate changes before payment, there will be an exchange difference which will be taxed or relieved as normal trading income. So, in principle, will hedging transactions, including options, which most countries now treat rationally for tax purposes.

Where there are debtors or creditors outstanding or open hedging

11. Most recently in John Chown and Ian Marsh, "Foreign exchange – taxation and more advanced techniques". *Treasury today*, 1(2), pp. 2-10.

12. *Foreign exchange gains and losses. Proposals for reform of the tax treatment of foreign exchange gains and losses. A consultative document.* Inland Revenue, March 1991.

transactions, timing on the accounting date has to be considered. Do unrealised profits or losses have to be brought into account for tax purposes? This only affects the timing of tax payments, and although this can be relevant at high interest rates, far less is at stake than with tax fragmentation proper. Generally, distortions tend to work in favour of the taxpayer as a "lower of cost or market" approach is often acceptable.

Capital market transactions

If a company operating with a domestic functional currency borrows Ecu or invests in Ecu instruments, the position is complicated, especially for a UK company. Minor market distortions apart, the Ecu rate of interest is the weighted average of interest rates ruling on instruments of the same quality and maturity in the component currencies.

If a company in a country with a higher-than-average rate of interest borrows Ecu, there will be a saving on interest cost which will increase taxable profit. The interest saving has, therefore, to be netted down by the tax rate. However, the market, expressed in the forward exchange rate, expects the Ecu to appreciate. The cost of repaying the Ecu in functional currency will rise. How will this increase be treated for tax purposes?

Similarly, a company in such a country which invests in Ecu securities or bank deposits will receive a lower rate of taxable interest but may expect a gain on maturity. The anticipated gains and losses should balance out because of interest arbitrage, before tax.[13]

The key words are "before tax". How are the exchange gains and losses on maturity taxed? If they are on "trading" account, they will be taxed and relieved in the same way as interest, and the treatment will be symmetrical.

Where a transaction is on capital account, the position is not so simple. The disposal of the asset may give rise to a capital gain. In continental Europe companies (though not always individuals) are generally taxed on such gains. In the UK (on present law) gains are taxed at the same rate as trading income, but indexation relief may be in question. There are also restrictions on the way in which capital losses can be offset. However, gains and losses on liabilities (and on certain long-term monetary assets which are not "debts on a security") are "nothings" – neither taxed nor relieved. This is the "tax fragmentation" trap.

The UK consultative document proposes that exchange gains on monetary assets and liabilities would, with very limited exceptions, become trading income and cease to be eligible for, or suffer from, capital gains or "nothings" treatment. The computation would be on an "accruals" rather than a "settled transaction" basis but with some scope for spreading forward liabilities.

When the new system comes into operation (Budget Day 1992?), it is proposed that existing transactions will be "marked to market". Tax will be calculated up to that day under the current ("fragmentation") rules, but the tax will not be collected, or relief granted, until realisation. This could result in a company being denied relief for a fragmentation loss accrued to that date and yet being taxed on a subsequent recovery. The consultative document does not look with sympathy at the "kink" relieving proposals made by the Group of Nine.[14] For the present, therefore, great care needs

13. In practice, of course, market predictions will usually be wrong, and the unanticipated changes are likely to be significant. The art of tax planning is to lock in the anticipated, ie forward market changes in a tax-efficient way, locking in the savings with a tax-neutral hedge.
14. The group was set up at the request of the Inland Revenue in 1987. The text of the report can be found, for example, in Chown, *Tax efficient foreign exchange management*, pp. 128-33. Professional Publishing Limited, London, 1990.

to be taken by UK companies, including UK subsidiaries of foreign companies, which have material long-term foreign currency liabilities, inter-company loans or cross-currency swaps. These changes will soon take place, and specialist advice is necessary.

The tax consequences of Ecu accounting

For tax purposes, a company must usually make up its accounts in domestic currency, even if it can and does keep its books and report to its shareholders in another currency. Normally this would mean taking apart each transaction.

Different rules already have to apply where a company trades through an unincorporated branch in another country. Most countries (France and the Netherlands are two limited exceptions within the EC) submit the profits of such branches to current taxation as if they were domestic enterprises. Others, like the UK and Germany within the EC, and the US and Japan, also subject certain separately incorporated "controlled foreign corporations" (CFCs) to current tax as if they were branches. Such foreign branches and CFCs will by nature do business and make up their accounts in the local currency as "functional" currency.

Under US law after 1986, if part or all of the business of a corporation is a QBU which can properly elect for a "functional currency" other than the US dollar, it can simply calculate its profits in functional currency and translate this into US dollars using (consistently) either the "closing exchange rate" or the "average rate" for the accounting period. There are 74 pages of Treasury regulations setting out the detailed rules on Sections 988 and 989.

Other countries in practice often permit such treatment, which is administratively simpler, although it can give a wildly different result when currencies are unstable. Where the branch is also liable to local tax, the effect of foreign exchange fluctuations can seriously distort the calculation of double tax relief.[15]

Such treatment has been available in the UK by concession. The consultative document proposes that the practice should be given legislative force, and there would also be a rationalisation of the rules for tax credit relief. Relief would be calculated with respect to the foreign tax that would be levied on the sterling-translated level of profit.

Could a US parent opt to use the Ecu as its functional currency for US tax purposes? The regulations[16] explicitly define a non-functional currency as "a currency (including the Ecu) other than ...". There is no specific mention of the use of the Ecu as a functional currency, but it appears that the IRS would, in practice, accept it as such.[17] The difficulty is that it would not typically be the currency in which it made up its domestic tax accounts in any one country. Thus, no major US company has yet taken this option. There should not be any difficulty if and when the Ecu becomes more generally acceptable throughout the EC.

At present, no member state permits a company to make up its domestic tax accounts for domestic operations in the Ecu or any other foreign currency.

In October 1989 a short paper[18] was written, now expanded as "The

15. See Chown, *Tax efficient foreign exchange management*, pp. 108-10. Professional Publishing Limited, London, 1990.
16. Reg 1.988-IT(c).
17. I am grateful to Dr Emil Sunley of Deloitte and Touche, Washington, and formerly of the US Treasury, for his comment on this point.
18. John Chown and Geoffrey Wood, "The right road to monetary union". *IEA Inquiry*, no. 11, 2 October 1989. Institute of Economic Affairs.

road to monetary union".[19] One of its recommendations was that, as part of the process of tax harmonisation, corporations within the EC should be given the option of making-up their tax accounts in Ecu. An appendix to the latter paper gives detailed examples, showing that the tax charge on a given level of real profits can be very sensitive to the rate of inflation of the currency used as a measuring rod. This option would be attractive to normal trading companies in those EC countries having a higher than average rate of inflation.

This thinking goes back at least to Hayek's Hobart Paper, "Choice in Currency".[20] A major advantage is that the arrangement would severely reduce the benefits to the tax collector of a higher rate of inflation. It goes back to the classic test of the distinction between good and bad measures of indexation.[21] A good measure of indexation is one which puts at least the whole of the cost of any inflationary correction on the inflation creating authority, namely the government.

The proposal appears to have found some favour in the UK, although the consultative document (para 2.21) states that "the government has decided that the use of a non-sterling functional currency should not be permitted for companies operating in the UK". This view appears to be at variance with the judgment in the Marine Midland[22] case. The document then says, "Ministers will in due course consider whether any special provision will be needed ... to encourage the wider use of the Ecu in business transactions."

The universal adoption of this measure, coupled with moves to a more harmonised tax base, would certainly simplify life for companies wishing to operate across Europe. It would solve more practical problems than the largely symbolic idea of the European company.

Can we pay taxes in Ecu?

Possibly, but does it matter? The liability will be calculated in Deutschmarks, lira, etc. That is the amount the Inland Revenue will eventually require. No businessman would permit his customer the benefit of hindsight to translate a debt in one currency into another, and it is unlikely the Inland Revenue will behave any differently. The one functional definition of "legal tender" that consistently applies everywhere is the acceptance that taxes and other debts are paid to the government. If an Ecu cheque was used and accepted to pay taxes a credit would only be given for whatever sum of the relevant currency it is in fact converted into.

As an aside, if a debt is payable at a future date, and no interest is accruing on it, it is generally better to have your liability in the weakest available currency. This would seldom, in practice, be the Ecu.

19. John Chown and Geoffrey Wood, "The road to monetary union. Price stability through tax reform", Institute of Directors, London, February 1991.
20. F A Hayek, *Choice in Currency*. Institute of Economic Affairs. Reprinted with a new introduction by Geoffrey Wood, October, 1990.
21. Generally, our aim is that EC harmonisation proposals should discourage any attempt by a national government to profit from inflationary money creation and eliminate ways in which government can use inflation as a soft option.
22. Pattison *v*. Marine Midland Limited. STC 540.

15 The legal context

J. T. Brown and A. M. Shea
Clifford Chance

Introduction

The relevance of the legal perspective

Lawyers can (and do!) argue over many aspects of the Ecu: whether it is merely a convenient unit of account or a currency in its own right; whether a creditor can insist on payment in Ecu; whether a court can award judgments in Ecu or apply conventional remedies for the enforcement of Ecu debts. Can a company have Ecu share capital or publish Ecu accounts? Can private individuals have Ecu bank accounts or take out Ecu mortgages and insurance policies?

In fact the Ecu will not wait for the lawyers to answer these questions. Many of them will remain unanswered until specific cases are brought before the courts or legislation and market practice has established a clearer context for the use of the Ecu in economic life. But this is not to say that the legal questions are merely academic. The impressive volume of transactions in Ecu and the ever-widening scope of its use in the EC, the financial markets and the business world, as documented elsewhere in this book, have come about largely through a collective faith in the value of the Ecu as a stabilising influence and a tool for enhancing cost-effectiveness in transactions.

Sustaining this faith depends mainly on the development of a better understanding of the nature of the Ecu and the obstacles to its wider use; that confidence can be undermined by ignorance or uncertainty concerning the legal implications of doing business in Ecu.

The scope of this chapter

The distinction has been drawn in Chapter 1 between the "official" and the "private" Ecu. The official Ecu is defined by Council regulations and has a central role as the basic accounting unit of the EC and in the European Monetary System (EMS). In short, it exists. The private Ecu is more elusive. Despite the billions of Ecus in circulation in the form of bonds, commercial paper, medium-term notes (MTNs) and syndicated loans, the private Ecu "exists" only as the result of agreement between transacting parties or as a creation of market practice. Yet this is the Ecu with which this chapter is primarily concerned.

Is the Ecu money? Is it a currency? What safeguards are necessary for lenders, borrowers and consumers when dealing with it? Not all of these issues can be adequately explored here, but some of the problem areas that an analysis of the legal context reveals will be highlighted.

The Ecu as money and as currency

The Ecu as money

Three functions characterise money: (1) it is a medium of exchange, obviating the need for barter; (2) it is a standard, a unit of measurement and account; and (3) it is a medium for storing value. Measured against these tests, the Ecu, both in its official and private forms, performs the role of money.

As a medium of exchange, the official Ecu is used to settle credit transactions and swaps between the monetary authorities of the EC. The private Ecu, as shown in preceding chapters, is now a serious rival to the dollar and the yen as a borrowing currency in the Eurobond markets. It is also used as a medium for invoicing and settlement.

As a standard or unit of account, the official Ecu operates as the *numéraire* for the Exchange Rate Mechanism (ERM) and has an ever-increasing role in the budgets of EC institutions, regulation of customs duties, agricultural policy and EC statistics. The part played by the private Ecu in the money markets, multicurrency lending and, increasingly, in the accounting of transactional companies also confirms this characteristic.

The use of the Ecu as part of the official reserves of EC central banks and the existence of Ecu deposits in the interbank and domestic markets demonstrates that both the official and private Ecu perform the function of a store of value.

The definition of money

The three functions of money described above do not, however, constitute a legal definition of money. English law does not provide a clear definition, even though the distinctions between monetary and non-monetary claims can have significant consequences.

The most respected authority on the English law position (A. F. Mann) concludes that only the coins and notes issued by the Bank of England ("legal tender") can properly be called money, on the basis that a creditor can refuse to accept anything else as being a proper discharge of a payment obligation. (Mann does go on to say that even coins and notes are themselves only a unit of value, as is, of course, the Ecu.) However, the position is different where the creditor has agreed to accept other methods of payment – for example, by cheque or transfer between bank accounts – in which case he cannot object to receiving payment in the agreed way. The key here is the creditor's express or implied consent to an alternative method of discharge, and this consent may well be implied by market practice and custom. The Ecu market has already achieved a substantial size and involves transactions which, increasingly, include payments between accounts in circumstances where there is no prior express agreement between the parties. It may be, therefore, that market practice has already evolved to the point that a sufficient element of implied consent exists for the Ecu to be considered as money by the parties using it.

Although English courts have, since 1976, been willing to grant judgment in foreign currency, it appears nevertheless that in some cases the courts may revert to the view that a claim for non-payment of foreign currency should be regarded as a claim for damages in respect of the non-delivery of a commodity (the "commodity" being the foreign currency). This would particularly be the case where a currency is being bought and sold, as on the foreign-exchange markets. In this respect, however, the Ecu would be no different from any other currency.

What are the practical consequences, under English law, of a court treating a claim as a money obligation or debt, as opposed to a claim for damages? First, a claim for a debt is self-contained; the plaintiff does not need to prove anything more than that the conditions that give rise to the debt becoming payable have occurred. The plaintiff does not have to prove "loss" nor is he/she under a duty to mitigate the "loss". Second, the plaintiff will usually be able to seek summary judgment rather than go through the more protracted procedures and proofs applicable to claims for damages. Third, the doctrine of "frustration" (analogous to what is generally understood by the expression *force majeure*) cannot apply to a monetary obligation, because such obligations are always theoretically capable of performance. Fourth, in bankruptcy, a debt can be proved for its face amount whereas other claims have to be proved for a "just amount" estimated by the trustee in bankruptcy.

French jurists, too, have difficulty in defining money and analysing the nature and consequences of claims for foreign currency debts. Again there are legal and practical consequences that result from whether a claim is characterised as a money obligation.

The problems associated with fitting foreign currency claims into the legal concept of money obligations will become even more complicated when the courts are confronted with the Ecu. The examples of English and French law are not exhaustive. Each country has its own jurisprudence, concepts of money and rules regarding the legal process of enforcing claims.

It seems likely, however, that a strict definition of money such as that quoted by Mann does not accord with the modern world. There are suggestions in several English cases to support the proposition that it would be inconceivable that the debtor of many millions of dollars or pounds could be obliged to transport coins and notes to settle this debt, where a bank transfer would suffice. By a similar process of market practice, it may well be that, although the courts have recognised as a foreign currency a unit of value which is legal tender in another country, this is no longer a necessary criterion. Thus the fact that the Ecu is not legal tender in any country may be irrelevant if it can be shown that the financial markets treat it as a currency in their everyday dealings.

The Ecu as currency

The Ecu is not issued by any country or by the law of any supranational institution. Officially, it is not (yet) the single currency of Europe, nor does it exist as a "parallel" currency, as proposals for the "hard Ecu" suggest that it might at some future date. Officially, the Ecu exists as a basket of currencies, each one being the sum of specified amounts of component currencies with "weightings" that can be revised from time to time in accordance with Council regulations. Privately, the Ecu, as a creature of contract, has to be defined by the contracting parties or by reference to a commonly accepted market practice, as in, for example, the interbank markets. It is normally defined by reference to the value of its official cousin.

No national statutes have granted legal status to the private Ecu (except for the limited amounts of commemorative coins minted in Belgium in 1987 and more recently in France, Ireland and Spain), nor does EC law impose on member states any regulations governing its legal treatment. This leaves governments, legislatures and courts free to respond independently to the private Ecu when confronted with it.

Regarding exchange control regulations, several countries, including France, Italy, Belgium and Luxembourg, have officially given the Ecu the status of a foreign currency. Others, including the UK, the Netherlands and Ireland, have recognised this status *de facto* without making specific rules.

Until June 1989, the German Federal Bank, notwithstanding the absence of exchange controls, had resisted the private use of the Ecu in Germany as a foreign currency. They perceived that use of the Ecu was tantamount to an indexation clause, prohibited by the anti-inflation legislation of the German Currency Law of 1948. Ecu accounts are now permitted and subject to the same minimum reserve requirements as foreign-currency accounts maintained by German banks.

In France and Italy, foreign-exchange regulations are more relaxed for Ecu transactions than for other foreign currencies, as demonstrated by the ability of importers to make forward purchases of Ecus for up to six months and for related charges invoiced in Ecu.

The different treatments of the Ecu as a currency or quasi-currency can expose the unprepared to risk, and care should be taken to investigate the possible application of exchange controls in the state where the transaction is being carried out or where the counterparty is located.

Other chapters in this book show how the markets treat the Ecu as a currency, particularly how banks operating in the interbank markets do not usually have to create Ecu out of the component currencies, but borrow, lend, buy and sell Ecu just as they do dollars or Deutschmarks.

Managing the private Ecu – the EIB and the EBA

That the private Ecu cannot readily be characterised as a currency is emphasised by the fact that there is no central banking institution to supervise its issuance or circulation. The arguments for and against the establishment of a European central bank, and the powers that it would need to be effective and politically acceptable are beyond the scope of this chapter. Two institutions that have been established, the European Investment Bank (EIB) and the Ecu Banking Association (EBA), have been successful in expanding the role of both the official and the private Ecu. Their legal status is outlined below.

The EIB

The EIB was established in 1957 by the Treaty of Rome. The board of governors is made up of the finance ministers of each of the member states. It operates as the EC's long-term financing institution and is primarily relevant regarding the official Ecu. One consequence of its increasing use of the official Ecu has been to stimulate the growth of activity in the private sector.

In March 1975, the board of governors decided that the EIB balance sheet should be expressed in European Units of Account (EUA) (the predecessor to the Ecu).

Subsequent capital increases have been denominated in Ecu. Loans made by EIB are expressed and paid in Ecu and are required to be credited to Ecu accounts. Its borrowings are also taken in Ecu, as are its drawings of short-term assets through money market paper. The EIB floated its first Ecu bonds in 1981.

The EBA

The EBA was formed in 1985 by a group of 18 commercial banks, developing out of the Mutual Ecu Settlement Account (MESA) clearing system that had been established three years earlier. Based in Paris, its members now number about 90 and include banks from the US and Japan as well as other European but non-EC member states. The concern of its members was to ensure more effective co-ordination of the developing Ecu markets, in particular by examining the legal aspects of the use of the Ecu in the EC member states. The EBA aims to promote the further development of transactions in Ecus and promotes its members' interests in negotiations with the EC authorities and national governments. The EBA has been influential in achieving the widespread (but not necessarily consistent) recognition by states that the private Ecu should be regarded as a foreign currency for regulatory purposes.

Despite its prominence and influence, the EBA should not be considered as similar to a monetary authority or as a European central bank. It does not operate as a lender of last resort nor does it contribute to money supply. Its influence on the clearing of the private Ecu is, however, substantial. This is an area dealt with in more detail in Chapter 13. The operation of the clearing system through the Bank for International Settlements (BIS) and the Society for Worldwide Interbank Financial Telecommunication (SWIFT) is achieved through contract rather than legislation or official regulation. Both BIS (which operates the clearing system) and SWIFT (which operates as a message system for payment instructions) act as agents for the EBA. Neither BIS nor SWIFT are exposed to significant risk or responsibility for losses or damage arising out of the clearing and netting of Ecu transactions. Again, the contrast with the position of central banks in domestic clearing and the role of a lender of last resort is significant.

In the absence of a European central bank or similar institution, the focus of the Ecu market can shift in response to market activity. This market originated in Brussels, moved to Paris and, with the announcement by the Bank of England in March 1989 that it would lend Ecu Treasury bills to market-makers in order to improve liquidity and settlements, on to London. It has been suggested that the Bank of England's undertaking to make a price to market-makers for bills offered has, in effect, obviated the need for a European central bank!

Documentation

The need for definition – the "open basket"

Because the private Ecu is not a currency in its own right and is not the same thing as the official Ecu, it exists only as a matter of agreement between the parties dealing with it or by reference to market practice. Thus, it has to be created, by express or implied contract, each time it is used, whether in a bond issue, a syndicated loan or a trader's invoice. The question of its definition is therefore of great importance.

As has already been mentioned, the composition of the official Ecu can occasionally be revised. This has a significant effect on the definition of the private Ecu.

The private Ecu can be defined in two ways: the "closed basket" and the "open basket" (see Chapter 1).

The first approach, the "closed basket", is to choose the same value as "today's" official Ecu, so that the private Ecu would keep its value even if the value of the official Ecu changed; the "fall-back" of breaking the Ecu down into its constituent currency amounts would ignore the inclusion into the composition of the official Ecu of further currencies or different weightings. This approach would create a "closed basket" Ecu which is one that did not necessarily reflect the value or composition of the official Ecu as time passed. One consequence of this approach would be the existence of private Ecus that had different values. For example, a "closed basket" created in 1988 would not be the same as one created in 1990, ie after the revision of the official Ecu incorporating the peseta and escudo and attributing new weight to the other component currencies.

Clearly, it is not conducive to the development of markets to have more than one type of Ecu being used at the same time. Hence the use of the "closed basket" approach has not generally been followed recently. The bond markets led the way in adopting an "open basket" definition, which defines the private Ecu as having the same value and composition as the official Ecu, as the latter might change from time to time.

The adoption of the "open basket" definition has led some commentators to describe the private Ecu as having shifted, conceptually, from being a "basket of currencies" to being a "basket currency". It has also facilitated the development of direct settlements in Ecu rather than in the component currencies. The use of the "open basket" has also encouraged the quotation of interest rates applicable to Ecu rather than by reference to the sum of the component currencies.

Other documentation issues

Most lawyers have tried to incorporate the Ecu into the documentation of bond issues, loans, commercial paper and other transactions in such a way as to treat it just like any other currency. This means that the documentation of an Ecu transaction, or a multicurrency facility including Ecus as an option, does not look very different to the "standard" US dollar or sterling form that it was modelled on. The mechanics of drawdowns, interest periods, repayments and the customary range of protective clauses (events of default, taxes, illegality and market disruption) remain largely undisturbed by the arrival of the Ecu. The lawyer must, however, make some concessions to it:

- the normal definition of "business day", as used regarding Ecu payments, must take into account the practice for interbank settlements of Ecu;
- the use of the expression "currency" ought to be specifically extended to include the Ecu;
- fall-back provisions are needed to cope with the (increasingly unlikely) possibility that the official Ecu (by reference to which the private Ecu is defined) ceases to exist;
- the document should address the possibility that the borrower (and/or the lender) may not have access to Ecu funds to meet their obligations; and
- indemnities will be incorporated to protect against the possibility of receipt of payment in other currencies or against the refusal of courts to award judgments in Ecu.

Examples of wording used in Clifford Chance's multicurrency documentation are set out in Exhibit 15.1.

"Health warnings" about the Ecu

As the use of the private Ecu spreads from EC institutions through the interbank and money markets to importers and exporters and personal bank accounts, cheque books and credit cards, the providers of credit and financial services should be prepared to explain to their customers some basic facts about the Ecu.

Consumers probably believe that their private Ecu is a currency issued by the EC, and that the EC "guarantees" its value. They may also believe that its value, on the exchange markets and in terms of interest rates, is the same as that of the official Ecu. As we have seen, none of these qualities are, in legal terms, attributes of the private Ecu.

They may assume that one Ecu will at least always be worth the sum of the "basket" of currencies current when the contract was signed, not appreciating the effect of the use of an "open basket" and the possible revision of the composition of the basket.

Exhibit 15.1

Documenting the Ecu

Clifford Chance, in common with other international law firms, have moulded their standard documentation to fit the Ecu without making major changes to the basic style and content.

Set out below are some extracts from their multicurrency loan documentation that specifically address the requirements of the Ecu:

Definitions

- The definition of "Ecu" equates it with the official Ecu, setting out the value of its components but creating an "open basket" by acknowledging that "this basis may be changed by the EC from time to time, including changes in the components, in which event the basis of valuation of the Ecu will change accordingly".
- "A **currency** includes, without limitation, Ecu."
- A **business day** shall be construed as a reference to a day on which ... if such reference relates to the date for the payment or purchase of any sum denominated in Ecu ... those banks which operate a clearing system in Ecu will generally clear payments in Ecu through such clearing system."

Market disruption/disappearance of the official Ecu – fall-back

"If the Agent at any time determines that:

(i) for reasons affecting the market in Ecu generally, Ecu are not freely available in the international interbank market;
(ii) the Ecu has ceased to be utilised as the basic accounting unit of the EC;
(iii) the Ecu has ceased to be used in the EMS; or
(iv) it is illegal, impossible or impracticable for payments to be made hereunder in Ecu,

then the agent may ... declare ... that the repayment of any Advance denominated in Ecu and any payment of interest thereon ... shall be made in a specified component currency ... computed ... in accordance with the provisions of [the Schedule]."

The relevant schedule sets out the procedure for conversion of the Ecu obligation into one denominated in a component currency as follows:

"The components of the Ecu ... (the Components) shall be the currency amounts that were components of the Ecu when the Ecu was most recently used in the EMS; provided however, that if the Ecu is being used for the settlement of transactions by public institutions of or within the EC or if it was so used after its most recent use in the EMS, the Components shall be:

(i) the currency amounts that are components of the Ecu as so used as of the Day of Valuation; or
(ii) the currency amounts that were components of the Ecu when it was most recently so used, as the case may be.

The equivalent of the Ecu in a component currency thereof shall first be calculated as the sum of the dollar equivalents of the Components, and the equivalent of the Ecu in such component currency shall then be calculated on the basis of the dollar equivalent of the Ecu, using the same rates as those used for determining the dollar equivalents of the Components."

Judgments awarded in other currencies – indemnity provisions

"If any sum due by the borrower under this agreement or any order or judgment given or made in relation hereto has to be converted from the currency (the first currency) in which the same is payable hereunder or under such order or judgment into another currency (the second currency) for the purpose of (i) making or filing a claim or proof against the borrower, (ii) obtaining an order or judgment in any court or other tribunal or (iii) enforcing any order or judgment given or made in relation hereto, the borrower shall indemnify and hold harmless each of the persons to whom such sum is due from and against any loss suffered as a result of any discrepancy between (a) the rate of exchange used for such purpose to convert the sum in question from the first currency into the second currency and (b) the rate or rates of exchange at which such person may in the ordinary course of business purchase the first currency with the second currency on receipt of a sum paid to it in satisfaction, in whole or in part, of any such order, judgment, claim or proof."

Customers would be well advised to check the fall-back provisions included in the documentation; these are normally designed to protect the bank or financial institution that is "selling" the Ecu, rather than the consumer.

Those providing financial services should take advice, when preparing their standard agreements, on whether they should publish "health warnings" about their "product" and its unusual qualities.

The validity and enforceability of Ecu claims

The payment obligation

Ecu bonds, loans, swaps and notes do not provide for payment to be made in the component currencies. The documentation may well provide for a fall-back of payment in one or more component currencies in the event that the Ecu disappeared, but the payment obligation is almost invariably expressed as an obligation to pay Ecu.

The private Ecu, however, is not "legal tender" or a currency. It exists as a creature of the agreement between transacting parties or of market practice. What happens if the debtor offers "real" money instead of Ecu? Can the creditor refuse to accept Ecu and insist on payment in "real" money? Will the courts recognise and enforce Ecu claims? What law will they apply in doing so if the transaction crosses national boundaries or if the parties have chosen a particular system of law to govern their agreement?

Making and accepting payments in Ecu

The courts of most countries will support the provisions of a contract that specifically requires payments to be made in Ecu and will not recognise payment in other currencies as discharging the payment obligation.

A debtor will be allowed to tender national currency if payment in Ecu would contravene relevant exchange control regulations, although most European states do now recognise the Ecu as a foreign currency either *de facto* or *de jure* for exchange control purposes.

Exceptions may apply in particular jurisdictions; for example, it may not be possible to force a Swiss national to make any payment in Switzerland in Ecu or to insist on payment in Denmark of any currency other than Danish kroner. In France, where international contracts stipulate payment in a foreign currency (including Ecu), a debtor could validly discharge his debt by payment in French francs.

Indemnity provisions or "judgment currency" clauses should be included in the documentation to protect the creditor against transaction costs or losses arising from exchange rate fluctuations in the event that payment is not received in Ecu as stipulated.

Conversely, the question arises: can a creditor validly refuse to accept Ecu payment, even though the contract stipulates Ecu payments, and insist instead on payment in one or more national currencies?

One would generally expect the creditor to be required to accept payment as agreed in the contract. However, the position is not always clear. For example, under English law there is some authority for the view that a creditor can refuse to accept any payment that is not made in "legal tender". In the 1970s and 1980s, the English courts recognised that payment orders and telex transfers were as valid a method of tendering payment as physical delivery of pound notes or dollar bills, but there are still cases where the courts and some legal writers regard currency as a commodity rather than as the subject of a money obligation. The greater use of the Ecu in the market place can only help to ensure that it will at least be treated as equivalent to foreign currency.

Enforcing the Ecu

Whether a court will issue a judgment obliging a debtor to pay Ecu will depend on the law of the place where the court is, rather than the law chosen to govern the contract. Courts in different places take different views and those that have shown themselves prepared to make orders for payment in Ecu include Italy, France, Luxembourg, Greece and the Netherlands.

The courts of Belgium and Denmark will countenance judgments only in the national currency. In Germany and the US, there seems to be no way of obtaining a judgment in Ecu.

This is not to say that courts which would not grant an Ecu judgment will not recognise the claim at all. These courts would grant judgments in local currency, converting the Ecu amount by reference to an exchange rate and a conversion date of its choosing. The selection of rates and dates can be significant to the litigating parties and different rules can apply in different jurisdictions. Whether or not the court would automatically award compensation for losses arising out of exchange rate fluctuations from the conversion date to the judgment date or payment date is another area where the practice differs from jurisdiction to jurisdiction.

In the face of such uncertainty, prudence dictates that the documentation of Ecu transactions should specifically provide for indemnities to protect the non-defaulting party against losses arising by reason of courts not awarding judgments in Ecu.

Even if a court were to issue a judgment in Ecu, enforcement of the judgment against assets of the debtor would involve a "conversion" process, with a selection of rates and dates, since the assets used to satisfy the judgment will most likely be valued in local currency terms rather than in Ecu (unless the debtor has Ecu account balances or Ecu bonds that can be attached). The conversion date might, in England for example, be the date of the enforcement order or the date on which realisation of the value of the assets is achieved.

The relevance of local exchange controls

In looking at the question of whether the courts might refuse to recognise the Ecu as a valid payment method or to award judgments in Ecu the alternative in each case has been to allow payment, or judgment, in a national currency. In some cases, it may be necessary to consider whether the use of the Ecu has a more fundamental effect on the very validity of the contract. If the contract is in conflict with the exchange control regulations of a state, the contract might be held to have been void from the start or to be unenforceable.

Conventionally, the courts of European states have tended to apply the law of the place where the case is being heard to the resolution of monetary disputes. Even if the contract specifically nominates another law as the governing law, the local regulations may well prevail. EC conventions on the laws applicable to contracts do not prevent mandatory local rules applying, particularly in the case of local exchange control regulations. This convention makes it difficult for parties to try to "contract their way out of" potentially applicable exchange controls. Contracting parties should therefore make themselves aware of the regulatory context in any state where it is likely that they may try to enforce payment obligations.

Many jurisdictions now recognise the private Ecu either *de facto* or *de jure* as a foreign currency for the purposes of applying exchange controls. This means that in France, for example, residents (other than banks) are restricted in their use of the Ecu and the cross-border transfer of Ecus.

In Germany, exchange controls do not exist and the prohibition of Ecu transactions has been relaxed since 1987. However, German residents still need authorisation from the Bundesbank to enter into Ecu-denominated contracts for goods or services.

Identifying the legal obstacles

The EBA and, more recently, the EC Commission have been trying to identify the legal obstacles that impede the current and future use of the Ecu. In November 1990 the Commission formally invited tenders to study the problems across the EC and to outline how the difficulties could be eliminated. The aim is two-fold: to promote the development of the official Ecu as the single common currency of the EC; and to increase confidence among the international business community and consumers regarding the use of the private Ecu in commercial transactions. The aims are complementary, and both focus on the need to establish greater uniformity between member states regarding exchange controls, recognition of the Ecu as a currency and the freedom of companies and individuals to make legally binding contracts in Ecu. Both aims also require an analysis of the institutional framework that is needed. If a central bank started issuing and guaranteeing Ecu notes, for example, and if these could be held by individuals, then many of the difficulties regarding definition and the complexities of fall-back clauses in documentation would disappear.

Broad topic areas in which legislation may need to be changed include:

- accounting rules;
- rules in connection with the capital of companies and shares;
- the assessment and collection of taxation;
- contracts and price fixing;
- rules concerning specialist industries such as insurance and banking.

This study would have to look at the issues in all member states and be sensitive to the differences that exist in their systems of law and the legal concepts that they employ.

Particular attention would need to be given to areas where political, rather than purely economic, considerations apply such as:
- the united Germany;
- the Belgium-Luxembourg monetary union;
- Monaco and France;
- the system of monetary union existing between states with different legal systems in the UK: England, Scotland, Northern Ireland and the Channel Islands.

Exhibit 15.2

Identifying the legal obstacles – some key issues

Billing and taxation

Are there any tax rules requiring value added tax (VAT) or other taxes to be stated in a given currency and billed in that currency?
Will customs require to see the bill and assess duty in the national currency?
Will the government accept payment of taxes in Ecu?
Where tax reliefs exist (eg in the UK for mortgage payments) will such reliefs be given for interest payments/capital payments made/calculated in Ecu?

Company law matters

What rules apply to the initial/nominal/authorised capital which companies are required to have by regulators? Can it be expressed in/paid in Ecu?
Can shares, bonds or other transferable securities be denominated in Ecu?
Can banks, local authorities, building societies or others issue CDs in Ecu?
Can companies express book debts in Ecu?
Can companies express/pay dividends in Ecu?
Can annual accounts be expressed in Ecu?

Use by individuals

Can private individuals have Ecu bank accounts (for either credits or debits)?
Are any Ecu coins/notes available for private use?
Can banks/building societies/insurers, etc, offer mortgages/insurance policies/other documents expressed in Ecu?
Can trustees invest in Ecu securities/maintain Ecu accounts etc where the trust instrument is silent?

General commercial matters

Are specific contracts affected by currency considerations: eg can salary/wages be paid in Ecu? Can contracts for public procurement be tendered for/paid in Ecu?
Can banks and others trade in Ecu? Can they do so on any officially recognised market?
Does any statute/law refer to a "currency" and if so, is the Ecu so regarded for the purpose?
There may be requirements to register certain details: for example, securities over land, ships, aircraft, and company property. If so, is it possible to express the relevant debt in Ecu?
Are there any standard contracts (such as in the UK the national conditions of sale for house purchase) requiring the price to be quoted in legal tender?
Can rents be expressed in Ecu?

Payment in Ecu

Can banknotes be denominated in Ecu?
Can fines imposed by authorities/courts be levied or paid in Ecu?
Can payment in Ecu be made by transfer or cheque?
Can payment in Ecu be made by bill of exchange? Is a bill drawn in Ecu a valid bill? (eg in the UK such a bill may not be valid because the sum is not a "sum certain").
Can payment in Ecu be made by credit cards or bank cards? (If not, as a matter of law or practice?)
Is payment in Ecu by set-off possible?

16 The future of the Ecu

Bertrand de Maigret and
Stefan Collignon
Association for the Monetary Union of Europe

The success of the Ecu as a financial instrument has been spectacular, as previous chapters clearly demonstrate. Yet the commercial use of the Ecu by companies remains very low: less than 1 per cent of European trade is invoiced in Ecu. Only a small portion of the supply of Ecu is effectively kept in Ecu accounts. Exhibit 16.1 shows the volume of credits and deposits in Ecu of the banking system in reporting countries. Note that most credits are extended to other banks, and only a small portion of Ecu deposits is held by the non-banking sector.

The Ecu is not yet functioning as money in the proper sense but is a successful financial instrument that serves as an efficient store of value. It still has to develop its roles as a widely used unit of account and an effective means of payment.

These facts clearly contradict the declared wish of many businessmen in Europe. They believe that a single European market is unattainable as long as many national currencies coexist, and therefore they want a single European currency.

Why are there these contradictions? When will fast-growing

Exhibit 16.1
Local positions in Ecu of banks in individual reporting countries, September 1990 (Ecu bn)

	Assets	*(Vis-à-vis non-banking sector)*	*Liabilities*	*(Vis-à-vis non-banking sector)*
Belgium	2.66	0.30	3.95	0.30
Luxembourg	3.80	0.53	4.40	2.36
France	7.83	1.44	6.08	0.76
Germany	0.23	0.15	0.15	0.08
Ireland	0.46	0.30	0.23	0.08
Italy	5.85	3.57	1.98	0.23
The Netherlands	0.46	0.15	0.76	0.46
Spain	1.90	0.99	1.44	0.53
UK	10.95	2.36	12.24	1.75
Japan	0.46	0.08	0.84	0.08

Source: BIS.

commercial Ecu use complement its financial use? When will the Ecu become money in its fullest sense?

The necessity of monetary union from a business point of view

The demise of the Bretton Woods international monetary system in 1972, with the subsequent regime of floating exchange rates between the major currencies, has led to a significant increase in currency volatility. This resulted in greater uncertainty and restrained long-term investment. Rapid shifts in real exchange rates altered the competitive positions of international companies. Europe was especially sensitive to such a development, as its markets are particularly open. Europe's response to international monetary instability has been the creation of the European Monetary System (EMS) in 1979. It is widely held to have been responsible for bringing down inflation and increasing exchange rate stability within the group of countries participating in the Exchange Rate Mechanism (ERM).

For businesses, this macroeconomic framework has had the following consequences:

1. High exchange rate volatility led to exchange rate risk and businesses had to protect themselves. This caused additional hedging costs.

2. While lower volatility followed from the success of the EMS, transaction costs in European trade and investment relations became more prominent. Stability in the EMS was obtained at the price of significant interest rate differentials, therefore distorting the financial cost structure in Europe. There were further costs due to the necessity of managing a multicurrency system; mainly banking commissions and fees. The consequent lack of market transparency caused higher information costs. All these conditions distorted market relations and led to unequal competition in Europe.

3. In some countries the disadvantages of a multicurrency system were further aggravated by monetary policy differentials such as different rates of inflation and fiscal policies. Thus, the possibility of exchange rate realignments was an additional risk factor and had to be reflected in interest rate differentials. All these factors established a currency hierarchy, with the Deutschmark as the strongest currency. It also created a competitive advantage for German industry.

The microeconomic consequences for businesses are, of course, inefficient allocation of resources and funds. Increased costs reduce profits, thus narrowing the scope for productive investment. Unified market decisions throughout Europe are not possible under these circumstances, and this environment is not compatible with the single market of 1993. This is the reason why economic and monetary union (EMU) in Europe has increasingly become a necessity for the European economy. The next step in completing the single market of 1993 is the creation of a single European currency. Many businessmen are convinced that greater exchange rate stability arguments will dominate in a future tripolar world between the three main monetary areas of yen, Ecu and dollar.

The advantages of a single currency

All the described disadvantages would disappear for European businesses if monetary union meant a single European currency for all EC countries. One single unit of account would be applicable to all transactions and operations within Europe, so that the single European market becomes the only "domestic" market. Only currency areas outside Europe would be considered as "foreign". Uncertainty, exchange risk and interest-rate differentials would all disappear. The condition of perfect competition would arise for the first time. Greater market transparency would allow a more efficient reallocation of existing resources, and greater stability in the economic environment would mobilise new resources for investment and growth. At the same time, Europe would become a major force in the world economy, with 24 per cent of world production and 40 per cent of world trade.

The benefits of EMU and a single currency have been clearly analysed by the Ernst & Young Report,[1] which looked at the assessment of them by European companies. They found that lower transaction costs could lead to Ecu15 billion savings in bank charges. Fifty five per cent of firms questioned claimed that their savings could be larger than, or equal to, 1.5 per cent of turnover and 25 per cent of firms believed that these savings could even exceed 1 per cent of turnover. Even banks felt that they would benefit from a single European currency. One-third of them expected increased income while another third did not expect any significant change. Only one-third expected a loss of income.

Of course, the introduction of a single European currency will also cause certain costs to companies. They will have to install new accounting systems, software and money machines. Most of these costs are one-off investment costs, while the resulting benefits will be perpetual. However, it may be that these costs will be unevenly distributed between different sectors in the economy. Large international companies may be affected more heavily than small local companies. Banks and financial institutions may have different one-off costs compared to small local shops. Consequently appropriate methods of burden-sharing, possibly by allowing tax credits, may have to be considered.

The role of the Ecu in the transition to EMU

The interest of European industry has been aroused by the utility of a single European currency. The question of how to get there is distinguished by three approaches.

1. The institutional approach

The institutional approach comes from the Delors Report in 1989 and has been followed by most governments since then. EMU means that all risks regarding exchange and interest rate differentials are to be eliminated by permanently fixed exchange rates. If exchange rates are to be permanently fixed, then this implies a single monetary policy for Europe. If exchange rates are permanently fixed and a single monetary policy is adopted, then

1. Ernst & Young, NIESR, AMUE, *A strategy for the Ecu*. Kogan Page, London, 1990.

the benefits of having a single currency, with all its related simplifications and increased market coherence, should not be overlooked. A market is not a system of barter but an institution of exchange against money. Therefore, EMU requires both a single monetary policy and a single European currency. This is equivalent to saying that there is a need for a European central bank (ECB) responsible for managing this currency. This bank will be established by an amendment to the Treaties of Rome at the end of the Intergovernmental Conference. The introduction of the Ecu as a single currency is then the consequence of a deliberate choice by democratically elected governments and parliaments.

2. The multicurrency competition approach

The alternative to such an approach would be multicurrency competition, with the idea of the "best" currency slowly crowding out all national currencies. It has been clearly proved by the experience of the 1970s and 1980s that multicurrency competition does not lead to stability, transparency or simplicity. In order to become the strongest currency and win such a competition, a currency would have to satisfy the following criteria:

- stable price levels;
- real exchange rates permitting a competitive industry;
- trade surpluses leading to the status of a creditor nation.

These criteria have been fulfilled by the Deutschmark, which can be claimed to have already won the currency competition. Nevertheless, no simplification or perfect currency substitution has taken place within Europe, and, as seen in Latin America, even in extreme hyperinflation situations, small daily currency transactions are still undertaken in local currency. One should expect an even greater stability of demand for national currencies in Europe. Therefore it is unlikely that the multicurrency approach will lead to a single currency.

3. The market-driven approach

One idea has been to restrict the multicurrency competition to a two-track race between the Ecu and the national currency in each country. The Ecu would then function as a "common" European currency, coexisting with the national currencies. This currency serves as a common unit of account for operations in all European countries. It coexists with other currencies, which are used for domestic operations and normally related to the internal consumer market. If the Ecu in its present basket form is used in this way, it is not necessarily identical with a parallel currency, which effectively competes with and replaces the domestic currency. As a basket, it is a weighted average and therefore never tends to be extreme. It can simply be used as a vehicle for specific operations on a European scale. The existence of the Ecu or any other common currency, together with other national currencies, is clearly not always optimal from the business point of view. It applies only to specific situations.

A common currency does not lead to savings in transaction costs but increases them. For example, bank commissions will need to be paid twice: once for buying Ecu and once for selling them again to obtain national currency. This is due to the fact that there is no end-user of Ecu as salaries, taxes, etc, ultimately need to be paid in national currencies. Furthermore, the additional cost of hedging long-term risks of exchange rate variations, transaction costs of using a 13th currency, etc, are also high because they involve significant management costs of running such a system.

However, there is a company structure where the Ecu as a common currency can really serve as an instrument of savings. If commercial transactions between different countries within one company group are frequent and the European production network is highly diversified, financial flows can be netted in terms of a common currency. Substantial savings can then be obtained by not having to change gross amounts but only incurring net currency transactions. This is a typical case for companies structured like Alcatel, but not for those companies which make up the bulk of European industry, such as Fiat, Rhône-Poulenc, Volkswagen, etc.

The commercial use of the Ecu has one major obstacle: it is only the bastard child of 12 national currencies. No central bank takes responsibility, so the Ecu has no fatherland guaranteeing it a monopoly of use by consumers. It is thrust into competition with the national currencies and has conquered a considerable part of the financial markets because it is a good instrument for protecting assets. It is heavily disadvantaged in business channels by its subordination to national currencies. The Ecu, burdened by the exchange cost and risk, is then only an outside currency weakened by the discrimination against it enshrined in national precedents.

A hard Ecu?

Given these difficulties, would it be a solution to make it "institutionally" the strongest currency by giving it a non-devaluation guarantee? From a free market point of view, this could be interpreted as an "infant industry" protection argument. This would make the Ecu a parallel currency, coexisting and competing with the other 12. The UK government proposed such an approach by suggesting the creation of a "hard Ecu" (see Chapter 17). However, Mrs Thatcher answered candidly when asked on 30 October 1990 in the House of Commons if this approach would work: "In my view, it would not become widely used."

Why is that so?

First of all, on a microeconomic level, a 14th currency that is in addition to the existing basket Ecu would create additional monetary complexity in Europe and destroy the already significant demand in Ecu markets. As pointed out above, the store-of-value function in financial markets is not enough to create money in the proper sense; the transaction functions also needs to be considered. Here, the hard Ecu represents no advantage whatsoever. Furthermore, the fact that it would be a 14th currency may easily destroy the financial success of the present basket-Ecu market. It took more than 10 years to build up the credibility of the basket Ecu. The new hard Ecu would presumably take this many years to reach the same degree of credibility. Such a split would not only have enormous consequences for the present dynamics in the Ecu market. It could create discontinuity of contracts and reduce the initial scope of the new Ecu market, increasing unit transaction costs and thereby preventing substitution of national currencies. Thus, even the discussion in the EC monetary committee came to the conclusion that a fundamental change in the Ecu's definition would have significant consequences for existing markets. This would be particularly serious if any definition gave rise to the coexistence of two different Ecus, a basket Ecu and a hard Ecu. It was also expected that the hard Ecu would have difficulties in competing with the basket Ecu, given the strength of existing markets and the instruments of the strong currency. This would be likely to reduce the attractiveness of the Ecu. Finally, it was thought that a formula which would entail discontinuity in the value of the Ecu would have adverse effects in the development of Ecu markets.

In addition to these microeconomic arguments, objections from a macroeconomic viewpoint may also be raised against the hard Ecu proposal. According to the UK plan, a repurchase obligation will reduce the inflationary impact of a parallel currency. This poses the question of a single monetary policy. Money is the hard budget constraint of a monetary economy. In case of a parallel currency, two constraints would exist if separate and diverging monetary policies are conducted. Therefore in some countries two different price levels would be observed, particularly if exchange rates between the hard Ecu and the national currencies within the EMS are fixed. Which one would be binding? Furthermore, interest rates are a mechanism for resource and fund allocation and, in the case of two currencies and two different interest rates, this can lead to distortions which would be incompatible with a proper market solution. All these factors indicate that the hard-Ecu proposals will not find acceptance in most of Europe.

Nevertheless, it has now generally been accepted that the hardening of the Ecu might be useful during transition towards EMU. The Spanish have presented a proposal which tries to bridge some of the different positions in the EC. It is still not entirely clear how the possible interest rate distortions between the strongest national currency within the EMS and a hardened non-devaluing basket Ecu can be overcome.

An increasing number of businesses want a single currency and a smooth transition, which would guarantee the preservation of numerous signed contracts and the long-term visibility of their monetary environment. Thus the discussion about the nature of the Ecu is virtually irrelevant. Indeed, the basket Ecu is a good and established way to measure uniformly throughout Europe the value of goods and merchandise. It easily fulfills the function of a unit of account. Businesses will use it more when they are sure that contract terms will not be modified by any political decision before the contract is honoured.

If the Ecu definition is frozen as it is, the Ecu will harden itself by the relative reduction of weight in the basket of those currencies which will depreciate, because their central banks conduct more permissive monetary policies. Most importantly, the hardening of the Ecu will be achieved by policies geared to price stability and virtuous public budgets.

This will certainly strengthen its store-of-value function. This measure may even be acceptable to the UK authorities, as documented by a remark from the Governor of the Bank of England: "The hard Ecu was the UK's favourite approach to the idea of moving further towards monetary union." However, he indicated that the UK "would not be adverse to considering other suggestions from moving in this direction. One such idea could consist of extending the use of the existing basket Ecu, a notional, financial unit based on the average weightings of existing European currencies, through freezing its value." (*Financial Times*, 23 January 1991)

Optimism and patience

However, even a reinforced store-of-value function will not necessarily remove the transactional costs and difficulties of the Ecu and help to make it money in the proper sense. If movement towards a single European currency is as strong as documented, the question remains, how can the Ecu be a useful tool in leading towards a single European currency? It is clear that a single European currency needs to be democratically chosen and then institutionally introduced at a certain given date, which can be called Big Bang. On that day, all national currencies will be replaced by the single currency. The basket Ecu can prepare the transition towards this final stage of monetary union by providing what the Germans call *kongruenten Anschluß*, ie a smooth transition towards the single currency. This means that the external value of the basket Ecu the day before Big Bang and of the new single-currency Ecu the day after Big Bang will be practically identical. Thus it will provide continuity of contracts, particularly if the present basket Ecu is frozen with regard to its present components.

For this solution to transition to have any impact on European businesses and the commercial use of the Ecu, it is important that there should be a credible announcement that the Ecu will be the single currency of Europe. A first step in this direction was made by the European Council in Rome in October 1990, when the heads of state and government formally announced, "With the achievement of the final phase of EMU, exchange rates will be irrevocably fixed. The EC will have a single currency, a strong and stable Ecu, which will be an expression of its identity and unity. During the transitional phase, the Ecu will be further strengthened and developed."

For the private sector to incur the sometimes considerable one-off costs involved in changing over to the Ecu, a clear deadline is needed as to when the change will come. This will allow the psychological preparation of contracts leading far into the future, such as the Italian 20-year bond issue. For companies and private industry, it will also allow the preparation of a pricing policy, possibly by the preparation of dual price tags and price lists to familiarise the consumer with future prices. This approach will also provide time to change accounting systems and prepare other money-related machines. Therefore the role of the Ecu will increase in the run-up to Big Bang.

These firms will remain "Ecu pioneers" until the governments have given a clear and credible description of the Ecu's future status, including an agenda for its introduction. Without such a political decision, a single currency for Europe will never come.

Major political decisions have been made by the European Council. Since December 1990, the Intergovernmental Conference on EMU has been in full swing. Optimists say it might finish its work in 1991, with its recommendations leading to the creation of a European central bank as early as 1994–5 and a single currency in 1997.

During the transition to a single currency, it is vital to maintain the political will that has brought so much progress toward monetary union over the last three years. The initiatives to be taken by the authorities to facilitate the use of the Ecu during the transition period will be signals to the markets. These markets are looking forward to measures which are at present being prepared to eliminate national obstacles to the use of the Ecu, as demanded by the European Council. This will be all the more efficient when an agenda for their implementation is agreed.

Government issues in the Ecu market in early 1991, the intentions revealed by the EC Commission, and the decision made by the European Council to set up a European central bank system at the start of 1994 are sources of encouragement and justify our optimism. Once the Treaty is signed and the European central bank is in a position to print Ecu bank notes for the individual customer's use, the time will be ripe for regular invoicing in Ecu. Then the Ecu will be real money.

17

Paul Richards
Samuel Montagu & Co. Limited

The UK proposals for an evolutionary approach to monetary union

Introduction

This chapter is designed to set the UK proposals for an evolutionary approach to monetary union in the context of the debate in the EC on transitional arrangements. The chapter is divided into three parts. The first assesses alternatives to the UK proposals for the transition; the second considers various proposals for hardening the Ecu during the transition; and the third explains how the UK proposals for a hard Ecu managed by a European Monetary Fund would overcome the problems identified in the first two parts with other proposals for transition and definitions of the Ecu.

Alternative routes to EMU

In the debate on monetary union, most attention has been given to stage three: that is, what should happen when monetary union has been achieved. Much less attention has been given in most member states to the transitional arrangements from stage one to stage three: that is, how to achieve monetary union in the first place. The term "monetary union" refers here to monetary union in the EC as a whole, not in part of the Community, and it is assumed that monetary union would require a single monetary policy and currency for the EC, not just irrevocably fixed exchange rates between national currencies.

A move to stage three soon

The Delors Report provided for a transitional stage two but failed to spell out in any detail what it should contain. The conclusion has sometimes been drawn that there is no need for a transitional stage of any substance at all. The Commission has proposed that stage two, which is due to begin on 1 January 1994, should be relatively short. The main purpose of a short stage two would be to set up the institutional arrangements at EC level for stage three proposed under the revision in the Treaty. Powers would then be transferred to the new institution when stage three was implemented shortly afterwards.

It may be simple in theory for member states to fix their exchange rates irrevocably and transfer the ultimate power to take decisions about monetary policy from national to EC level. But it is becoming increasingly clear that it would not be feasible in practice for the whole EC to move to stage three shortly after the revision in the Treaty is ratified. Doubts about the feasibility of a speedy transition towards monetary union would have surfaced even if the Gulf crisis had not intervened to accentuate them. Apart from the UK, the higher-inflation countries would not be able to make the necessary commitment required to implement stage three soon. Even if they were prepared to do so, the low-inflation countries would be very unlikely to accept that the higher-inflation countries were sufficiently convergent, either in terms of the degree of economic cohesion necessary between different regions of the EC or in terms of their expected inflation performance, for monetary union to be feasible soon in the EC as a whole.

The UK is not alone then in believing that there would be unacceptable risks in moving quickly to a single currency. The experience in Germany since German monetary union has reinforced the view there that premature monetary union in the EC would increase unemployment and the need for transfer payments, at least in the short term. Nor would the Bundesbank Council be prepared to vest its decision-making powers in an EC institution, unless it was confident that the single monetary policy pursued would result in at least as low inflation in Germany as the Bundesbank itself expected to achieve. A track record of this kind would take time to build and require support from governments and citizens throughout the EC for the principle of achieving price stability over other objectives. The President of the Bundesbank has pointed out that there would be no advantage in saving transaction costs by introducing a single currency if the new monetary system was not as effective in countering inflation as the old monetary system that it was designed to replace.

A prolonged stage one

Although a move by the EC as a whole to stage three soon appears not to be feasible, two other options for the transition (apart from the UK proposals) have been considered so far. One would be to prolong stage one for a considerable period after ratification of the Treaty, in the hope that a move could be made to stage three at a later date. A prolonged stage one of this kind would be unattractive to some advocates of monetary union, for two opposing reasons:

1. One school of thought is that the Exchange Rate Mechanism (ERM) is inherently unstable. The argument goes that, unless the EC were to take new steps soon towards monetary integration, speculative pressures would break up the ERM.
2. The other school of thought is that, on the contrary, the complete abolition of exchange controls and the advent of the single market would bind the EC closer together by making control of monetary policy more difficult at national level. The assumption here is that the market would begin to arbitrage out interest differentials between national currencies,

though this would not necessarily have the effect of reducing the underlying rate of inflation in the EC.

In both cases, a prolonged stage one would be regarded as undesirable: in the first case, new institutional arrangements would be needed to stop the EC from losing momentum and the ERM from falling apart; in the second case, new institutional arrangements would be needed to reflect the fact that the EC had moved closer together.

These opposing views are probably overstated and too mechanical. What is more likely to happen is that the ERM will continue to develop as it has done over the last 10 years, with less and less frequent realignments. This view would be consistent with institutional changes in the EC, though institutional changes in practice would be likely to occur, not because they were essential, but because they were the necessary result of a revision in the Treaty. There would after all be no need for a revision in the Treaty, unless it were to lead to the establishment of a new EC institution with decision-making powers of some sort. Previous experience (for example, in the case of the European Monetary Co-operation Fund (EMCF)) also suggests that a new EC institution would lack credibility if there was too long an interval between the date on which it was established and the date when it could begin to exercise its powers.

A two-tier EC

The other option would be for the EC to move towards monetary union at two speeds, as provided for in the Delors Report and proposed by the Bundesbank. The idea here would be that all member states, with the possible exception of the UK, would sign a Treaty which would set out the arrangements for stage three as a goal. However, only a few member states would be in a position to implement stage three quickly. They would probably consist largely of the original Schengen area: ie Germany, Benelux and France. The rest would be expected to follow later, possibly on specified future dates according to an agreed timetable. Their currencies would continue within the ERM in the meantime and would eventually all move within 2¼ per cent bands.

There is general agreement that a two-speed approach would be quite likely to happen in the absence of a realistic EC-based alternative. It would be an unattractive option for those who consider that a two-speed EC would lead to a two-tier EC for five main reasons:

1. A two-tier approach to monetary union would be likely to lead to a two-tier approach in other areas of economic policy.
2. One of the reasons why some member states (like France) would favour monetary union in the EC as a whole is to reduce the relative power currently exercised by the Bundesbank in the ERM by absorbing it in a EC institution in which all members could have an effective say. Under the two-tier approach, however, the Bundesbank would probably carry even more weight in the first tier than it has carried in the ERM, and the operational centre of the system would no doubt be located in Germany.
3. The monetary policy of countries in the second tier (such as the UK) would be at least as heavily influenced by a monetary institution in which they had no say as in the ERM in practice at the moment.

4. It would not be clear whether countries in the second tier who wished to join the first tier as soon as possible (such as Italy and Spain) would automatically be able to do so. If they did, this would probably reduce the support for monetary union from the Bundesbank. If they did not, then decisions about entry would effectively be taken by the first tier rather than in an EC context.
5. There would be no specific provision for enabling countries in the second tier to catch up with those in the first tier.

Alternative definitions of the Ecu in the transition

A number of ways have been proposed of hardening the Ecu during the transition to monetary union. The second part of this chapter identifies the problems which would arise during the transition with the existing Ecu basket, a frozen-Ecu basket, a hard-Ecu basket, a two-tier hard Ecu and an official hard Ecu.

Existing Ecu basket

The Ecu is currently defined as the sum of a basket of fixed weights of the component currencies of member states. The basket has been revised every five years, when the currencies of new member states have been included, and the weights given to existing members' currencies adjusted according to a set of economic and financial criteria. Generally, when revisions take place, the weights given to currencies that have been strong are reduced, and the weights given to weak currencies are increased. The external value of each new basket is always the same as the old basket at the point of change in the Ecu's definition. From that point onwards, the values of the different baskets diverge. The value of the basket Ecu and the value of the Ecu as the EC's future single currency would only be the same on a continuous basis, if exchange rates were irrevocably fixed first between the national currencies of all the member states included in the basket.

There would be four main problems during the transition with the Ecu as currently defined.

1. The most important problem is that, while the underlying value of the Ecu would harden if and when the national monetary policies of member states became more counter-inflationary, the Ecu itself could not be used to promote convergence throughout the EC on low inflation, which would be an essential precondition for bringing a viable monetary union about. The Ecu would simply represent the weighted average of the component currencies in the basket and the interest rate on any given maturity on the Ecu yield curve would be influenced by the interest rate on the component currencies for the maturity concerned. Consequently, if a direct attempt was made to change Ecu interest rates, arbitrage opportunities would normally arise between the interest rate on the Ecu and the interest rate on the component currencies in the basket. The main limitations on arbitrage of this kind would be transaction costs, liquidity constraints and other distorting factors, such as tax advantages from investing in financial

instruments denominated in Ecus or market expectations of a future change (eg a hardening) in the definition of the Ecu. The only other circumstances in which arbitrage opportunities would not arise would be circumstances in which a monetary authority at EC level was able to impose its chosen interest rate on national authorities, with the effect that they had no choice but to follow any change in Ecu interest rates. In practice this would be virtually equivalent to stage three.

2. The intention is that the Ecu should increasingly be used during the transition to monetary union. The Rome Communique in October 1990 proposed that the use of the Ecu should be promoted in stage two.

Promotion of the use of an Ecu which represented "the average" would probably be more difficult, particularly in countries used to low inflation, such as Germany, than promotion of an Ecu which represented "the best": that is, an Ecu which could never be devalued at realignments against the Deutschmark (or any other national EC currency). In addition, if the Ecu's circulation did increase during stage two while it remained a basket average, this would be consistent with a monetary policy representing the EC average. However, it would not be consistent with a monetary policy designed to ensure a rate of inflation in the EC as low as Germany (or any other member state).

While it would not much matter that the Ecu consisted of a basket average if the Ecu was not intended to be extensively used during stage two, the problem that would need to be confronted in those circumstances would be a different one, because the Ecu would be unknown when it replaced national currencies. This would be especially difficult if the measures necessary for the introduction of the Ecu as the single currency were to be taken immediately after the beginning of stage three.

3. It is not clear why a revision in the Treaty would be needed at all at this stage unless powers were granted at EC level to manage the Ecu. National monetary policies could be co-ordinated, monetary techniques standardised and the use of the Ecu promoted in stage one without a revision in the Treaty. The reason for revising the Treaty now could be limited solely to the need to make preparations in stage two for the transfer of powers from national level to EC level in stage three. However, if stage two began on 1 January 1994 as planned, there would then either be a long delay until all member states were sufficiently convergent to move together to stage three, during which the new EC institution set up at the beginning of stage two would (like the EMCF) effectively have no powers; or, if there was a short delay, only selected member states would initially be willing and able to move to stage three. So, instead of forming a monetary union of the EC as a whole, they would be forming a monetary union among themselves in one tier, leaving other member states behind in a second tier.

4. In those circumstances, the exchange rate of the first tier of member states (whose own exchange rates would have been irrevocably fixed) would not be the same as the exchange rate on the basket Ecu, which would contain currency components from the second as well as the first tier. The implication is that either the first tier would have to wait before introducing a single currency until all the second tier had joined or, if a single currency was introduced in the first tier, it could not be the basket Ecu.

Frozen-Ecu basket

A second option would be to freeze the composition of the Ecu basket. The effect would be to avoid a revision in the basket every five years. A frozen-Ecu basket would arguably have two advantages over the existing Ecu basket, but otherwise it would have the same disadvantages. One advantage would be that, if membership of the EC expanded during the transition to monetary union to include countries from European Free Trade Association (EFTA) and Eastern Europe, their currencies would not have to be included in the basket as there would be no subsequent basket revision in which to include them. Consequently, continuity between the basket Ecu and the Ecu as the future single currency would only have to await irrevocably fixed exchange rates between existing member states and not a similar commitment by any new members. The other advantage over the existing Ecu basket would be that the value of the proportions represented by strong currencies in the basket would continue to increase instead of being reduced every five years, and the proportions represented by weak currencies would diminish. The underlying value of a frozen basket Ecu could be expected to be marginally stronger than the existing basket Ecu. But it would still represent a weighted average. The only difference from the existing Ecu basket would be a marginal change in the weights.

Hard-Ecu basket

A third option would be to redefine the weighted average Ecu basket at the beginning of stage two into a hard-Ecu basket, along the lines proposed by Germany and Spain. The Ecu would consist of a basket of component currencies, but at realignments it would not be devalued against any national EC currency. In other words, it appears that there would be two changes to the existing basket Ecu: first, revisions in the weights would take place at each realignment rather than every five years; second, revisions would be based on "the best" rather than "the average". This would overcome the problem that the value of the basket Ecu has traditionally not been as strong as the Deutschmark. However, it would not overcome other drawbacks with the basket Ecu, and it could raise new problems.

The main problem would be the apparent inconsistency between basing the Ecu on a basket (ie a weighted average) between realignments, on the one hand, while revising the basket at realignments so that the Ecu was not devalued against any national EC currency on the other. The revision in the basket could be achieved by increasing the weights of either all the component currencies equally, or the strong currencies or weak currencies disproportionately. But whichever way, tensions would arise between the influence of the basket and the influence of the exchange guarantee at realignments, particularly during periods when realignments were expected in the market.

If the yield on the hard-Ecu basket initially reflected the yields on the component currencies in the basket, then the market could arbitrage out the yield differential on the basket over the lowest-yielding national EC currency without taking an exchange risk. However, if on account of the exchange guarantee the yield on the basket fell to (or below) the level of the yield on the strongest national currency, then interest rates on the hard-Ecu basket would no longer be determined by the component currencies in the basket, and might be capable of being influenced by intervention on the part of national authorities.

In the case of the hard-Ecu basket exchange rate, either a premium would develop over the value of the component currencies in the basket, particularly when the market anticipated a realignment, or there would be additional downward pressure on short-term interest rates on the basket to compensate for the step change in the basket's value on realignment, at which point additional amounts of component currencies would be added to the basket.

Two-tier hard Ecu

A fourth option would be to define the hard Ecu in terms of the national currencies of those member states which had fixed them irrevocably to it. This could happen, for example, under a multispeed approach to monetary union, during which a number of member states, including (say) Germany, France and Benelux, would fix their exchange rates irrevocably first, while other member states would join the monetary union later, when they were willing and able to do so. The hard Ecu would become a common currency for the first tier or, alternatively, a single currency if it were to replace the national currencies of the first tier. Either way, it would become a parallel currency in the second tier. This approach would have the significant disadvantage that the hard Ecu would be managed by the first tier, not by the EC as a whole. The monetary policy of member states in the second tier would be influenced by decisions taken by member states in the first tier, but without the second tier having any say in formulating them or even the final say over when they could join. A two-tier hard Ecu would also raise questions of discontinuity with the basket Ecu in the period after the first tier had moved to stage three, but before the second tier had done so. There could even be three Ecus in existence at the same time: the hard Ecu, the basket Ecu, and the official Ecu.

Official hard Ecu

A fifth option would be to confine the hard Ecu during the transition to transactions between national central banks. One suggestion is that the official Ecu should become an instrument of monetary control over the national central banks of member states by means of reserve requirements. If the reserve requirements were effective, the impact would be similar to stage three: control over the Community's monetary policy would be transferred from national to EC level. If not, there would be no point in introducing them in the first place. Another suggestion is to make the hard Ecu the common denominator for the central parities of member states in stage two, use it for central bank intervention at or within intervention points in the ERM and in settlement of intra-central bank debts and remove the distinction between official and private Ecus through the abolition of the official Ecu as currently defined. This approach would not be inconsistent with the UK proposals for a hard Ecu managed by a European Monetary Fund (EMF).

The UK proposals for hard Ecu managed by an EMF

The UK proposals for a hard Ecu managed by a European Monetary Fund (EMF) are designed to overcome the problems identified with other proposals and definitions of the Ecu for the transition. In the third part of this chapter, the UK proposals are assessed in three sections: the first contains an outline of the UK proposals; the second emphasises the attractions of the UK proposals; and the third answers the main lines of criticism of them.

Outline of the UK proposals

Under the UK proposals, the EMF would have an obligation to manage the hard Ecu so that it was never devalued at realignments against any national EC currency. The EMF would issue hard Ecu liabilities on demand in exchange for national EC currencies. Narrow central bank money would be controlled through the exercise of the repurchase requirement, under which the EMF would present excess holdings of national currency to the relevant national central bank for payment in hard Ecus or other hard currencies. Broad money (ie including deposits in hard Ecus with the commercial banking system) would be influenced through the EMF's ability to control hard-Ecu interest rates. Once the credibility of the EMF was established, hard-Ecu interest rates should normally be as low or lower than interest rates on the strongest national EC currency. The hard Ecu could, if member states agreed, replace the basket Ecu as the common denominator of the EMS. The exchange rates of member states would then float in the ERM within narrow margins of central parities expressed in terms of the hard Ecu. Member states would be free to fix their exchange rates on the hard Ecu by eliminating narrow margins, forming a *de facto* monetary union if they chose to do so, but the hard Ecu, would continue to be managed by the EMF, representing the central banks of the EC as a whole, and not by the central banks of those member states which chose to fix their exchange rates.

Attractions of the UK proposals

The UK proposals themselves are complete and free-standing. They do not indicate what, if anything, should supersede them. Nor would any further development be technically necessary. Consequently, they are in line with the UK government's insistence that it will not accept the imposition of a single currency. However, quite apart from their attractions as a self-contained scheme to follow stage one, the UK proposals should be attractive to those who support the aim of a single currency and are concerned that the transition to full monetary union should proceed as smoothly as possible. The main attractions of the UK proposals can be summarised as follows:

1. They would enable the EC to take institutional steps in the relatively near future that would constitute stage two in the process of transition to monetary union and require a revision in the Treaty, while recognising that monetary union itself would take a longer period to achieve and could not be achieved successfully until a much greater degree of convergence had occurred between member states.

2. At the same time, the UK proposals would promote convergence throughout the EC on low inflation. This would help create the conditions in which a viable monetary union could come about, if and when there was the political will in the EC to achieve it.

3. Under the UK proposals, the EC would move forward together. The EMF would be owned by the national central banks of all member states. The board of the EMF could be independent, if member states so decided. The European system of central banks in stage two, consisting of the EMF alongside national central banks, would evolve into the European system of central banks and consist of the European central bank (ECB) and national central banks, if and when the Community moved to stage three.

4. Finally, the UK proposals would enable the EC to gain practical experience in managing the hard Ecu as a common currency before irreversible decisions were taken about whether to fix exchange rates irrevocably and replace national currencies with a single currency. They would avoid a "leap in the dark" involving the transfer of powers away from national level to EC level, unless and until it was clear to all member states that the new system would be at least as counter-inflationary as the system it replaced.

Critique of the UK proposals

The three main criticisms of the UK proposals are that the hard Ecu would be a parallel currency; that the establishment of the new institution required to manage it would create a grey area in the EC's monetary policy; and that the use of the hard Ecu would be a poor guide to the need for a single currency. None of these criticisms is justified.

The hard Ecu would be a common currency which would not be subject to either of the criticisms made of parallel currencies in the Delors Report. First, it would not be inflationary. On the contrary, the hard Ecu could only subtract from inflationary pressures, not add to them. Second, it would not complicate the process of transition to monetary union, but by promoting convergence on low inflation, the hard Ecu would be a common currency which would help to create the conditions in which a viable monetary union in the EC as a whole could come about, if there was the political will to achieve it.

The second criticism – that the UK proposals would create a grey area in the EC's monetary policy in stage two – is also unjustified. Decisions about national monetary policy would continue to be taken at national level. Responsibility for the hard Ecu would rest solely with the EMF, which would manage it without interference from national governments in the light of its legal obligation not to let the hard Ecu be devalued. In the first case national central banks would co-operate, and in the second they would act collectively, through the EMF. The effect would be to leave much less ambiguity in the EC's monetary policy in stage two under the UK proposals than under the alternatives. One of these alternatives would involve a solution that relied exclusively on co-ordinating national monetary policies through peer pressure. The other alternative would involve a two-tier solution, in which the policy of member states in the second tier would be influenced by the policy of member states in the first tier without any say in making it, or the final say over when they could join.

The third criticism – that the use of the hard Ecu would be a poor guide to the need for a single currency – can be answered as follows:

1. The use of the hard Ecu could be expected to develop over time in response to market choices. The attraction of the hard Ecu to investors would be the commitment not to devalue it at realignments against their national currency. The attraction to borrowers would be the low interest rate, which should normally be at least as low as on the strongest national currency and probably lower once the hard Ecu's liquidity and the EMF's credibility in the market had been established.
2. The hard Ecu would probably be used initially for transactions by businesses and their banks at the commercial level rather than by individuals at the retail level. Individuals are traditionally reluctant to give up the use of their national currency, whereas businesses and banks trade across borders in different currencies all the time.
3. The use of the hard Ecu would probably grow more quickly in substitution for national currencies if market participants considered that it would one day become the EC's single currency. That would not mean that irreversible decisions about the single currency would need to be taken now.
4. The UK proposals should not be judged solely on the circulation achieved by the hard Ecu. Their objective would be to reinforce convergence on the lowest rate of inflation in the EC through the monetary discipline that they would exert on national central banks. Consequently, the hard Ecu would act as a European standard.
5. Finally a decision by member states about when to move from stage two to stage three would not depend on complete substitution of hard Ecus in place of national currencies first. But the exercise of market choices in favour of the hard Ecu would be one of the factors that member states would take into account in deciding when the time was right to do so.

As under other proposals for hardening the Ecu during the transition, the question would arise under the UK proposals of how best to handle contracts in basket Ecus.

One option would be to replace the basket Ecu with the hard Ecu at the beginning of stage two, with continuity in the Ecu's external value at the point of change similar to previous changes in its definition. The other would be to allow basket-Ecu contracts to run off and leave the market to devise ways of exchanging basket Ecus into hard Ecus once the hard Ecu was launched. Whichever option was chosen, there would be no need for any confusion to arise in the market.

Conclusion

In summary, the UK proposals represent an evolutionary approach to monetary union for the whole EC. They constitute a practical way forward beyond stage one, given that it would not be feasible for the EC as a whole to move from stage one to stage three soon. They would provide businesses and individuals with a common currency at an early stage; enable the prospective monetary institution for the EC to establish its credibility, and gain practical experience of a common currency, before irreversible decisions were taken about a single currency; help to create the conditions for monetary union by promoting convergence on low inflation; and have the advantage of avoiding a two-tier EC.

18 Country studies

Benelux and the Ecu

Bernard de Thomaz

Banque Bruxelles Lambert

During the 1960s, while the first major monetary upheavals were shaking the Bretton Woods monetary system, Belgian banks realised that the "Belgian dentist" was on the outlook for investments intended to circumvent the troubles which were brewing on exchange markets.

The Eurobond market had just been created. The European Payments Union had been dissolved in 1958. Thus the idea was born of issuing bonds denominated in the unit of account used by the former European Payments Union. "Unit of account 17" bonds were rapidly successful with these investors who were anxious to make investments without a monetary risk. After 1973, when the links with gold were dropped by domestic parliaments, these bonds went through a difficult time. Indeed, a clause stipulated that the currency of repayment would be that which still had a link with gold if by chance the other currencies broke this link. The last currency to maintain this link was the Swiss franc, which, it will be remembered, appreciated substantially against the other currencies after this period. For borrowers, this was a costly clause; indeed, it was necessary to redeem some bonds at over 170 per cent of their initial value.

To keep this market alive, Belgian banks, in particular, began to use the unit of account 9, defined on the basis of a basket of the nine currencies of the countries which made up the European Community at that time. Although this market had a considerable success, the "currency basket" which was its mainstay had a major flaw; no supranational body had authority over it or gave its moral backing to this currency.

Yet the calculations made at the time clearly show that bonds denominated in unit of account 17 or 9 enabled their holders to obtain returns in line with their expectations. These investments yielded a substantial return and the currency was stable in a world harrowed by monetary maelstroms.

When, in 1979, President Valéry Giscard d'Estaing and Chancellor Helmut Schmidt agreed to set up a European currency, the embryo of the single currency, Belgian banks found among their customers investors willing to subscribe to these bonds denominated in this new currency, which in their eyes presented many advantages, not the least the fact that this new unit of account enjoyed the moral backing of the Community and that its vocation was to become the European currency. For these savers eager for stability, this meant a stable currency from an exchange rate point of view, offering considerable returns, as they were based on the yields offered by all the currencies participating in the system, including those of the Southern European countries.

Until the end of 1982, this Ecu-denominated Eurobond market remained the prerogative of the banks of the Belgo-Luxembourg Economic Union. Yet these banks rapidly realised the danger of such specificity. Therefore they welcomed with open arms the interest shown by banks from neighbouring countries in the Ecu, for this would allow them to avoid such geographic concentration. At the outset, it was the Italian banks which were extremely interested in investments in Ecu. Gradually, other banks followed suit, to such an extent that the market opened up harmoniously and grew to its present respectable size.

During 1985 and 1986, the momentum of Belgian investors decreased due to the fact that, as the pound sterling was dropping steadily against the other European currencies, the value of the Ecu weakened against the Belgian franc. As the return on Eurobonds in Ecu was close to that of those available in Bfr, the attraction of these investments for Belgian investors waned.

Obviously, these investments are not the only ones on offer to savers wishing to invest in Ecu. Although, given the dynamism of investors, Paris has become the leading market for investments in bonds and London has taken first place in the Ecu interbank market, Brussels continues to play a major role with regard to the investment capacity of Ecu-denominated Eurobonds. Furthermore, Belgian banks continue to play a significant role in Ecu transactions in the non-banking sector.

In this regard, Belgian banks made a point of developing an extremely full range of Ecu services for their clients. From the very beginning, in the early 1980s, they offered the possibility of opening current accounts denominated in Ecu. Needless to say, they did not stop there. Customers can now open term accounts in Ecu, make transfers or collections, draw cheques and transfers, issue letters of credit for the purpose of exports and imports, carry out spot and forward operations in Ecu, carry out interest and currency swaps, take out options and conclude FRAs, obtain short- or long-term loans in Ecu with fixed or floating rates, and obtain syndicated loans and issue Eurobonds denominated in Ecu. It can be said that in Belgium it is easy to carry out Ecu operations and that the scope in this field is very wide. All these services are available to both companies and private individuals.

Furthermore, it is a well-known fact that Belgian banks were among the founding member of the MESA group which made it possible to clear interbank transactions denominated in Ecu under the patronage of the Bank for International Settlements (BIS).

A few figures will give an idea of the scope of these different possibilities.

The structure of banking intermediation in Ecu over the past three years (the statistics available to date stop at the end of the third quarter of 1990) shows that the net position of banks belonging to the Belgo-Luxembourg Economic Union with regard to non-resident's stood at Ecu23.4 billion for assets and at Ecu22.5 billion for liabilities. The assets belonging to non-banks amounted to Ecu7.9 billion and liabilities to Ecu3.5 billion. Therefore, it can be said that the banks of the Belgo-Luxembourg Economic Union represented 21.3 per cent of assets in Ecu on non-residents and 20.1 per cent of liabilities in Ecu towards the non-resident non-financial sector. As for liabilities towards residents, the banks of the Belgo-Luxembourg Economic Union held Ecu6.5 billion, ie 18.5 per cent of residents' assets in Ecu and gathered Ecu8.4 billion, ie 25.9 per cent of residents' deposits in Ecu. In the latter figures, banks' non-financial residents' assets represented Ecu0.8 billion, ie 7.7 per cent of the total, and liabilities represented Ecu2.7 billion, ie 40.3 per cent of the total.

To develop the Ecu market, all Luxembourg and Belgian-based banks have always worked closely together. Admittedly, this co-operation was probably facilitated by the fact that many Luxembourg banks are branches or subsidiaries of Belgian banks, and that banks in both countries have a very similar customer base.

As for the expansion of the Ecu market in the Netherlands, it would be fair to say that Dutch banks wholeheartedly supported the efforts deployed by the Belgian and Luxembourg banks. Yet Algemene Bank Nederland should be singled out as the one to have pioneered the introduction of Ecu-denominated certificates of deposit.

At the end of last year, Dutch banks had accumulated Ecu5.5 billion in Ecu assets (4.0 per cent of their total assets) and collected Ecu5.1 billion in Ecu deposits (3.78 per cent of total deposits). These are mainly interbank positions, since non-bank assets amounted to only Ecu0.8 billion, and non-bank Ecu deposits to Ecu1.0 billion, or 5.47 per cent and 2.99 per cent of total non-bank positions respectively.

Dutch banks accounted for some 3.99 per cent of all Ecu bank assets as at that date, and for 3.78 per cent of all Ecu bank liabilities. Also, the Ecu was used as a transaction currency for 0.7 per cent of Dutch exports and 0.6 per cent of imports, against 0.4 per cent and 0.3 per cent respectively for total Belgo-Luxembourg exports and imports.

The participation of banks of the Belgo-Luxembourg Economic Union in issues of Eurobonds remains considerable. Total issues in Ecu during 1990, carried out through 83 different operations, gathered Ecu13,525 million. For the first three months of 1991, this figure already amounted to Ecu11,815 million, carried out through 20 operations.

In this regard, according to the data provided by the IFR database, according to statistics established on the basis of the issue date, all lead-managers and co-managers of 1909 Ecu-denominated Eurobond issues in terms of largest volume, BBL is the leading bank with Ecu9,266.1 million, carried out through 94 operations. Générale de Banque is the ninth bank with a volume of Ecu6,061.5 million and 59 operations, while Kredietbank is the fourteenth bank with Ecu5,176.1 million and 54 operations.

The European currency as seen from Brussels

The adoption by member states of a single currency implies choices: if one decides to use a single currency, one must decide at the same time to harmonise the economic and fiscal policies of the countries involved. For a country as small as Belgium such a choice raises a number of questions. For many years Belgian monetary policy has been dominated by the fact that Belgium belongs to the EMS. This implied that Belgium had to follow German monetary policy and, consequently, the same policy as that of the Netherlands. The Belgian monetary authorities were not left much room to manoeuvre. Nonetheless, it was necessary first to bear the weight of the past. The existence of an immense public-sector debt implied that the authorities needed to rationalise government spending. Broadly speaking, this effort has now been achieved. The Belgian public-sector net borrowing requirement is now comparable to that of the Netherlands. However, this effort is not yet sufficient. It should be noted that it is still necessary to align economic policy. This is being achieved through the steps taken to adapt Belgian statutory and fiscal working conditions to Community guidelines. However, a few extremely sensitive issues remain.

The alignment of the Belgium franc with the Deutschmark, which was decided unilaterally by the central bank of Belgium, entails consequences which can be considered entirely favourable in the long term for Belgium. In the short term, however, there is no institutional mechanism which guarantees success. The risk is that the adjustments required within the Belgian economy will be painful for certain portions of the population. This may require a policy of income transfers. Indeed, once economic and monetary Europe is set up, it will be essential to set up fiscal and social Europe. These priorities and the importance of what is at stake implies that no time should be lost in setting up monetary Europe.

Eastern Europe and the Ecu

Alfonso Jozzo

Istituto Bancario San Paolo di Torino

The return to democracy and the beginning of the transition to a marked economy in the East and Central European countries (ECECs) represents one of the two fundamental developments in Europe at the end of this century. The other is the acceleration of the process towards Economic and Monetary Union (EMU) for the EC member states.

In our highly interdependent world the former process cannot be carried on without a comprehensive view of the new European environment. The role of the Ecu, as the future currency of Europe, in the ECECs thus represents an opportunity to understand these trends and possibly forecast certain developments in that area.

The actual use of the Ecu in these developing markets, the official attitude towards the Ecu, the relevance of Ecu-oriented supranational institutions in the ECECs and the opportunities that the Ecu offers to the countries and companies of the former Comecon will be examined here, from both a micro- and macroeconomic viewpoint.

The use of the Ecu in the ECECs

It is well known that in planned economies "money" played a different and far less relevant role than in the market economies. In the ECECs it is "the entire sphere of the currency policy which, until recently, has been expelled not only to the periphery of practical politics, but it was ousted to the periphery of the theory and research as well".[1]

In fact, banking systems and financial markets were non-existent in the countries of the Comecon. The sole ECEC players on the international financial market were the central banks, while foreign trade-related operations were delegated to the national foreign trade banks. After the introduction of two-tier banking systems and more business-oriented rules, these habits are expected to change in a few years, with the new commercial banks and ECECs' domestic companies allowed to borrow in foreign currencies.

Due to the above constraints, from October 1984 to August 1989 Vnesheconombank, the Soviet bank for foreign economic affairs (named Vneshtorgbank until 1988), had been the sole Eastern European beneficiary of Ecu loans. At the end of 1990, it had received a total amount of Ecu767 million, under several types of credit facilities.

On the Eurobond market, Czechoslovakia, Hungary and the USSR launched seven issues, worth the equivalent of a US$1.4 billion total in Deutschmarks, US dollars and Austrian schillings as denomination currencies in 1990. The National Bank of Hungary has so far been the only ECEC borrower to tap the Ecu sector. In August 1989 it issued an Ecu75 million seven-year Eurobond.

At present, the Ecu is officially quoted on a daily basis by the National Bank of Hungary, the National Bank of Poland, the State Bank of the USSR (with both an official rate and, from the end of October 1990, a commercial rate) and the Yugoslavian Banking Association.

The institutions of the former Comecon are also looking to the Ecu as a useful means for their reshaping, as shown by the experience of the International Bank for Economic Co-operation (IBEC). The IBEC acted as clearing agent of the transferable rouble-based system. After the break-down of the latter, the members of the IBEC decided it will carry on its activity on a commercial basis and in convertible currencies.

As a way of underlining its new role, at an extraordinary meeting of the IBEC's Council in December 1990 the nine members decided to re-denominate its capital in Ecus. It has been established at Ecu400 million (with a 46 per cent stake for the USSR).

The European currency has already been used for large public contracts with the Soviet Union, and has proved a useful tool for overcoming problems in East-West joint ventures. The most important examples concern the USSR, ie the Sherotel (ACCOR Group) at Moscow airport and the Fiat plant in Yelabuga.

The Sherotel joint venture has Ecu-denominated and paid-in capital, Western credits are in Ecus and the accounts of the hotel are kept in Ecus. Choosing the Ecu was a natural choice for a Soviet joint venture, with London-based bank accounts, a Belgian construction company and financing bank and French shareholders and management.

1. As stated by Josef Tosovsky (President of the Czechoslovak State Bank) in an address delivered at the Conference on "The role of the Ecu in the developing relations between Eastern and Western Europe", organised by the Ecu Banking Association in Prague, 22 June 1990 (now in *Ecu Newsletter – Central and Eastern Europe Supplement*, Istituto Bancario San Paolo di Torino and Inter-Europa Bank, September 1990).

The Yelabuga plant, with investments worth Ecu1.2 billion, is expected to act as an Ecu enclave in the Soviet economy. All transactions, both domestic and foreign, will be denominated and actually paid in Ecus, while within the Soviet Union a sort of clearing house will convert Ecus into roubles for domestic clients and suppliers. This experiment could open wide-ranging prospects for multinational companies to do business in Ecus with the Soviet Union.

International financial co-operation and the Ecu

A major role in developing the knowledge and use of the Ecu in the ECECs will certainly be played by initiatives of East-West financial co-operation in the years to come.

The G-7 meeting in Paris in July 1989 decided to grant assistance to Hungary and Poland and asked the other industrialised countries of the G-24 to join this programme. The EC Commission was given the role of co-ordinating all the interventions. This resulted in the setting-up of PHARE (Poland and Hungary: Assistance for the Recovery of the Economy), to be extended to the other countries of the area.

In this way the Ecu has become the unit of account of the programme and the main currency used by the EC Commission to tap the market in order to fund the project. Funds allocated for grants in the framework of PHARE amounted to Ecu300 million at the beginning of 1990 and increased to Ecu500 million at the end of the year; they are planned to reach Ecu820 million in 1991 and Ecu1 billion in 1992.

On 22 February 1990 the Council of the EC also approved a medium-term loan to the Republic of Hungary for a maximum of Ecu870 million. The first tranche was linked to a Ecu350 million Eurobond issued in April 1990.

In 1990 the European Investment Bank (EIB) was authorised to lend up to Ecu1 billion to Hungary and Poland. Last February the programme was extended to Czechoslovakia, Bulgaria and Romania, for an amount up to Ecu700 million. In October 1990 the first global loan ever granted by the EIB in the ECECs (Ecu25 million, 12-year) was channelled through the Hungarian Inter-Europa Bank, to be extended to local small and medium-sized companies.

Most relevant among the initiatives launched by Western countries to support the reform process in the ECECs has been the setting-up of the European Bank for Reconstruction and Development (EBRD). As stated in the agreement signed by the 42 founding members on 29 May 1990 in Paris, the EBRD "is a multilateral financial institution which is European in its basic character and broadly international in its membership".

The EBRD has been the first supranational institution with its capital denominated and financial accounts kept in the European currency. EBRD's capital stock amounts to Ecu10 billion (30 per cent of which is paid in). The 12 EC member states (including the EC Commission and the EIB) control 51 per cent of the capital stock, while the US holds 10 per cent and Japan 8.5 per cent of the shares. ECECs have a 13.5 per cent stake, with 6 per cent subscribed by the USSR (which for the first time is participating in an international financial institution).

At least 60 per cent of the amount of the Bank's total committed loans, guarantees and equity investments will be provided for the private sector, with the aim "to foster the transition towards open market-oriented economies and promote private and entrepreneurial initiative in the ECECs committed to and applying the principles of multiparty democracy, pluralism and market economics" (article 1 of the agreement).

The EBRD will probably play a major role in fostering the use of the Ecu in the ECECs. It is expected to have large recourse to the Ecu as a funding currency and will have several opportunities of using it in its highly diversified interventions in the ECECs (loans, investments in equity capital, provision of guarantees, etc), notably in the private sector.

Possible roles for the Ecu in the ECECs

The benefits of increased Ecu use by the ECECs can be evaluated from both a micro- and a macroeconomic point of view. Generally speaking, the Ecu would enable the ECECs to avoid the instability of the US dollar, while its "neutrality" would favour it with respect to the Deutschmark. This evolution will be enhanced, as stated above, by the acceleration of the process towards European economic and monetary union (EMU) in the EC. After the two European Councils in Rome at the end of 1990, there is a clear political commitment to the Ecu as the single European currency. This announcement will strongly influence end-users' expectations, thus contributing to a further growth of the Ecu markets.

As regards the ECECs' political economy, the definition of exchange rate policy represents a fundamental aspect of any reform programme. Moreover, these countries lack a market price system, while the exchange rate is the most important relative price in the economy. As a way to reduce uncertainty and support monetary stabilisation policies, the exchange rate could be fixed, by pegging ECECs' national currencies to the Ecu, at a realistic and sustainable rate.

At the end of 1990, Czechoslovakia pegged the crown to a basket of currencies, including the US dollar, the Deutschmark, the Austrian schilling, the Swiss franc and sterling, largely reflecting the Czechoslovak trade basket. As reform continues and trade and financial relations with the EC tighten, the Ecu could represent a better reference, as a ready-made basket with a strong "European identity" and a well-developed market, in which EC central banks already play an important role. This strategy would also represent a clear signal of ECECs' interest in future EC membership, as the natural goal of their economic reforms.

In March 1991 a draft economic plan drawn up by a group of experts was presented to Yugoslavia's federal parliament. It recommended the introduction of a single, convertible currency "closely tied to the Ecu".

Once their currency is pegged to the Ecu, national central banks would have an evident interest in holding a large part of their reserves in Ecus and borrowing in the same currency, as they would have to intervene mainly on the Ecu market.[2]

A major consequence of the breaking-down of the former Comecon was the dramatic shrinking of the volume of bilateral trade between the member countries. Following the experience of Western Europe after

2. On this point, and for a comprehensive analysis of the issue, see "Reforms in Eastern Europe and the role of the Ecu". Macro-financial study group of the Ecu Banking Association, a report presented at the conference in note 1.

World War Two, the setting-up of a Central European Payments Union (CEPU) was proposed, notably by the United Nations Economic Commission for Europe (UNECE),[3] as a temporary solution in the transition of the ECECs towards a multilateral trade and settlement system.

In the UNECE proposal the Ecu would be the accounting and payment currency of the CEPU. Moreover, "this solution would not only invite the CEPU members to manage their foreign exchange regime in tandem with that of the European Monetary System (EMS): it would also subject them to the discipline of the EMS".[4]

A group of commercial banks from both Western, Central and Eastern Europe, with the support of the Ecu Banking Association (EBA), is also developing a project for the establishment of a private Ecu-denominated settlement system between East European countries. This would reduce the need for foreign exchange, maintain the existing trade relationships between them and facilitate the development of relations with the EC member states.

Regarding the microeconomic benefits of the Ecu, ECECs' enterprises need to start developing stronger links with the Western economy, especially the single market, as well as the European economic space resulting from the future agreement between EC and EFTA members.

The Ecu would be the natural choice for the currency to manage these relations, as it would simplify both the cash management and the accounting and invoicing problems of these enterprises. Due to its composition, the Ecu would also offer an "automatic" hedge to companies trading with several countries of the EC.

Other opportunities deserve attention and further study, ie the possibility of having one price list for Europe and obtaining/accepting more flexible terms of payment with Western creditors/debtors, thanks to the built-in stability of the European currency. The Ecu can also play a useful and wide-ranging role for joint ventures between ECEC companies and EC partners, as seen above.

France and the Ecu

Paul Mentré

Banque CSIA

When President Giscard d'Estaing suggested the composite name of Ecu for the new European currency to his European partners at Bremen in 1978, he knew that his actions meant reviving the name of a traditional currency in France, prior to the French franc of the Revolution, the Ecu. As such, the Ecu has always been viewed in France as a native, worthy of special care and sympathy. The Ecu has been widely used by French dealers and promoted by the French authorities. At a time when there is a swing towards monetary union, unanimity is less certain in the debates about European currency against national currency and common currency against single currency.

3. UNECE, *Economic Survey of Europe in 1989-1990*, 43rd Report. (pp.147-50.). New York, 1990.
4.UNECE, *op. cit.*, p.149.

The public Ecu

Ever since the bilateral negotiations on the creation of the European Monetary System (EMS) began, the French advocated the concept of a neutral unit at the heart of the system, the Ecu. The Germans, however, remained greatly attached to the previous idea of the snake, that is the grid of bilateral parities, which would maintain a privileged role for the Deutschmark in relation to other national currencies.

In the first 10 years of the EMS, France has continually aimed at wider use of the Ecu, at the heart of the EMS. The French authorities, committed to defending the relationship between the French franc and the Ecu, when it came to the five-yearly reviews of the Ecu basket, have always pushed for the restoration of the share initially agreed for the French franc. This has been eroded by the increased power of the Deutschmark (see Exhibit 18.1).

In addition to prestige considerations, there was the desire to keep the Ecu in a central position, without it being dragged too far up by strong currencies.

France has always favoured a wider use of the Ecu in business dealings between central banks. It contributed to the Palermo agreements, which improved the status of the Ecu, and the Basle-Nyborg agreements, which made intra-marginal dealings easier, leading to the presumption that integral payments in Ecu were acceptable. It supported the enlargement of facilities for mutual assistance, and in particular the flexible amalgamation of medium-term procedures for EC funding through loans.

Finally, the desire to promote the Ecu was shown in the management of exchange controls. Where loans made to foreign countries by French banks in French francs were forbidden, loans in Ecu, hence their component in French francs, which was approximately a fifth, were fully allowed, and this was used by French banks, especially when converting the debts of borrowing countries.

The first breach in the prohibition on individuals holding credits in foreign currency was the authorisation given to French residents to hold deposits in Ecu. The abolition of exchange control at the beginning of 1990 put an end to these incentives, and the free regime then applied to all dealings with foreign countries, whatever the currency used. These were nonetheless an indication of the intense desire to actively promote the Ecu, as was the support given by the French Treasury to the development of the Ecu market by private dealers.

Exhibit 18.1

Composition of the Ecu, 1979–89

	1979 basket		*1984 basket*		*1989 basket*	
	Initial weighting 13/3/79 (%)	*Weighting on 14/9/84 (%)*	*Initial weighting 17/9/84 (%)*	*Weighting on 17/9/89 (%)*	*Initial weighting 21/9/89 (%)*	*Weighting on 31/12/90 (%)*
Share of Ffr	19.9	16.7	19	18.7	19	18.2
Share of DM	(33.0)	(36.9)	(32)	(34.6)	(30.1)	(30.6)

Source: Euromoney.

The private Ecu

The Ecu, which was initially very little used by central banks, has been used directly in the markets. Because of its eventual status and composition, it appeared to offer a balanced compromise between lenders and borrowers, strong and weak currencies and interest rate and exchange risks.

Consequently, the role of the Ecu in international issues of bonds has now reached about 5 per cent, in flows and stocks, during the course of recent years. French borrowers have contributed more than proportionately to this development. International issues by French borrowers have in fact developed as follows during these same years (see Exhibit 18.2).

At the end of 1990, the running total of international bonds issued by French borrowers amounted to Ecu10.5 billion, that is 27 per cent of EC issues and 18 per cent of total issues. This placed France in second position, after Italy, in the list of market users (see Exhibit 18.3).

French banks have actively contributed to the advancement of the Ecu on the banking market, at both the end-user and interbank transaction level, where French banks have been especially active in launching and developing the clearing system between banks in Ecu.

Banks set up in France provide 18 per cent of banking business in Ecu (and 19 per cent of the activity of banks in the EC). This places them in second place, after banks set up in the UK (28 per cent), in a market which on 30 June 1990 represented 2.6 per cent of all the various international claims held by banks in the Bank for International Settlements (BIS) area and 3.3 per cent of all the bank claims in foreign currencies.

However, as in other EC countries, the use of the Ecu as an invoicing

Exhibit 18.2

Ecu issues by French borrowers, 1986–90 (Ecu bn)

	1986	*1987*	*1988*	*1989*	*1990*
Gross French issues in Ecu	1.1	1.1	1.6	2.5	2.4
Share of international issues in Ecu	16%	15%	18%	22%	17%

Source: Euromoney.

Exhibit 18.3

Running total of international issues in Ecu, 31 December 1990 (Ecu bn)

Community institutions	5.9	International Institutions	1.7
Member countries of the EC	30.0	European countries outside the EC	7.5
of which:		of which:	
Italy	(11.8)	Scandinavia	(3.4)
France	(10.5)	(others)	(4.1)
Benelux	(3.2)	US/Canada	(5.0)
Denmark	(1.9)	(Japan)	(2.7)
Others	(2.6)	(Others)	(1.7)
EC total	38.9	Total outside EC	(18.6)
Grand total	57.6		

currency by businesses has remained very limited, around 0.7 per cent of imports and 0.4 per cent of exports (1.3 per cent at the level of current transactions, which include interest paid and received). Examples often quoted (internal invoicing in Ecu by the Saint Gobain group, the holding in Ecu of the accounts system of the Netherlands holding company of Alcatel and the Gaz de France-Gasunie contract) should not mask the reality, which is that industrialists are waiting for an irreversible swing towards the single currency before committing themselves.

The French authorities wished to contribute actively towards this essentially financial development in the use of the Ecu. Alongside the Bank of England and the Bank of Italy, the Bank of France began to hold and make use of private Ecu assets. The total amount of central banks' private Ecu assets amounted to Ecu4 billion at the end of 1987, Ecu11 billion at the end of 1988, Ecu17 billion at the end of 1989 and Ecu27 billion at the end of 1990, representing 18 per cent of the Ecu banking market at that date. Like the Bank of England, the Bank of France declared that it was prepared to provide liquidity facilities for the French banks, for their settlements in the Ecu interbank clearing system.

Similarly, in the French Treasury, long-term domestic issues of public bonds were developed in Ecu. Ecu1.6 billion were issued in 1989 and Ecu3.8 billion in 1990, placing France second in Europe, after Italy, for these issues. Under the pressure of competition from London, it will undoubtedly also be forced to issue short-term Ecu bills.

The French Treasury announced its intention in 1991 to continue covering a significant part of its domestic borrowing needs in Ecu. With the aim of competing with LIFFE and MATIF, it has just launched a fixed-period Ecu bond contract, first from the French Treasury (OAT) and then for a fixed period from other independent issuers in the EC.

Thus, the French authorities want to see Paris stand at least second in Europe, after London, for the Ecu, and first in Continental Europe.

Exhibit 18.4

Domestic issues in Ecu, 1987–90 (Ecu bn)

	1987	*1988*	*1989*	*1990*
Long-term bonds				
New issues				
Italy	1,500	7,250	6,000	5,250
France	–	–	1,652	3,857
Greece	217	–	1,537	2,260
EC total	1,717	7,250	1,537	11,367
Running total at the end of this period				
France	–	–	1,652	5,300
EC Total	9,182	16,432	24,255	34,805
Short-term bonds				
Italy			7,476	4,750
UK			2,800	3,600
EC Total			10,276	8,350

The future of the Ecu

Although they have promoted the Ecu in this way, both in public and private use, the French authorities are rather ambivalent regarding the future of the Ecu and the movement towards the single currency.

Together with private dealers, they support every action which could facilitate the use of the Ecu, including reinforcement of the clearing system in Ecu between banks and setting-up a system for instantaneous payments in Ecu. Furthermore, it is not certain that all the consequences of this last option have been appreciated. This would mean, in fact, that for the common agricultural policy all prices would henceforth be fixed in Ecu, ending the system of monetary compensatory amounts.

As it is very difficult to envisage a price fall in national currency, this would practically prevent any revaluation being carried out against the Ecu and would lead to the "hard Ecu" being set up, as advocated by the UK. This makes the French, from their point of view, inclined to accept the freezing of the basket. The stability of the French franc in relation to the Deutschmark, maintained since 1986, has become a political axiom and therefore the previous trend towards the reduction of the share of the French franc in the basket, between two reviews, is now thought to be historical. In wiping out the impact, for example, of devaluations of individual currencies on the value of the Ecu, the French may even be prepared to accept a more pronounced "hardening" of the Ecu, subject to continuity being maintained in relation to the existing Ecu.

The idea of giving the central body of the European system of central banks a role in promoting the Ecu, from the second phase onwards, in accordance with the UK proposals, is in line with certain French arguments. It is, however, doubtful whether the Bank of France would be prepared quickly to accept the issue of banknotes in Ecu.

It is the passage to the third stage, the move towards the single currency, which will in reality constitute the decisive step. Although part of the opposition, and certain dealers, favour the common currency as against the single currency, the majority choice in France is for the single currency. National traditions do not appear to be totally prepared to accept all the consequences of this transition: autonomy of the European Central Bank (ECB) in charge of the issue of money (in its memorandum, France puts forward the idea of a European centre for economic policy), practical abandonment of the responsibilities of governments as regards exchange rates; and independence of national central banks, particularly the Bank of France, which is at present only in charge, according to the statutes, of implementing the monetary policy set by government.

France has shown its attachment to the Ecu. The positions it has adopted in public, and the action of its private dealers, have helped strengthen the place of the Ecu in the European market. If the negotiating process leads to a quick adoption of the single European currency, it will be well satisfied. The possibility cannot be excluded that, in certain bureaucracies, this enthusiasm is fed by the trust in the braking systems which could be exerted by other countries. If political goodwill reigns at every level, France's campaign in favour of the Ecu shows every prospect of leading to a single currency.

Germany and the Ecu

Werner Becker
Deutsche Bank AG

The Ecu in German financial markets

In contrast to the Ecu's increasing and successful use in several European financial markets, the unit has played only a marginal role in Germany. The main reason is the confidence the business and banking community has in the strength and stability of the Deutschmark as a mature international reserve, investment and transaction currency with normally relatively low (nominal) interest rates. The Ecu, on the other hand, was created as a basket containing a weighted average of strong and weak EC currencies bearing traditionally higher interest rates than the Deutschmark. Although the share of hard currencies in the Ecu has risen following increasing economic convergence (to around 70 per cent; Deutschmark share: 30 per cent), thus increasing the stability standard of the Ecu, its competitive disadvantage in "currency competition" with the Deutschmark has prevailed in Germany.

This argument is a strong one because virtually all financial transactions in Germany can be conducted in Ecu. The Ecu is *de facto* treated as a foreign currency. However, as in all other EC countries, the Ecu is not legal tender. While the purchase of Ecu claims on non-residents has never been restricted in Germany, the complete dismantling of the remaining restrictions was implemented in two steps:

1. With effect from 16 June 1987, the Bundesbank generally permitted German residents to incur Ecu liabilities in the domestic market. Previously, such liabilities were subject to authorisation by the Bundesbank, which was, on principle, not given. The reason was that use of the Ecu in loan contracts was interpreted as an index clause, which is deemed to endanger monetary stabilisation policy. This liberalisation move meant in practice that bank customers were allowed to raise certain loans on the domestic market and that domestic banks were allowed to manage Ecu accounts for their customers.
2. In January 1990, the legal basis was created for listing Ecu bonds on German stock exchanges. Furthermore, the Bundesbank fully permitted the issuance of Ecu bonds and borrowers' note loans (*Schuldscheindarlehen*) in Germany. Consequently, there are no legal impediments to issuing and trading Ecu bonds in Germany.

Following the Ecu liberalisation and the ongoing process of economic and monetary integration in Europe (EMU), the business community and banks' retail clients have become increasingly interested as more information about the Ecu emerges. Demand for Ecu financial products in Germany remains muted, however, and is concentrated on very few products.

Ecu bonds are the most common Ecu instrument used by German residents. About a dozen German banks have tapped the international Ecu bond market since 1984 under their own name. They raised a total of more than Ecu1.5 billion, a major part of which was placed with German investors. The market share of German issuers, only banks, in total Ecu issues since 1981 is roughly 2 per cent. In March 1990, the government-owned Kreditanstalt für Wiederaufbau (KfW), a specialist bank providing *inter alia* preferential funding terms for export credits and investments within the framework of structural credit programmes, launched the first German domestic Ecu bond issue. This issue, together with some Ecu bonds of EC institutions, is listed on the Frankfurt Stock Exchange.

German institutional investors are increasingly active in Ecu bonds, although the ratio of Ecu to total funds is still very small. They prefer liquid paper, such as Ecu issues of governments and EC institutions, which were increasingly available in 1990 to 1991. The Ecu is used as a means of diversifying assets within Europe. Banks' retail clients also sometimes buy Ecu bonds. These investors are generally still reserved *vis-à-vis* the Ecu because it lacks some essential features of a natural currency, such as a responsible central bank. In this context, one important aspect is that the interest rate advantage of the Ecu *vis-à-vis* the Deutschmark has shrunk substantially in past years. For comparable bonds, the interest rate differential was between 50 and 100 basis points in the first quarter of 1991, depending on maturity. Although the exchange rate risk of the Ecu/Deutschmark rate is limited, it could easily erase the Ecu's small interest rate advantage. Consequently, Ecu bonds no longer offer German investors a special "yield appeal". This is one side effect of the increasing economic and interest rate convergence between countries in the European Monetary System (EMS).

Some other minor Ecu business in Germany deserves mention. According to Bundesbank statistics, the Ecu assets and liabilities of domestic banks *vis-à-vis* residents total around Ecu300 million and Ecu200 million respectively (December 1990), of which more than 50 per cent is *vis-à-vis* non-banks. They account for around 5 per cent of banks' total assets and liabilities in foreign currencies. Ecu liabilities against non-banks are a component of the German monetary aggregate M3. With a share of roughly 0.01 per cent in M3 they are, however, negligible for the conduct of monetary policy. While Ecu time deposits, especially from corporate clients, are attracting some attention, Ecu savings deposits are, generally not offered by German banks because of a lack of demand. On the other hand, there is virtually no domestic credit business in Ecu, mainly because of the higher cost than in Deutschmark, and therefore no incentive for banks from that side to offer Ecu savings deposits. There are reports that some banks are considering introducing savings accounts as a new product in Germany. The number of Ecu accounts being opened with German banks is increasing in connection with the purchase of Ecu bonds by residents.

At the daily foreign exchange (FX) fixing in Frankfurt, the Ecu is not officially quoted against the Deutschmark. However, the major banks in Germany deal in Ecu and quote spot and forward rates in the over-the-counter (OTC) market against all important currencies. Compared to other currencies, daily turnover in Ecu is very small.

In commercial transactions the Ecu also plays only a marginal role in Germany. Although a number of trade agreements with European partners are based on Ecu, the unit has practically no importance in this area:

around 80 per cent of German exports and more than 50 per cent of imports are invoiced in Deutschmarks; the corresponding figures for the Ecu are less than 0.05 per cent for exports and 0.1 to 0.2 per cent for imports. The modest use of the Ecu in German firms' hedging of FX risks in intra-EC trade is even receding because the exchange rate stability within the EMS since January 1987 is expected to continue for now.

There is no national Ecu clearing system in Germany. Ecu payments can be settled through the clearing system of the Ecu Banking Association (EBA) under the agency of the Bank for International Settlements. Several big German banks are members of EBA.

Official attitude: no enthusiasm

The Bundesbank and the Ministry of Finance, which is responsible for German exchange rate policy *via-à-vis* third currencies, seem to take a somewhat ambivalent stance on the use of the Ecu in the process towards EMU.

The Bundesbank argues that the Ecu plays only a marginal role in the workings of the EMS, which has been increasingly successful in recent years in terms of price and exchange rate stability due to the anchor role of the Deutschmark. Furthermore, the Bundesbank has often referred to the Ecu as a financial innovation and not a genuine currency. The Bundesbank strongly denies the basket unit any useful role as a parallel currency, because it will undermine stabilisation policies in the EC and complicate monetary policy co-ordination on the way to EMU. Finally, the German monetary authorities reject every artificial promotion of the use of the Ecu by politicians at national and EC levels.

However, the Bundesbank fully recognises the success of the Ecu in the financial markets. It has removed domestic barriers to the use of the Ecu, as mentioned above. The Bundesbank consents to the notion, as laid out in the Delors Report, that the Ecu has the potential to be developed into the single, unique European currency. Furthermore, a smooth transition from the old basket Ecu to the single currency Ecu (*rekurrenter Anschluß*) is deemed desirable to support legal certainty for Ecu-denominated assets and liabilties. The German government (in close co-ordination with the Bundesbank) also proposed a "hardening" of the Ecu for the beginning of stage two (in the draft for the amendment of the EC Treaty presented to the Intergovernmental Conference in February 1991, a similar proposal was made by the Spanish government). Such a hardening is to be achieved by suspending the regular (five-year) basket revisions and by not devaluing the Ecu against any EC currency in future realignments. This is expected to increase the attractiveness of the Ecu in the markets. A hardening of the Ecu is conceived to be a useful intermediate step towards a stable EMU aiming at a single currency and not a common, parallel currency.

Although German monetary authorities are not euphoric about the Ecu, they are ready to give the Ecu a fair chance in currency competition. The Ecu will, however, not be allowed to undermine monetary stabilisation policy on the road to EMU.

Prospects

The future role of the Ecu in German financial markets will depend somewhat on the progress made towards a stable EMU in the years to come. The message of the European Council (formulated at the Rome Summit in October 1990) to establish "a single currency, a strong and stable Ecu" will increase the popularity of and demand for information on the Ecu in Germany. Nevertheless, in the short run the prospects for greater use of the Ecu seem modest given the current environment. Provided a hardening of the Ecu will be concluded for stage two of EMU, the Ecu might benefit in the longer term. This seems to be especially true as a store-of-value. Above all, Ecu bonds and perhaps Ecu time deposits might be favoured in the process. German investors will become increasingly aware that the Ecu provides an optimum opportunity to diversify assets "Europe-wide" using only one instrument. One "disadvantage" might be, however, that, as a consequence of economic convergence, interest rates might continue to converge, thus more or less eliminating the interest rate advantage of the Ecu against the Deutschmark. The same seems true in the event of a hardening of the Ecu, when the risk of a devaluation of the Ecu against the Deutschmark will disappear. Use of the Ecu as an investment unit will also be positively influenced by the substantially increased liquidity of Ecu bonds and the availability of virtually all maturities. This was partly due to several large Ecu issues of EC sovereign borrowers.

While the majority of EC governments have already tapped the Ecu bond market in order to finance their budget and/or to push Ecu business in their financial markets, Germany has not issued any Ecu bonds (except the KfW). No doubt, such a large-volume German issue would be welcomed because it would be a clear, political signal to the EC partners that Germany is firmly committed to EMU; it would also help establish an Ecu bond market in Frankfurt. One argument against "Ecu Bunds" is that market confidence in the Deutschmark sector might be negatively affected where high German budget deficits caused higher Deutschmark funding costs for the government sector. Seen in perspective, this argument is, however, not very convincing. The issuance of Ecu bonds by Germany would mean a change in borrowing policy because German government funding has always only been in Deutschmarks. Whether the German federal government will tap the Ecu market is an open question. The Bundesbank has repeatedly expressed its reservations about such a step.

Apart from Ecu bonds, there is little Ecu business which is expected to gain major importance in Germany in the future. Especially in credit business and commercial transactions, there is no incentive to substitute the Ecu for the Deutschmark. Any official artificial support of the Ecu cannot be expected. Therefore, purchasing Ecu bonds seems to offer a readily available instrument for experiencing the Ecu as a European currency well before a genuine single Europe currency materialises.

Italy and the Ecu

Rainer Masera
Istituto Mobiliare Italiano

Italy was one of the first countries to issue Ecu-denominated bonds on international markets and, at the same time, Ecu-linked bonds on the domestic market. In the past, the restrictions on residents holding foreign-currency assets obliged the Treasury to make issues that were indexed, rather than denominated, in Ecus.

The issue of Ecu-linked securities not only encouraged national investors to diversify their portfolios, but also promoted the Ecu's role in the process of monetary integration.

In recent years there has been a substantial increase in issues by the Italian Treasury and public and private bodies. This has been accompanied by a parallel growth in banks' Ecu-denominated assets and liabilities, just as in other EC countries.

Nevertheless, there are further steps yet to be taken, at domestic and international level, in order to strengthen the Ecu market while helping the EC to progress towards full monetary union. In this connection a number of reform proposals are outlined, following a brief survey of the situation of the Italian market.

Issues by the Italian Treasury

The first Ecu-indexed issue made by the Treasury dates back to 1982, when Treasury certificates denominated in Ecu (CTEs) were issued, carrying fixed rate yearly coupons, redeemable in a single instalment at expiry and with maturity of four to eight years. The early issues were made in two tranches, one of Ecu-indexed certificates issued on the domestic market and the other destined for the Euromarket. For residents, coupon and principal are paid either directly in Ecu or in lire at the lira/Ecu exchange rate that is the average of Milan and Rome stock exchange quotations (Italian Exchange Office average) two working days prior to the settlement date. Non-residents are paid directly in Ecu. Since September 1987, interest payments on new issues are subjected to a 12.5 per cent withholding tax, on a par with other categories of government securities.

At the outset, CTEs were subscribed by an *ad hoc* placement consortium, but since September 1990 they have been issued under the uniform-price auction system. The Treasury, fixing the coupon and a minimum starting price, equal to 100, establishes the maximum return above which it refuses to borrow. The value of the subscription right, equal to a multiple of five basis points, which clears the market, is calculated at the auction. The subscription price is therefore the sum of the floor price set by the Treasury and the value of the right. Both commercial banks and financial companies may take part in the auctions.

The Treasury allots the securities according to the following procedure. The bids submitted are arranged in decreasing order of price. Applications are satisfied for the full amount, starting with the highest price offered, until all the certificates are allocated. The stop-out price is the tender price for all the operators.

These CTEs have become an important instrument of Treasury borrowing and have also encouraged the growth of the Ecu swap market. Because of the 12.5 per cent tax, CTEs must carry a higher coupon than similar Ecu-denominated Eurosecurities. Hence, when the law allows the 12.5 per cent withholding tax to be recovered as a credit, there is a bias in favour of using CTEs in swap operations. Foreign operators acting as counterparties in Ecu swaps can cover themselves by purchasing CTEs and have a profit margin. The margins are especially high (up to 100 basis points) when the swaps are finalised in conjunction with the auctions, whereas they are much smaller in the case of arbitrage on the secondary market. How extensively Ecu certificates are used in swap operations is seen from the close correlation (approximately 50 per cent) between the amount of swaps arranged with Ecu issues and the volume of CTEs issued (see Exhibit 18.5).

In October 1987, the Italian Treasury began issuing a second type of Ecu-denominated security. These are 12-month Treasury bills (BTEs) issued under the uniform-yield auction system. For an issue price of 100, the Treasury announces the quantity in supply and the maximum yield at which it will borrow. Bidders' submissions are arranged in increasing order of return and are satisfied beginning with the lowest yields. The redemption price, which is the same for all successful bidders, entails a return equal to the stop-out yield.

BTEs are also subjected to a 12.5 per cent withholding tax and redeemed in lire or Ecu in the case of residents and in Ecu in the case of non-residents. With the issue of these securities, Italy became the first sovereign debtor to enter the short-term end of the Ecu market. The exchange liberalisation measures of July 1990, under which non-bank residents are permitted to invest in foreign currency bonds with a residual life of less than 180 days, should now allow a programme of under

Exhibit 18.5 **Swaps on issues of Ecu and CTEs (quarterly data in Ecu m)**

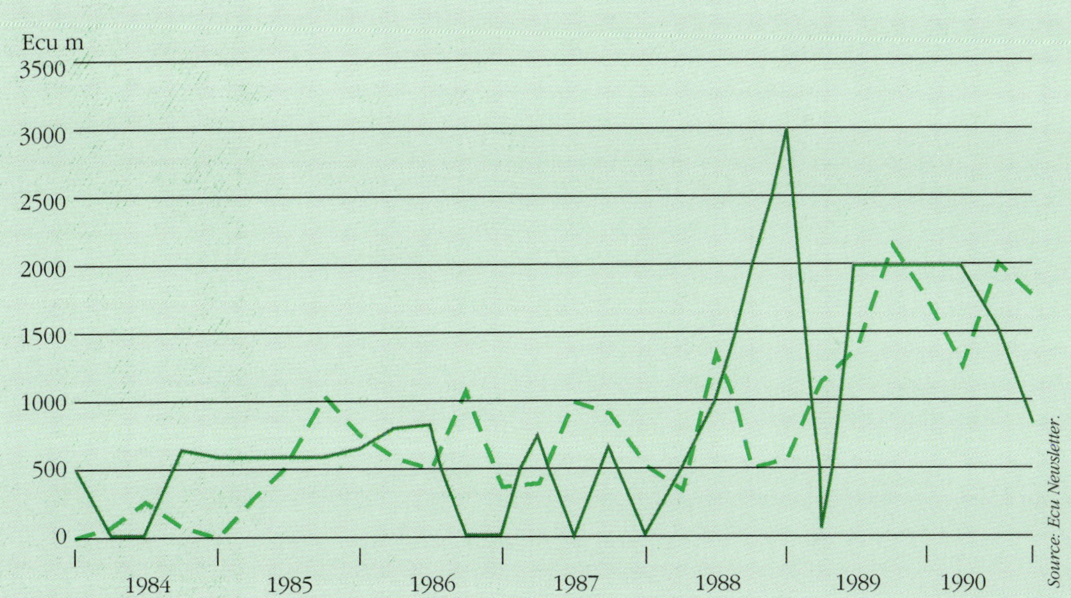

12-month Ecu issues to be launched. Among other things, such a decision would increase the liquidity of the domestic Ecu market.

At the end of 1990, the nominal value of Ecu securities issued by the Italian Treasury represented approximately 3.7 per cent of the stock of government securities in circulation, compared with 3.4 per cent in 1988 and 1.5 per cent in 1986. Of issues made in 1990, those denominated in Ecu amount to a value of Ecu9.25 billion, which in lire terms is equal to 1.9 per cent of total gross issues by the Treasury.

While Ecu issues to date may appear fairly small in comparison with the aggregate amount of the Italian public debt, Italy is nevertheless the EC member with the highest nominal value of Ecu securities in circulation, followed by France, the UK and Greece. Furthermore, the Italian Treasury's Ecu-denominated domestic securities account for over a third of all Ecu securities circulating on the Euromarket (see Exhibit 18.6).

The banking market in Ecu

The Ecu has been constantly increasing over the years as a component of bank assets and liabilities. During the period 1988 to 1990, the growth of Ecu liabilities of Italian banks reporting to the Bank for International Settlements (BIS) was close to 61 per cent, and that of Ecu assets nearly 57 per cent.

Thus Italian institutions have gradually been stepping up their role in the Ecu banking market. Today they occupy third place as regards volume of intermediation of Ecu assets and liabilities, after UK and French banks.

Among non-bank borrowers of bank funds the presence of Italian residents is also considerable. Their share of total bank assets of BIS reporting countries has risen from 32 per cent in 1988 to 36.4 per cent in September 1990. At the same time, the share of French non-bank borrowers has dropped from 35.2 per cent to 15.1 per cent of the total, to be overtaken by English non-bank borrowers, up from 17 to 24.4 per cent.

In terms of bank liabilities, the UK, Belgium and Luxembourg remain

Exhibit 18.6

Domestic markets for Ecu securities (Ecu m)

	1990 issues	*Securities in circulation at 31 December 1990*
France	3866	5509
Italy (Cte)	5250	25350
Italy (Bte)	4000	4750
Spain	500	500
Greece[1]	1850	3389
UK (ETB)	11700	3600
Total	**27166**	
for reference:	27166	
Eurosecurities in Ecu	13710	58588

[1] Figures for Greek securities refer to 31 October 1990

Source: Ecu Newsletter.

the countries with the largest Ecu-denominated deposits. They have been joined recently by Spain. The BIS estimates that the percentage of total Community Ecu deposits of residents in Belgium and Luxembourg is 23 per cent and of residents in the UK 31 per cent, while in Italy the share is less than 15 per cent.

Eurobonds in Ecu

With regard to international issues of Ecu-denominated bonds, Italian operators have also been among the most active during the period from 1986 to 1990. Italian issues on the Euromarket, by the government, special credit institutes, public bodies and firms, during the period 1986 to 1990 amounted to Ecu5.4 billion, or 22 per cent of the total.

At June 1990, Ecu assets represented 3.7 per cent of the foreign-bond portfolio of Italian unit trusts and, at December 1990, constituted 68 per cent of the foreign portfolio of Italian life insurance companies. Out of a total of Lit196 billion of investments in foreign currency securities in the last quarter of 1990, more than Lit130 billion related to financial or liquid assets denominated in Ecu. Foreign-currency portfolios consisted of government securities and bonds issued by EC institutions such as European Investment Bank (EIB), International Bank for Reconstruction and Development (IBRD), European Coal and Steel Community (ECSC) and Euratom. It should be noted that life insurance policies in foreign currency represent a minute part of the nearly Lit30,000 billion administered by life insurance funds.

The author's viewpoint

Before monetary union can be achieved a number of national and international problems still remain to be tackled. In the specific case of Italy, the main internal problems are wage trends and the large public deficit.

On the wage front, a process that will bring the trend of unit labour costs into line with standard European levels needs to be encouraged. This is especially important in the sphere of general government in Italy. Because the sector is not exposed to international competition, it has failed in the past to match the increases in productivity achieved in the private sector and, particularly, industry (excluding construction).

Figures for the first 10 years of operation of the European monetary system (EMS) illustrate the situation very clearly: on the one hand, we see nominal wages in general government increasing at a faster pace than in industry; on the other, the trend of productivity in general government is practically stationary, while industry shows a marked growth in productivity. During the period 1978 to 1988, the productivity index for industry (excluding construction) rose by 58 per cent, while for general government the increase was under 10 per cent. By contrast, the indices of real per capita wages for these sectors have increased by 23 per cent and 38 per cent respectively.

Regarding the private sector, and especially the industrial sector, Italy's problem is one of divorcing pay claims from inflationary expectations in order to link the trend of nominal wages to productivity gains. This is the only possible way to interrupt a vicious circle of inflation fuelled by costs and inflationary expectations. The reform of the mechanism of wage formation, which would contribute significantly to curbing the growth of current government expenditure, could be accompanied by monetary reform. Italy could anchor the "new lira" to the Ecu. This would allow the public debt to be converted into "new lira", with a large saving in interest payments.

Models based on the approach developed by Barro and Gordon (1983) make it clear that the credibility of the government is the crucial factor determining prices and wages in the private sector. Even more than the commitment to a stable exchange rate, and hence to control over the money supply, it is the action of the government in fixing public sector wages and salaries that determines businessmen's expectations.

Anchoring the "new lira" to the Ecu would officially eliminate the gap separating Italy from its partners regarding rates of increase in real and nominal wages and prices. The monetary reform would also defuse expectations of inflation and confirm the switch to the new régime.

This virtuous circle would be further strengthened by a mechanism

Exhibit 18.7 **Real ex-post returns on government securities**

	Real ex-post returns on CCTs (yearly percentages)						
	Dec 84	*Dec 85*	*Dec 86*	*Dec 87*	*Dec 88*	*Dec 89*	*Dec 90*
Dec 80	5.5	5.7	6.3	6.1	5.8	5.7	5.8
Dec 81	7.3	7.1	7.5	7.1	6.6	6.4	6.4
Dec 82	8.7	8.0	8.3	7.6	7.0	6.6	6.7
Dec 83	9.3	7.9	8.4	7.5	6.7	6.4	6.5
Dec 84		6.5	7.9	6.9	6.1	5.8	6.0
Dec 85			9.3	7.1	5.9	5.6	5.9
Dec 86				4.9	4.3	4.4	5.1
Dec 87					3.6	4.1	5.1
Dec 88						4.6	5.9
Dec 89							7.1

	Real ex-post returns on BTPs (yearly percentages)						
	Dec 84	*Dec 85*	*Dec 86*	*Dec 87*	*Dec 88*	*Dec 89*	*Dec 90*
Dec 83	8.2	6.9	8.5	7.2	6.7	6.1	6.0
Dec 84		5.6	8.6	6.9	6.3	5.7	5.6
Dec 85			11.6	7.6	6.5	5.7	5.6
Dec 86				3.7	4.1	3.8	4.2
Dec 87					4.5	3.9	4.3
Dec 88						3.4	4.3
Dec 89							5.2

	Real ex-post returns on CTRs (yearly percentages)					
	Dec 85	*Dec 86*	*Dec 87*	*Dec 88*	*Dec 89*	*Dec 90*
Dec 84	3.3	9.1	6.2	4.2	3.5	4.8
Dec 85		15.1	7.6	4.6	3.6	5.1
Dec 86			0.6	−0.4	0.0	2.7
Dec 87				−1.4	−0.3	3.4
Dec 88					0.8	6.0
Dec 89						11.5

Source: Calculations based on IMI and ISTAT data.

Exhibit 18.8 **Differentials between long- and short-term interest rates**

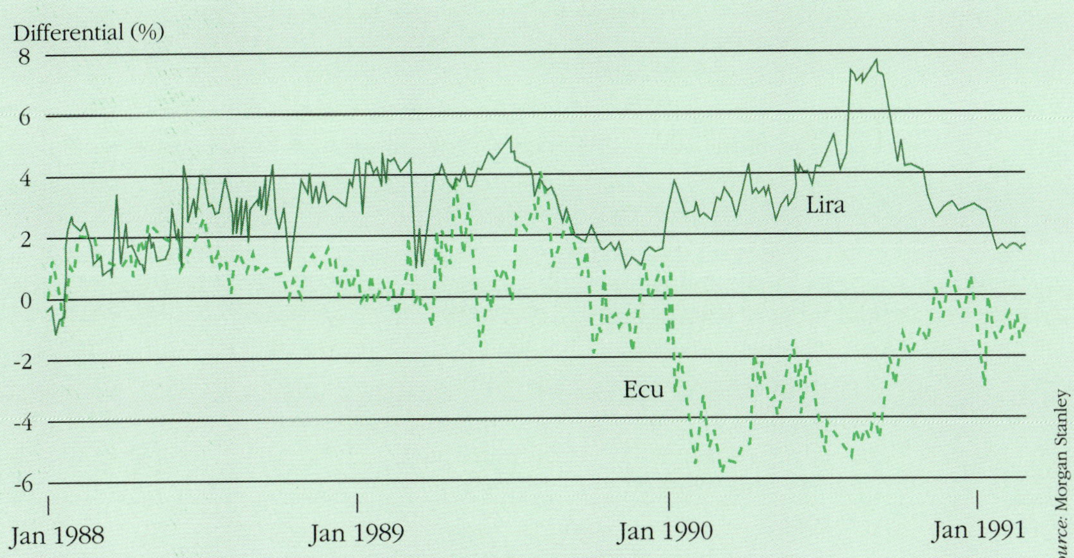

N.B.: Theoretical rates calculated according to the Cox, Ingersoll and Ross model.

that has been described elsewhere (Masera, 1986). A reduction in the rate of inflation brings an immediate reduction in the debt burden because, in the short term, changes in the cost of servicing the public debt in real terms are related in a directly proportional manner to the rate of inflation.

The saving in interest payments obtained by converting the public debt into Ecu appears even more substantial if we consider how high real interest rates have risen in Italy during the 1980s. For instance, investments in Treasury credit certificates (CCT) and Treasury bonds (BTP) made in 1984 and settled in December 1990 would have yielded a real rate of return of respectively 5.8 per cent and 6.0 per cent per annum (see Exhibit 18.7). While the high real rates of interest have not over-burdened the private sector, insofar as firms have been able to borrow abroad and on international markets, they have constituted a serious burden for the Treasury.

It would be useful to combine conversion of the public debt into Ecu and the establishment of a stable lira/Ecu exchange rate with other measures to contain the cost of debt servicing, such as forms of real indexation of government stock and strong currency issues. In a working hypothesis which simulates the consequences of total substitution in the period 1983 to 1989 of the stock of BTPs and CCTs (which actually gave a real return of approximately 6.5 per cent) with real indexed securities giving a 4.5 per cent return, the debt/GDP ratio in January 1990 would have been 0.926 instead of 0.970 (Masera, 1990a). Comparable simulations assuming the stock of BTPs and CCTs to be replaced by securities denominated in Deutschmarks give similar results.

The two proposals offer a way to contain the costs attached to the high-risk premium for uncertainty as to future rates of inflation, which is a component of nominal interest rates on government issues. The adoption of forms of indexation of the government and thereby not only reduce the risk premium demanded by subscribers of medium- and long-term securities but also help to extend the average maturity of the debt. The average life of Italy's public debt is less than three years. This is extremely low when compared with UK bonds (10.9 years on average) or German bonds (5.4 years).

The saving which can be obtained in interest payments by converting the public debt into Ecu is well illustrated by an analysis of the term structure of lira and Ecu interest rates, estimated daily between the end of 1987 and February 1991 (see Exhibit 18.8). Briefly, the structure can be seen from the difference between long- and short-term interest rates. Throughout the period studied, the slope of the term structure in lire has always been positive, unlike that in Ecu. Moreover, Ecu interest rates have been almost constantly lower than the corresponding rates in lire, whatever the maturity. Had the debt been converted into Ecu, therefore, the combination of the two complementary circumstances would have given the government the twofold advantage of paying less interest in Ecu than in lire and being able to make long-term issues at lower rates than shorter ones.

The two measures taken together therefore – one to reform wage formation mechanisms and the other of monetary reform based on anchoring the lira to the Ecu – would produce the desired effect of defusing inflationary expectations. A virtuous circle would be started whereby the decrease of the deficit in nominal terms is both cause and consequence of its reduction in real terms.

Concerning the questions to be tackled at international level, the starting-point could be the fact that, although the Ecu has won itself a place on international financial markets, at official level it use is still hampered by problems of transferability and convertibility. The acceptability restrictions were originally adopted to avoid the dangers of a glut of Ecu, but now they restrict use of the Ecu as a reserve currency, for central banks must be able to use official Ecu in market intervention.

In the author's opinion, an appropriate link should be created between the official Ecu and the Ecu traded on the various markets. The best way to establish such a link is via a clearing house, acknowledged as lender of last resort in Ecu. The model for the system has already been presented in earlier works (Masera, 1987 and 1990) and, very briefly, operates along the following lines. Central bank A, which wants to buy foreign exchange for intervention in support of its own currency, before it reaches the compulsory intervention margin, enters into a triangular operation with a commercial bank resident in country B and the clearing house. Commercial bank B obtains official Ecu from central Bank A and, not being allowed to hold them, deposits them with the clearing house. Thus, central bank A gets a deposit in private Ecu with commercial bank B, which it can use directly for its currency support interventions.

Commercial bank B records an increase in its liabilities (the Ecu deposit of bank A) and its assets (its official Ecu deposit with the clearing house). At the close of these operations, the clearing house holds assets in Ecu, deposited with the European Monetary Co-operation Fund (EMCF) (the official Ecu), and liabilities *vis-à-vis* commercial bank B. Subsequent transactions between commercial bank B and other commercial banks only affect the amount of B's deposit with the clearing house, not the amount of official Ecu.

Among other things, this scheme does not call for any changes in the current laws. All that is needed to make the system operative is a joint decision on the part of the governors of the EC central banks, the EMCF and the BIS. At the end of 1986, the earlier Ecu clearing system, MESA (Mutual Ecu Settlement Account), was reinforced by the participation of over 30 commercial banks and by the BIS, which now acts as agent for the clearing system.

If the official and private Ecu markets were sufficiently integrated, the currency would take on a truly central role as an international reserve asset and a European currency in parallel with national ones. Of course, the creation of private Ecu would be subjected to similar controls to those existing for individual currencies and would take account of the latter growth.

The European Monetary Board would be entrusted with the task of supervising the Ecu and acting as the nucleus of the system of central banks. The Board would also be responsible for the centralised management of a part of the European foreign currency reserves, in accordance with the original plan for the EMS, and for the short-term credit mechanism for the support of currencies, designed to fight speculative attacks on the currencies of participating countries.

I believe that these proposals could help to more firmly establish the Ecu's role in Europe and Italy and strengthen the EMS by promoting that convergence of monetary policies among EC countries which is prerequisite of progress towards full monetary union.

Japan and the Ecu

Toshinaga Koizumi

The Industrial Bank of Japan, Limited

The Ecu is still a relatively unfamiliar currency sector to most Japanese participants in the capital markets. This is largely because the perceived political importance of the currency and its profile as a result of the debate associated with European monetary union differ markedly in Japan from those in Europe.

The principal involvement of Japanese institutions with the Ecu has been as investors in Ecu-denominated bonds, although borrowing through the Ecu market has developed since the mid-1980s.

Japanese issuers of Ecu bonds

Despite their relative unfamiliarity with the currency, the number of Japanese borrowers considering Ecu issues and the issued amount of Ecu bonds are increasing. For example, since The Industrial Bank of Japan, Limited (IBJ) opened the market for Japanese borrowers in 1983, the total number of Japanese issues reached 60 by the end of 1990, and the total amount issued increased from Ecu80 million in 1983 to Ecu1.1 billion in 1990.

Exhibit 18.9

Issuing history of Japanese issuers, 1983–90 (Ecu m)

	1983	*1984*	*1985*	*1986*	*1987*	*1988*	*1989*	*1990*
No of issues	2	4	16	5	15	3	6	9
Amount	80	160	781	480	985	350	740	1,135

Source: IFR Bondbase.

An analysis of borrowers over this period reveals that banks launched 40 per cent of the issues, corporations from a variety of industries launched 47 per cent and government-guaranteed borrowers launched 13 per cent (see Exhibit 18.10).

The bank issuers of Ecu bonds have mainly taken advantage of attractive swap arbitrage opportunities to generate sub-Libor US dollar funding.

Of the 28 corporate bond issues, 12 were issued through overseas subsidiaries. The proceeds of these issues are likely to have been swapped into US dollars or major European currencies and utilised by the issuers' overseas operations. The proceeds of the directly-issued corporate bonds were probably swapped into yen for domestic use.

The outlook for Japanese issuance of Ecu bonds

Japanese institutions are closely watching the progress of the EC towards the goal of a single market. A recent IBJ survey of one representative group, the treasurers of large corporations, revealed a predisposition towards the Ecu bond market as a funding source. These borrowers generally have simple funding requirements, which are cost-effectiveness and availability in size to meet their investment needs in the currencies of their choice.

The IBJ survey established that almost all of the corporate treasurers interviewed are interested in issuing Ecu bonds, including those issuers who have not done so before. The most common reason for focussing on the Ecu market is the belief that the international status of the Ecu will rise in future. The second most common reason is the view that the Ecu market may offer better swap arbitrage opportunities than other currencies. Other reasons include the relative stability of the Ecu in the currency markets and the expectation of significant market growth. Concerns about the market expressed by interviewees included questions relating to the bond and

Exhibit 18.10

Issuer breakdown (%)

Banks	*Corporations*	*Government-guaranteed*	*Total*
24	28	8	60
40	47	13	100

Source: IFR Bondbase.

swap markets' liquidity and the likely size achievable by corporate issuers.

Clearly, however, increased usage of the Ecu by this borrower category, as with other Japanese borrowers, will primarily depend on the relative cost of funds available.

Japanese investors in Ecu

Foreign currency investments by Japanese institutions generally have a relatively short history, and the Ecu is a relative late comer in tapping Japanese sources. It was in the 1960s, as Japan's trade balance turned positive, that some financial institutions started to allocate a proportion of their assets to currencies other than yen. However, this process was reversed in the 1970s as the yen appreciated substantially, encouraging most of these investors back to the domestic markets, having discovered that foreign currency bond investment was not a profitable business.

Then, in the early 1980s, banks seeking asset growth commenced heavy investment in US dollar-denominated floating rate notes (FRNs). The Japanese life insurance companies followed the banks, investing in straight Eurodollar bonds even more heavily. These investors moved on to invest in US Treasury bonds after their exemption (as non-US holders) from withholding tax by the Treasury department in 1984.

It is likely that the first Ecu-denominated investment by Japanese investors was made soon after this time as well, given the availability of higher coupon bonds and a relatively stable currency. Until 1986, however, US Treasury bonds remained the main foreign investment of Japanese institutions.

In 1986, investors began to seek other products offering higher yields and relative currency stability. As the Ecu offered high coupons and represented a currency basket, it appealed strongly to investors suffering from a US Treasury bond market in the doldrums and heavy US dollar currency losses against the yen. In 1987, US Treasury bons represented around 70 per cent of the total foreign long-term investments of institutional investors, but by 1990 this figure was slightly over 50 per cent and Ecu bonds had increased their share from slightly under 4 per cent to almost 7 per cent. Over the same period, European currencies including the Ecu increased their proportion of foreign long-term bond holdings from about 10 per cent to more than 20 per cent of the total.

Investor categories

The Ecu has proven a difficult currency for Japanese banks to invest in, given its relatively flat or negative yield curve. Ecu deposits from clients have been limited and borrowing through the interbank market to invest in long-term bonds has not been beneficial. Furthermore, the banks have generally not been as prepared as others to take currency exposure. The bulk of Japanese investors in Ecu bonds have therefore been institutions obtaining Ecu by selling yen in the currency markets.

Those investors that have been able to obtain the long-term funding required to profitably invest in Ecu bonds are principally the life insurance companies, pension funds and some governmental investment funds.

This investor base broadly comprises two categories: long-term bond holders, concerned with the issuers' credit and achieving higher coupons; and short-term holders seeking currency plays and requiring a high degree of liquidity, through investor puts for example. These short-term investors, accounting for about 10 per cent of the total Ecu investments (by volume), have purchased significant quantities of Ecu FRNs with quarterly put options, to take advantage of the inverted yield curve.

Conventional Ecu bond investment also increased over the 12 months to spring 1991, particularly following the spate of sovereign and supranational jumbo issues, peaking in mid-February 1991 with the issues of the UK, Belgium and Italy. Interest in the market was heightened by the commencement of Ecu bond future contract trading through the MATIF in October 1990 and LIFFE in March 1991.

In broad terms, Japanese investors are targetting a 10 per cent coupon, and the alternative investments are Deutschmark and French franc bonds. Some investors increasingly shuffle their assets between these three currencies according to their currency views.

Official attitude towards the Ecu

In 1983, the Japanese authorities authorised the use of the Ecu as a book-keeping currency, in support of the EC movement towards economic unity. This represented an earlier authorisation than that of some major European countries.

Japanese officials consider it wise for Japanese issuers to tap the Ecu bond market in order to diversify issuing currencies. By doing so, they

Exhibit 18.11

Composition of non-yen-denominated assets by currency for eight top Japanese life insurance companies

shown as a proportion (%), as of the end of September 1990, with end of March 1990 figures in the lower line

	US$	*C$*	*A$*	*£*	*DM*	*FFr*	*Ecu*	*Others*	*Total (Yen bn)*
Nippon	57.0	13.8	8.7	4.8	5.0	4.1	2.5	4.1	4,639
	60.6	9.6	8.6	5.9	4.7	2.9	0.9	6.8	4,820
Dai-Ichi	65.8	9.5	3.2	7.7	1.3	7.5	2.1	2.9	3,312
	69.7	12.9	1.9	5.4	4.2	2.1	0.9	2.9	3,123
Sumitomo	44.1	14.9	7.1	9.8	5.6	3.1	5.7	9.7	3,286
	59.3	13.0	4.8	7.9	2.0	1.9	7.8	3.3	3,135
Meiji	55.0	19.1	7.8	1.7	2.7	8.1	2.7	2.9	1,894
	57.2	17.3	4.1	2.8	7.2	6.0	2.0	3.4	1,899
Asahi	48.6	23.6	9.6	10.8	0.6	3.8	1.5	1.5	1,800
	60.9	20.1	4.4	6.8	1.3	2.9	1.5	2.1	1,606
Mitsui	47.9	20.0	7.4	6.2	7.1	4.9	2.1	4.4	1,144
	46.0	19.7	8.0	6.3	10.2	4.0	1.5	4.3	1,001
Yasuda	51.1	13.2	4.2	8.4	1.1	2.8	3.7	15.5	1,308
	50.8	11.8	4.8	8.4	1.9	4.3	1.4	16.6	1,274
Chiyoda	52.8	10.0	7.2	6.4	8.2	10.5	4.5	0.4	848
	57.9	11.4	5.2	8.0	6.7	7.0	3.2	0.6	849

Source: The Nikkei Financial Daily, 3 December 1990.

believe they can avoid conflict and confusion due to concentrated fund-raising operations in particular markets, such as the US dollar or Swiss franc, by many Japanese issuers. Diversified issuing currencies are also viewed as being beneficial for issuers in reducing the risk of extensive currency losses on redemption.

Spain and the Ecu

Jonathan Grosvenor

Banco Bilbao Vizcaya

Spain's contemporary economic experience has been one of rapid demand-led growth, increasing interdependence with trading partners and convergence in economic and monetary policy development. Perhaps the most striking feature of this change has been the nation's cultural, political and economic integration into the EC. Since entry into the EC on 1 January 1986, Spain's political and economic profile has risen substantially within both the OECD and the EC, particularly during Madrid's presidency of the EC Council of Ministers from January to June 1989. Immediately following this period the peseta simultaneously joined the Ecu basket with a 5.4 per cent weighting and the Exchange Rate Mechanism (ERM) of the European Monetary System (EMS), initially within a 6 per cent fluctuation band. This increasing rapprochement between Spain and EC member states has been not only indicative of the climate of change in Madrid, but also a clear measure of the Spanish government's commitment to an active role in European affairs.

Spain's financial markets have proved a useful barometer of this change and development, undergoing widespread structural reforms and performing commensurately. The greater integration and transparency of the Spanish financial sector has also been symptomatic of the authorities' intention to establish Madrid as a competitive and attractive international financial centre for the 1990s. Not only have the stock, bond and derivative market structures been modernised, but the authorities have tried to develop an adequate regulatory environment with an appropriate infrastructure compatible with ongoing EC requirements. It would also seem more useful to assess the Ecu's projection in Spain through its penetration of the domestic markets, since the use of the Ecu for trade finance, general commerce or retail banking has yet to be developed.

Renewed interest in the Ecu

Although the Ecu has not enjoyed widespread use in Spain to date, there is considerable interest in its applications and advantages for trade, financing and investment purposes. Exchange controls, borrowing restrictions and a wide differential between domestic peseta interest rates and Ecu rates have diminished the latter's short-term prospects. Nevertheless, the progressive liberalisation and modernisation of Spain's capital markets, and the steady erosion of Ecu/peseta yield spreads have prompted renewed interest, particularly in view of Spain's own proposals on economic and monetary union (EMU) within the EC.

In trade finance, the US dollar has long been favoured by Spanish industry, although more recently the use of the peseta itself has grown. However, the Ecu's lack of popularity does not appear to be limited to Spain, because the private Ecu market is still in its infancy throughout the EC. Official figures also show that the largest growth area for Ecu applications has actually been in Portugal and Spain, although this may be partly explained by the level of EC transfers in Ecus. Future prospects will depend on the agreements reached in the Intergovernmental Conferences (IGCs), since Spanish exporters will be unwilling to assume additional currency risks.

Perhaps the most notable trend in the Spanish market has been the growing proportion of Ecus in terms of total foreign-currency debt for the whole economy. From 0.69 per cent of total foreign debt in 1983, Ecu financing grew to represent 12 per cent of a US$43.7 billion total by the end of 1990, in which period US dollar liabilities halved (see Exhibit 18.12). This trend has been accelerated by the Spanish Treasury's initiation of an Ecu funding programme in 1990. Corresponding figures for central bank reserves are not available broken down by currency, although a commensurate rise in Ecu assets would not be unduly surprising, given the recent dramatic growth in reserves (US$53 billion at December 1990).

The growing dimensions of the Ecu bond market were recognised by borrowers and intermediaries in Spain at an early stage. However, a 30 per cent compulsory non-remunerated central bank deposit for all foreign currency transactions, imposed in February 1989 to curb the inflationary impact of heavy corporate borrowing programmes, meant that the Ecu market was effectively off-limits to Spanish borrowers. This restriction was lifted in March 1991, although the Spanish Treasury anticipated the move with an inaugural Ecu500m domestic issue of five-year *bonos del estado* in

Exhibit 18.12 **Spain's gross outstanding debt by currency, 1983–90**

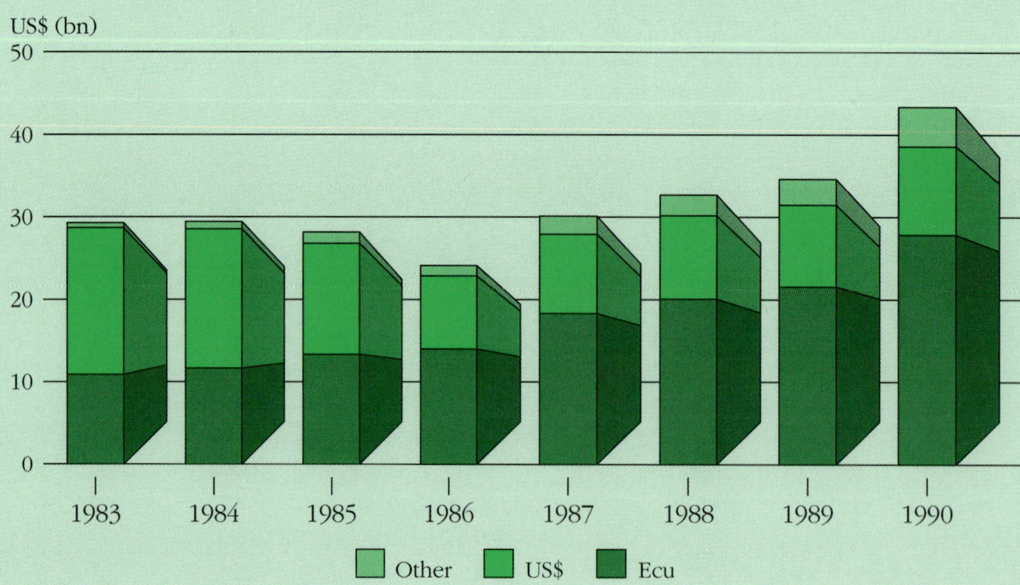

Source: Bank of Spain

April 1990. The decision to issue in Ecus represented a redefinition of Spain's borrowing policy, since in previous years a major reform of the domestic capital markets had allowed it considerably more flexibility at home. The origination, syndication and distribution of Ecu government bonds through the domestic market also represented an important political move, since Madrid wished to be seen actively promoting the Ecu market. Although the bonds are listed on the four domestic stock exchanges (Madrid, Barcelona, Bilbao and Valencia), they were structured to be perfectly homogeneous with conventional Eurobonds, and trade over-the-counter (OTC). Although the syndicate was composed exclusively of Spanish financial institutions and foreign banks with adequate representation in Spain, a commitment was extracted from the leading and five co-leading banks that prices would be made from Madrid, following certain guidelines. Despite substantial media publicity, the bonds were principally sold abroad, perhaps 10 per cent being subscribed by Spanish accounts. The novelty of the product, the strength of the peseta and the crucial 4 per cent negative yield spread between *bonos del estado* in pesetas and Ecus at that time proved decisive in this respect. Although the possibility of a second fungible tranche being issued later in 1990 was not excluded, this option was not exercised.

Spain's second Ecu issue, launched in April 1991, maintained the momentum achieved the previous year, despite the market having been saturated by "jumbo" issues from France, Italy, the UK and Belgium and several supranational borrowers. The adoption of the fixed-price re-offer system in the domestic market allowed the Spanish Treasury to launch on a yield basis, rather than price themselves against market reference, which proved more attractive in the absence of any adequate benchmark. It also allowed much finer pricing, with tighter commissions. Although the Treasury invited tenders for a variety of maturities, a five-year term was preferred, in recognition of the finer margins and greater demand in that term. Domestic familiarity with the product had certainly improved, yet despite the larger issue size (Ecu1 billion), relatively few bonds were placed with end-investors in Spain. Given that many institutional investors prefer to build their synthetic currency baskets, with flexible weightings, and private investors have yet to develop interest in this sector, domestic placement has been restrained.

Hybrid Ecu financing vehicles remain relatively rare, particularly in Spain. Nevertheless the innovative issue of Ecu70 million of mandatory convertible debentures by Central International Cayman Islands (a Banco Central subsidiary) in February 1991 proved attractive for the borrower, since it raised Tier I capital, and for investors, who receive an attractive yield, with conversion into peseta-denominated equity at a fixed 5 per cent premium (Ptas4,545.45). Similarly, a novel Ecu107 million nine-year loan arranged for EAIPSA (an Elf Aquitaine subsidiary) by Banco Bilbao Vizcaya (BBV) in 1987 prompted much interest in the Spanish market, although borrowing restrictions later prevented repetitions. Prior to the peseta's integration into the ERM of the EMS, Ecu currency swaps had little commercial application in Spain. Borrowers wishing to hedge out of more volatile US dollar liabilities have, however, opted for this route.

EMU in Spain

Since Spain's integration into the EEC in 1986, the Spanish government's contributions at IGCs have developed at a pace compatible with the nation's commitment to its European responsibilities. Indeed, it was inevitable that Spain's role in EC policy development, and the move towards EMU, would accelerate following the success achieved at the Madrid summit in 1989. Spain has wanted to put the case for the southern EC member states, and at the September 1990 IGC presented proposals for Stage two of EMU and a greater use of the Ecu. Significantly, the Spanish proposals lent some support to the UK's hard-Ecu plans.

However, it was at the January 1991 IGC that Carlos Solchaga, Minister for the Economy, presented an independent Spanish draft Treaty proposal for stage two of EMU, drawing on the strengths of the UK, German and EC Commission projects. This proposal, dubbed the "hardened Ecu" plan for its advocacy of increased use of the Ecu, was built around the foundation of an independent EC institution to co-ordinate and supervise the domestic monetary policies of the 12 EC members: a *de facto* European central bank (ECB). Although the ECB would be responsible for promoting the development of the private Ecu market, it would also be charged with developing a pan-European Ecu market to substitute individual national currencies. The Spanish proposal emphasised the importance of an independent central bank, while also signalling that national sovereignty should not be prejudiced by the functions of this institution, which should be passive at this stage. This point was reiterated in April 1991 by Manuel Conthe, Director General of the Spanish Treasury, who indicated that the Spanish authorities would be prepared to confer independent status on the Bank of Spain at the start of stage two.

The Spanish proposal also embraced the UK concept of a hard Ecu but pointed out that this should not detract from the Ecu's future role as the single European currency with the introduction of stage three. However, Spain recognised the weaknesses of an abstract Ecu, particularly as a 13th currency in the ERM, as mentioned in article 47 of the Delors Report. Thus Spain proposed a compromise solution, through the re-definition of the Ecu itself into a hard-Ecu basket, or 'hardened' Ecu. The weighting of each currency within this basket would be adjusted after each realignment, thus allowing the currencies not being devalued to maintain their central parities against the Ecu. Furthermore, the Ecu itself could not be devalued against any constituent currency. Thus the Ecu would not become the 13th currency and could continue to be developed as a means of payment for intra-EC trade. In this manner, the sensitive question of sovereignty, and the *modus operandi* of national central banks would not be upset, because the ECB would not be pursuing an active monetary policy role.

The strategic compatibility of this proposal with existing EC institutions and mechanisms would eliminate the problems associated with a parallel hard Ecu, even though some doubts have been raised about the negative implications of an adjustable Ecu on the capacity of commercial banks to generate synthetic assets and liabilities in hard Ecus. An adjustable Ecu would also prevent any artificial interest-rate competition between the ECB and the 12 national central banks, since Ecu interest rates would always represent an average of constituent currency rates.

The Spanish draft treaty also advanced proposals for the ECB to issue Ecu coin and paper currency, and generate deposits in Ecu against constituent currencies. The ECB would enjoy exclusive seignorage rights in this respect, although Ecu currency would only be considered legal tender in those EC member states in agreement. Neither would the ECB create net new liquidity, since it would be obliged to respect a 100 per cent reserve–asset ratio. Furthermore, the responsibilities of the ECB might thus be developed to include intervention within the EMS when any currency approached its divergence limit. The objective of these proposals would be to create maximum transparency for Ecu exchange rates, according to the EMS founding Treaty of 1978.

In general, the Spanish proposal was well received, although the simultaneous presentation of an alternative draft by the French government, proposing greater monetary discipline within stage two, means that some of the important issues being raised have been clouded by the large number of different proposals. Considering the tight schedule before the timetabled introduction of stage two on 1 January 1994, there still remain widely varying opinions among national governments on the best route to convergance. The Spanish authorities have also made it clear, subsequent to their initial proposals, that their agreement to economic, monetary and political union is conditional upon the creation of an EC fund to accelerate the convergence of north and south in the EC, having already rejected a nominal increase in existing regional spending programmes. This is essential if greater economic convergence is to be achieved. Similarly, for fiscal reasons the Spanish authorities do not wish to surrender control of their external trade and finance positions. Greater transparency of information about intra-EC transfers may satisfy this hard line.

While the drift towards EMU seems inevitable, it is equally inevitable that national governments will want special dispensations or compromises. Spain wishes to avoid watering down the conditions for monetary union or delaying the introduction of stage two, but it has made clear that the EC should recognise that Spain has tried to ensure that progress on its integration programme is ahead of schedule. Cohesion between member states will only be achieved through economic covergence, and this requires a greater transfer of resources to the EC's poorer economies. Some further structural adjustments will be necessary in Spain before the introduction of stage two, and the peseta has yet to join the tight 2.25 per cent ERM band, but these decisions are not far off.

Furthermore, although the Spanish authorities recognise that stage two of EMU requires discipline, and will represent cost as well as benefits, they also accept that the implied loss of sovereignty means that progress must be slow. Nevertheless, Spain has also recognised, and stated clearly in its draft Treaty proposal, that progress depends upon the natural evolution of the private Ecu market and the early creation of an independent ECB.

The UK and the Ecu

Ian Plenderleith

Bank of England

Consistent with London's pre-eminent role in international financial transactions, it has emerged as the leading centre for Ecu-based financial services, with important roles in creating, distributing and trading Ecu-denominated and Ecu-related financial products. These products range from deposits through bills and bonds to more esoteric derivative instruments such as swaps, options and futures. There has been considerable growth in the useage of these products in the last few years as the Ecu market has become a liquid one where major financial participants can undertake large transactions in pursuit of their balance-sheet objectives. This process has been market-led, but the UK authorities have sought to encourage it and create conditions where markets can grow freely. This section discusses the more significant initiatives of recent years, after a brief description of the main Ecu instruments.

Ecu instruments

The markets for Ecu securities rely crucially on banks to create Ecu deposits as the means of payment for Ecu instruments, because for the "private" Ecu there is no official "issuer" of Ecu (as distinct from the "official" Ecu used for a range of transactions among official holders in the EMS); London is an important centre of this activity, which involves "bundling" of component currencies as counterpart to selling Ecu to customers. This effectively expands banks' balance sheets, because they have as assets deposits denominated in Ecu component currencies, and have an Ecu deposit as liability. This activity requires capital and management time, usually producing a systematic premium in the price of Ecu deposits relative to a weighted basket of component currencies. This premium shows up in two ways, though the balance between them can vary considerably: Ecu interbank deposits generally have a lower yield than the weighted average of component current deposits; and the Ecu is generally expensive relative to a theoretical valuation of its components

Associated with this activity there is a long-established and reasonably deep market in Ecu time deposits. At March 1990, the market amounted to US$160 billion (Ecu133 billion at May 1991 exchange rates), with the biggest single contribution (US$50 billion, (Ecu42 billion) from banks in London. A market has now emerged in liquid money market securities (CDs, Eurocommercial paper and the UK government Ecu Treasury bills) and in derivative products such as FRAs and the LIFFE three-month interest rate contract.

There is also an actively traded bond market, principally involving fixed coupon "straight" issues from top-quality borrowers, but with growing floating rate note (FRN) and medium-term note (MTN) issues. There was very strong growth in 1990 and the first quarter of 1991, with issues of Ecu9.8 billion by sovereign and supranational borrowers. Much of it was underwritten and distributed through London.

The more recent bond issues are usually much larger than earlier issues

(Ecu500 million to Ecu2.75 billion, rather than a few hundred million Ecu); and more long-term, with more issuance at final maturities of 10 years or even longer. There has also been a significant increase in secondary market activity in Ecu. For example, Ecu turnover in Euroclear in February 1991 was US$68 billion (Ecu57 billion), 15 per cent of the all-currency total and surpassed only by Deutschmark and US dollar securities. This increased liquidity has been helped by the development of Ecu securities' lending markets, mainly by London dealers and large international final investors. A number of dealers now run 'matched books' in international securities, involving several repo traders borrowing and lending securities and cash so as to fund their securities dealers' long and short positions. They also aim to make money from arbitraging the financial demands of other players, including sophisticated large final investors. This activity is rapidly developing and has a growing Ecu component. It may, however, be somewhat hampered by the characteristics of the international securities settlements systems where Ecu securities are normally settled.

The increase in liquidity has created suitable conditions for the launch of Ecu bond futures, initially in Paris and more recently in London, at LIFFE. These contracts help to reinforce liquidity, increasing investor interest in what is now seen internationally, particularly by many US and Japanese investors, as a liquid market for an "index" of European yields.

The role of the UK authorities

The UK authorities have consistently encouraged the development of these activities. This initially involved fostering a friendly environment where market participants could initiate new and evolving instruments in a variety of currencies and forms. As the Ecu came to be more established in the markets, reflecting the preferences of issuers and investors alike, the authorities judged it appropriate to provide more direct infrastructural support through several initiatives developed progressively from the late 1980s.

The first of these was the launch of a Treasury bill programme in October 1988. UK government Ecu Treasury bills are discount instruments, denominated and settled in Ecu via the usual international clearance systems. The Bank of England holds a monthly auction for pre-announced quantities of one-, three- and 6-month bills, with bills allocated at whatever yield is bid, up to the market clearing level. There are currently Ecu3.6 billion of bills outstanding, with monthly issuance of Ecu1 billion.

The programme has a panel of market-makers, who commit to making active two-way markets in all outstanding bills and participate in the auctions (though other dealers and investors may participate directly if they wish). Bills trade on a quoted spread of five basis points in yield in reasonable size, with closer spreads often available. Turnover was at monthly levels of around Ecu4 billion in 1990. Since March 1989, the Bank of England has promoted liquidity by creating an extra Ecu50 million of each new issue for lending to market-makers.

These Treasury bills have developed into the leading money-market product in Ecu. At the time the programme was launched in 1988, there were few Ecu money market securities and these were largely confined to occasional issuance by sovereign or supranational borrowers, typically seeking to generate dollar borrowing via a swap. There was an increase in participation and volume in response to the liquidity and investor interest demonstrated by the UK's Treasury bills. Investors have shown interest in Euronotes from other high-quality borrowers, and issuers have responded to the opportunity to borrow at attractive yields. This market now has outstandings of nearly Ecu4.5 billion, sharply up since 1989. The related MTN market has seen less activity, but has nearly a further Ecu1 billion outstanding. Moreover, most new note issuance programmes now have an Ecu option built into them, suggesting scope for further growth.

This developing interest in Ecu money markets was accompanied by the introduction on LIFFE of a three-month interest-rate contract. The contract was relaunched, after a period of light activity, in October 1990, with five designated market-makers. It provides a useful hedging vehicle for traders of money market instruments and deposit derivatives such as FRAs and options (see Chapter 8).

The markets for long-dated instruments have also grown in the last few years, with the Ecu's share of the international bond market growing from 5 per cent in 1985 to 10 per cent in 1990. This process of growth was by no means continuous as new issuance fell in 1986 after the uncertainty created by the two EMS parity changes in 1985. However, subsequent years show steady growth both in new issuance (from Ecu9 billion in 1988 to Ecu14 billion in 1990) and average issue size.

In response to growing volume and liquidity, the UK authorities felt it appropriate to allow the gilt-edged market-makers (GEMMs are committed to making markets in UK government gilt-edged securities) to enter the Ecu markets. After a period of consultation, GEMMs were allowed to extend their activities to include a wide range of Ecu-denominated instruments, as well as some hedging instruments denominated in Exchange Rate Mechanism (ERM) currencies.

This step was taken in recognition of the emerging interest in Ecu instruments among domestic UK institutional investors, with whom GEMMs have particularly close broking relationships. This interest, which has been further encouraged by sterling's entry into the ERM, offers the prospect of greater broadening of the Ecu investor base and should in the years ahead help to expand further this level of activity in the Ecu markets in London.

These markets have recently been enhanced by the lengthening list of Ecu bond market-makers operating in London. Of the 38 market-makers who have obtained a listing from the Association of International Bond Dealers (AIBD), 20 trade from London. These firms, and others who make markets without complying with all the AIBD's requirements for listing, have already helped develop the interest of investors in Ecu, particularly internationally orientated investors both in London and abroad.

To promote the Ecu markets in London, the UK issued a 10-year Ecu fixed coupon bond in February 1991, a so-called Ecu gilt. The issue was the largest fixed coupon issue ever sold in the international bond market, at

Ecu2.75 billion, and, despite being priced on finer terms than any existing issue in the market, it met instant and widespread demand. The issue was closed only seven days after pricing, the shortest interval ever achieved for an international distribution, and helped reduce settlement risk in the markets generally. A further innovative feature was the provision of bond-lending facilities made available through the Bank of England, which retained Ecu250 million of the issue for this purpose. These securities are lent to dealers to facilitate their market-making in the issue, at rates a little higher than those normally prevailing in the Ecu securities "repo" market.

The UK issue has established itself as the most actively traded and lowest-yielding 10-year Ecu bond, thus providing a benchmark in the sector. Its weekly turnover in Euroclear in February 1991, shortly after issue, was over Ecu10 billion, three times as much as the next most actively traded Ecu bond, and more than twice as much as the most active Eurodollar bond. In recognition of this, two London securities firms have issued warrants on the bond, allowing investors to have a liquid and highly geared interest in the movement of the Ecu gilt's price. There are encouraging signs that this liquidity has attracted particular interest from UK institutional investors not hitherto involved in the Ecu markets.

Domestic involvement in the Ecu market might be fostered by the provision of Ecu securities settlement facilities in London. This topic is currently under study by the Bank of England. One possibility would provide same-day settlement facilities in Ecu parallel to those already available for gilts and sterling money markets in the Bank's CGO/CMO settlement systems. This facility might be attractive to domestic investors already familiar with short settlement intervals in sterling instruments, as well as to more sophisticated international investors and dealers, who would value the improved opportunities for managing their Ecu securities and cash positions via the 'repo' markets. This might not only help create the appropriate infrastructure for a highly liquid market, but also reduce settlement risk.

The future

The markets have responded with some enthusiasm to the opportunities presented by expanding interest in the Ecu, and Ecu instruments have rapidly developed into a market which is as big in terms of volume and turnover as the domestic markets of some of the smaller EC countries. Use of these markets by companies for commercial financial activity has thus far grown somewhat more moderately. However, as the Ecu financial markets in London have developed, there is evidence of growing interest by UK companies in using the Ecu and the facilities in Ecu offered by banks. This use would extend particularly to their business with EC countries as a means of holding liquidity, a source of borrowing and a medium for pricing, invoicing and payment. The same holds for firms across the community and beyond. The next period will be one in which market participants and users will have a close interest in the evolving debate about the future extent and form of economic and monetary integration in the EC. There are reasons to believe that the financial markets in London will continue to grow in a dynamic and innovative way during this process, thereby promoting the general well-being of economic structures in the EC and worldwide.

The US and the Ecu

Thierry Porté and James O'Brien

Morgan Stanley & Co, Inc.

Both issuers and investors from the US have had a long-standing relationship with the Ecu. The first Ecu bond issue by a US entity, Citicorp, dates from 1983. In November 1984, the first Ecu-denominated security was introduced in the US market with an issue by the European Economic Community (EC). Ecu currency futures were first listed in the FINEX, a division of the New York Stock Exchange on 7 January 1986 (see Chapter 8) and on the International Monetary Market (IMM) on 15 January 1986.

The Ecu is treated as any other foreign currency in the US and is actively traded on the foreign exchange market. Over the past decade, financial market participants have fully familiarised themselves with the Ecu as they have with other financial innovations. This section will explore the use of the Ecu by American issuers and investors and will particularly focus on the increased interest in the Ecu as a vehicle for investing in European currency markets.

The Ecu and US issuers

US corporate entities have been relatively frequent issuers of Ecu bonds in the international capital markets. Important US corporations such as Citicorp, Walt Disney, IBM and General Motors have been issuers. Exhibit 18.13 presents the annual issuance statistics of US issuers in Ecu.

The pattern of issuance is erratic. In general, US corporations are not using the Ecu as such in their financial management strategy. Instead, US corporates have used the Ecu market for arbitrage purposes. Thus, they have sought to issue bonds denominated in Ecu in order to swap from Ecu to the desired currency, most frequently US dollars on a fixed or floating

Exhibit 18.13

US Ecu issues, 1983-91 (Ecu m)

Year	*Number of issues*	*Amount (Ecu m)*
1983	1	40.0
1984	3	98.0
1985	15	1,192.5
1986	13	827.8
1987	4	350.0
1988	8	685.0
1989	15	1,700.0
1990	5	525.0
1991[1]	3	275.0

Through April 1991.

rate basis, on highly favourable terms. With the substantial reduction in the available market arbitrage, US corporate interest in issuing Ecu bonds has diminished. This reduction in arbitrage can be largely traced to the increasing institutionalisation of the Ecu market, which has reduced the spread between swap and bond yield levels.

The Ecu and the US bond market

The EC's Ecu bond was a path-breaking issue. The issue was marketed with an extensive roadshow in major US cities and attracted interest from a variety of American financial institutions and fund managers. The initial issues in 1984 and 1985 generally attracted investors seeking a high current yield and a potential currency play againt the US dollar. Since this first issue there have been a handful of Ecu bond issues, including several floating rate note (FRN) issues. These are listed in Exhibit 18.14.

While these issues have generally been successful, Ecu bonds in the US market remain basically a sideshow. This is not surprising, because the home market for Ecu bonds is in Europe. Nonetheless, these issues have been important in initially capturing the imagination of key bond market participants and raising the visibility of the Ecu with US investors in sovereign bond issues by EC member states. In the past several years, interest in European Ecu bonds has blossomed and represents the most interesting success story for the Ecu in the US market.

The Ecu and US investors

The growth and development of the non-US bond markets is being reflected in US fixed income portfolios as fund managers seek access to the risk-diversification and return enhancement benefit of non-dollar bonds. Perhaps most impressive has been the recent growth in the Ecu bond sector. US portfolios have clearly embraced both the Ecu and Ecu bonds. The reasons for this growth are several. A look at Morgan Stanley's non-dollar bond business in the US reveals the following:

Exhibit 18.14

Ecu bond issues in the US (Ecu m)

Issuer	*Amount*	*Coupon (%)*	*Issue date*	*Maturity date*
EC	200	9⅞	1/12/84	1/12/96
Hercules Chemical	70	10⅛	15/3/85	15/3/92
Crédit Foncier de France	150	9¾	1/4/85	1/4/95
Kingdom of Denmark	100	FRN[1]	15/5/85	15/5/90
Banque Nationale de Paris	100	FRN[1]	15/10/85	15/10/95
Crédit National[2]	100	FRN[1]	1/12/85	1/12/95
Federal Home Loan Bank	100	8¾	15/2/86	15/2/96
J P Morgan	100	6¾	24/7/86	15/12/91
Student Loan Marketing Association	100	9½	10/1/90	30/1/92
General Electric Capital	100	9½	7/1/91	15/1/93

[1] FRN = Floating rate note.
[2] Dollar issue convertible to Ecu.

- non-dollar bond turnover with US clients (excluding currency-linked issues denominated in US dollars) rose by approximately 250 per cent from 1986 to 1990;
- the percentage of overall non-dollar bond turnover represented by Ecu bonds rose from 1.6 per cent in 1986 to 9.4 per cent in 1990;
- reflecting the explosion in benchmark-sovereign issuance in 1990 and consequent greater liquidity, Ecu bond turnover rose from 5.7 per cent of non-dollar bond turnover in 1989 to 9.4 per cent in 1990.

Ecu bond investment varies depending upon the type of portfolio. For portfolios with limited non-dollar exposure and low position turnover, the benefits of Ecu-bond investing are as follows:

- excellent diversification properties for US dollar-based portfolios. As with the underlying European markets, Ecu bond returns are not highly correlated to US bond returns, providing diversification in an overall portfolio context;
- Ecu represents a diversified European currency and interest rate play. Morgan Stanley studies indicate, not surprisingly, that Ecu bond and currency volatility closely tracks the volatility of the underlying markets. This would indicate that Ecu bonds are a simple and low-cost way of establishing a European market position, as the need to analyse and transact in individual markets is reduced;
- yield-conscious US portfolios have also found ways to make Ecu bonds fit their US dollar asset needs via the Ecu interest rate and currency swap markets. Morgan Stanley has structured a number of transactions for its clients using Ecu-denominated Italian government debt – CTEs (*Certificati del Tesoro in Euroscudi*), which are Ecu-denominated treasury bonds.

A sample transaction is shown in Exhibit 18.15, where a taxable US portfolio purchases Italian CTEs and swaps the cash flows to an after-tax yield of US Treasuries plus 120 basis points, a minimum of 50 basis points higher yield than similar-quality, dollar-denominated debt.

For portfolios with better-developed non-dollar exposure and high position turnover, the Ecu bond market offers similar benefits, with additional value derived from the many trading opportunities offered by a rapidly developing growth market. Many of these opportunities reflect a necessary shift in relative value assessment of Ecu bonds and the desire to exploit these changing relationships.

The historic means of assessing relative value in Ecu bonds included a comparison of Ecu bond yields to a "synthetic" Ecu yield level. Lacking any Ecu-denominated government bond market to use as a benchmark, Ecu analysts construct a synthetic yield curve using the underlying European bond market yields in the appropriate weights that comprise the Ecu. By comparing actual Ecu yields to this "basket", traders are able to ascertain the value of their positions *vis-à-vis* the basket. In theory, arbitrage between the individual European markets and the Ecu market should keep Ecu bond rates close to the basket rate. In practice, factors such as the choice of bonds, transaction costs, withholding taxes and illiquidity in certain maturities and bond markets have created gaps between actual and synthetic yield levels. In fact, the rapid growth of a liquid, benchmark sovereign/supranational Ecu bond sector in 1990 to

Exhibit 18.15 **Sample transaction**

1. The situation

An investor needs five-year US dollar bonds with a yield of 100 to 120 basis points over the five-year Treasury. The investor is authorised to purchase foreign debt.

2. transaction

The investor purchases Ecu-denominated Italian government bonds. The Republic of Italy is rated Aaa by Moody's. The investor then enters into a currency swap to convert its fixed Ecu cash flows into fixed US dollar cash flows.

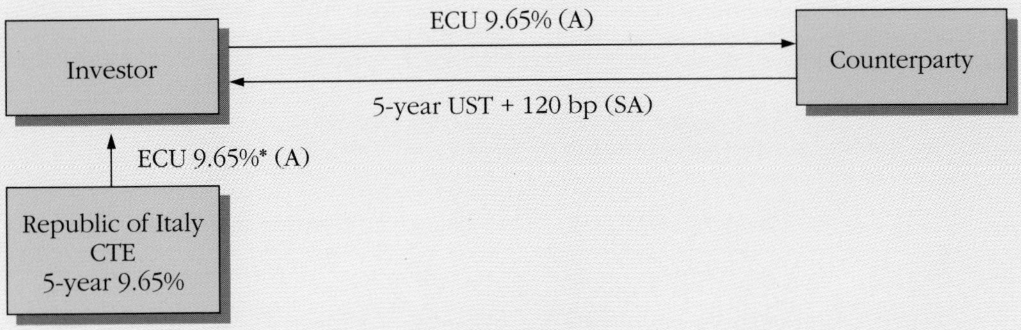

** Coupon is subject to 12.50 per cent withholding tax, but investor claims a tax credit against US taxes for taxes withheld in Italy. Investors should consult their own tax advisors to clarify their particular tax situation.*

3. Principal exchange at maturity

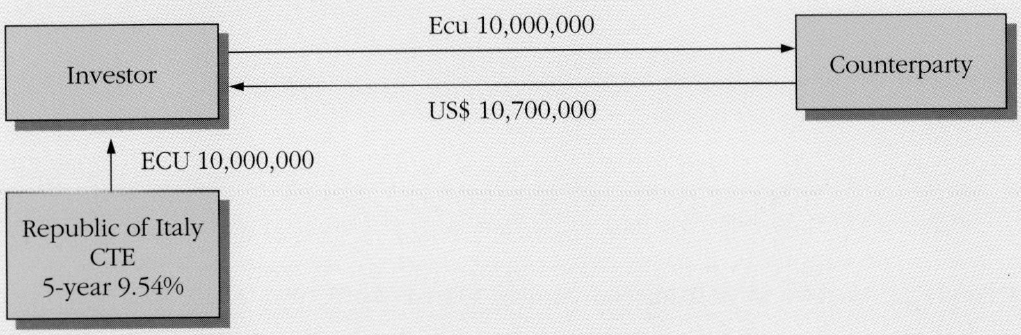

4. The result

Assuming a US$/Ecu exchange rate of 1.07, the investor will have converted an Ecu 10 million 9.65% fixed asset to a US$ 10.7 million fixed asset at UST + 120 bp (assuming tax credits mentioned above). The spot exchange rate is set at the time of the initial trade so that the investor knows exactly the size of the US$ asset created.

Should the investor prefer to create a floating-rate asset, the US dollar leg of the swap can be structured to create a Libor-based security

Note: A = Annual coupon payment. SA = Semi-annual coupon payment.

Source: Morgan Stanley.

1991 has caused Ecu bond yields to trade significantly through synthetic yields, as shown in Exhibit 18.16.

This shift in relative value and improved liquidity in Ecu bonds has led to other trading opportunities, as portfolios have begun to trade Ecu bond positions versus the Ecu interest rate swap market and major European bond markets.

Exhibit 18.17 shows the yield spread between the Ecu OAT 9½% due 25/4/2000 and the Ecu 10-year interest rate swap level. This history shows

Exhibit 18.16 **Ecu yield spread, September 1990 to April 1991**

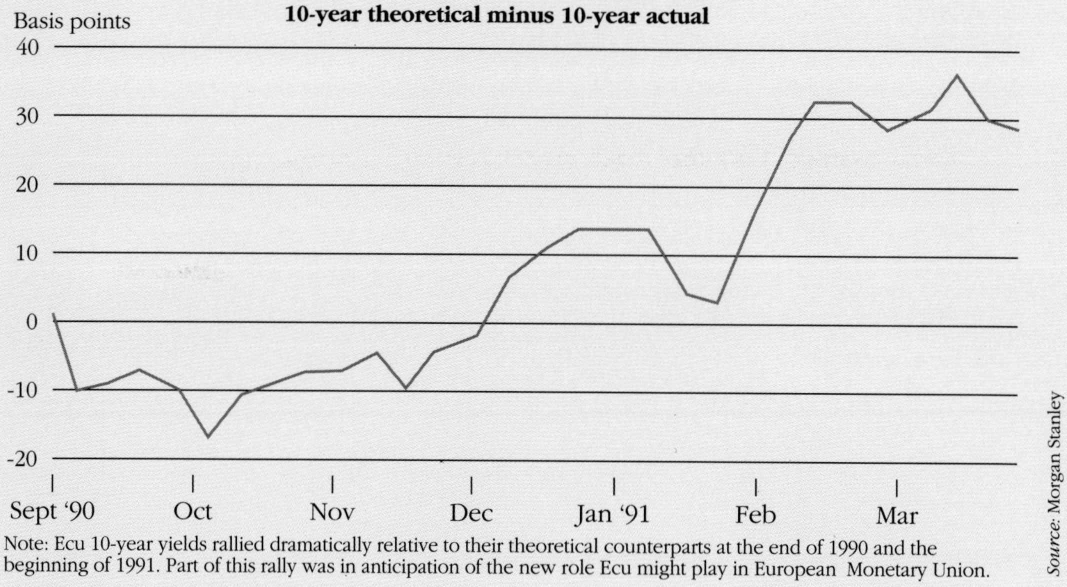

a fair amount of volatility, with a mean reversion of approximately 25 basis points, which suggests that this spread is in fact being traded.

The Ecu market offers opportunity derived from the inherent inefficiencies of a growth market. As an example, (Exhibit 18.18), the yield spread between two benchmark Ecu 10-year bonds is looked at: Italy 10¾% due 18/04/2000 and OAT 9½% due 25/4/2000. This yield spread moved in a range of 22 basis points from 18/4/90 to 28/3/91.

The past two years have also witnessed a convergence of high- and

Exhibit 18.17 **Ecu bond yield spread, August 1990 to April 1991**

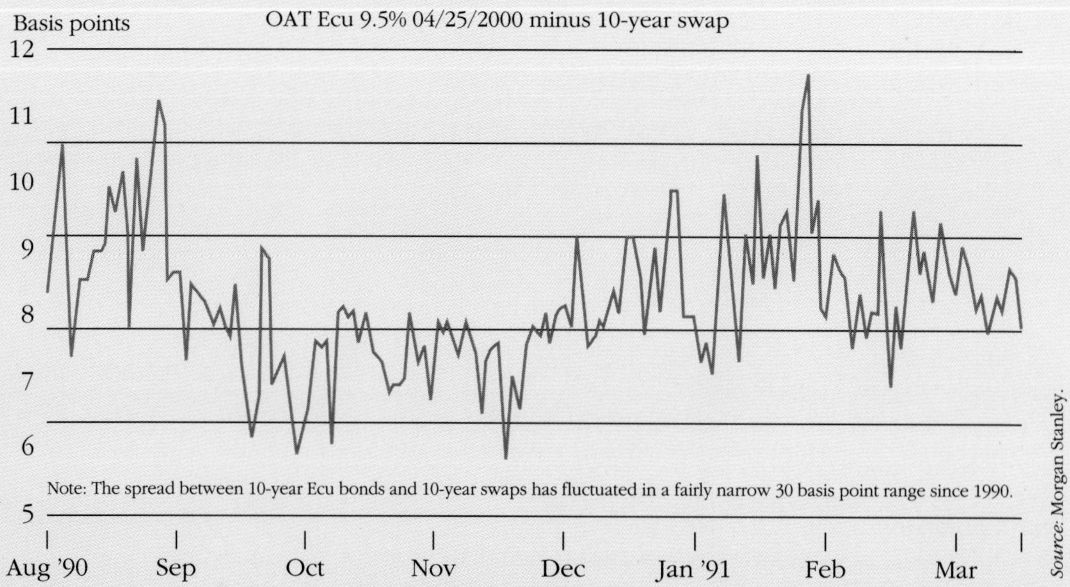

Exhibit 18.18 **Ecu bond yield spread, May 1990 to April 1991**

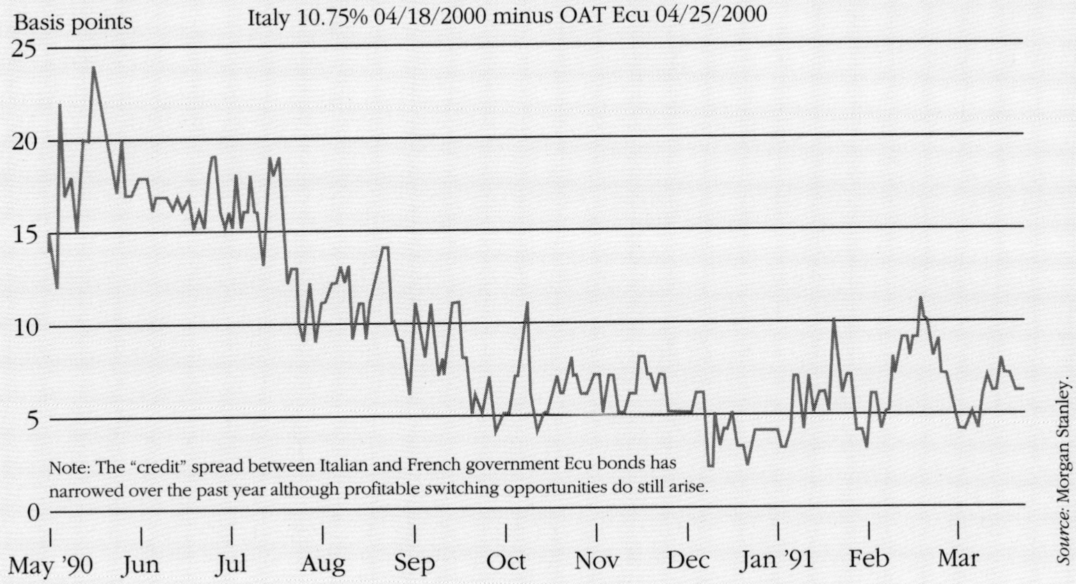

low-yielding European bond markets to Ecu bond yields, which again would indicate that there has been active trading between underlying government bond markets and Ecu bonds. Morgan Stanley's business with US clients corroborates these observations, and these investors increasingly view the Ecu bond market as another European government bond market which broadens their trading and investment opportunities (Exhibit 18.19).

Derivative trading and financing markets have been the engines of growth and development for the European bond markets over the past few

Exhibit 18.19 **European bond yields, January 1988 to January 1991**

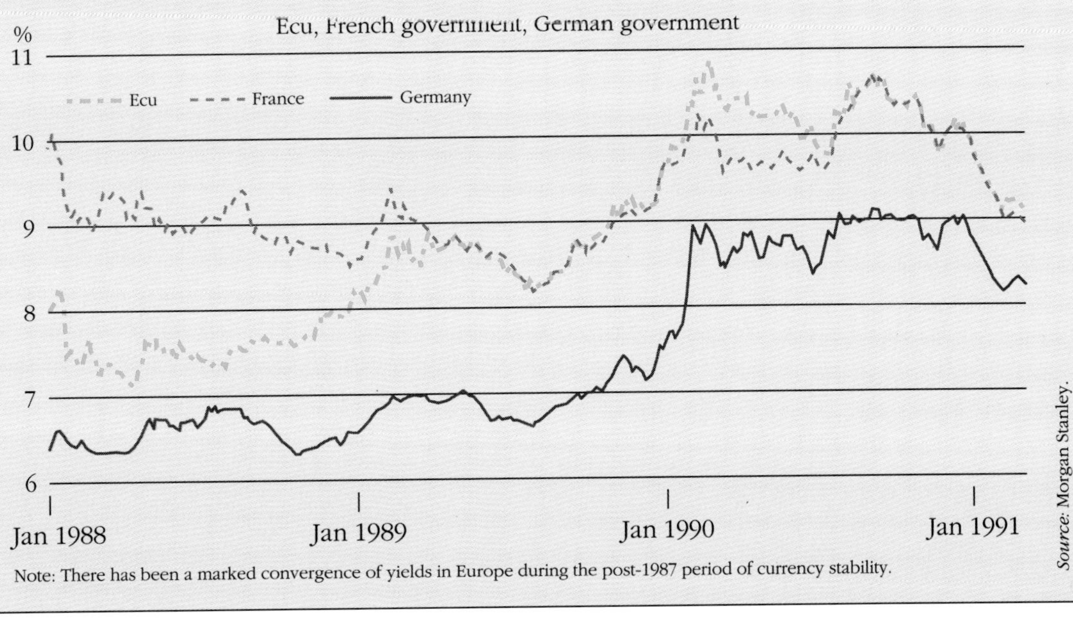

Note: There has been a marked convergence of yields in Europe during the post-1987 period of currency stability.

Exhibit 18.20

Bond	Yield (S/A)	FX Spot	FX Forward	Hedged yield	Breakeven spread change
UK (Ecu) 9⅛% 21/2/2001	8.71%	1.2087	1.1982	5.33%	11
US Treasury 7¾% 2/15/2001	8.02%	–	–	–	–

years. The Ecu market is just beginning to benefit from the liquidity enhancement and trading opportunities offered by derivative products trading and the development of a financing market; a growing number of North American investors are utilising their experience in derivative trading to take advantage of these market opportunities. Morgan Stanley has established an execution and settlement structure in the non-dollar derivative market, especially for dollar-based clients. Currently, both the MATIF in Paris and LIFFE in London offer Ecu bond futures contracts. LIFFE also offers a three-month Ecu interest rate futures contract (see Chapter 8).

US investors still count currency risk as the primary obstacle to the expansion of non-dollar bond exposure in their portfolios. The futures/options and financing markets offer an efficient way for portfolios to separate the interest rate and currency components of foreign bonds. Exhibits 18.20 and 18.21 explore the return profile of positions which offer non-US interest rate exposure with minimal currency risk.

In Exhibit 18.20 the forward currency market is used to hedge Ecu currency exposure back to US dollars for three months. The rate differential implied in the forward produces a standstill "hedged" yield of 269 basis points through US Treasuries of the same maturity.

We see that a narrowing of the 10-year Ecu bond to 10-year US Treasury yield spread of 11 basis points is needed to offset the cost of the hedge. Any further tightening of the US/Ecu yield spread over the three-month horizon represents out-performance of the currency-hedged Ecu bond to US Treasuries. Therefore, if an investor feels that Ecu bonds have the potential to out-perform US bonds by more than 11 basis points over the next quarter, he can take advantage of the superior price performance with limited currency risk.

Another way to obtain Ecu interest rate exposure with minimal currency risk involves the use of futures. Exhibit 18.21 looks at the return profile of a 10-year Ecu bond position versus a position of US dollar cash plus an Ecu bond future in varying interest rate and currency level scenarios. Exhibit 21 a) shows the return generated by an investment in an Ecu bond, the Italy 10¾% due 18/4/2000 for a six-week investment horizon. Exhibit 21 b) shows an investment in a factor-weight amount of Ecu bond futures plus a US dollar CD at a rate of 6 per cent for the same horizon.

We see that the return profile for a dollar-based investor is much smoother in the cash and futures position because the currency volatility has been reduced. US investors have utilised this strategy to express a

Exhibit 18.21 a) and b)

Ecu bond investment

(a) shows the return generated by an investment in an Ecu bond, the Italy 10¾% due 18/4/2000 for a six-week investment horizon.

(a) Yield shift

Exchange rate	*Money market rate of return to cash (%)*				
1.13	−10.06	−20.52	−30.77	−40.83	−50.69
1.19	29.23	18.21	7.42	−3.17	−13.56
1.25	68.52	56.95	45.61	34.48	23.57

(b) shows an investment in a factor weight amount of Ecu bond futures plus a US dollar CD at a rate of 6 per cent for the same horizon.

(b) Yield shift

Exchange rate	*Money market rate of return to CD + Future (%)*				
1.13	23.20	15.17	5.57	−4.49	−14.35
1.19	24.11	15.66	5.54	−5.05	−15.43
1.25	25.03	16.14	5.52	−5.60	−16.51

number of interest rate and currency views (eg sterling cash plus yen bond futures).

Finally, the rapidly developing non-dollar financing market has provided participants with a number of short-term products which serve the needs of the Ecu bond holder and cash investor. Liquidity in this market has been greatly enhanced due to the growth of derivative products such as options, futures and matched-book trading.

For leveraged accounts, funding can be obtained and costs lowered through the repo-ing/lending of Ecu securities. For bond holders of fully paid-for securities, securities lending provides a mechanism for generating incremental returns on the entire portfolio. This is accomplished through the lending of "specific issues" whose demand is driven by short positions, fails-to-deliver and other delivery requirements. And finally, for cash investors repo is an attractive money market investment alternative which provides competitive rates of return on Ecu cash.

The dynamic growth and development of the Ecu bond market and the growing trend toward further diversification into non-dollar bonds by US portfolios ensures sustained growth in Ecu bond investment in the US.

Conclusion

Over the past decade, growing interest in the Ecu as a vehicle for US issuers and investors has been witnessed. However, not surprisingly, the US market for Ecu bonds remains relatively underdeveloped. The growing use of the Ecu by US institutional investors as an investment vehicle is a trend which looks set to continue.

19 The Ecu as a coin

Sue Moore

Numismatic history

That the acronym derived from the initials of the European Currency Unit should spell Ecu is a happy coincidence, for the word "ecu" has long been a significant term in the history of European currency. It describes a varied collection of gold and silver coins issued all over Europe from 1262 until 1793. The ecu was primarily used in France, and although the last coin officially to bear the name was struck in 1793, the word continued to be applied to five-franc pieces until well into the nineteenth century. It retains a degree of contemporary currency in a number of French phrases: *Avoir des écus* (to have money); *Etre au bout de ses écus* (to have no more money); and the elaborate but astute comment *Celà ne lui fait plus peur qu'un écu à un avocat* (he'll be no more frightened of that than a lawyer is scared of money).

The word derives from the old French *escu*, which in turn traces its roots back to the Latin *scutum*, meaning shield, an image which appears on the obverse of every kind of old ecu. There are a number of pan-European variations on the French term, including *schild* in the Low Countries, *escudo* in Spain and Portugal, and *scudo* in Italy. The shield image and the words relating to it are in fact the only links between the many different types of ecu minted between the mid-thirteenth and late eighteenth centuries. The coins were never conceived as an international currency. They were issued in different metals, with widely differing designs, and different denominations according to the needs of each individual province or state, or in line with the policies or whims of whichever monarch happened to be in power. The present understanding of the term Ecu puts the international character of the historic ecu in a somewhat misleading light. In truth, the proliferation of so many different ecus all over the continent represents less an historic quest for pan-European monetary union than a desire for novelty and diversity.

There is no coherent numismatic history, ie no straight line of descent through which one may trace the genealogy of the ecu and its international versions. However, there are a number of occasions on which the old ecu, in an early (and entirely unintentional) prefiguration of the present desire

Exhibit 19.1

Summary of Ecus, 1262–1793

Country/date of issue	*Coin name*	*Value*
France 1262	*Ecu d'or*	10 sous
France 1328	*Ecu à la chaise*	1 livre/ 20 sous
France 1385	*Ecu à la couronne*	22 sous
Burgundian Netherlands 1425	*Ecu de Hollande/clinquart/klinkaert*	25 sous
Belgium 1491	*Ecu au soleil*	*25 sous*
Sicily/Naples 1495	*Scudo di oro*	160 soldi
Milan 1522	*Ecu au porc epic*	36 sous
Spain 1537	*Escudo d'oro*	11 reales
Italy 1551	*Scudo*	160 soldi
France 1624	*Ecu d'argent/Ecu blanc*	60 sols
Portugal 1720	*Escudo*	1,600 reis
France 1791-3	*Ecu de six livres*	6 livres

for European monetary harmonisation, crossed frontiers and provided an international solution to a series of currency problems.

The first instance of the ecu's role as an Anglo-French currency was during 1494, when coins originally issued by the French King Charles VIII were packed into ships at Calais and sent across the Channel to England, where Henry VII was trying to cope with a dearth of gold coinage. There were no English gold coins from 1490 until 1509, and the French ecus were renamed in the Privy Purse Expenses records as "newe crownes". £13,153 worth of the French money went into circulation on 30 April 1494. Another temporary shortage of coins in 1522 caused the English Treasury to declare that several foreign gold and silver pieces, including the French *écu au porc épic* issued by Louis XII, were to be accepted as legal tender at the rate of four shillings and four pence sterling. Versions of the coin had originally been issued in Milan as part of the Franco-Italian series of coinage, and the pairs of spiney, whiskered porcupines on either side of the obverse shield and in the angles of the floriated cross on the reverse of the coin caused them to be referred to in England as "crownes named porpynes".

By 1625, when the operations of the Royal Mint were suspended during an epidemic of bubonic plague, the English Treasury was again short of coins. It permitted the use in England of the French *quart d'écus* (quarter ecu pieces), which became corrupted to "cardecus" by plague-stricken Londoners. Three years later the *écu d'or* appeared even further north of its native France, in the form of a Scottish coin, which was later re-issued in 1543.

For all its cross-Channel ventures, the ecu was primarily conceived as a French royal coin. The earliest known ecu is the *écu d'or* issued by the canonised crusader Louis IX. It was introduced in 1262 as the final element in Louis' new monetary policy, struck in pure gold, and valued at ten *sous tournois*. The coin was intended to supply the requirements of international trade more appropriately than the lower-denomination denier but never proved particularly popular. Only eight examples remain, a similar rate of survival to that of Henry VII's English gold penny, which also failed to find acceptance in the market place.

Of the numerous gold ecus minted in France throughout the Middle Ages, the ecus *à la chaise* and *à la couronne* were the most widely circulated. The former, so widespread that it is sometimes simply referred to as the ecu, was the first French coin to be struck in really large quantities. It was minted by Philip VI of Valois in 1337 on the eve of war with Edward III, and the coin's design was later imitated by the English king in his Anglo-Gallic series of coins struck for the French provinces he won during the 100 years' war. Another foreign imitation of Philip VI's *écu à la chaise* also appeared in the Burgundian-occupied Netherlands, in the form of the *écu de Hollande*, also called the *clinquart* or *klinkaert*, which was struck by Philip the Good, Duke of Burgundy, in 1425.

As France's principal standard gold coin for nearly 100 years, the *écu à la couronne* holds the record for ecu "longevity". It was first struck under Charles VI in 1385 and remained in circulation until 1475, when Louis XI's slight modification (the addition of a rising sun behind the armorial shield) transformed it into the *écu au soleil*. The reverse of this design was in turn copied by Henry VIII when he issued the "crown of the rose" in England in the sixteenth century.

Despite the success of various gold ecus, no silver ecu appeared in France until 1624, when Louis XII struck the *écu blanc*. By this time, silver versions of the ecu were already in circulation in many other European countries. A silver *scudo* had been struck in Milan in 1551, and an assortment of "bi-lingual" ecus with French and Flemish names were widely circulated in northern Europe, including the *écu à la croix de Bourgogne* which was minted by Philip II of Spain in 1567 for use in Brabant and the Spanish-occupied provinces of the Low Countries, where it was called the *kruisdaaler* or *kruisrijksdaalder*. By 1576, Anthony of Brabant had also issued the silver *écu au lion* or *leeuwendaalder* for circulation in Brabant and Flanders, and the *écu à l'aigle* was in use throughout Friesland.

The rapidity with which the European rulers of the Middle Ages exchanged and occupied each others' territories is reflected not only by the proliferation of ecus with names in two different languages but also by the large number of coins issued by the administrations of one country for the use of another. This explains why the first Italian equivalent of the gold ecu was issued by a French ruler. The *scudo di oro* was first struck in 1495 by Charles VIII of France, in his capacity as King of Sicily and Naples. He also issued a variant called the *scudo di oro del sole*, which depicted a rising sun behind the royal armorial shield on the obverse of the coin. A silver *scudo* appeared in Milan in 1551 and then a wide variety of different denominations and designs swiftly followed in Lucca, Venice, Mantua, Modena and the papal states. Thus, the silver *scudo* was the most widely used silver coin in the country and the monetary equivalent of the German *Thaler* and English crown.

The first Spanish *escudos* were minted in 1537 to replace the *excelente* which had been in circulation since its introduction in the fifteenth century by King Ferdinand and Queen Isabella, but it was not until 1720 that the Portuguese *escudo* appeared. Since then it has been struck in a variety of different metals (including the current bronze), undergone a range of revaluations but remained in circulation for over 270 years. Provinces and previous colonies of Portugal also use the *escudo*, with the coin remaining legal tender in Timor, used in Cape Verde until 1968 and in Angola until as recently as 1975. Costa Rican and Ecuadorian *escudos* were also in circulation until the mid-nineteenth century.

The very last in a long line of French gold and silver ecus was the *écu de six livres* or *grand écu*, issued between 1793 and 1794. Struck by Louis XV, this coin was also copied in Prussia, where it was known as the *Laubthaler*, and it was counterstamped for use in Berne. After 500 years of fairly constant use in over 25 different varieties, the French ecu was finally taken out of monetary circulation.

Contemporary coins and medals

Ever since the Ecu's official "birth" as the European currency unit in 1979, there has existed a fascination with the idea of its physical presence, of the notes and coins that might be carried in one's pocket and spent in any shop from Lisbon to Dresden. Although that day remains a long way off, many European countries have already endowed the Ecu with a physical presence by striking commemorative coins and medals. The popularity of

Exhibit 19.2

Summary of commemorative Ecus, 1985-91

Country/date of issue	*Metals*	*Denominations (Ecu)*
Belgium		
1987	Gold	50
	Silver	5
Spain		
1989	Gold	10
		50
		100
	Silver	5
		1
France		
1990	Gold	70
	Silver	15
Ireland		
1990	Gold	50
	Silver	10
		5

these Ecus began some five years ago, and since then the striking of commemorative Ecus has grown into a small but thriving Europe-wide cottage industry.

To date, a bewildering assortment of national and private issues from Belgian, French, Spanish, Irish and Dutch sources has put several million gold and silver coins into circulation. Although the majority are recognised as legal tender in their countries of origin, it would be profligate to start spending them, because their value as collectors' items considerably outweighs their nominal value according to the current rates of exchange.

The first commemorative Ecu was a private venture, issued in April 1985, unauthorised by any one country and bore a zodiac composed of the national insignia of the then 10 member states of the EEC. Two years later the Belgian commemorative Ecu was issued to mark the 30th anniversary of the treaty of Rome. The 50- and five-Ecu pieces, struck in gold and silver respectively, featured an image of Charles V, whose sixteenth-century monetary reforms were considered by the Belgians to be an early prefiguration of the European open market. The coin design is based on a reproduction of the *carolus d'or* first struck in 1521, and it bears a legend proclaiming the international power base established by "Charles, Emperor of the Romans, King of Spain, Duke of Burgundy and Count of Flanders".

In 1989 the Spanish commemorative Ecu appeared with one and five denominations minted in silver and the 10-, 50- and 100-Ecu pieces struck in gold. The French 15- and 70- Ecu coins designed by Carole Tiete followed in May 1990, each bearing an imposing portrait of that early advocate of pan-Europeanism, Charlemagne, complete with a flowing beard.

The most recent national bank issue of a commemorative Ecu has been from Ireland, where a set of particularly attractive medals was minted to commemorate the Irish presidency of the European Council of Ministers. They were initially presented to visiting heads of state before going on sale in June 1990. Unlike their Belgian and French equivalents, the Irish pieces are medals and not officially recognised as legal tender. The same is true of the Dutch 25-Ecu piece issued in March 1991 to commemorate the wedding of Prince Claus and Beatrice. Like many of the recent, privately issued commemorative coins which bear the name "Ecu", this coin does not appear in any standard catalogues. The enthusiasm with which mints and collectors alike have warmed to the idea of a tangible (if unspendable) European currency should bode well for the time when the current glut of commemorative pieces is replaced by "real" Ecus destined for the cashier's till rather than the collector's cabinet.

20

Christopher Johnson
Association for the Monetary Union of Europe

The Ecu – statistical section

The exhibits in this section numbered 20.1 to 20.8 are taken from *Recent developments in the use of the private Ecu: statistical review*, by the Committee of Governors of the central banks of the member states of the EC, Basle, February 1991, which we gratefully acknowledge as their source. The percentage exhibits numbered nine to 13 are derived from these. Other statistics will be found at the relevant place in the various chapters of the book. A brief commentary on the exhibits is given, incorporating some further information from the above publication. Like most of the tables, the commentary refers to the third quarter of 1990. It should be noted that there was a strong expansion of the Ecu bond market in early 1991, as shown in some of the tables elsewhere in the book.

Banking markets

Exhibits 20.1 and 20.9 show that the main use of the Ecu in banking is for cross-border transactions between EC residents. This accounts for half the total balance sheet, and domestic transactions between EC residents just over a fifth. The interbank market, including central banks, accounts for about four-fifths of the total, non-banks one-fifth. Assets outnumbered liabilities by a margin of 17 per cent in 1987, but since then liabilities have grown even faster than assets, and the two sides of the balance sheet are equal. The growth in Ecu deposits by non-EC residents has been particularly rapid; they nearly trebled in just over three years, and account for over one-sixth of total liabilities. The growth rate of Ecu banking assets in the year to end-September 1990 was 20 per cent, and that of liabilities 33 per cent, so that the whole market more than doubled in size over the previous three years.

Exhibits 20.2 and 20.10 show that London has moved well ahead of Paris since 1988 to become the leading Ecu banking centre, with 30 per cent of the total banking balance sheet, compared with 17 per cent for Paris. This is partly due to the higher proportion of non-resident business because of London's position as an international financial centre. Italy comes third with 13 per cent, followed by Belgium and Luxembourg, which between them account for 21 per cent of the market.

Bond markets

Exhibits 20.3 and 20.11 demonstrate the extent to which the Ecu bond market has become dominated by EC member governments, accounting for 60 per cent of the 1990 total, or Ecu15 billion. This is a compound growth rate of over 50 per cent a year since 1983. The business sector accounts for 30 per cent of total bond issues, roughly equally divided between EC and non-EC corporations; large multinationals such as IBM and NTT are among those which have used the Ecu market. Non-EC issuers account for only 18 per cent of the total market, however. The benchmarking role of the EC institutions has shrunk to 8 per cent of the total, as other issuers have followed their lead.

Exhibits 20.4 and 20.12 show that Italian issuers take up over a third of the total Ecu bond market, French a quarter and Greek 9 per cent. Among major countries, Germany and the UK have only recently begun to enter the market as issuers. The attraction of Ecu finance to relatively high-interest countries enjoying Exchange Rate Mechanism (ERM) exchange rate stability is obvious. In Italy and France, three-fifths of all Ecu issues were targeted at domestic investors in 1990, and in Greece all of them were.

Domestic Ecu bond issues outstanding are Ecu35 billion, and have quintupled in the four years to the end of 1990. There are also just over Ecu8 billion in Italian and UK Treasury bills outstanding (see Exhibits 20.5 and 20.6).

Share of Ecu among currencies

The Ecu's share is highly variable as between markets (see Exhibit 20.13). It is the sixth banking currency, with 2.7 per cent, after the US dollar, Deutschmark, yen, Swiss franc and sterling, in terms of outstandings. In terms of growth rates, it has moved to fifth place, with 5.6 per cent of flows, ahead of the Swiss franc. As a foreign currency held by banks, it is also in fifth place with 3.5 per cent, thus outranking sterling but not the Swiss franc in terms of outstandings; however, it has moved up to third place after the US dollar and the Deutschmark, with 7.2 per cent of the increase in foreign currency holdings.

The Ecu is also the fifth currency in international bond markets. It accounts for nearly 5 per cent of international bonds outstanding, and 11 per cent of gross new issues in the year to end-September 1990. In terms of turnover, it rose to nearly 14 per cent of the total Eurosecurities market in the third quarter of 1990.

Ecu interest rates, in Exhibit 20.7, show relatively flat yield curves through time, and usually a significantly lower yield on long-term bonds than that on the average of currencies in the Ecu basket. This point was made in a number of chapters in the text.

Exhibit 20.8 shows the return in each currency base for investors in the Ecu compared with domestic and foreign currencies, which are sensitive to the holding period. The Ecu has, since the late 1980s, been relatively attractive to investors in the US, Japan and low-interest EC countries. It has been relatively unattractive to investors in high-interest EC countries, in view of its interest-averaging, risk-hedging characteristics. The converse holds for borrowers. For most investors and borrowers, Ecu returns or costs have been more volatile than those of domestic currency, but less volatile than those of other foreign currencies. This is partly due to the averaging effect and the important weight of major EC domestic currencies in the Ecu basket.

Exhibit 20.1

Structure of Ecu bank intermediation by customers (outstanding amounts in Ecu bn)

	Positions vis-à-vis *non-banks*					*Positions* vis-à-vis *other entities*[2]					
End of Period	*EC residents*[1]	*of which crossborder*	*Non-EC residents*[1]	*Unallocated*	*Total*	*EC residents*[1]	*of which crossborder*	*Non-EC residents*[1]	*Unallocated* [3]	*Total*	*Grand Total*
					Assets						
87 Q.2	11.8	6.0	3.0	3.0	17.8	42.5	29.1	6.5	8.6	57.5	75.3
88 Q.2	16.4	8.0	2.9	4.5	23.7	54.1	36.4	7.8	9.6	71.5	95.3
89 Q.2	20.0	9.1	3.0	6.6	29.6	72.0	50.2	10.3	9.3	91.5	121.1
89 Q.4	20.6	10.0	3.1	7.0	30.7	69.3	49.2	11.7	11.5	92.5	123.3
90 Q.1	21.3	10.4	3.0	7.8	32.1	79.7	56.5	12.8	12.0	104.5	136.6
90 Q.2	21.7	11.1	3.4	8.3	33.4	81.6	60.4	13.1	9.7	104.5	137.8
90 Q.3	21.7	11.9	3.2	9.1	34.1	85.2	61.0	15.1	10.6	110.8	144.9
					Liabilities						
87 Q.2	4.5	1.9	1.1	.8	6.4	44.2	30.7	7.7	6.0	57.9	64.3
88 Q.2	5.3	1.9	1.2	1.1	7.6	56.1	37.8	10.6	6.9	73.6	81.2
89 Q.2	7.0	2.5	2.0	1.8	10.8	75.5	52.5	13.0	9.0	97.5	108.4
89 Q.4	8.6	2.9	2.7	2.5	13.8	72.3	51.5	16.0	9.5	97.9	111.7
90 Q.1	8.0	2.9	3.2	2.8	13.9	85.8	60.2	18.2	13.2	117.3	131.2
90 Q.2	8.5	2.9	3.0	3.1	14.6	86.3	63.8	19.4	14.4	120.2	134.8
90 Q.3	9.8	3.2	3.6	3.4	16.7	89.8	65.0	23.2	14.4	127.5	144.2
					Net balances[4]						
87 Q.2	7.3	4.1	2.0	2.2	11.4	–1.7	–1.6	–1.3	2.5	–.4	11.0
88 Q.2	11.1	6.1	1.6	3.3	16.1	–2.0	–1.4	–2.7	2.7	–2.0	14.0
89 Q.2	13.0	6.5	1.0	4.8	18.7	–3.6	–2.3	–2.8	.3	–6.1	12.7
89 Q.4	12.1	7.1	.4	4.5	17.0	–3.0	–2.3	–4.4	2.0	–5.3	11.6
90 Q.1	13.3	7.5	–.2	5.0	18.1	–6.1	–3.6	–5.4	–1.3	–12.8	5.3
90 Q.2	13.2	8.2	.4	5.2	18.8	–4.8	–3.3	–6.3	–4.7	–15.7	3.0
90 Q.3	12.0	8.7	–.3	5.7	17.4	–4.7	–4.1	–8.2	–3.8	–16.7	.7

Discrepancies in totals are due to rounding.
Break in series: 1987 Q1, 1988 Q1. For explanations, see notes.
[1] A few missing values in individual country series for 1986 and 1987 have been treated as zeros.
[2] Includes banks as well as other entities (for instance central banks) not explicitly identified as non-banks by the banks reporting to the BIS. [3] Including short- and long-term securities. [4] – = net liability position.
Source: BIS, *Quarterly Statistics on International Banking Developments.*

Exhibit 20.2

Structure of Ecu bank intermediation by countries (in Ecu bn)

Banks in the countries below	*Third qtr.*	*Positions* vis-à-vis *non-residents* *Total*		*o/w: non-banks*		*Positions* vis-à-vis *residents*[1] *Total*		*o/w: non-banks*		*Total*		*Of which: non-banks*	
		Assets	*Liab.*	*Assets*	*Liab.*	*Assets*	*Liab.*	*Assets*	*Liab.*	*Assets*	*Liab.*	*Assets*	*Liab.*
Belgium	1988	10.9	7.7	3.6	1.1	2.9	3.0	.3	.2	13.8	10.6	3.9	1.3
	1989	12.2	9.1	4.0	1.0	2.2	2.3	.3	.2	14.4	11.5	4.3	1.2
	1990	13.1	13.9	4.7	1.4	2.7	4.0	.3	.3	15.7	17.8	5.0	1.7
Luxembourg	1988	6.6	5.0	2.2	.9	2.5	3.4	.2	1.3	9.1	8.4	2.4	2.2
	1989	7.9	6.4	2.5	1.2	2.8	3.8	.4	1.7	10.7	10.2	3.0	2.8
	1990	10.3	8.6	3.2	2.1	3.8	4.4	.5	2.4	14.1	13.0	3.7	4.4
Denmark	1988	.9	.6	.0	.0	.0	.0	.0	.0	.9	.6	.0	.0
	1989	.5	.3	.0	.0	.0	.0	.0	.0	.5	.3	.0	.0
	1990	1.3	1.1	.1	.1	.0	.0	.0	.0	1.3	1.1	.1	.1
Germany	1988	3.2	2.7	1.1	.1	.0	.1	.0	.1	3.2	2.8	1.1	.2
	1989	3.3	3.2	1.0	.5	.1	.1	.1	.1	3.5	3.3	1.0	.6
	1990	5.0	4.7	1.1	.7	.2	.2	.2	.1	5.2	4.9	1.2	.8
Spain	1988	.4	.9	.1	.1	.8	.2	.6	.0	1.2	1.1	.7	.1
	1989	.9	1.5	.2	.1	1.1	.3	.7	.0	1.9	1.8	.9	.1
	1990	1.9	2.5	.4	.3	1.9	1.5	1.0	.6	3.8	4.0	1.4	.9
France	1988	15.3	14.6	1.8	.4	8.2	5.0	3.1	.3	23.5	19.6	4.9	.7
	1989	16.5	15.9	2.1	.8	8.0	5.4	2.5	.5	24.5	21.3	4.7	1.3
	1990	16.4	19.6	1.4	.6	7.8	6.1	1.5	.8	24.3	25.7	2.9	1.4
Ireland	1988	.1	.2	.0	.0	.3	.1	.2	.0	.4	.2	.2	.1
	1989	.2	.2	.0	.0	.2	.0	.1	.0	.4	.2	.1	.0
	1990	.3	.4	.1	.0	.4	.2	.3	.1	.8	.6	.5	.1
Italy	1988	8.0	11.1	.0	.2	5.1	1.5	2.8	.0	13.1	12.6	2.8	.2
	1989	10.4	15.7	.1	.8	8.4	2.7	5.1	.1	18.8	18.4	5.2	.8
	1990	12.4	17.5	.1	.9	5.9	2.0	3.6	.2	18.3	19.5	3.7	1.1
Netherlands	1988	3.8	3.0	.6	.3	.2	.5	.1	.3	4.1	3.5	.7	.5
	1989	4.1	3.3	.7	.4	.4	.6	.3	.4	4.5	3.9	.9	.8
	1990	5.0	4.3	.9	.5	.4	.8	.2	.5	5.5	5.1	1.1	.9
UK	1988	20.5	15.6	4.9	1.2	6.1	7.0	1.5	.7	26.6	22.6	6.4	2.0
	1989	26.7	20.6	6.8	1.9	8.8	11.0	1.4	.9	35.5	31.6	8.2	2.8
	1990	33.2	29.0	9.0	2.8	11.0	12.3	2.4	1.7	44.2	41.3	11.4	4.6
Non-EC countries[2]	1988	3.4	3.1	.8	.2	.6	.5	.3	.2	3.9	3.6	1.2	.4
	1989	5.8	5.4	1.7	.4	.6	.7	.2	.1	6.4	6.1	2.0	.6
	1990	10.8	10.2	2.8	.6	1.0	1.1	.5	.2	11.8	11.2	3.3	.8
Grand total	1988	73.1	64.6	15.3	4.5	26.7	21.3	9.1	3.2	99.8	85.9	24.4	7.7
	1989	88.5	81.6	19.1	7.1	32.7	27.0	11.2	3.9	121.2	108.6	30.3	11.1
	1990	109.9	111.8	23.7	10.0	35.1	32.4	10.4	6.7	144.9	144.2	34.1	16.7

Discrepancies in totals are due to rounding. Break in series following the inclusion of Switzerland as from 1988. For explanations, see notes.
[1] In the case of Belgium and Luxembourg, residents of the BLEU. [2] Austria, Canada, Finland, Japan, Norway, Switzerland and Sweden.
Source: BIS, *Quarterly Statistics on International Banking Developments.*

Exhibit 20.3

Ecu bond issues by category of borrowers[1] (Ecu m)

Period	*Business sector*			*Governments*			*Institutions*			
	EC	*Other*	*Total*	*EC*	*Other*	*Total*	*EC*	*Other*	*Total*	*Grand Total*
1983	740	300	1,040	690	50	740	550	185	735	2,515
1984	895	968	1,863	1,456	200	1,656	950	275	1,225	4,744
1985	3,264	3,566	6,830	3,339	200	3,539	955	585	1,540	11,909
1986	2,188	2,314	4,502	2,158	350	2,508	1,285	115	1,400	8,410
1987	2,258	2,181	4,439	2,767	303	3,070	1,345	250	1,595	9,104
1988	3,190	3,338	6,528	7,350	575	7,925	1,845	200	2,045	16,498
1989	4,100	4,521	8,621	9,839	350	10,189	1,461	200	1,661	20.471
1990	4,170	3,565	7,735	15,167	550	15,717	1,535	500	2,035	25,487
1988										
I	530	200	730	750	125	875	200	–	200	1,805
II	675	848	1,523	1,600	–	1,600	225	–	225	3,348
III	890	950	1,840	2,000	–	2,000	615	100	715	4,555
IV	1,095	1,340	2,435	3,000	450	3,450	805	100	905	6,790
1989										
I	735	851	1,586	1,300	–	1,300	385	–	385	3,271
II	1,125	875	2,000	2,691	150	2,841	516	100	616	5,457
III	1,110	1,490	2,600	2,824	–	2,824	200	–	200	5,624
IV	1,130	1,305	2,435	3,024	200	3,224	360	100	460	6,119
1990										
I	815	1,025	1,840	3,684	–	3,684	560	175	735	6,259
II	1,220	1,165	2,385	4,105	300	4,405	975	225	1,200	7,990
III	960	400	1,360	4,042	–	4,042	–	100	100	5,502
IV	1,175	975	2,150	3,336	250	3,586	–	–	0	5,736

Data are based on payment dates.
For explanations, see notes.
[1] Including issues targeted to residents, excluding Ecu-indexed bonds denominated in domestic currency, except for Greece.
Source: EC Commission.

Exhibit 20.4

Geographical breakdown of Ecu bond issues[1] (Ecu m)

Country of borrower or borrowing institution	*1986*	*1987*	*1988*	*1989*	*1990*	*1989 Jan-Jun*	*1989 Jul-Dec*	*1990 Jan-Jun*	*1990 Jul-Dec*
Belgium/Luxembourg	231	325	50	1,185	400	710	415	400	–
Denmark	490	850	175	150	30	150	–	–	30
Germany	–	–	–	75	675	–	75	275	400
Greece[2]	165	217	–	1,537	2,260	491	1,046	1,980	280
	(165)	(217)	(–)	(1,537)	(2,260)	(491)	(1,046)	(1,980)	(280)
Spain	100	–	–	–	550	–	–	500	50
	(–)	(–)	(–)	(–)	(–)	(–)	(–)	(–)	(–)
France	1,076	1,083	1,660	4,112	6,272	2,150	1,962	2,419	3,853
	(–)	(–)	(–)	(1,652)	(3,857)	(1,000)	(652)	(1,259)	(2,598)
Ireland	100	200	–	–	–	–	–	–	–
	(–)	(100)	(–)	(–)	(–)	(–)	(–)	(–)	(–)
Italy	2,093	1,950	8,080	6,165	8,750	2,000	4,165	4,000	4,750
	(1,600)	(1,500)	(7,250)	(6,000)	(5,250)	(2,000)	(4,000)	(2,750)	(2,500)
Netherlands	206	100	275	490	–	225	275	–	–
Portugal[2]	–	150	13	–	–	–	–	–	–
UK	50	–	300	225	400	135	150	250	150
EC Institutions	1,285	1,345	1,845	1,461	1,535	901	560	1,535	–
Total EC	5,796	6,220	12,398	15,400	20,872	6,762	8,648	11,359	9,513
Other European countries	860	268	2,125	1,506	1,460	426	1,080	710	750
European multinationals	200	375	253	325	320	100 *	225	200	120
Other European instit.	–	–	–	100	275	100	–	175	100
International institutions	115	250	200	100	225	–	100	225	–
Non-European countries[3]	1,604	1,990	1,535	3,040	2,335	1,350	1,690	1,580	755
Total non-EC	2,779	2,883	4,113	5,071	4,615	1,976	3,095	2,890	1,725
Grand total	8,575	9,103	16,511	20,471	25,487	8,738	11,743	14,249	11,238
				Memorandum items					
Total issues:									
international	6,810	7,286	9,261	11,282	14,120	5,247	6,045	8,260	5,860
domestic targeted	1,765	1,817	7,250	9,189	11,367	3,491	5,698	5,989	5,378

[1] Including issues targeted to residents. The latter are given between parentheses. Excluding Ecu indexed bond issues denominated in domestic currency. For explanations, see notes. [2] Including index linked bonds. [3] Mainly US and Japan. Figures include loans raised by foreign branches and subsidiaries of German enterprises with the guarantee of the parent company (Ecu440 million in the period 1984 to Nov. 1988). * Including the Ecu 75m loan raised by the National Bank of Hungary.
Source: EC Commission. Data are based on payment dates.

Exhibit 20.5

Evolution of domestic Ecu bond issues and outstanding stock (Ecu m)

Period	*Gross new borrowing*	*Total repayment*	*Net new borrowing*	*Stock outstand.*
1986	1,765	0	1,765	7,365
1987	1,817	0	1,817	9,182
1988	7,250	0	7,250	16,432
1989	9,188	1,365	7,823	24,255
1990	11,367	817	10,550	34,805
1988				
I	750	0	750	9,932
II	1,500	0	1,500	11,432
III	2,000	0	2,000	13,432
IV	3,000	0	3,000	16,432
1989				
I	1,000	500	500	16,932
II	2,491	0	2,491	19,423
III	2,673	0	2,673	22,096
IV	3,024	865	2,159	24,255
1990				
I	2,184	106	2,078	26,333
II	3,804	111	3,693	30,026
III	1,542	0	1,542	31,568
IV	3,837	600	3,237	34,805

Source: EC Commission.

Exhibit 20.6

Ecu Treasury bills (Ecu m)

	Italy			*UK*
End of quarter	*New issues*	*Repayment*	*Stock Outstand.*	*Stock Outstand.*
1989				
II	NA	NA	6,033	2,400
III	960	750	6,243	2,500
IV	1,733	500	7,476	2,800
1990				
I	500	1,783	6,193	3,000
II	1,000	2,000	5,193	3,300
III	500	1,000	4,693	3,600
IV	2,000	1,943	4,750	3,600

Source: EC central banks.

Exhibit 20.7

Ecu market interest rates

Period	Euro deposit rates 1					Bond yields 2			Avg. national rates 3	
	2 days not.	1-month	3-month	6-month	12-month	short-term	med.-term	long-term	short-term	long-term
Annual averages										
1985	8.8	9.1	9.2	9.3	9.3	8.9	9.4	9.6	9.0	9.7
1986	7.8	8.0	8.0	7.8	7.6	7.7	8.2	8.3	7.8	8.2
1987	6.8	7.0	7.1	7.2	7.2	7.9	8.2	8.5	6.9	8.2
1988	6.4	6.7	6.9	7.0	7.2	7.7	7.9	8.2	6.8	7.9
1989	8.9	9.1	9.3	9.4	9.5	8.9	8.8	8.8	9.2	8.6
1990	9.9	10.1	10.3	10.6	10.7	10.8	10.4	10.4	10.5	10.3
Monthly figures										
89 Jun	8.7	8.8	9.0	9.2	9.3	8.8	8.7	8.7	9.0	8.4
89 Jul	8.9	9.0	9.1	9.2	9.3	8.8	8.5	8.6	9.0	8.2
89 Aug	9.0	9.2	9.3	9.3	9.2	8.8	8.6	8.6	9.0	8.3
89 Sep	9.2	9.5	9.8	9.8	9.8	8.9	8.6	8.7	9.7	9.1
89 Oct	10.2	10.3	10.3	10.3	10.3	9.4	9.1	9.2	10.3	9.2
89 Nov	10.3	10.5	10.6	10.6	10.5	9.7	9.3	9.3	10.6	9.5
89 Dec	10.5	10.8	10.9	10.9	10.8	9.9	9.3	9.2	10.7	9.5
90 Jan	10.6	10.9	11.2	11.3	11.3	10.8	10.3	10.0	10.9	9.9
90 Feb	10.5	10.8	11.1	11.4	11.5	11.4	10.9	10.8	10.9	10.5
90 Mar	10.0	10.3	10.7	11.1	11.4	11.6	11.0	10.7	10.7	10.4
90 Apr	10.1	10.1	10.4	10.7	10.9	11.5	10.9	10.7	10.4	10.5
90 May	10.0	10.1	10.3	10.5	10.7	10.5	10.4	10.3	10.3	10.3
90 Jun	9.7	9.9	10.1	10.4	10.5	10.5	10.3	10.2	10.2	10.2
90 Jul	9.8	9.9	10.1	10.3	10.4	10.2	9.9	9.9	10.2	10.0
90 Aug	9.7	9.9	10.2	10.4	10.5	10.6	10.4	10.5	10.4	10.5
90 Sep	9.4	9.6	9.9	10.3	10.5	11.0	10.6	10.7	10.3	10.7
90 Oct	9.5	9.7	9.9	10.1	10.2	10.3	10.3	10.4	10.1	10.5
90 Nov	9.6	9.7	10.0	10.0	10.1	10.7	10.2	10.3	10.3	10.4
90 Dec	9.7	10.3	10.3	10.3	10.3	10.6	10.0	10.0	10.7	10.4

[1] Bid rates: averages of daily observations at the opening of the market. [2] End-month observations. [3] Weighted average of representative market rates of the currencies represented in the Ecu basket; in the case of short-term rates the three-month Euro market rates have been taken, whereas in the case of long-term rates domestic rates have been used; weights have been calculated on the basis of the respective currencies' Ecu market rates.

Sources: BIS and Luxembourg Stock Exchange.

Exhibit 20.8

Exchange-rate adjusted yield-cost of three-month investment indebtedness*
(a) July 1988 to June 1989, (b) July 1989 to June 1990

					Euro-							
	Domestic currency		*Ecu*		*DM*		*US$*		*Jpy*		*CHF*	
	a	*b*	*a*	*b*	*a*	*b*	*a*	*b*	*a*	*b*	*a*	*b*
Base country: Benelux												
Average	7.8	9.8	7.8	8.1	5.6	6.1	12.6	−11.8	1.6	−15.2	2.2	9.5
Standard deviation	.6	.8	1.2	3.0	.8	2.2	19.1	13.2	10.8	21.1	8.9	10.8
Variation co-efficient	.1	.1	.2	.4	.1	.4	1.5	−1.1	6.9	−1.4	4.1	1.1
Base country: Denmark												
Average	8.1	11.1	9.6	8.1	7.4	6.0	14.4	−11.9	3.4	−15.2	4.0	9.5
Standard deviation	.4	1.1	2.3	4.4	1.4	2.6	19.1	13.6	12.5	22.1	8.0	12.0
Variation coefficient	.0	.1	.2	.5	.2	.4	1.3	−1.1	3.7	−1.5	2.0	1.3
Base country: Germany												
Average	5.8	8.0	7.9	9.9	5.7	7.9	12.7	−10.1	1.7	−13.5	2.3	11.4
Standard deviation	.8	.5	1.3	4.6	.8	.5	19.2	14.7	10.7	20.7	8.9	12.6
Variation coefficient	.1	.1	.2	.5	.1	.1	1.5	−1.5	6.5	−1.5	3.9	1.1
Base country: France												
Average	8.5	10.2	7.8	9.0	5.6	7.0	12.5	−11.0	1.6	−14.3	2.2	10.4
Standard deviation	.6	.7	2.1	2.8	2.5	2.6	17.6	12.8	11.7	20.5	9.9	10.7
Variation coefficient	.1	.1	.3	.3	.4	.4	1.4	−1.2	7.4	−1.4	4.5	1.0
Base country: Ireland												
Average	8.3	11.4	8.4	9.4	6.3	7.4	13.2	−10.6	2.2	−14.0	2.9	10.8
Standard deviation	.6	.9	1.3	2.8	.7	2.9	18.8	12.6	11.2	20.7	8.9	10.3
Variation coefficient	.1	.1	.1	.3	.1	.4	1.4	−1.2	5.0	−1.5	3.1	1.0
Base country: Italy												
Average	11.8	12.6	4.9	12.5	2.7	10.5	9.6	−7.7	−1.3	−11.1	−.7	13.9
Standard deviation	.9	.3	2.4	2.9	2.9	5.6	18.2	10.8	11.6	20.8	8.0	8.4
Variation coefficient	.1	.0	.5	.2	1.1	.5	1.9	−1.4	−9.0	−1.9	−11.3	.6
Base country: Netherlands												
Average	6.2	8.3	7.8	9.8	5.6	7.8	12.6	−10.1	1.6	−13.5	2.2	11.3
Standard deviation	.8	.6	1.6	4.5	.8	.6	19.1	14.4	10.9	21.1	9.0	12.5
Variation coefficient	.1	.1	.2	.5	.1	.1	1.5	−1.4	6.8	−1.6	4.1	1.1

* On the basis of monthly averages of daily interest-rate observations adjusted for exchange-rate changes occurring three months later.

Source: BIS and EC central banks. Calculations by EC Secretariat.

Exhibit 20.8 (cont'd)

Exchange-rate adjusted yield-cost of three-month investment indebtedness*
(a) July 1988 to June 1989, (b) July 1989 to June 1990

	Domestic currency		*Ecu*		*Euro-* *DM*		*US$*		*Jpy*		*CHF*	
	a	*b*	*a*	*b*	*a*	*b*	*a*	*b*	*a*	*b*	*a*	*b*
Base country: UK												
Average	12.6	14.8	11.0	13.8	8.8	11.9	15.9	−6.5	4.5	−10.4	5.4	15.0
Standard deviation	1.0	.5	9.1	17.5	10.4	21.1	23.4	19.6	4.5	14.4	15.0	12.8
Variation coefficient	.1	.0	.8	1.3	1.2	1.8	1.5	−3.0	1.0	−1.4	2.8	.9
Base country: Greece												
Average	17.5	19.7	15.2	23.2	13.0	21.2	20.0	2.6	8.9	−1.2	9.5	24.7
Standard deviation	3.4	4.2	2.3	6.2	2.9	7.8	18.1	14.8	11.7	14.8	9.0	10.5
Variation coefficient	.2	.2	.2	.3	.2	.4	.9	5.6	1.3	−12.8	.9	.4
Base country: Spain												
Average	13.3	15.3	2.5	8.7	.3	6.8	7.2	−11.4	−3.8	−14.7	−3.0	10.0
Standard deviation	1.7	.3	9.1	6.4	10.6	9.5	21.2	9.6	7.5	19.1	15.0	5.3
Variation coefficient	.1	.0	3.7	.7	31.6	1.4	2.9	−.8	−2.0	−1.3	−5.0	.5
Base country: Portugal												
Average	12.8	13.3	10.4	15.4	8.2	13.1	15.2	−4.9	4.1	−8.5	4.8	16.8
Standard deviation	.2	.4	2.6	2.7	4.0	6.5	17.8	11.0	9.7	17.5	10.6	6.6
Variation coefficient	.0	.0	.2	.2	.5	.5	1.2	−2.2	2.3	−2.1	2.2	.4
Base country: US												
Average	8.6	8.1	5.1	29.9	3.0	27.8	9.1	8.5	−.9	5.2	−.2	31.2
Standard deviation	.7	.1	18.4	13.9	18.6	16.3	.7	.2	24.0	22.2	23.2	12.2
Variation coefficient	.1	.0	3.6	.5	6.2	.6	.1	.0	−27.4	4.3	93.5	.4
Base country: Japan												
Average	4.2	5.8	11.2	32.2	9.0	30.1	16.2	11.0	4.7	6.6	5.7	33.5
Standard deviation	.2	.8	10.8	20.5	11.7	22.1	24.9	21.8	.2	.8	16.9	18.6
Variation coefficient	.0	.1	1.0	.6	1.3	.7	1.5	2.0	.1	.1	3.0	.6
Base country: Switzerland												
Average	5.0	7.8	10.9	7.1	8.7	5.2	15.9	−12.9	4.7	−16.4	5.1	8.3
Standard deviation	1.4	.9	8.8	7.6	8.3	11.4	24.4	10.9	15.2	16.6	1.4	.9
Variation coefficient	.3	.1	.8	1.1	1.0	2.2	1.5	−.8	3.2	−1.0	.3	.1

* On the basis of monthly averages of daily interest rate observations adjusted for exchange rate changes occurred three months later.

Source: BIS and EC central banks. Calculations by EC Secretariat.

Exhibit 20.9

Ecu bank intermediation by customers

Percentage analysis, end-Q3 1990

	Assets	*Liabilities*	*Average*
EC residents:			
Domestic	23.5	21.8	22.6
Cross-border	50.3	47.3	48.8
Non-EC residents	12.6	18.6	15.6
Unallocated	13.6	12.3	13.0
Total	**100.0**	**100.0**	**100.0**
Non-banks	23.5	11.6	17.6
Banks, etc	76.5	88.4	82.5
Total	**100.0**	**100.0**	**100.0**

Source: Exhibit 20.1.

Exhibit 20.10

Ecu bank intermediation by countries

Percentage analysis, end-Q3 1990

	Average of assets and liabilities	*Rank order*
UK	29.6	1
France	17.3	2
Italy	13.1	3
Belgium	11.6	4
Luxembourg	9.4	5
Netherlands	3.7	6
Germany	3.5	7
Spain	2.7	8
Denmark	0.8	9
Ireland	0.5	10
Non-EC	8.0	
Total	**100.0**	

Source: Exhibit 20.2.

Exhibit 20.11

Ecu bond issues by category of borrower

	Percentages, 1990
Business sector	30.3
Governments	61.7
Institutions	8.0
Total	**100.0**
EC	81.9
Other	18.1
Total	**100.0**

Source: Exhibit 20.3.

Exhibit 20.12

Ecu bond issues by country of borrower

	Percentages, 1990	*Rank order*
Italy	34.3	1
France	24.6	2
Greece	8.9	3
EC institutions	6.0	4
Germany	2.6	5
Spain	2.2	6
UK	1.6	7
Belgium/Lux	1.6	8
Denmark	0.1	9
Total EC	81.9	
Non-EC	18.1	
Total	**100.0**	
International	55.4	
Domestic	44.6	
Total	**100.0**	

Source: Exhibit 20.4.

Exhibit 20.13

Currency shares of Ecu in financial markets

	Percentages, end-Q3 1990
Assets/liabilities average	
International banking market	
Outstandings	2.7
One-year change	5.6
Banks' foreign currency	
Outstandings	3.5
One-year change	7.2
International bond market	
Outstandings	4.9
Latest year gross new issues	7.1
Turnover of Eurosecurities Q3	13.6
Official forex reserves end-Q4 1989	9.1

Source: Committee of Governors of EC central banks, International Monetary Fund

The Sponsors

BANCO BILBAO VIZCAYA
THE ECU BANK IN SPAIN

Banco Bilbao Vizcaya was founded on 1st October 1988, through the merger of Banco de Bilbao and Banco de Vizcaya. Both banks were long established banking groups with traditional strengths in retail, corporate and international banking. The merger aimed to create a Spanish-based bank of European dimensions, with the human, capital and technological resources to compete in the increasingly competitive environment of global financial markets.

History and Development

Banco de Bilbao and Banco de Vizcaya were founded in Bilbao in 1857 and 1901 respectively. Both banks were originally established in order to meet the needs of local industrialists and traders, but they soon expanded throughout the Basque region itself and eventually the rest of Spain. The greatest regional strengths of the two banks came to centre in Madrid, Cataluña and the Basque country, which have among the highest per capita incomes in Spain.

Both banks were active in promoting and financing the development of the Spanish economy, with particular emphasis on the coal mining, iron and steel, shipbuilding, the utilities, ports and railway industries. Apart from their own substantial investments in those sectors over the years, the two banks played a significant role in the channelling of overseas investment funds into Spanish industry and commerce.

The importance of the international perspective was appreciated by each bank at an early stage, and overseas expansion was actively pursued, initially in Europe with the opening of branches in London and Paris at the beginning of the century. This process was accelerated after the late 1960's and took a variety of forms, with the establishment of branches, subsidiary banks and offices in the world's major financial capitals (London, Paris, Frankfurt, Zurich, New York, Hong Kong, Tokyo), specialized banking subsidiaries and branches in important off-shore centres (Andorra, Jersey, Gibraltar, Cayman Islands, Bahamas) and the creation of a network of representative offices to serve the interests of customers in Europe, Central and South America, and the Middle and Far East.

The process of financial liberalisation in Spain, commencing in 1962, stimulated the development of integrated banking services and both banks embarked upon strategies leading to the creation in each case of a major banking group offering a wide spectrum of financial services with subsidiaries specialising in credit card operations, leasing, hire purchase, merchant banking, investment banking and unit trusts, venture capital, trading, factoring and real estate services. At the same time greater emphasis was placed on activities in the domestic and international capital, money and foreign exchange markets.

When merged, Banco Bilbao Vizcaya ranked 32nd largest European bank in terms of assets (ptas 6,200bn), and 4th in terms of pre-tax profits (ptas 97.9bn),

according to "The Banker" magazine (July 1988 edition). Since merger, the BBV Group has consolidated its position not only as Spain's leading provider of financial services, but also as a conglomerate of diversified industrial and commercial businesses. Furthermore, Banco Bilbao Vizcaya is now Spain's premier banking group in terms of income from services, and has a market capitalization amongst the highest of all companies listed on the Spanish stock exchanges.

BBV Group now encompasses four major business areas: firstly, mainstream corporate and retail banking in Spain through the Banco Bilbao Vizcaya branch network, and through that of its eight regional subsidiary banks; secondly, international banking through BBV's extensive overseas presence, with115 offices in 25 different countries; thirdly, upstream specialized activities, such as fund management, treasury, capital markets, stock brokerage and leasing; and fourthly, diversified industrial and real estate holdings, comprising 180 companies with an aggregate investment of Ptas 125bn, concentrated particularly in the energy, oil and water sectors. Banco Bilbao Vizcaya is also an important sponsor of the arts in Spain, having founded the BBV Foundation in 1990 to develop cultural and academic latitude.

Registered Head Office

Banco Bilbao Vizcaya
4 Plaza San Nicolás
Bilbao
Province of Vizcaya
Spain

BBV

BANCO BILBAO VIZCAYA

BBV Capital Markets Group

The Capital Markets Group of BBV has played a major role in the domestic capital markets, achieving overall pole position in the peseta markets in 1988, 1989 and 1990. The group's global approach has been characterized by flexibility, innovation and leadership in a market which has emerged into the mainstream of European finance. For this division of the bank, the 1988 merger represented more than a simple addition of one plus one; the bank's origination and placement capacity has grown exponentially. In addition, the group has developed a highly specialized role in international markets, allowing it considerable exposure to European, U.S. and Far Eastern markets. Syndicated lending, interest rate and currency swap arbitrage, fixed income origination, intermediation and distribution, private placements and stock market listings have formed the bedrock of BBV's transactional business.

Traditionally BBV's strength has been built upon a combination of strong international links and closely-knit domestic relationships. Indeed, the Capital Markets team's knowhow has been built on hands-on experience in foreign markets and financial centres. The chemistry of this approach has afforded the team a distinctive, competitive philosophy to financing techniques in capital markets both at home and abroad.

BBV Capital Markets Group has been active in promoting the ecu throughout the Iberian peninsula, building on its strengths as Spain's ecu clearing bank. The peseta's integration into the ecu basket and the exchange rate mechanism of the European Monetary System in June 1989 encourged a growing awareness for the ecu market in Spain, where relatively high domestic interest rates have encouraged interest in foreign currency markets. The Kingdom of

Spain's inaugural ecu bond issue, launched in May 1990, and lead managed by BBV, further developed this trend, whilst providing an excellent benchmark for corporate and local government treasurers keen to grasp the intricacies of the ecu market. BBV's ecu team is uniquely placed to advise, structure, underwrite, syndicate and distribute transactional business in this sector of the Spanish market, having worked with sovereign, supranational and corporate borrowers in the ECU market since 1987.

This announcement appears as a matter of record only

April 1990

KINGDOM OF SPAIN

BONOS DEL ESTADO EN ECUS

Ecu 500,000,000
10.75% Bonds Due 1995

BANCO BILBAO VIZCAYA, S.A.
BANCO ESPAÑOL DE CREDITO, S.A. (BANESTO)

BANCO CENTRAL, S.A.
BANCO HISPANO AMERICANO, S.A.
BANCO SANTANDER DE NEGOCIOS, S. A.
BANQUE PARIBAS, Sucursal en España
J.P. MORGAN, S.V.y B.

BANCO COMERCIAL TRANSATLANTICO, S. A. (Grupo Deutsche Bank)
BANCO EXTERIOR DE ESPAÑA, S.A.
BANCO POPULAR, S. A.
BANCO URQUIJO, S.A.
B.N.P. ESPAÑA, S.A. (Grupo Banque Nationale de Paris)
CAIXA DE PENSIONS (La Caixa)
CAJA DE MADRID
CREDIT COMMERCIALE DE FRANCE (C.C.F.), Sucursal en España
CREDIT LYONNAIS, Sucursal en España
DRESDNER BANK A.G., Sucursal en España
MIDLAND BANK PLC, Sucursal en España
NIKKO ESPAÑA, S. V., S. A.

A. B. ASESORES BURSATILES, S.V., S.A.
BANCO DE CREDITO INDUSTRIAL
BANCO PASTOR, S. A.
BANQUE BRUXELLES LAMBERT, Sucursal en España
BETA CAPITAL, S.V., S.A.
CAIXA DE CATALUNYA
CITIBANK ESPAÑA, S. A.
CONFEDERACION ESPAÑOLA DE CAJAS DE AHORROS (CECA)
INTERDEALERS, S.V.B., S.A.
MAPFRE INDOSUEZ, S. V.
S.B.S., SOCIEDAD DE VALORES, S.A.
TOKYO SOCIEDAD DE VALORES (España), S.A. (Bank of Tokyo Group)
BANCA CATALANA
BANCO NATWEST, S. A.
BANKERS TRUST, S.V., S.A.
BENITO Y MONJARDIN, S.V.B.
BRAVO Y GARAYALDE, S. V. B.
CAJA POSTAL DE AHORROS
COMMERZBANK A.G., Sucursal en España
FG INVERSIONES BURSATILES, S. A., S.V y B.
ISTITUTO BANCARIO SAN PAOLO DI TORINO, Sucursal en España
RENTA 4, S.A., S.V.B.
SOCIÉTÉ GÉNÉRALE DE BANQUE EN ESPAGNE
WESTDEUTSCHE LANDESBANK, Sucursal en España

Paying Agent
BANCO ESPAÑOL DE CREDITO (BANESTO)

BBV BANCO BILBAO VIZCAYA   Banesto

BBV's commitment to international capital markets is absolute and long-term; to this end BBV joined the Association of International Bond Dealers (AIBD) in 1973, and remains the only Spanish bank to be an appointed reporting dealer to that association. In addition BBV is a board member of the International Primary Market Association (IPMA), and a full member of the Securities and Futures Authority (SFA) of the U.K. The bank is also a founder member of Spain's Asociación de Intermediarios Financieros (AIAF). Furthermore, the BBV Capital Markets Group maintains a round the clock presence in global financial markets, via its complimentary London, New York and Tokyo teams.

Capital Markets Head Office

Banco Bilbao Vizcaya
Calle de Alcalá, 45
Madrid 28014
Spain

BBV

Deutsche Bank

Deutsche Bank is one of the world's leading banks and has been the biggest bank in Germany for many years. As a universal bank, it offers the full range of modern banking services. Besides deposit and lending business, two of the main activities are securities and issuing business. In 1,860 business offices, of which 360 are abroad, the Group serves seven million customers worldwide: private individuals, the corporate sector – from small companies to multinational groups – public corporations, institutional investors and banks.

The service for private customers is continually being improved, most recently, for example, by the addition of further self-service facilities. Thus, the bank now has over 800 cash dispensers, and intends to have over 1,000 installed by the end of 1991. With its more recent entry into the building savings and life insurance business, Deutsche Bank has further consolidated its position as the leading provider of financial services in Germany. The bank goes beyond traditional banking activities in providing small and medium-sized companies, especially in the new federal states, with advice on business questions. Deutsche Bank settles the financial side of roughly a fifth of Germany's foreign trade.

German reunification was the key feature of 1990 for Deutsche Bank. Since 1 July, the bank has had a comprehensive network in east Germany – initially through a subsidiary bank, and since the end of 1990 through its own branches. There are now a good 160 offices, and in the medium term it is intended to increase their number to 250. About 9,000 staff are working in the new federal states, including 630 apprentices. In the UK, the merchant bank Morgan Grenfell Group plc is a 100 per cent subsidiary of Deutsche Bank, and in Spain, Deutsche Bank has a roughly 97 per cent stake in Banco Comercial Transatlántico, S.A. In Portugal, Deutsche Bank de Investimento, S.A., has taken over the business activities of MDM Sociedade de Investimento, S.A., and has expanded the scope of its operations.

Deutsche Bank at a glance

Deutsche Bank Group	*1990 DM m.*	*1989 DM m.*
Business volume	404,700	348,800
Balance sheet total	400,200	344,000
Funds from outside sources	361,200	312,500
Total credit extended	273,300	233,800
Capital and reserves	15,566	14,367
Equity ratio	3.9%	4.2%
Income on business volume	9,084	7,619
Income on services business	3,611	2,788
Staff and other operating expenses	8,165	6,536
Partial operating profit	4,530	3,871
Operating profit	5,126	4,673
Taxes	1,371	2,193
Net income for the year	1,067	1,340
Net income per share of DM50	DM23.20[1]	DM33.10[1]
Allocations to revenue reserves	748	604
Withdrawals from revenue reserves	422	–
Staff	68,552	56,580
Customers (excl. banks)	7.66m.	6.98m.
Offices	1,856	1,640

[1] Excluding minority interests in profit

Deutsche Bank – Your Partner Worldwide

The services of Deutsche Bank Group are provided in particular by the following companies

Commercial banks

German

Deutsche Bank AG
Frankfurt am Main
Capital and reserves DM 15,538.3m.*

Deutsche Bank Berlin AG
Berlin
Capital and reserves DM 890.6m. Holding 100%

Deutsche Bank Lübeck AG vormals Handelsbank
Lübeck
Capital and reserves DM 128.7m. Holding 92.3%

Deutsche Bank Saar AG
Saarbrücken
Capital and reserves DM 102.6m. Holding 69.2%

International

Banca d'America e d'Italia S.p.A.
Milan
Capital and reserves Lit 602.7 bn. Holding 98.6%

Banco Comercial Transatlántico, S.A.
Barcelona
Capital and reserves Ptas. 20.4 bn. Holding 96.9%

Banco de Montevideo
Montevideo
Capital and reserves U.N$ 18.4 bn. Holding 95.4%

H. Albert de Bary & Co. N.V.
Amsterdam
Capital and reserves Guil. 191.8 m. Holding 100%

Deutsche Bank (Asia Pacific) Ltd.
Singapore
Capital and reserves S$ 67.4 m. Holding 100%

Deutsche Bank Australia Ltd.
Melbourne
Capital and reserves A$ 133.1 m. Holding 100%

Deutsche Bank (Austria) AG
Vienna
Capital and reserves AS 283.1 m. Holding 100%

Deutsche Bank (Canada)
Toronto
Capital and reserves Can.$ 94.6m. Holding 100%

Deutsche Bank Luxembourg S.A.
Luxembourg
Capital and reserves LF 14.7 bn. Holding 100%

DB (Belgium) Finance S.A./N.V.
Brussels
Capital and reserves BF 2.4 bn. Holding 100%

DB U.K. Finance p.l.c.
London
Capital and reserves £24.2 m. Holding 100%

Mortgage banks

German

Deutsche Centralbodenkredit-AG
Berlin – Cologne
Capital and reserves DM 836.5 m. Holding 92.2%

Frankfurter Hypothekenbank AG
Frankfurt am Main
Capital and reserves DM 861.8m. Holding 93.8%

Lübecker Hypothekenbank AG
Lübeck
Capital and reserves DM 274.2 m. Holding 100%

Schiffshypothekenbank zu Lübeck AG
Hamburg
Capital and reserves DM 103.8 m. Holding 100%

International

Europäische Hypothekenbank S.A.
Luxembourg
Capital and reserves DM 29.8 m. Holding 100%

Investment banking, capital market and capital investment companies

German

Deutsche Asset Management GmbH
Frankfurt am Main
Capital and reserves DM 39.5 m. Holding 100%

degab Deutsche Gesellschaft für Anlageberatung mbH
Frankfurt am Main
Capital and reserves DM 0.8 m. Holding 100%

Deutsche Gesellschaft für Fondsverwaltung mbH
Frankfurt am Main
Capital and reserves DM 53.3 m. Holding 100%

DWS Deutsche Gesellschaft für Wertpapiersparen mbH
Frankfurt am Main
Capital and reserves DM 176.5 m. Holding 93%

Deutsche Grundbesitz-Anlagegesellschaft mbH
Frankfurt am Main
Capital and reserves DM 3.6 m. Holding 60%

Deutsche Grundbesitz-Investmentgesellschaft mbH
Frankfurt am Main
Capital and reserves DM 24.5 m. Holding 60%

Deutsche Vermögensbildungsgesellschaft mbH
Bad Homburg v.d.H.
Capital and reserves DM 5.5 m. Holding 100%

Grunelius KG Privatbankiers
Frankfurt am Main
Capital and reserves DM 33.6 m. Holding 86.5%

*The participatory certificates with warrants issued in February 1991 lead to liable capital pursuant to the German Banking Act of DM 16,978.3 m.

International

Bain & Company Ltd.
Sydney
Capital and reserves A$ 52.8 m. Holding 50%

Deutsche Bank Capital Corporation
New York
Capital and reserves U.S.$ 103.0 m. Holding 100%

Deutsche Bank Capital Markets Ltd.
London
Capital and reserves £77.0 m. Holding 100%

Deutsche Bank de Investimento, S.A.
Lisbon
Capital and reserves Esc. 3.8 bn. Holding 100%

Deutsche Bank Government Securities, Inc.
New York
Capital and reserves U.S.$ 76.9 m. Holding 100%

Deutsche Bank (Suisse) S.A.
Geneva
Capital and reserves SF 114.2 m. Holding 100%

DB Capital Markets (Asia) Ltd.
Hong Kong
Capital and reserves Yen 8.0 bn. Holding 54.5%

Internationale Investment Management Gesellschaft S.A.
Luxembourg
Capital and reserves DM 97.8 m. Holding 100%

McLean McCarthy Ltd.
Toronto
Capital and reserves Can.$ 8.5 m. Holding 100%

Morgan Grenfell Group plc
London
Capital and reserves £333.3 m. Holding 100%

Instalment financing and leasing companies

German

ALD AutoLeasing D GmbH
Hamburg
Capital and reserves DM 79.0 m. Holding 51%

ComCo Datenanlagen GmbH & Co. KG
Berlin
Capital and reserves DM 9.5 m. Holding 52%

DB Export-Leasing GmbH
Frankfurt am Main
Capital and reserves DM 0.05 m. Holding 100%

Deutsche Immobilien Leasing GmbH
Düsseldorf
Capital and reserves DM 36.3 m. Holding 50%

EFGEE Gesellschaft für Einkaufs-Finanzierung mbH
Düsseldorf
Capital and reserves DM 18.0 m. Holding 100%

GEFA Gesellschaft für Absatzfinanzierung mbH
Wuppertal
Capital and reserves DM 173.0 m. Holding 100%

GEFA-Leasing GmbH
Wuppertal
Capital and reserves DM 55.0 m. Holding 100%

International

BAI Factoring S.p.A.
Milan
Capital and reserves Lit 6.1 bn. Holding 100%

BAI Leasing S.p.A.
Milan
Capital and reserves Lit 6.9 bn. Holding 100%

Deutsche Credit Corporation
Deerfield/U.S.A.
Capital and reserves U.S.$ 55.5 m. Holding 100%

Leasing Bancotrans, S.A.
Barcelona
Capital and reserves Ptas. 743.3 m. Holding 100%

P.T. Euras Buana Leasing Indonesia
Jakarta
Capital and reserves Rp. 3.4 bn. Holding 60%

Specialised institutions

German

Deutsche Bank Bauspar-AG
Frankfurt am Main
Capital and reserves DM 29.4 m. Holding 98%

Deutsche Beteiligungsgesellschaft mbH
Frankfurt am Main
Capital and reserves DM 3.6 m. Holding 92.5%

DPE Deutsche Projektentwicklungs-Gesellschaft für Grundvermögen mbH
Frankfurt am Main
Capital and reserves DM 1.0 m. Holding 50%

Lebensversicherungs-AG der Deutschen Bank
Wiesbaden
Capital and reserves DM 38.3 m. Holding 100%

International financing companies

International

Deutsche Bank Finance N.V.
Curaçao
Capital and reserves U.S.$ 5.9 m. Holding 100%

Deutsche Bank Financial Inc.
Dover/U.S.A.
Capital and reserves U.S.$ 0.5 m. Holding 100%

Deutsche Finance (Netherlands) B.V.
Amsterdam
Capital and reserves Guil. 10.3 m. Holding 100%

Consultancy companies

German

Roland Berger & Partner Holding GmbH
Munich
Capital and reserves DM 23.6 m. Holding 75.1%

DB Morgan Grenfell GmbH
Frankfurt am Main
Capital and reserves DM 1.0 m. Holding 100%

Deutsche Gesellschaft für Mittelstandsberatung mbH
Muncih
Capital and reserves Dm 2.8 m. Holding 100%

Immobiliengesellschaft der Deutschen Bank mbH
Frankfurt am Main
Capital and reserves DM 7.5 m. Holding 100%

Development of business volume 1980–1990

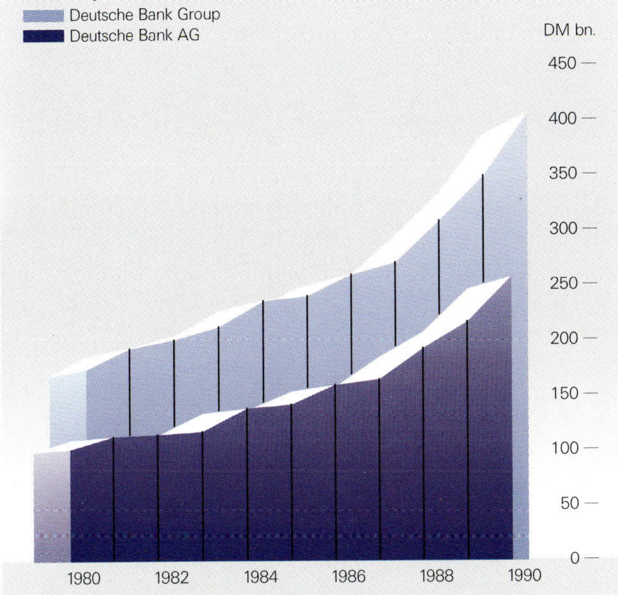

Development of capital and reserves

Deutsche Bank AG

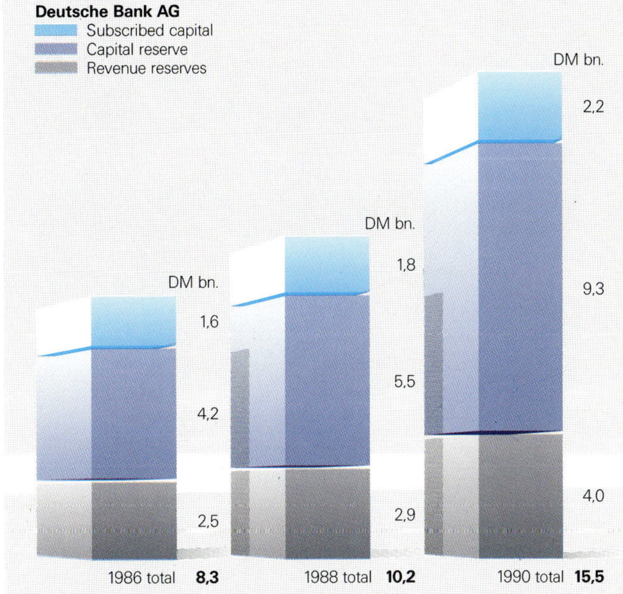

Breakdown of aggregate business volume, end of 1990

Deutsche Bank Group

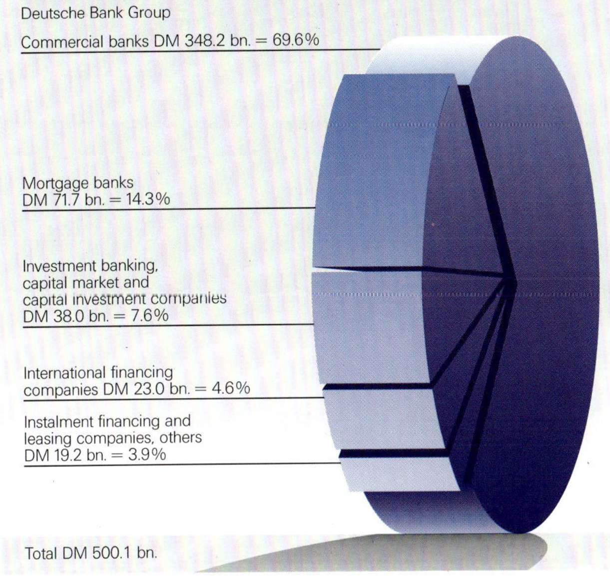

Who owns Deutsche Bank?

Number of shareholders

Employed persons and pensioners (incl. 45,000 members of staff)	195,700
Self-employed persons	33,600
Institutional investors and companies	7,300
Other private individuals	68,400
Total	305,000 shareholders

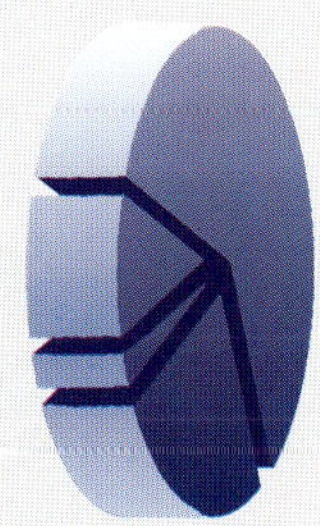

Breakdown of share capital ownership

Employed persons and pensioners	29.1%
Self-employed persons	12.8%
Institutional investors and companies	43.6%
Other private individuals	14.5%

Total DM 2,200 million in January 1991

IBJ and the Ecu

The Industrial Bank of Japan, Limited (IBJ) was established in 1902 as a government financial organisation, and is the oldest and largest of Japan's long-term credit banks. In 1952, IBJ became a private bank and currently it ranks among the world's 10 largest banks in terms of both assets and capital. On 30 September 1990, IBJ's total assets amounted to US$326 billion (at ¥ 138.05 per dollar) and its shareholders' equity totalled US$8.93 billion.

The institution has a reputation for exceptional reliability and depth of service and its strength is reflected in its high credit ratings. In the annual poll of accounting and finance executives conducted by *Nihon Keizai Shimbun,* Japan's leading financial newspaper, IBJ has consistently been ranked first in the quality of its overall banking services in every year since the commencement of the survey.

IBJ's Head office, Tokyo.

Through its uniquely strong Japanese domestic base, where it maintains banking relationships with 90 per cent of the top 200 Japanese corporations, a principal objective of the group is to contribute to the development of the world's financial markets as a leading transnational financial institution. The IBJ Group is a market leader in international commercial and investment banking, encompassing the full range of banking and securities services.

In London, IBJ first established an office in 1965 (upgraded to a branch in 1971) and its London-based securities arm, IBJ International Limited (IBJI), was inaugurated in 1975.

IBJ's London branch offers full commercial banking services and IBJI's principal activities encompass securities underwriting, trading and distribution, financial engineering – including providing a wide range of swaps and derivative products and associated liability management services – and investment management and advisory services.

The IBJ Group has been an active participant in the Ecu Euromarket since 1988, through new issue underwriting and bond and swap market-making. Through its commitment to marketing and trading Ecu Eurobonds, IBJI established itself as a leading Japanese participant in the Ecu market at an early stage. In addition, IBJ's London branch became a member of the Ecu clearing system in November 1988, being the first Japanese bank to do so. At that time, IBJ was one of six non-European Community banks of a total of 33 banks participating in the clearing system. Since then the number of clearing members has increased to 45, of which non-EC banks total seven.

Ecu-denominated debt securities have gained popularity not only with European institutions but also increasingly with Japanese investors, attracted by the combination of relatively high yields and, as a composite currency, greater stability. By the beginning of 1991, for example, the top eight Japanese

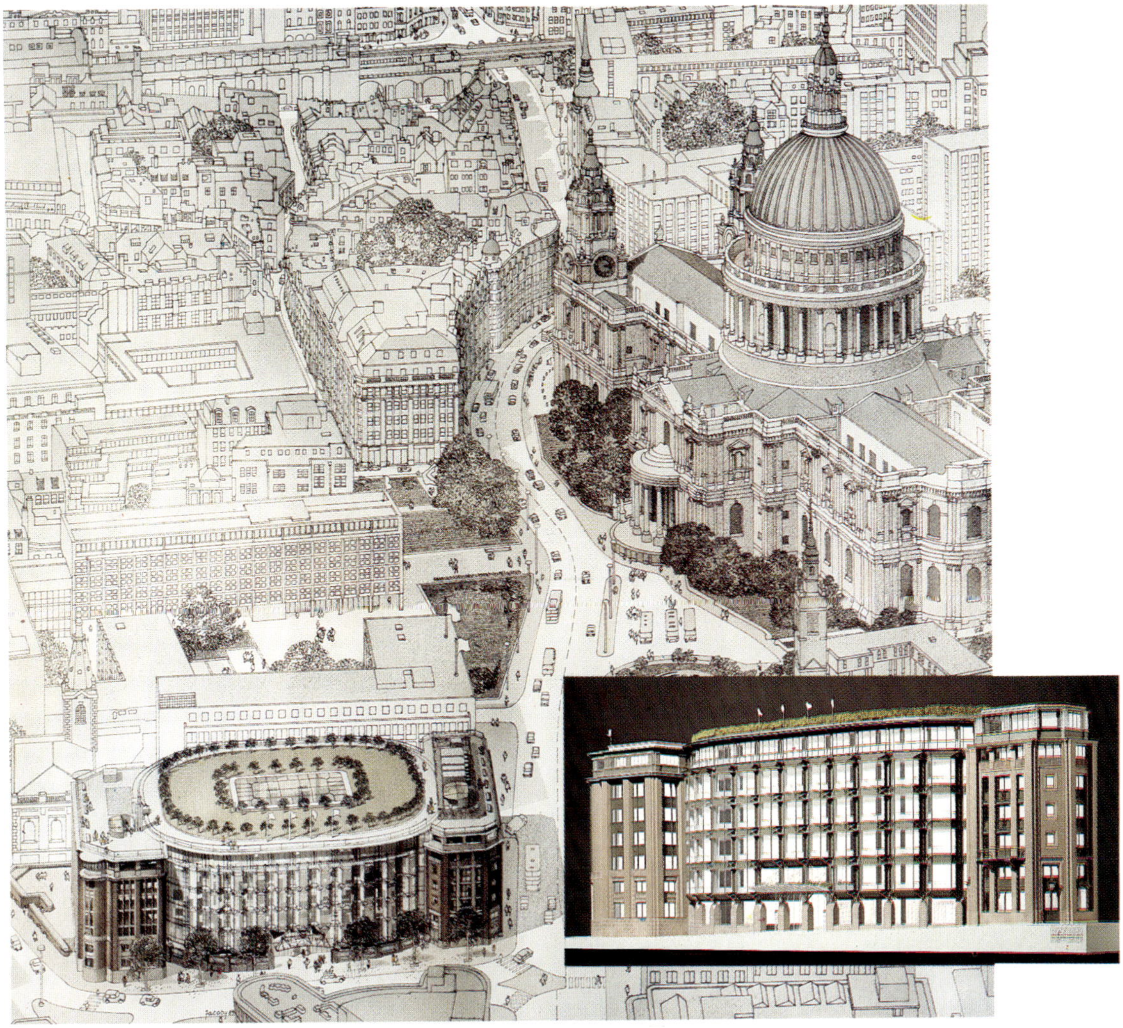

Artist's interpretation of IBJ's new London office at Bracken House.

insurance companies held approximately 5 per cent of their foreign assets in Ecu, a total then of Ecu3.6 billion of paper.

The Ecu bond market

The surge in the volume of new Ecu issues has been one of the most significant trends in the Eurobond market in the last fifteen months, with new supply of Ecu Eurobonds nearly doubling in the first half of 1990 to almost Ecu9 billion, increasing to Ecu14 billion by the year end and further boosted by a spate of politically-driven sovereign issues in mid-February 1991, with a total of over Ecu12 billion issued in the first quarter of 1991 alone. Institutional investor activity in the market has been spurred by the Ecu's increasing political and economic significance, and liquidity in the sector has been boosted by the recent issues of the United Kingdom (a 10-year Ecu2.75 billion issue), the Kingdom of Belgium (a 5-year Ecu1.25 billion issue), the Kingdom of Spain and the Kingdom of Norway (both 5-year Ecu1 billion issues) and the Republic of Italy (a 20-year Ecu 2.5 billion issue) as well as by major issues of Ecu1 billion or more by the European Investment Bank and the Republic of France.

Electric Power Development Co., Ltd.

CARIPLO

EUROPEAN INVESTMENT BANK

International Bank for Reconstruction and Development

European Economic Community

SNCF

SOCIÉTÉ NATIONALE DES CHEMINS DE FER FRANÇAIS

THE EXPORT-IMPORT BANK OF JAPAN

OESTERREICHISCHE KONTROLLBANK AKTIENGESELLSCHAFT

CAISSE CENTRALE DE COOPERATION ECONOMIQUE

EUROFIMA

Société européenne pour le financement de matériel ferroviaire

Republic of Finland

IBJ believes this growth will be maintained through the early 1990s, driven by the further integration of Europe and the emergence of major new Ecu users such as the European Bank for Reconstruction and Development.

Having selected the Ecu as one of four principal currencies on which to focus its resources in the Eurobond and swap markets, IBJI lead-managed its first Ecu Eurobond in December 1986, becoming an active secondary market-maker by January 1988. During 1989 IBJI firmly established itself as the leading Japanese bank in the Ecu market and one of the top ranking Ecu Eurobond underwriters. In this period, the bank lead-managed four new issues totalling Ecu295 million, and ranked 12th in the Ecu Eurobond lead manager league table for the year.

In 1990, IBJI consolidated its position in the Ecu financial markets, lead-managing issues totalling Ecu370 million – including its first Ecu-denominated bond issue for a Japanese government-guaranteed borrower, that of the Electric Power Development Company, and an issue for a second European supranational borrower, Eurofima. Since the beginning of 1989, IBJI has also co-lead managed issues by the World Bank, Oesterreichische Kontrollbank, Republic of Italy, Kingdom of Denmark, Republic of Finland, EXIM Bank of Japan and five French sovereign borrowers.

IBJI's success in the Ecu Eurobond market stems from its long-term commitment to the currency, its strong placement and secondary market trading capabilities and its extensive swaps and financial engineering expertise. With over 60 institutional bond sales professionals in Europe, Asia and the Americas, IBJI's Eurobond sales coverage encompasses all of the major central bank and institutional investors throughout these and other regions.

Selected borrowers for whom IBJI has lead and co-lead managed recent Ecu Eurobond issues.

IBJ London branch dealing room.

Ecu clearing services

IBJ provides a flexible and cost-effective clearing service enabling its client base to meet Ecu obligations highly efficiently. The bank has a well established team of Ecu administrators with real-time access to account data and an in-house information system producing statements on the value date of each transaction. Quarterly adjusted balance statements and interest analyses are available as a matter of course in easily understandable formats. The bank operates a system whereby individual transaction expenses are recouped by offsetting daily operating balances through a given period, rather than being charged to customer accounts. A realistic minimum balance requirement is set on a reviewable basis, with credit balances accruing interest, making the Ecu a particularly attractive currency from a cash-management point of view.

IBJ's customer base in this field, numbering close to 50 account-holders, is principally comprised of Japanese regional banks. Whilst currently generally cautious about large-scale involvement in the developing Ecu markets, such Japanese banks and their associated corporate clients are potentially large investors in Ecu business and financiers of Ecu-backed commercial trading. As the Ecu develops as a major international trading currency, members of the Japanese banking community will increasingly become familiar names in the Ecu financial market place. Furthermore, IBJ's own extensive corporate client base has enormous growth potential for Ecu investment, in European infrastructure projects and joint-venture schemes for example, or to diversify general investment portfolios in Eastern and Western Europe.

In summary, the IBJ Group combines all the elements necessary to provide its capital markets and commercial banking clients with competitive terms in the Ecu sectors of the public and private international capital markets and international clearing system.

IMI Group

A leading Italian financial services group, whose distinctive features are entrepreneurial management and a constant commitment to quality and to innovation

An overview

Istituto Mobiliare Italiano ranks within the top class of European financial institutions.

On the strength of its traditional role in Italy, providing medium- and long-term financing to domestic manufacturing and service sector companies, IMI has built a diversified financial services structure. This undertaking has been accomplished mainly during the 1980s.

IMI Head Office in Rome.

In many of its business segments the Group is a leader:

- Among medium- and long-term credit institutions, IMI claims a 20 per cent share of the domestic market.
- Through its subsidiaries, IMI has earned in Italy a market share of almost 30 per cent in mutual fund management and distribution.
- IMI Group ranks as the leading broker in the domestic securities market, largely through Sige.
- In the life insurance market, entered only six years ago, IMI ranks fourth in Italy by annual premium income.
- Through the network of IMI International, IMI is the most active Italian institution in international investment banking.

In Italy IMI operates through its head office in Rome and 10 regional offices. It acts as the sole manager of a large government concessionary lending programme, the Fund for Applied Research and Development.

It provides commercial banking through Banca Manusardi's head office in Milan and 11 branches also located in the country's prime urban centres.

Its subsidiary Sige, with headquarters in Milan, provides the typical services of an investment and merchant bank. Mainly through the company Sige Investimenti, the Group undertakes investments in the risk capital of medium and small-sized Italian companies.

Fideuram's nationwide sales force of personal financial consultants provides the Group's principal direct link with retail savers, and an additional point of contact with small and medium-sized firms. The Fideuram consultants represent a selling and placing franchise which is nearly unique in Italy.

IMI also operates, through subsidiaries, in leasing, factoring, shipbuilding credit, real estate development, and advisory services.

IMI Group international activities

IMI is committed to providing a full range of financial services in Europe and the United States. IMI International S.A., incorporated in Luxembourg with share capital of Ecu500

IMI's trading room.

million, co-ordinates the activities of foreign subsidiaries and provides them with financial assistance.

Subsidiary companies are present in New York, London, Luxembourg, Frankfurt and Zurich, offering brokerage and market-making in Eurobonds and equities, under-writing and syndication, portfolio management services, banking and an increasingly important research capability.

Recently IMI International concluded the merger of its business activities in the US through its subsidiary IMI Securities Corp. with Mabon, Nugent & Co., which has enabled the Group to significantly increase its presence in the US market. The renamed Mabon Securities Corp. (51 per cent controlled by IMI International), operating in New York, provides the whole spectrum of securities trading and investment banking services. It is the only Italian-controlled institution with broker/dealer licences in all US stock exchanges. In addition, its 100 per cent owned subsidiary Cedar Street Securities Corp. is active as an inter-dealer broker in the US market.

In London IMI International subsidiaries are IMI Capital Markets (UK) and IMI

Mabon Securities Corp.'s offices are located in the Wall Street financial district of New York.

Securities. IMI Securities was admitted to the membership of the International Stock Exchange in November 1988. It is a recognised market-maker in the shares of Italian blue-chip companies listed at SEAQ.

Cedar Street Ltd (a subsidiary of Cedar Street Securities Corp. New York) is one of the major inter-dealer brokers in Eurobonds and UK equities.

IMI Invesco Ltd, a joint venture between IMI and Invesco MIM, formed in 1989, combines the investment skills and distribution strength of both partners in order to access better the progressively unified European economy for investors inside and outside the Community.

This venture complements the Group's long-standing international asset management services provided in Luxembourg by IMI International's subsidiaries, Interfund Advisory Company, Fonditalia Management Company, and International Securities Advisory Company.

In Luxembourg the Group is active in the international bond market through IMI Bank (Lux) which recently obtained full banking licence. The company is a member of the Luxembourg Stock Exchange and is an active member of the Association of International Bond Dealers (AIBD).

Early in 1989 the IMI Group entered the German market by establishing IMI Bank AG in Frankfurt with a mandate to specialise in investment banking products and securities-related business. IMI Bank AG is a member of the Frankfurt, Berlin and Düsseldorf Stock Exchanges.

Through its Channel Islands and Swiss subsidiaries, IMIL and TURIS, IMI participates in traditional banking syndications, maintaining a dynamic presence in a market of strategic importance.

IMI International recently set up an operational presence in France with IMI-CPR Finance, formed in joint venture with Compagnie Parisienne de Réescompte. The new company will mainly operate in the trading of Italian and French securities.

This document is intended for distribution only in Europe (as defined herein) and, in particular, is not intended for distribution and should not be distributed nor should any offer or sale of the securities described herein be made to persons with addresses in Canada or Japan, or to persons with addresses in the US, its territories or possessions or to any corporation, partnership or other entity created or organised under the laws thereof or to estates and trusts subject to US, Canadian or Japanese taxation, except in connection with the Overseas Offers as described herein. Any such distribution could result in a violation of relevant law. This document may not be distributed in the United Kingdom ("UK") otherwise than in compliance with all applicable provisions of the Financial Services Act 1986.

This Offering Circular includes the text of the Prospectus (the "Prospectus") for the Offers for Sale of shares (the "Shares") of National Power PLC ("National Power") and PowerGen plc ("PowerGen") together (the "Companies") by Kleinwort Benson Limited on behalf of the Secretary of State for Energy (the "Secretary of State"). The Prospectus comprises listing particulars relating to each of the Companies prepared in accordance with listing rules made under Section 142 of the Financial Services Act 1986. This Offering Circular has not been submitted for formal approval by the Commission des Opérations de Bourse ("COB") in France and the information contained herein may not be supplied to the public in France or anywhere else in Europe. The securities described herein have not been registered under the United States Securities Act 1933, as amended. The Shares are subject to certain sales restrictions (see page E-4).

European Offering of up to 654,800 Units each comprising 62 Shares of 50p each in National Power PLC and 38 Shares of 50p each in PowerGen plc and International Tender Offers

The Offer Price in the European Offering is 175p per Share, payable as to 100p per Share on 12th March, 1991 and as to 75p by 3 p.m. (London time) on 4th February, 1992. The Offer Price per Unit will therefore be £175 of which £100 will be payable on 12th March, 1991. The prices of Shares sold in the International Tender Offers will be determined following the International Tender Offers and will be payable on the same dates as, and will be greater than, the Offer Price in the European Offering.

Credit Suisse First Boston Limited

ABN AMRO

Banque Nationale de Paris

Deutsche Bank
Aktiengesellschaft

IMI Capital Markets (UK) Ltd

Banque Bruxelles Lambert S.A.

COMMERZBANK
AKTIENGESELLSCHAFT

Crédit Lyonnais

Dresdner Bank
Aktiengesellschaft

Paribas Capital Markets Group

Swiss Bank Corporation

Banque Indosuez

Crédit Commercial de France

Creditanstalt-Bankverein

Enskilda Securities
Skandinaviska Enskilda Limited

Girozentrale Vienna Capital Markets Group

Pictet International Ltd

Société Générale

Svenska Handelsbanken Group

Swiss Volksbank

Westdeutsche Landesbank
Girozentrale

Co-ordinator of the European Offering
Credit Suisse First Boston Limited

Financial Advisers to the Secretary of State
Kleinwort Benson Limited

Financial Advisers to National Power PLC
Lazard Brothers & Co., Limited

Financial Advisers to PowerGen plc
S.G. Warburg & Co. Ltd.

Offering Circular dated 22nd February, 1991

MATIF

A few months after its launching, which took place on 18 October 1990, the MATIF Ecu bond futures contract has already secured international interest. The trading activity is regularly increasing, as well as the open interest. Volume reached a daily average of 2,351 for the month of March 1991, while the open interest at the end of the month was 7,109, as compared to the end of February open interest of 4,155 contracts. The contract shows every sign of building up into a well-traded contract: volume continues to be on the up side and open interest consolidates.

More than 100 financial institutions, mainly international ones, have already benefited from the advantages of the MATIF Ecu long-term instrument, namely its liquidity, the homogeneity of its bond pool and, naturally, the security of the MATIF.

In a context of jumbo issues and rumours and reactions about the Ecu, MATIF SA and the MATIF members are well aware of the Ecu contract potential. More than that, they are aware of the technical edge that the MATIF contract has over other proposed instruments.

First, the transparency of the deliverable bond pool composition. Minimum requirements for deliverable securities have been clearly defined and made public from the outset. Just as the specifications of the contracts were designed with the help of Ecu market experts, the definition of which bonds could be included in the MATIF Ecu bond pool was decided on the advice of professionals.

The underlying securities have to be sovereign or supranational fixed rate issues, with a residual maturity of six to 10 years at settlement/delivery date and must be Ecu-denominated. A new issue may be admitted into the bond pool for a given delivery month up to four months prior to the settlement/delivery date of the said delivery month. Besides, the outstanding amount of bonds must be over Ecu1 billion. The selected bonds are actively traded in the secondary market and are deliverable through Euroclear, Cedel and Sicovam.

Consequently, and this is the second point, the MATIF Ecu bond pool is international and homogeneous. It is made up of top quality and actively traded securities, chosen by MATIF SA for their liquidity in the secondary market, on top of the above mentioned criteria.

Traders and users know ahead of time what the bond pool will comprise and can then act accordingly.

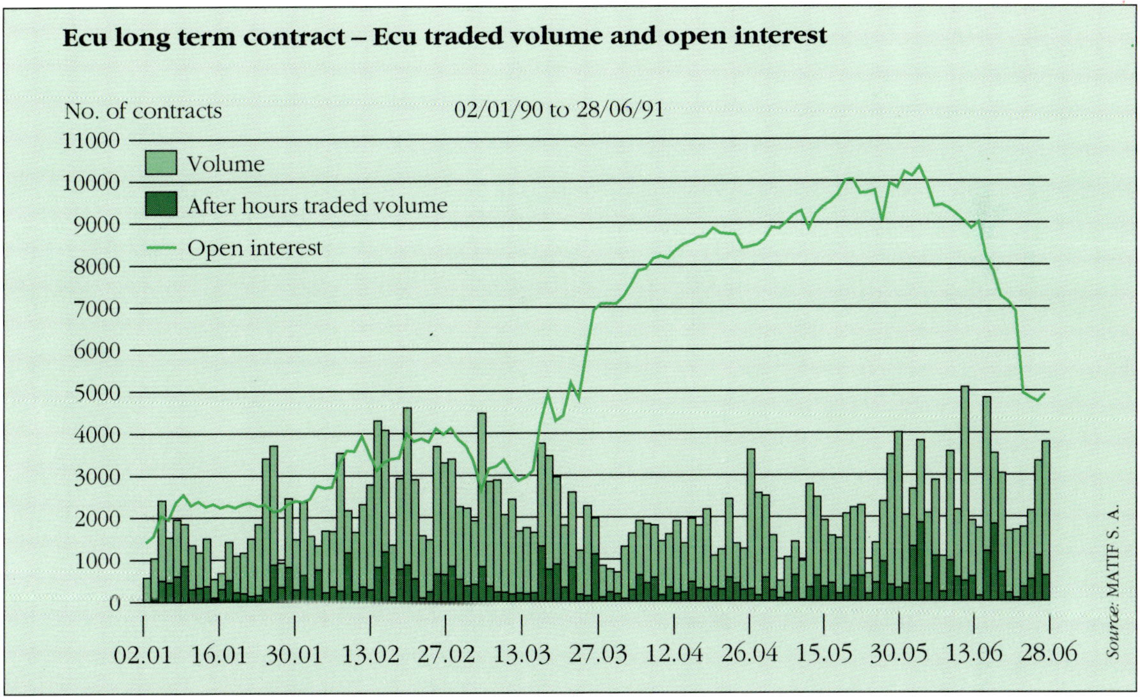

Third, the contract specifications, designed with care and the help of professionals outside MATIF SA's research and development team, follow the market's trading conditions.

Specifications of the contract are clear: a nominal value of Ecu100,000, which is adapted to the cash market trading habits; two quarterly delivery dates are open for trading at any one time with settlement dates identical to those of the MATIF Notional bond futures contract, which is the top European long-term interest rate contract in terms of volume; an initial margin of Ecu2,000 per contract and of Ecu1,000 for a straddle, payable in the following currencies: Ecu, French francs, US dollars, Deutschmarks, or in the following securities: French Treasury Bills and Treasury Notes, US Treasury Bills will soon be accepted.

MATIF SA set up a multi-currency coverage system in 1990 and made the payment of initial margins for all its contracts in various currencies.

Finally, the market-making scheme: in order to provide further liquidity to the nascent contract, four market-makers have been selected by MATIF SA. They started their market-making activities on 21 January 1991.

The four liquidity nurterers are BNP, Crédit Lyonnais, San Paolo and Société Générale. Of course other MATIF members, in particular international brokerage houses, did a lot to accompany the market in its liquidity search.

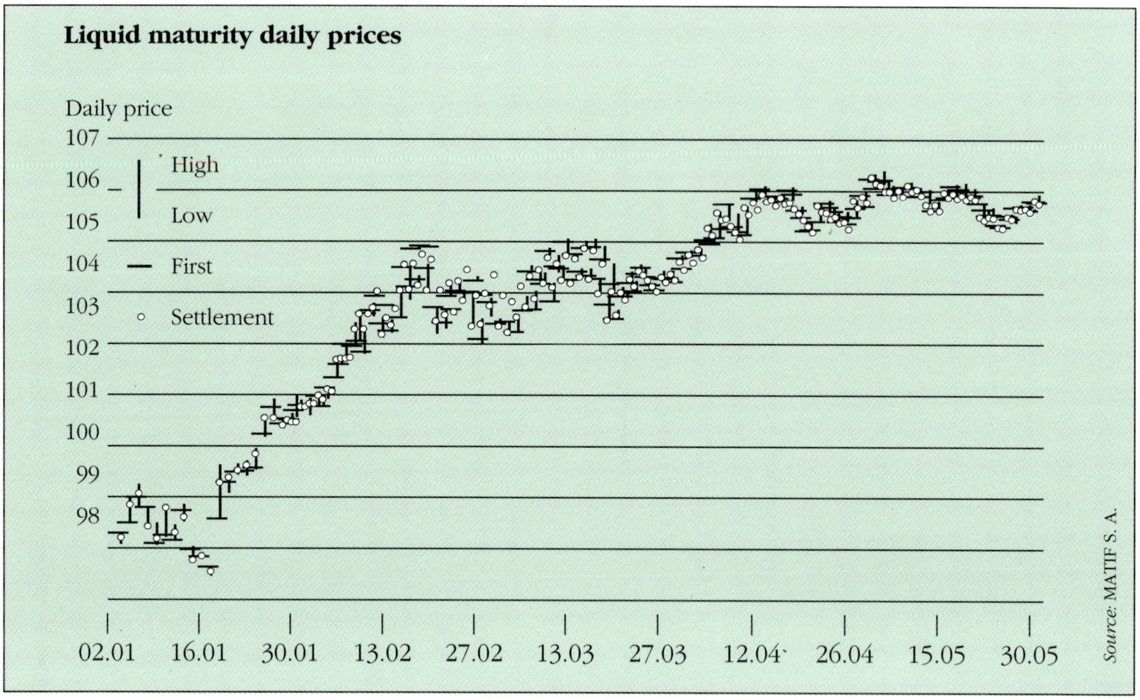

Liquid maturity daily prices

Although liquidity is an elusive recipe, the Paris market-makers have succeeded in attracting new business in Paris as the chart shows.

In return for a reduction of their clearing fees, MATIF Ecu bond futures market-makers are under the following obligations:

- they must have a team constantly present in the pit, during the open outcry trading session – in fact most selected market-makers put in well seasoned and extremely qualified traders and set up computer programmes to help them and their clients get the best prices and the most cost efficient strategies; and
- they must quote a set number of contracts, with a maximum spread: up to 30 contracts with a maximum spread of 2 ticks (4 basis points) and up to 50 contracts with a maximum spread of 3 ticks (6 basis points).

The Paris market place already benefits from the Notional bond futures recognition; options trading is widely accepted as its forte. The dynamism of MATIF members and their search for excellence in terms of service make the Paris market place all the more attractive. But Paris has another ambition: to become the Ecu market place.

The MATIF contracts can make the difference for you.

The MATIF has been helped by French Treasury policy and its regularly and large Ecu-denominated issues. The attractiveness of the MATIF Ecu contract, its liquidity, the homogeneous nature of its bond pool as well as the quality of the market itself, whether in terms of depth or in terms of security, are its best assets.

NIP

Nomura: Towards the new Europe

Nomura Securities is Japan's largest securities company, with around five million account holders and more than ¥50 trillion of customer assets in its custody. Its extensive network comprises 148 branches in Japan and 61 offices in 23 countries throughout the world. This unrivalled global reach encompasses virtually every securities sales and trading business. Nomura is a member of every one of the world's major stock markets, and an active participant in all the world's leading bond markets.

For more than 65 years, Nomura has been serving its clients with the best in investment advice on and research into equity and bond markets. Nomura's commitment to new and developing markets, like the Ecu markets, has the resources of the entire Nomura group network behind it.

Nomura International, Nomura Securities' London-based European headquarters, was a leading player in the Euromarkets throughout the 1980s, and is well placed to maintain that role throughout this decade. For three straight years since 1987, Nomura International has been the number one lead manager of Eurobond issues.

In 1990, Nomura International lead

View of the City of London from the Thames.

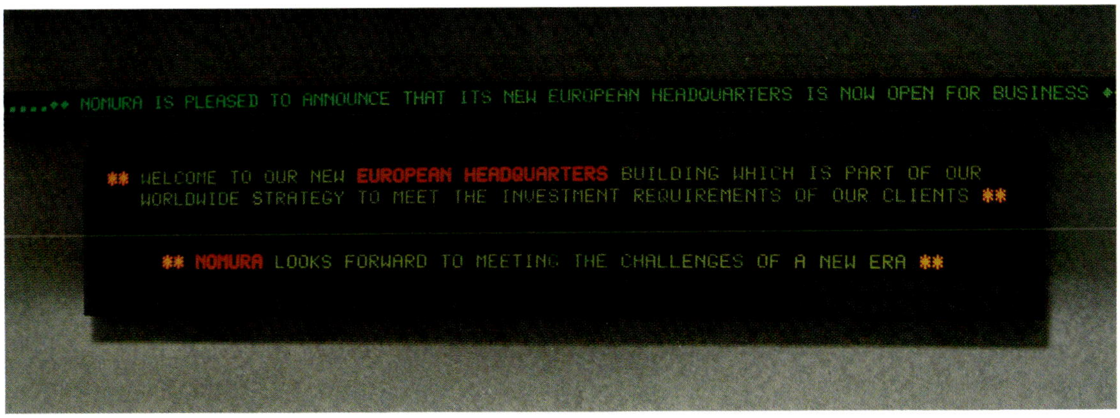

Tickerboards are displayed on the walls of both the upper and lower dealing floors.

managed 104 Eurobond issues totalling US$16.1 billion in value. Among other leading borrowers, Nomura has brought issues for the European Investment Bank, the Republic of Finland and the Nordic Investment Bank to the Eurobond market as lead manager and arranger. Although Nomura International is the market leader in the arrangement of equity-related issues for Japanese corporate borrowers and for Euroyen bond issues, 40 per cent of the Eurobond issues brought to the market by Nomura International last year were for non-Japanese borrowers.

Nomura has for many years been the foremost underwriter in the Japanese government bond market, and has more recently extended its expertise to the government bond markets of overseas nations. Since 1986 Nomura has been a primary dealer in US government securities. In 1988, Nomura Securities' subsidiary Nomura Gilts gained the status of market-maker in UK government bonds, and in 1990 Nomura became the first Japanese financial institution to be designated a primary dealer of French government securities. Nomura's Frankfurt office has been a member of the German government bond underwriting syndicate since 1987.

Nomura is also an active participant on the London International Financial Futures Exchange (LIFFE) and also has a seat on the Paris futures exchange, the Matif. Ten-year Ecu bond futures contracts are traded on both these exchanges.

Together with Nomura's pre-eminence in Eurobond underwriting, the skills and resources it has built up in Europe's domestic bond markets amount to a formidable strength. This strength is firmly behind Nomura's presence in the Ecu marketplace, a marketplace which Nomura is convinced will play an increasingly important role in global fixed income markets. Nomura's experience in government bond markets in particular has engendered an understanding of the importance of the use of the Ecu in sovereign government financing by the UK, Italy and France and in the wider acceptance of the Ecu among international investors.

In 1990, in terms of new issues, the Ecu sector was the Eurobond market's third largest, after the US dollar and Japanese yen-denominated sectors. It is also the fastest growing Eurobond sector in terms of new issue volume, and Japanese investors are becoming a major force in its development. Given this, Nomura's involvement in the Ecu market might appear inevitable.

However, Nomura's role in the Ecu market cannot be explained purely in terms of the everyday activities of a major international securities house. The concept of *Dochakuka* (literally "nurturing new roots" or adapting to local markets) is a key tenet of

Nomura's corporate philosophy. The Ecu marketplace is perhaps the ultimate European marketplace, a currency without national borders is the logical product of the idea of a single European market for capital and investment. Nomura's commitment to the Ecu reflects Nomura's commitment to the Europe of today, and of Europe post-1992.

Nomura also has banking licences in six European countries, notably in the UK where Nomura Bank International is involved in lending, foreign exchange trading and asset management operations. Nomura's other European banks emphasise service tailored to local needs. Nomura Bank Nederland (NBN), Nomura Bank (Deutschland) and Nomura Bank (Belgium) focus on universal banking services, including equity transactions. The core business of Nomura Bank (Switzerland) is private banking including asset management services. Nomura Bank (Luxembourg) offers mainly custodial services.

Nomura's involvement in the Ecu market also reflects its long history of financial innovation. It was the first securities house to introduce dual currency bonds and collateralised mortgage obligations (CMOs) to the Tokyo market, for example.

Although Nomura is a company of extraordinary size, its 14 subsidiary and affiliate companies are engaged in a diverse number of financial and information-related businesses. The Nomura Research Institute

Nomura House, 1 St. Martin's-le-Grand, London EC1.

Lower dealing floor.

(NRI), for example, is ranked as one of the world's top five economic think-tanks. Nomura considers research to be the backbone of its securities business, and the NRI works closely with Nomura Securities' in-house Investment Research Division.

The Nomura Group also includes the Nomura Securities Investment Trust Management Co Ltd, a leading investment trust management company, and the Nomura Investment Management Co Ltd (NIMCO) which deals exclusively in asset management.

This diversity is another deliberate strategy of the Nomura Group, which is constantly seeking to break new ground in the world's financial markets. As a relatively new market – and one with enormous potential – the Ecu securities market is a natural focus of activity for Nomura.

As the Ecu market grows, investors will demand increasingly sophisticated research and trading capabilities in the Ecu marketplace. Nomura is confident of its ability to meet those demands. The range of technical problems associated with such a financing are enormous, but no more insurmountable than the complexities involved in the birth of the Ecu itself in 1979.

As well as an underwriter and distributor of Ecu securities, Nomura International in London also forms a cornerstone of the secondary market for Ecu bonds. Nomura International makes markets in all outstanding liquid Ecu bond issues, displaying two-way prices on the Reuter screen system, on page NONO.

Nomura's formula for success has been a simple one. It has consistently worked to match the ever more demanding requirements of investors with new investment ideas, and services. As the Ecu market grows, Nomura and its clients will grow with it.

The Paribas Group

The principal activities of the Paribas Group are concentrated in four business units: Banque Paribas, Compagnie Bancaire, Crédit du Nord and a portfolio of industrial equity investments. These are grouped under the ultimate holding company, Compagnie Financière de Paribas, whose stock is quoted on the Paris Bourse and listed, also, in Tokyo, Belgium and Switzerland. In 1990 Paribas was the 23rd largest banking group by balance sheet. In 1990, Paribas' net consolidated income (excluding minority interests) was Ffr2.5 billion, after a major increase in risk provisions. The estimated net share value was Ffr686 after self financing per outstanding share on 31 December.

The Paribas Group is present in 57 countries.

Banque Paribas

Banque Paribas was founded in 1872 in four European countries: France, Belgium, Switzerland and the Netherlands. An investment bank, from the very beginning, Paribas is today a European-based international bank. Banque Paribas has a strong European base, capable of responding to the needs of large companies in the European Community and Switzerland. In France and Belgium a network of branches makes Paribas more accessible to small and medium-sized enterprises and reinforces its activities in private banking. On an international level, Banque Paribas holds strong positions in market operations (Paribas Capital Markets), exchange operations, investment banking, private banking, as well as portfolio management (Paribas Asset Management).

Compagnie Bancaire

Compagnie Bancaire is the leading specialised financial services group in Europe. It focuses on business equipment and consumer finance, life assurance, savings and property development. The Compagnie Bancaire group is characterised by its innovative approach in creating new financial instruments (Cortal, Carte Aurore, etc.) and by its growing European base. Specialised subsidiaries or joint ventures have been established in the United Kingdom, Germany, Belgium, the Netherlands, Switzerland, Italy, Spain and Portugal. In 1990, Compagnie Bancaire's Group net operating income was Ffr1,479 million, down 11 per cent from 1989. Total loans granted reached Ffr83.5 billion, 25 per cent outside France.

Crédit du Nord

Crédit du Nord is the retail banking arm of the Group, with 380 branches and six subsidiary regional banks in France. Crédit du Nord developed its activities in the areas of individual asset management and services to small and medium sized enterprises. In Europe the bank has pursued a strategy of co-operation in Belgium (Banque Paribas), Scandinavia (NordBanken) and Spain (Banco Urquijo).

Equity investments

Compagnie Financière de Paribas manages a large portfolio of equity investments which represent an important part of its activities as an investment bank. In 1990, these investments represented nearly half of the Group's income. The strategy for this activity is based on Paribas' position as major shareholder in large industrial groups such as Poliet (cement), the Sema Group and Axime (computer services) and Guyomarc'h (agri-business) and the formation of large industrial holding companies quoted in France (Nord-Est and Saulnes-Chatillon) and Belgium (Cobepa). On 30 December 1990, the estimated value of the investment portfolio amounted to Ffr50 billion.

Paribas' investment strategy gives priority to sectors which offer profitable prospects for development in a European perspective: healthcare, hotel and leisure, communications, agri-business, electronics. In order to encourage the European growth of the portfolio and support international mergers and acquisitions activity, Paribas has established national holding companies of this type in the Netherlands, Germany, Portugal and Spain.

Shareholders and management organisation

In 1990, the Paribas Group put in place a new management structure, consisting of Management and Supervisory Boards and an International Committee, whose members are chosen for their international experience in business and finance. The Supervisory Board, presided over by Michel François-Poncet, represents Paribas' core shareholders, including Compagnie de Navigation Mixte, the Axa group, AGF, the Pargesa/Frere/Power group and UAP. Since its privatisation in 1987 Paribas has a large number of individual shareholders, who numbered approximately one million at the end of 1990.

The Management Board of Compagnie Financière de Paribas, presided over by André Lévy-Lang, is made up of Gilles Cosson, Philippe Dulac, Christian Manset and Hubert de Saint-Amand. Each member of the Board is responsible for one of the main activities of the Group and the subsidiaries related to that activity. Banque Paribas has adopted the same structure with a Supervisory Board, presided over by André Lévy-Lang, and a Management Board, headed by Hubert de Saint-Amand.

Paribas Capital Markets

The Group worldwide

One of the Paribas Group's major strategic objectives has been to develop its capital markets capabilities through its international network formed of a range of specialised institutions. This positions the Group as a leading debt and equity intermediary in many domestic markets and a major participant in the international capital markets. In 1984, the Group broadened its well-established retail base in the international capital markets by launching an institutionally-directed business under the title Paribas Limited in London. Today, these domestic and international activities are managed as an integrated worldwide capital markets group known as the Paribas Capital Markets Group.

As is necessary for a genuinely international business enterprise, the Capital Markets Group of Banque Paribas draws on more than 1,000 personnel from all corners of the world, wherever the talent is available. 28 different nationalities are represented in the London office of the Capital Markets Group alone, bringing a cosmopolitan dimension to handling a multinational clientèle that few other houses can match. In addition to the 500 staff in Paribas Limited in London, there are 75 each in Tokyo, New York and Geneva, with smaller numbers in Singapore, Sydney and Frankfurt. In Paris there are 300 staff working on capital markets activities of the Group, with a further 100 in Courcoux Bouvet, the Group's French stockbroking firm.

To complement its own international representation, the geographical spread of the Group's capital markets representation is extended through liaison with personnel in Banque Paribas offices in other areas of the world, such as Amsterdam, Brussels, Luxembourg, Milan, Madrid and Hong Kong. In London, Paribas Limited is closely associated with Banque Paribas' largest branch outside

France, which has been established in the City for more than 25 years.

Products and services

The Paribas Capital Markets Group delivers a comprehensive range of products and services required by investors, corporations and sovereign entities in both the domestic and the international markets. Two qualities distinguish the Group from its major competitors in the investment banking field: the constant search for innovation and the ability to supply superior and speedy service to all our clients. These qualities characterise every facet of our wide range of products and services, which include:

- corporate finance;
- structured finance;
- fixed income, equity and commodity derivatives;
- equity and bond new issues;
- fixed income sales and trading; and
- equity sales and trading.

The company's traditional strengths in the fields of underwriting and distributing bond issues and arranging swap transactions are well known. Whilst growing in prominence for those activities, Paribas' repertoire has been extended to include a full range of services supporting the primary and secondary markets for both bonds and equities. Paribas Limited has also developed a broad spread of corporate finance capabilities, which supplement its skills in investment banking on an international scale.

Among non-American houses, the Paribas Capital Markets Group has been one of the most active arrangers of international issues for US and Canadian borrowers, and a leading book runner of collateralised financing for American thrift institutions on the international markets. On the other side of the world, the Capital Markets Group has lead managed many issues for Japanese and Australian corporations and official bodies. To consolidate its command of the international environment, the Group is also an acknowledged authority on swaps in many currencies.

Overall, the geographical mix of new bond and equity issue business is well balanced between Europe, the Pacific Basin and North America. The issuing activity is supported by the Paribas Capital Markets Group's substantial placing power. Our distribution capabilities are complemented by both bond and equity trading expertise and volume. Paribas is the number one lead manager of Ecu-denominated issues, and is among the top 10 Eurobond lead managers worldwide.

The Group is also by far the largest non-US participant in interest rate and currency swaps, both as underwriter and intermediary. The European Equity Group, trading and broking equities on all European stock exchanges, is one of the leaders in this market and is well placed to consolidate its position in 1992 and beyond. A highly motivated corporate finance department is consistently liaising with origination, sales, trading and swaps experts in the structuring and closing of complex and innovative transactions. Paribas has obtained a leading position in European mergers and acquisitions because of the close rapport which exists between its office in the different network locations and from their in-depth knowledge of the local industrial landscapes.

The research departments make a further significant contribution to the Group's products, offering a unique service to investors across a wide range of international securities, in support of secondary markets sales teams, who maintain close contact with issuers of debt and equity instruments, as well as institutional investors.

This whole client-related activity is supported by a large administrative group, concerned with providing transaction facilities and the very sophisticated technology required to ensure that the corporate activities can be both effectively managed, and at the forefront of financial innovation.